Writers from Brazil and Portugal, Mozambique and Angola all use the same language — Portuguese, for stories from a thousand locales in a hundred styles.

Brazil — almost a continent by itself — has a tremendous set of talented writers turning over its rich tropical, urban and racial mix.

Portugal (like England) is a tiny country that has contributed far beyond its size to the world's cultural and literary wealth.

Drawing from both these traditions and their own African heritage writers from Angola and Mozambique have recently begun to chronicle their own strange story...

The Babel Guide is your way in to this wide world of reading — inside are details on *all* the novels and short stories from these countries available in English with 70 'trailers' to the best books of 35 major writers to aid your purchasing or borrowing choices.

Take a journey to the heart and soul of another world; here is the guide.

'a brilliant idea'

— BBC Radio 3

The Babel Guide
to the Fiction of
Portugal, Brazil & Africa
in English Translation

by Ray Keenoy, David Treece & Paul Hyland

with

David Brookshaw
Marina Coriolano-Lykourezos
Maria-Amelia Dalsenter
Maria-Manuela Lisboa
Tom MacCarthy
Pat Odber
Carmo Ponte
Giovanni Pontiero
Caroline Shaw

Illustrations by Jackie Wrout

BOULEVARD

Babel Guide to the Fiction of Portugal, Brazil and Africa in English Translation

©Boulevard Books 1995.
(Paul Hyland's contributions ©Paul Hyland 1995)
First published 1995 by Boulevard Books
8 Aldbourne Road
London W12 OLN, UK
Tel/Fax 0181 743 5278

Special thanks to

Michael Collins
Maria-Amelia Dalsenter
Giovanni Pontiero
Luis de Sousa Rebelo
David Treece
Siân Williams
Jackie Wrout

Published with support from the Camões Institute Lisbon,
Gulbenkian Foundation UK/Portugal 600
The publisher acknowledges financial assistance from the Arts Council of
Great Britain

ISBN 1 899460 055

Boulevard Books are distributed in the UK by Central Books.
Cover Art: Chris Hyde
Typeset & Design: Studio Europa (0181 743 5278)
Printed and bound by the Guernsey Press, Guernsey, C.I.

for Célia

CONTENTS

Introducing the Babel Guides...

This is the second Babel Guide, part of a new series that lists and discusses fiction in translation available in English, with the accent on contemporary writing. This edition focuses on the lands that use the Portuguese language and has two parts — the *Database* section has the details of *every* book by authors from Portugal, Brazil, Angola and Mozambique translated since 1945 and the *Reviews* section introduces seventy of the best and most representative books with a quotation to give you a taste of the writing.

The Babel Guides are here to help readers, librarians and booksellers to locate and appreciate international literature by emphasizing the new foreign writing amidst the mass of titles available in today's bookshops. We're sure that having this information in an accessible, portable form will enrich and extend your reading.

PORTUGAL

ANTHOLOGY

Dedalus Book of Portuguese Fantasy

Eds. Lisboa, E & Macedo, H

The Portuguese are notorious as a people somehow immersed in dreams, or at least prone to feeling the famous *saudade* (not wholly translatable by the word 'nostalgia') and so perhaps 'fantasy' has been a happy genre for their writers. The independent publisher Dedalus has a series of short story collections that explore the riches of 19th and 20th century fantasy, surrealism etc. in various European literatures. *The Dedalus Book of Portuguese Fantasy* is a collection that has been lovingly researched and effectively translated; the result is satisfying and enjoyable even for someone not necessarily invited by the word 'fantasy' in the title.

For one thing this is because some of the greatest Portuguese writers, such as Eça de Queirós and Mário de Sá-Carneiro are here in 'fantastic' mode alongside other accomplished authors including Ferreira de Castro and Manuel Texeira Gomes. Another factor is that this is quite a big book, allowing the reader to skip one or two pieces that may be too gothic or mysterious and still find plenty of good stuff. Highlights are *Our Lord of All Seafarers* by Ferreira de Castro which is a romantically-set ironic dialogue with the Creator on his creation — a clever and radical story; Sá-Carneiro's *Myself the Other* is an avant-gardist interrogation of madness and the struggle to be oneself, with a magnificent line that berates those that 'don't even have enough genius to want to be a genius'; Texeira Gomes's *Blood Lust* is as enjoyably decadent and archly funny as an Almodovar film with its strange-sex angle and finally of especial note is António Patrício's *The Fountain Man,* a touching celebration of Italy and her cities. Patrício has really 'seen' the grandeur of Rome in its soft but magnificently glowing light and this is also the fascinating story of a bizarre and beautiful young man, a story that takes the possibilities of the fantastic as a genre and uses it to express some realities of aesthetic and sexual existence. Which could also be said for many of the other stories in this marvellous book. R K

'Then I returned to Rome where I had first seen Harry months before.

I often thought about him with a persistent, complicit sympathy, for I too love fountains. At the time, I used to go to the Piazza del Popolo at night in order to savour the rough, tragic wine of its solitude. I would stretch out on the broad alabaster rim of the fountain, opposite the Pincio; and allow myself to be impregnated by that memoryless soul, by that august chronicle of silence: the magical atmosphere of Rome's squares when they are empty of people and filled only by liquid voices. I would stay there for hours at a time filled by an almost sensual sadness, a kind of delirium of grandeur that allowed me to converse with Rome, to calm my doubts about my failures in the supernatural beauty of that great dead city and fuse my destiny with hers, like that of a hero in an old poem.

To experience that ecstasy of the psyche you must either have lived a great deal or else be touched by the premature old age of the artist who, even in the full flush of youth and strength, seizes happiness by her hair and grows sad when he kisses her eyes. During my time in Rome that was my most silent hour.

In the middle of the square the four lions spouted water, guarding the Egyptian obelisk like sphinxes keeping perpetual watch. At night, in Rome, time takes on an almost monastic quality. It is the perfect city in which to live out a dream or an idea, watched over by millenary figures poised to receive your confession.' *The Fountain Man* António Patrício

ANTHOLOGY

Passport to Portugal

Eds. Gerrard, M & MacCarthy, T

This recent anthology is the result of a real effort to get a representative selection of fresh and powerful writing from Portugal and Portuguese-speaking ('Lusophone') Africa.

Reading the whole anthology through a British reader might be struck with parallels between the experience of the UK and Portugal. There is even an End-of-Empire colony (Macao) awaiting the fateful day of takeover by the Peoples' Republic of China. There is a fascinating picture of Macao in the story *6 August* by João Aguiar.

There is a also certain atmosphere of living in a land resolutely looking backwards, that post-imperial condition suffered by Britain and perhaps now the United States too. One of the best stories is from the pen of Lídia Jorge, considered Portugal's greatest woman writer. A story that suggests Portugal — perhaps as a result of post-imperial fatigue — is a country where some people at least take the time to meditate on eternal questions.

Another side of Portugal, the famous rural backwardness carefully cultivated during the long years of the Salazar dictatorship, is revealed, reveled in perhaps, by the young writer (b.1965) José Direitinho in *Portents;* a very good short story that conjures up the reactions of people caught up in fatalistic folk-beliefs. Helena Neves' *Deolinda* alludes, in a poetic, experimentalist way, to the other great interrogator of Portuguese life, the huge ocean that it faces, forever tempting its people to foreign adventure.

That too is a parallel with the British experience. Less British is the story that emerges from the African writers in this anthology; Lina Magaia's searing tale of life and sudden death in Mozambique, where a whole people have been sadly abused by warriors from or sponsored by Portugal and South Africa. Manuel Rui gives an amusing but in fact interestingly detailed picture of everyday life in 'revolutionary' Angola while José Luandino Vieira, again set in Angola, contributes *The Loves of João Vêncio* which is quite Runyonesque; spirited and with an undercurrent of violence. The last African writer here (Portuguese is used officially in five African countries; Angola, Mozambique, Cape Verde, São Thomé e Principe and Guinea-Bissau) is Mia Couto, a veteran short-story writer from Mozambique, with an extract from his first novel, fascinating and sad, preoccupied, like Lina Magaia with the effects of the long civil war there.

There are also pieces (including an interview) by José Saramago, the lively António Lobo Antunes and Maria Isabel Barreno, last heard of in English in the famous book *New Portuguese Letters*, recently re-issued.

The Passport anthology is aimed, like this Babel Guide, at bringing the news to the English-speaking world about the fascinating but neglected literature written in the Portuguese language by writers in four continents. Now there's no excuse to miss out! R K

'Deolinda loved the sea so much that she even understood its rages. Because the sea was small it didn't need to be limited by high walls and ports. She felt its sharp longing for land, its desire to see the fields close-up, to feel the nearness of the cornfields, to crush the corn with the white teeth of its waves, to change itself into the playful streams, impregnating the neighbouring land with even more salt.' p115 (Neves Deolinda *The Sea*)

ANTHOLOGY
Ed. Bartes, R.A.

Portugal through her Literature

This is a mini-anthology of Portuguese literature in parallel text format, with each extract side-by-side in both languages, especially helpful for people learning or thinking of learning the language. At the moment it is the only book of its kind available, and only in library copies as it's thoroughly out-of-print.

The book is divided into separate prose and poetry sections and in both its editor has decided to show a very wide range of writing in Portuguese. The collection therefore runs from the fifteenth century Padre H Francisco Álvares via Fernão Mendes Pinto's extraordinary *Peregrinations*, an early travel book, up to Manuel Texeira Gomes who is included in the *Dedalus Book of Portuguese Fantasy*, also reviewed in this guide.

The extracts are rather shorter than is usual with anthologies as they've all been fitted on to one page each, but they do shed some light on authors and books otherwise completely inaccessible to English-speaking readers who don't read Portuguese. *Portugal through her Literature* also includes in its poetry section seventeen poets spanning the 15th to the early 20th century. R K

'In this period (September and October) every self-respecting Englishman.....prepares ten or twelve trunks and leaves for the countries of sun, wine and happiness.....Sometimes he travels with his wife, his sister-in-law, a female friend of the sister-in-law, an acquaintance of this friend, seven children, six servants, ten dogs, and other doggy acquaintances of these dogs, and pays for all this without grumbling! No: I do not put that correctly, always grumbling. This pleasure trip, the Englishman almost always spends it grumbling.

The truth is that the Englishman does not amuse himself on the continent; he does not understand the language; he finds the meals strange; everything that is foreign shocks him; he suspects that they want to rob him; he has a vague belief that the sheets on the hotel beds are not clean; to see the theatres open on Sunday and the crowd amusing itself embitters his Christian and puritan soul; he dare not open a foreign book because he suspects that there are obscene things in it; if his guide informs him that such and such cathedral has six columns and if he finds only five, he remains unhappy for a whole week and furious with the country he is passing through, like a man who has been robbed of a column; and if he loses a walking-stick, if he does not arrive on time for the train, he shuts himself in the hotel for a whole day composing a letter to the 'Times', in which accuses the continental countries of being in a completely savage state and wallowing in putrid demoralization. In a word, the Englishman when he is travelling, is a miserable creature. (p73) (Eça de Queirós; newspaper article)

ANTUNES

António Lobo

Act of the Damned [Auto dos Danados]

Act of the Damned is a portrait of two things; the corrupt ruling class which fattened itself for decades under Salazar and of Portugal's revolutionary year of 1974–75. We're fed our picture of both things from within the bosom of a rich family trying to escape a fate worse than death — having its wealth seized by militant soldiers and peasants. As the family struggles to cut some quick, semi-legal deals to get their money out of the country, Antunes depicts a series of marvellously grotesque characters; one important member of the clan spends his whole life playing with his train set without realising it's a toy while Old Grandpa has had sex with his daughter and his daughter's daughter (who is also *his* daughter). The narrator, estranged politically and emotionally from this bunch, is one of literature's few heroic dentists, a man under pressure who spends the novel trying to navigate past a cacophony of over-weening receptionists, lovers on drugs and angry wives. Meanwhile the awkward squad down in the street want to make a revolution.

A very funny book in places, with a lot of genuinely striking description as, with a disgusted tone, Antunes drags skeletons out of cupboards and parades various unpalatable realities. Antunes himself is from a social background similar to the one he describes and some of his family apparently view his books as 'acts of betrayal'. R L

'We'd arrived in Évora an hour earlier and begun to decay with the rest of the two thousand-year-old town in the first hotel we found: a family operation with vinyl couches and a TV in the lobby and flags of many nations planted in a wooden disc on the counter, where a squint-eyed geriatric whose fingers were longer than conductor batons or lobster antennae handed out keys and had guests fill in cards. We dragged the luggage up two flights, the squint-eyes leading the way with a jittery cockroach's energy, we entered the room, the old man's snare-drum skipping faded out in the corridor along with his grumbling about the tip, and within a few minutes we'd discovered that the light bulb in the bedside lamp was burned out, that the window lock was jammed, that pressing the lever on the toilet made its empty stomach swallow the tank ball in vain, and that dozens of insects patrolled the baseboard, probing the cracks in the wood with their feelers.' p101

An Explanation Of The Birds [Explicação dos pássaros]

Lobo Antunes employs a colloquial, omnivorous language that digests trauma and black comedy and nourishes readers hungry for literature which meets life head on. *An Explanation of the Birds* is the work of a consummate technician, a shocking artist. He writes in the first or third person but always from within someone's head — where past and present cohabit with hope and fear — and earns the right to psychological if not theological omniscience. His style must be read to be believed, and it compels belief.

Rui S., political historian, skips an academic conference and takes his Marxist second wife Marília away for a weekend — the book's long chapters are Thursday, Friday, Saturday, Sunday — to tell her it's all over. He's estranged from his rich father, his mother's dying, his first wife plays on his nerves, his politics are compromised.

He remembers his father tenderly telling him tales to explain the birds, the birds that will peck at his corpse in Aveiro's lagoon; 'his father smoothed his hair against his temples and handed him the paper-knife. "I'm going to help you grasp the birds," he said. "I'm going to help you understand them."'

At the novel's heart, long before his inexorable death, is Rui's obituary which salutes, satirizes, mocks his life. Then Marília pre-empts him, leaves him before he can leave her. It's a fine plot, a big top, a broad comedy, a bleak life ending when the spotlights are all on and whirling helter-skelter around the ring, the stands, the balcony, the ceiling, highlighting and forgetting countless objects and faces... P H

'My tonic, Dona Almerinda,' the blind man ordered in a voice without echo or inflection, searching with his vacant eyes for the long, transparent bottle that must be (he thinks) a kind of moonlight in his darkness.

'One more beer,' I said. 'And some nuts please.'

My father leant towards you with an urbane smile on his plastic ageing-actor's face: 'So what is it you teach at the university?'

Dona Almerinda wove among the men with glass in hand, and I thought, 'It's not that he wants to make conversation, he just wants to make fun of you in front of the others.' He thinks, 'What sordid, venomous telescopes their smiles are.'

South of Nowhere [Os Cus de Judas]

This is a book that came out of, or perhaps exploded out of, Portugal's colonial war in Africa of the late 60s/early 70s — the struggle Antunes himself called 'our poor man's Vietnam'. There's the explosion of cynicism, desperate sexuality and nihilistic pleasure-seeking that seeing friends and enemies meaninglessly slaughtered can induce in ex-combatants. The tone is reminiscent of Curzio Malaparte sifting through ruined Europe in 1945 or Anthony Burgess' Malayan campaign; witnesses to 'dirty wars' feel dirty and sometimes write books like this as an expiation.

South of Nowhere sold half a million copies in Portuguese, which is a tribute to Antunes' edgy and sardonic prose. It also in a very timely way reflected an amazing moment of awakening for Portugal, an awakening to a hopeful revolutionary and democratic dawn in 1975, with the end of both the war and the long Salazarist dictatorship. From this book it is clear it was simultaneously an awakening to what a tawdry, wasteful period the dictatorship had imposed on an inventive nation. For this it's interesting to read *South of Nowhere* in conjunction with José Saramago's *Year of the Death of Ricardo Reis*, which is set during the high noon of the Salazar regime; between one book and the other, between one generation of writers and another, is the closed epoch from which Portugal emerged twenty years ago.

Apart from its importance as a landmark piece in Portugal's contemporary history, *South of Nowhere* is an engaging, thrilling read; Antunes very effectively unwinds his stark scenes; of a war organised by the Secret Police as much as by the military, of late 60s sexual and political liberation and of tangled, tender family life. R K

'You know, I imagine you in a scenario halfway between oriental philosophy and the judicious, lucid Left...a lot of pillows on the floor, the smell of incense and patchouli floating over the Indian bibelots, a Siamese cat disdainful as a prima donna, books by Reich and Garaudy promulgating their vehement prophecies on the shelves, the febrile voice of Léo Ferré on the record player. Moustached architects with their studied rumpled look occasionally occupy your antique brass bed from Sintra, filling your ashtrays with the butts of unfiltered cigarettes or scratching the shaggy hair on their chests. In the mornings the concierge, fat and intractable, collects the garbage cans, insulting you with her thick bulldog eyebrows. From the apartment next door come the furious growls of a marital argument, accompanied by the sounds of breaking china. A sun as happy as the smile of a policeman plays on the blinds.' p76

The Sin of Father Amaro [O Crime do Padre Amaro]

Zola said this Portuguese writer, who, to be honest, has been barely heard of in Britain, was 'greater than Flaubert'. One could look for the truth of that in *The Sin of Father Amaro,* his first published novel, and it is certainly a jolt to read it, to stumble upon the great Eça unawares. For one thing there's the 'shock of the modern' here; Eça's uninhibited eroticism, his hostility to religion, his cynicism about human nature might come as a surprise in a nineteenth-century novel.

Eça is famous for creating a world within his books and here it is the world of a small provincial town where the clergy have a lot of influence, an influence the rationalist Eça shows them misusing in the most appalling ways. Much of the book is a long dissection of the psychology of the celibate priesthood as we follow Father Amaro (Amaro means 'bitter' in Portuguese) from youth through to cynical middle age. In a nutshell the story of the book is of a series of women being exploited sexually, financially or emotionally by a collection of avaricious and rapacious priests.

His main characters, Amaro included, are created however with understanding; the origins of their villainy and cynicism are revealed. The reader can make his or her own judgement; Eça provides the evidence for both the prosecution and the defence. Here is part perhaps of his 'naturalist' method, making an effort to give a rounded, total view. The citizen-reader is enabled to think the world through for him or herself and this is the alternative to running to the shelter of handed-down moral certainties. Amaro in fact is shown as a weak and put-upon youth who grows up into an immoral, selfish man; who exactly is to blame for that?

While the trip around Eça's moral maze is important, the joy of the book is the observation of a certain moment of life in provincial Portugal, re-created in a way that is both detailed and enveloping — Eça knew the town and the story he tells in reality and they both become very real to the reader. A great, utterly enjoyable work of art. R K

'It was now the end of August. In the macadamized path which stretched along the river one caught a glimpse of the bright-coloured clothes of the women as they walked to and fro between the two rows of old poplars. In the row of poor dwellings at the side of the Archway, the old women sat at their doors, spinning; the dirty, ill-nourished children played on the ground, showing their nude, swollen bellies; and the hens went round voraciously picking among the dirt and filth. Round the fountain all was noise; vessels were dragged over the stones, servants abused one another, soldiers in dirty uniforms and enormous laced down-at-heel boots waved their malacca canes and made love; girls with fat-paunched pitchers on their heads walked in pairs swinging their hips; two lazy officers, with their uniforms unbuttoned and hanging loose over their stomachs, chatted together as they waited to see who might arrive. The coach was late. When twilight descended a flame from the lamp in the saint's niche over the archway became visible. From the hospital windows in front lights appeared one by one, throwing out a dull glow.' p13

Cousin Bazilio [O Primo Bazílio]

Cousin Bazilio is one of Eça's greatest works, his *Madame Bovary*. It's a fairly long book one is forced to read slowly because the writing is so replete with poetic genius and Eça is always inventive enough to tackle a hackneyed image and recast it freshly and movingly; 'Her golden hair, still burnished by the warmth of the pillow'.

The novel is set amidst a stifling coterie of Lisbonites in cozy government jobs and Eça has good fun with several hilariously pompous minor characters, such as the Counsellor, who talks about a rural province with a lot of pigsties as having 'great porcine wealth', while a minor female character, Aunty Victoria, finds her favourite nourishment in 'catarrh pastilles'.

Throughout the novel a great contrast is made between the two main female characters, the sensual, romantic Luiza, who falls for a wealthy cad — her cousin Bazilio — and Luiza's servant, the scrawny, embittered (and virginal) Juliana. The heights of Luiza's sensual abandon in her illegitimate affair, the lush evocation of her lively, rosy body, her delighted playfulness with Bazilio are all subject to the constant counterpoint of Juliana's scorn, her moral scorn and the unwitting scorn of the comparison with her ill-favoured body and existence as Luiza's undernourished, ailing servant. Eça creates in this contrast an exquisite amalgam of social critique, sexual fire and psychological truth.

The sensuality of Eça's prose, translated with a certain swing by the South African poet Roy Campbell, has to be read to be believed, Luiza preparing to sink into adultery is described promenading; 'the lassitude of her gait broke her waist-line in a languorous and promising manner' and later Bazilio discovers 'a delicious turbulence in her gesture and looks'. Eça could manage something lacking in the Anglo-Saxon literary tradition, — enjoy and celebrate his female characters, revel in and share their femininity and sexual grace even while revealing their snobbery and naiveté.

Something else he seems to reveal, as in another of his great sexy novels *The Sin of Father Amaro*, is the frustrated condition of fin-de-siècle womanhood which made them prone apparently to overblown romantic emotions and eventual 'moral downfall'.

One of the fascinations of this book is to ask where exactly Eça's sympathies lie. Cousin Bazilio is a radically strange drama of married morality where the author takes all sides, of the cheating wife and the doting husband and the blackmailing but oppressed servant and the protective friend — all sides except that of caddish Bazilio. Perhaps he didn't want to arrive at a final moral standpoint and avoids the issue by rapidly coming to a contrived ending which has shades of Flaubert's *Madame Bovary.* R K

'Afterwards came to her mind all the classical episodes of Lisbonese love-affairs which had blossomed in Cintra; the walks by moonlight at Sitiais, taken slowly, with long hushed rests on the Penedo da Saudade, looking over the valley, with the sands in the distance, full of a nostalgic, idealistic, pale lustre; warm siestas in the shade of the Green Peak, hearing the fresh dripping murmur of water falling from boulder to boulder: afternoons in the fields of Collares, rowing an old boat on the dark water in the shade of the ash trees — and what laughter, when they were going to moor in the tall reeds, and her straw hat got caught in the lower branches of the poplars!

She had always loved Cintra. As soon as she entered the dark and murmurous groves of the Ramalhão she felt a sweet, happy melancholy.' pp12-13

The City & the Mountains [A Cidade e as Serras]

The City & the Mountains is a later and less-regarded work by Portugal's master novelist, Eça de Queirós (1843-1900). However this tale of a (very) rich young man from rural Portugal who emigrates to Paris 'capital of the nineteenth century' as Walter Benjamin called it, is today suddenly very relevant and far-seeing.

Eça describes a life-style frighteningly like that lived by many in today's big cities. His aristocratic hero becomes infatuated with a kind of trendy gadget-filled consumerism. His luxurious villa on the Champs-Elysées is loaded with telephones, ticker-tapes, music and listening tubes connected to the Paris Opera or the Comédie Française. He has all the principal newspapers from around the world delivered every day and has every possible kind of book acquirable. In effect he's on the Nineteenth Century Internet.

He cultivates exclusively 'artificial', highly elaborated pleasures and can't bear to step outside the centre of Paris. His friends are all sophistication, guile and free-loading. He is in the Heart of Darkness and the City of Light simultaneously. He is blessed and damned as is anyone living in a high-tech world. To round out his point Eça provides a moral crisis for his protagonist which transports him back to the 'good life' in rural Portugal where this ex-urban sophisticate takes up a deeply unconvincing interest in the welfare of cows and peasants.

An astonishingly prescient and haunting book, which is well worth dragging out of its obscurity. The current edition was translated by the noted South African poet Roy Campbell.

R K

'Almost immediately she reappeared: and Madame Oriol....seated herself at the table, where Jacinto found Maltese tangerines for her, frozen chestnuts, and a biscuit soaked in Tokay.

She refused them with her hands kept in her muff. She was neither tall, nor strong, but every fold of her dress, or curve of her cloak, fell and rippled harmoniously, with perfections covering perfections. Under her close veil you could scarcely perceive the whiteness of her powdered skin or the darkness of her large eyes. What with those black silks and velvets and a little, hot reddish-gold hair, strongly twisted, which showed over the black furs on her nape, she gave forth a sensation of smoothness and fineness everywhere. Persistently I considered her as a flower of 'Civilisation' — and I thought of the centuries of toil, refinement and culture that were required to produce the soil from which such a flower could bud, and then bloom fully, as now, in full perfume, even more beautiful for being a flower of conscious cultivation and the hot house, and for having something in her petals that seemed about to fade and wither.' p39

The Illustrious House of Ramires [A Ilustre Casa de Ramires]

Like his French contemporary Huysmans, Eça de Queiros started his writing career as a disciple of Zola but came of age as a satirist rather than a realist. His protagonist in *The Illustrious House of Ramires*, Gonçalo Ramires or 'The Nobleman of the Tower', is a decadent aristocrat who entertains whimsical fantasies of future success as novelist and politician. Where Huysmans used the aimless Des Esseintes to explore a sterile aesthetic hell, Eça sets up in Ramires an allegory of Portugal itself. While Portugal plans to sell off its colonies, Ramires is forced to rent out his ancestral lands and as Republican rumblings threaten from Italy and Spain, Ramires, who sees the fatherland as 'a beautiful estate' governed by 'those who receive and rule', is disturbed by the insubordination of a local commoner.

In his well-stocked library, Ramires attempts to write a novel based on the exploits of his predecessors, vamping up his

source material with heroic detail in the same way as an under
confident Portugal was piecing together its own history in
the form of a Romantic epic.

As the narrative jumps between Ramires' life in a late
nineteenth-century province and the Golden Age of his work-
in-progress, the latter reproduces, in the form of a
Shakespearean subplot, the particulars of Ramires' situation
in symbolic form. Ramires' ancestor Tructesindo finds his
castle assailed by Baião 'The Bastard,' who, holding his son
to ransom, demands the hand of Tructesindo's daughter.
Similarly, Ramires finds himself importuned by the Civil
Governor, a heartless womaniser, who offers him a future in
politics in return for entry into his family circle, where he
intends to seduce his sister. This two-tier system generates
the novel's driving irony, playing off Tructesindo's heroic
integrity against Ramires' cowardice and willingness to
compromise. As critics have pointed out, Ramires, in his
obsession with a largely imaginary past, is a Don Quixote.
But whereas Don Quixote, like a naive reader, interprets his
chivalric fables literally, believing himself to *be* a knight-errant,
Ramires understands all too well his own pathetic nature.
Like Ebeneezer Scrooge he is haunted in his sleep by the
ghosts of Ramireses past; the *fados* sung by his guitar-playing
sidekick Videirinha to celebrate his family name, mock and
torment him. In desperation, he sees a vision of his ancient
tower 'split apart, revealing an unexpected pile of rubbish
and dirty skirts.'

Things pick up for Ramires when, almost inadvertently, he
attacks the disrespectful ruffian whose constant insults provide
one of the novel's leitmotifs. Through a chain of Chinese
whispers the episode is elaborated and exaggerated throughout
the region until it is eventually reported in the Lisbon newspapers in a form no less heroic than Ramires' own accounts
of Tructesindo's adventures. Swept into office on a wave of
popularity, Ramires feels purified but also somewhat hollow,
the novel thereby ending ambiguously, its satire scathing but
not vindictive, its general tone more affectionate than
subversive. T M

'In the broad, lofty room where the broad, pallid rays
of moonlight..."Broad, broad"! And the pallid rays, the eternal "pallid
rays"! And this cursed castle was so complicated, too! And Don

Tructesindo, whom I just can't see clearly, and so ancient! Horrible, the whole lot! He knocked aside his leather chair, bit into his cigar angrily and marched out of the library, slamming the door behind him, thoroughly bored with his work, with that complicated and confused Manor of Santa Ireneia, and with his ancestors — huge iron-clad men with ringing voices who remained as elusive as wisps of smoke.'

The Maias [Os Maias]

Eça de Queirós was one of the leading intellectuals of the 'Generation of 1870', highly concerned with the future of his country in the aftermath of the civil war of 1828–1834. Portugal had emerged from this internal struggle as a constitutional monarchy, politically and economically dependent on Great Britain, while culturally dominated by France.

The Maias was first published in 1888, against this historical background, and is not only Eça's acknowledged masterpiece but also the novel in which the Portuguese most recognise themselves, even today.

It traces the moral decline of a wealthy and powerful aristocratic family over three generations. Their destinies reflect ideological, cultural and political developments in Portugal from the beginning of the nineteenth century to the mid-1880's. *The Maias* displays a social determinism to which they are all subjected; thus Afonso da Maia the elderly head of the family upholds the old, traditional values which are gradually lost in the next generations who, by adopting imported foreign ideas, turn the 'march to progress' into a 'march into decadence'.

At its simplest level the plot is melodramatic and even implausible with an all too obvious historical symbolism. But the dominantly ironic tone of the novel makes it a 'comic tragedy' that deflates the emotional tension built around the central motif of unwitting incest between brother and sister. The malevolent turn played by fate serves less to illustrate tragic events than to draw attention to the inward-looking, decadent society that wastes itself in idle pursuits.

Although based on characters and events belonging to a specific geographical and historical context, the novel's continuing appeal rests as much with the writer's masterful use of language in voicing his pointed social critique as with the actual themes: the dynamics of wealth, power and politics.

C P

'When Craft came down a few moments later in evening dress - fresh, white, starched, correct, he found Carlos still covered in the dust of the road, his hat on his head, pacing about the room, in this radiant commotion.

"You're sparkling, man!" said Craft, stopping before him with his hands in his pockets and contemplating him for a moment from above his resplendent collar. "You're afire! You look as though you've a halo round your head! Something or other very good has happened to you!"

Carlos stretched himself and smiled. Then he gazed at Craft for a moment in silence, shrugged his shoulders and murmured:

"One never knows, Craft, whether what happens to one is, in the final analysis, good or bad."

"Usually it's bad", replied the other coldly as he went up to the looking-glass and adjusted the knot of his tie.' pp303-304

The Mandarin (and other stories)

Critics waste time on dating Eça de Queiros's movement from Romanticism to Realism to Fantasy, for these — along with satire, the macabre, farce and, latterly, the sentimental — were ready on his palette when he needed them. *The Mandarin* has a prologue, from an unpublished play, which leaves no doubt about the colour with which he chose to load his brush; we are urged to:

> 'rest a while from the harsh study of human Reality. Let us depart instead for the fields of Dreams and wander those blue, romantic hills where stands the abandoned tower of the Supernatural, where cool mosses clothe the ruins of Idealism. Let us, in short, indulge in a little fantasy!'

Teodoro, the government clerk who tells the moral fable, is a pipsqueak nonentity with 'certain ambitions' who suffers routine indignities with rational resignation and a little hope.

> 'Happiness would arrive one day and to hasten its arrival I did everything that a good Portuguese and a constitutionalist could do: I prayed every night to Our Lady of Sorrows and bought lottery tickets, the cheapest available.'

At his lodgings he drugs himself with old books from the flea market; one day he reads about a fabulously wealthy mandarin:

> 'all you have to do is to ring the bell placed on a book by your side. In that remote corner of Mongolia, he will utter a single sigh. He will then be a corpse and at your feet you will see gold beyond the dreams of avarice. Mortal reader, will you ring the bell?'

Teodoro debates with the Devil he doesn't believe in before he rings the bell. The story follows the consequences of that act, his life of indulgence and extreme pleasure, of *ennui* and guilt, his pilgrimage to China to offer reparation, his discovery that humanity does not deserve justice, his attempted return to his old life (the picture of his lodgings in Lisbon's Travessa da Conceição is more enjoyable than any oriental extravagance) and his irremediable haunting by the dead mandarin.

When he was consul in Havana, before taking up the post in Newcastle upon Tyne, Eça bore an unfulfillable responsibility for thousands of Chinese labourers shipped from Portuguese Macao. Did this burden find perverse expression in Teodoro's mind?

> 'The flowers in my rooms wither and no one replaces them; the dullest of lights dazzles me as if it were a blazing torch; and when my lovers in their white peignoirs come to lie in my bed, I weep, as if they were the shrouded legions of my dead joys.'

At the point of death Teodoro challenges us with his own choice.

The Mandarin is a novella about getting what you dream of and wishing to be rid of it. Also in this volume, along with part of *The Relic*, is the wonderfully mature, delicately realised short story, *José Matias*, about not taking what you desire. From the perspective of his funeral, it contemplates a rich man's decline, consumed by unconsummated passion for the married, widowed and re-married Elisa. His obsession takes hold:

> 'And love began to seep out of our impenetrable friend José Matias, like thin smoke through the invisible cracks in a locked house engulfed by flames.'

When we learn that José turned Elisa down, perception shifts, the tale becomes a critique of Romantic alienation and, at last, we understand the phrase 'a locked house.' Whose victim is he? P H

'Convinced that I would never be able to placate Ti Chin Fu. I spent the whole of that night in my room in my palace on the Largo do Loreto, where the innumerable candles still dappled the damask curtains with reds the colour of fresh blood, and I considered how best to rid myself of those supernatural millions, as if I were ridding myself of the trappings of sin. That way I might perhaps free myself once and for all of that paunch and that hateful kite!

I left my palace and gave up my nabob existence. I put on a threadbare jacket and went back to Madame Marques' house. I returned to the office, my spine bent, to beg for my 20 *mil-reis* a month and my beloved quill!

But a greater suffering came to sour my days. Assuming I was bankrupt, all those whom my wealth had once humbled now heaped insults on me, the way people smear with filth the fallen statue of a ruined prince. In a triumph of irony. the newspapers mocked my poverty. The Aristocracy, who had fallen tongue-tied with adulation at the feet of the nabob now ordered their coachmen to run down in the streets the flinching figure of the ministry scribe. The 'Clergy, whom I had enriched, accused me of being a 'wizard', the People threw stones at me and, when I complained meekly of the granitic toughness of her steaks, Madame Marques planted two hands on her hips and shouted:

"Well, what do you expect, Pipsqueak? You'll just have to put up with it! Beggars can't be choosers, you know!"' p72

The Relic [A Relíquia]

The Relic (1887) is one long romp through a world polarised by piety and debauchery, Lisbon's credulity and decadence, Egypt's old stones and fleshpots, Palestine's corrupt nostalgia and — jumping 1800 years — 'one day in the month of Nisan, when Pontius Pilate was the procurator of Judaea'! It is also a hard look at religion and hypocrisy, love and lust, truth and the fateful lie. It was a risk: like *The Mandarin* it released Eça from realism's shackles but didn't endear him to Catholic critics.

It may have been timely for him. Its writing coincided with his marriage, at forty, and drew on the travels of his twenties with his wife's brother to Egypt and the Near East. Fantasy was another satirical edge with which to flay society; Eça's sensual writing may have been compensation for his colluding with it.

Wealthy, devout, puritanical Aunt Patrocínio's adoption of the young Teodorico costs the boy dear.

'Eyes lowered I would say the creed and list the Ten
Commandments, all the time aware of the smell she gave off,
the bittersweet odour of snuff and formic acid.'

As a graduate, the brief moments he steals away from the
stifling religiose home, the prison he must still endure for his
inheritance's sake, are given over to real devotion.

'Trembling, I knelt down on the rug and pressed my chest
against her knees, offering myself up to her like a mere beast.
She opened wide her shawl and mercifully took me in.'

She, this time, is Amelia, an energetic lover who soon cools
and teaches Teodorico, not for the last time, about betrayal.
He too refines duplicity; his aunt's commission to visit
Jerusalem to acquire a healing relic grants him freedom at
last, and scope for indulgence, such as Mary from Yorkshire
who gives 'her brave little Portuguese lover' her nightdress in
Alexandria, while his companion, the German scholar Topsius,
is a suitably didactic foil in the holy places and whore houses
of Palestine. Teodorico obtains a branch of thorns that are
plaited up into a crown.

Then he and Topsius awake, transported back in time, and
set off for Jerusalem on the eve of Passover:

'The whole city was bathed in sumptuous light... And within
the wall, facing the cedar trees that shaded us, stood the Temple,
proud and splendid... Walled in by polished granite, protected
by ramparts of marble, it looked like the shining citadel of a
god!'

In his holy delirium, Teodorico meets Pharisees and
prostitutes, Saducees and soothsayers, Essenes and Jesus
himself; a portrait of a society painted with sensuous precision.
He hears Pilate's question, 'What is the truth?'; he sees the
crucifixion, and the grave from which the still-living Jesus is
smuggled. The empty tomb is the big lie upon which
Christendom is founded.

Back in his own century, he approaches another Jerusalem:

'Trembling, I galloped forward. And I saw the city below me...
sombre, packed with monasteries and crouched behind its
crumbling walls, like a poor, flea-ridden woman who crawls
into a corner to die, wrapped in the ragged remnants of her
cloak.'

After many adventures he returns to his aunt, loaded with
relics, longing for her death and his inheritance. The tale
unwinds with a kind of recalcitrant logic. Of course the parcels
— crown of thorns and nightdress reeking of sin — get

swapped; plot and moral creak alarmingly as they work themselves out, but this book has so many unexpected delights that perhaps it doesn't matter whether Eça earns or gives the lie to his final paragraph; '...I had lost it all...because for one moment, I lacked the "shameless heroism needed to tell a lie", which thanks to some universal illusion, is responsible for creating all sciences and all religions, whether it loudly strides the earth or merely lifts its eyes palely to Heaven.' P H

'He gave us two ears of corn and, following behind him, our Gentile feet entered the forbidden courtyard of Judah.

Walking by my side, Eliezer of Silo, courteous and gentle, asked me if my country lay far off and if its roads were dangerous.

I mumbled something vague, evasive:

"Yes. We've just arrived from Jericho."

"Has the balsam harvest been good there?"

"Wonderful!" I assured him ardently. "Blessed be the Eternal One, for in this year of His grace, we're up to our eyes in balsam!"

He seemed pleased. He told me then he was one of the doctors who live in the Temple, since the priests and those who perform the sacrifices suffer continually from 'intestinal disorders', because they're always walking about, sweating and barefoot, on the cold flagstones of the courtyards.

"That's why', he murmured, his kind eyes glinting playfully, "the people in Zion call us 'gut doctors'!" "I bent double with laughter and pleasure at that joke whispered to me in the austere dwelling place of the Eternal One. Then, recalling my own intestinal disorders in Jericho, provoked by my passion for the divine but treacherous melons of Syria, I asked the amiable physician if in these circumstances he would prescribe bismuth.

The learned man cautiously shook his woollen mitre. Then, raising one finger in the air, he entrusted me with this incomparable remedy:

"Take glue from Alexandria, saffron from the garden, an onion from Persia and dark wine from Emmaus, mix it all up, then boil it. Leave it to cool in a silver vase and place it at a crossroads at sunrise....' pp186-7

The Yellow Sofa and Other Stories

In *The Yellow Sofa* one of Eça's clerky Lisbon characters, Godofredo Alves, is resoundingly cuckolded by his supposed best friend and office colleague the elegant Machado. Over the span of a hundred-odd pages Godofredo goes from a world of innocent domestic bliss where 'when one is well brought up, everything turns out right' through the trauma of losing friend and wife in one blow, his subsequent loneliness and then, finally, to a reconciliation with wife/adulteress and friend/adulterer.

The genius of the book is how Eça captures all the emotional fluctuations the eminently weedy and Pooterish Godofredo endures during this trajectory, and with such accuracy. The result is an enjoyably humorous novella that is simultaneously breathtakingly ironic.

Godofredo Alves seems like a marvellous example of a benighted conformist, the man who will put up with anything for the sake of a quiet, moderately comfortable existence. In that way he seems very English, a 'Portuguese soul' with the opposite of the fiery jealous temperament that Latin peoples are supposed to possess. Eça brings us this character in a treatment that is both sardonic and tender, achieving the effect of his famous and genial *truthfulness*. R K

'But worst of all were the lonely evenings. He had always been a home-loving man, fond of coming home early putting on his slippers, enjoying his own domestic scene. In the old days, Ludovina would play the piano in the drawing room for a while; he would go round and light the lamps, like a devotee preparing an altar, for he loved music and he would finish his cigar in his armchair, listening to her playing, gazing at the mass of her dark hair hanging over her shoulders in graceful abandon and intimacy. Certain pieces that she played him gave him a feeling of having his heart caressed by something soft and velvety, and made him swoon; one especially, a certain waltz, *Souvenir of Andalusia*... How long it had been since he had heard it played!

While the summer lasted, he went for a walk every evening. But even the sight of the streets revived memories of lost happiness. There would be an open balcony, with a young woman in a bright dress, enjoying the air, and this made him think of his lonely house, now lacking the swirl of a woman's skirts; and at nightfall, there was a window which revealed the subdued light of a pleasant evening party, and coming from it the gentle sound of a piano...And worn out, his shoes dusty, he then acutely felt the unhappy evidence of his loneliness.' pp90-91

Travels In My Homeland [Viagens na minha terra]

'Garrett was not only a man of letters,' wrote the critic Rebelo da Silva, 'but an entire literature in himself.' He revitalised the theatre of his time, wrote its finest lyric poetry, struggled all his life to liberalize the Portuguese psyche and society, and wrote two of the first novels in the literature. *Travels in my Homeland* is his prose masterpiece.

Mix Laurence Sterne and Sir Walter Scott, combine a travel book with a romance and a political tract; do it playfully and passionately and you'll get some idea of the texture of Garrett's innovative novel. It's said that the Inquisition and the Lisbon earthquake of 1755 delayed the birth of the Portuguese novel by the best part of a century, but when Garrett took hold of it he dragged it into the world kicking and chuckling.

João Baptista da Silva Leitão was born in Oporto in 1799 into a well-to-do family who lost their wealth when they fled to the Azores to escape the 1807 French invasion. A politically active law student at Coimbra University, he was stirred to write poetry and plays by the liberal revolution of 1820. The names Almeida and Garrett he took from his mother and grandmother. In 1822 he married the barely fifteen-year-old Luisa Midosi, who may be the model for his heroine Joana, and was forced into exile in England and France by the absolutist faction in 1823. There Garrett found spiritual comrades in the romantic movement.

Political tides carried him home, into prison, to England again and out to the Azores Islands where he joined the constitutionalist forces under Pedro IV which besieged Oporto in July 1832. The anguished romantic novel at the heart of *Travels in my Homeland* takes place in the context of this fratricidal war between Dom Pedro and Dom Miguel. Garrett was on the winning side; he became a deputy; he undertook diplomatic missions and government posts. He was created a viscount in 1851 and minister of foreign affairs in 1852. Patriotic and generous, vain and pretentious, charming and ingenuous to the end, he died in Lisbon in 1854.

It was in July 1843 that he made his journey to Santarem, just fifty miles up the Tagus from Lisbon, to visit an old friend, Passos Manuel, leader of the Progressive Party who lived in the fortress of the first king of Portugal, Afonso Henriques. Only six weeks after this visit the first chapter of *Travels...* appeared in a Lisbon magazine; by the end of 1846 all forty-nine had appeared and the book was published in two volumes.

It begins with a reference to Xavier de Maistre's popular *Voyage autour de ma chambre:*

'That a person who lives near the Alps, in Turin, which is nearly as cold as St. Petersburg, should travel around his bedroom, is understandable... I myself, on these stifling summer nights, often travel as far as my window to get a sight of the snippet of the Tagus at the end of the street... And I have never written down these travels of mine or my impressions of them; well, there was so much to see! My pen was always ambitious: poor yet presumptuous, it needs a broader theme. That is just what

I shall give it. I shall go to Santarem, no less, and I swear that everything I see and hear, everything I think and feel, shall be chronicled.'

Garrett's short journey may seem to have been conceived in whimsy and narrated with irony but he insists, with reason, that it is his odyssey. His models give him the freedom to mix past and present, fiction and history, genres and literary styles:

'These interesting travels of mine shall be a masterpiece, erudite, sparkling with new ideas, something worthy of our century. I need to inform the reader of this, so that he may be forewarned... Now this journey of mine up the Tagus symbolizes the march of our social progress: I hope the reader has understood this by now.'

His destination is the cradle of Portuguese national pride and his own disillusion, redeemed perhaps by satire:

'Santarem is a book of stone in which is inscribed the most interesting and poetic part of our chronicles. Rich in illuminations, in cut-outs, in floral pieces, in illustrations, in superb arabesques and tracery, it was the most beautiful, most precious book in Portugal...[it] should have lasted for ever, until the hand of the Creator stretched forth to erase the memory of His creature.

But this Nineveh was not destroyed; this Pompeii was not submerged by any gigantic catastrophe. The people whose history is in the book still exists. But this people fell into childish ways: they were given the book to play with and they tore it, mutilated it, pulled out its pages one by one and made kites and dolls and paper hats with them.'

When he tells the story of seventh-century Saint Iria, for whom the town was named, he plumps for the popular version, not the monks' sanctimonious tale. Monks and 'barons' he hates. He attacks the barons, who are destroying his country, with all the venom of one whose ideals have been betrayed by opportunists. They have redefined themselves, who had been classical heroes — *barões* — in the first line of Camões's *Lusiads*. Meanwhile, in the Vale of Santarem, the *romance* develops:

'The trees, the window, the nightingale...the hour of day... late afternoon...what more was needed to complete the romance?

A female figure to come and sit at that balcony, in a white dress — oh, it must be white!...

The eyes, the eyes...', I said, by now thinking aloud, but still enraptured, 'the eyes...black.'

'Well, they were green!'

'Her eyes green...hers, the figure at the window?'

'Green as two priceless, gleaming, transparent oriental emeralds.'

'No, really!...Is that a joke or is there really a pretty woman there?'....

This dialogue obviously took place between myself and one of my travelling companions. We did indeed dismount; we sat down and this is the story of the *maiden of the nightingales*... a simple, naïve little story, unpretentiously and honestly told.'

Believe that if you like. Green-eyed Joana has her source in the sixteenth-century *Livro de Saudades* of Bernardim Ribeiro. Her beloved Carlos advances with Dom Pedro's forces. The cottage where she lives with her blind grandmother is Dom Miguel's last outpost. But who is the old monk who visits them every Friday? What secrets possess them? Lust, faithlessness, incest?

'In this preposterous, unclassifiable book of my *Travels*, the thread of the stories and observations does not so much break as become intertwined, and in such a manner that, I am fully aware, much patience is needed to unravel and trace it....'

Garrett weaves his yarns with such wit, experimental zest and angry satire, that the book's a delight for anyone interested in the matter of Portugal. It's relevant too. Ten years after the liberal victory Joana's grandmother continues to wind yarn, insentient, a dead woman awaiting burial like Pessoa's 'postponed corpse'. Twenty years after the Revolution is not a bad time to go travelling with Garrett in the barons' Portugal. P H

The Book Of Disquiet (Tr. M J Costa)/The Book Of Disquietude (Tr. Richard Zenith)/The Book Of Disquiet (Tr. Iain Watson) [O Livro do desassossego]

Lisbon: What The Tourist Should See [Lisboa: O Que O Turista Deve Ver] (Livros Horizonte: Lisbon 1992)

Fernando Pessoa is a colossus of Portuguese culture, though an unlikely one: slight of build, a clerk's neat clothes, almost asexual, bow-tie, homburg, face punctuated by a trim moustache, myopic eyes behind gold-rimmed spectacles, he sits still outside the Lisbon writers' cafe *A Brasileira*, a bronze figure at a table with an empty bronze chair beside him, waiting for whom?

The two big names regularly and reverently breathed by those with the smallest knowledge of Portuguese literature are Pessoa and Camões. What a contrast Pessoa is to the rugged, randy, one-eyed sixteenth-century epic and lyric poet Luis Vaz de Cames who sailed the seas, was wrecked in the

Mekong river, stranded in Goa and Mozambique and commemorated in Jerónimos monastery with an exuberant sarcophagus opposite that of Vasco de Gama. Pessoa has a bleak marble and metal pillar poised uneasily in the cloister, inscribed with verses by some of the poets that he was.

Pessoa (his real name) means 'person' or 'individual', but he assumed many names that he called 'heteronyms'; or perhaps we should say that Pessoa's pen was assumed by many of the multiple personalities of which he — and, he maintained, each person or *pessoa* — was made. His universe, his theatre was within him.

'The idea of travelling nauseates me.
I've already seen what I've never seen.
I've already seen what I have yet to see.

The tedium of the forever new, the tedium of discovery (as if there were a difference between things and ideas), the unchanging identity of everything...Life makes me suffer a vague nausea, and any kind of movement aggravates it.

Tedium is absent only from landscapes that don't exist, from books I'll never read. Life, for me, is a somnolence that never reaches the brain. This I keep free, so that I can be sad there.' (*The Book of Disquietude* tr Richard Zenith)

Fernando Pessoa was born in Lisbon in 1888. After his father died of TB, his mother married the Portuguese consul at Durban and they emigrated to South Africa in 1895. He returned to Lisbon in 1905 to live with his grandmother and great-aunts.

'I went among them as a stranger, but not one of them saw what I was. I lived among them as a spy, but nobody — not even myself — suspected what I was. All of them imagined I was one of their kinsfolk, but not one knew that there had been a substitution at my birth. So I was like others without resembling them....'(*The Book of Disquiet* tr. Iain Watson)

Soon abandoning his Philosophy course at the university, he tried unsuccessfully to set up a printing press. For the rest of his life he worked for various businesses as a commercial translator and moved from lodgings to rented rooms to relatives again.

'And if the office in the Rua dos Douradores represents Life for me, the second floor room I live in on that same street represents Art. Yes, Art, living on the same street as Life but in a different room; Art, which offers relief from life without actually relieving one of living, and which is monotonous as life itself but in a different way. Yes, for me Rua dos Douradores embraces the meaning of all things, the resolution of all mysteries, except the existence of mysteries themselves which is something beyond resolution. (*The Book of Disquiet* tr.M J Costa)

One night in 1914 Pessoa stood at his chest of drawers and wrote 'about thirty poems straight off, in a kind of ecstasy whose nature I cannot define.' It was, he said, an unrepeatable day of triumph. The poet who appeared in him was Alberto Caeiro, the Keeper of Sheep, whom he regarded as The Master for himself and for two other major heteronyms, Ricardo Reis and Álvaro de Campos. Pessoa had his own disciples, though, until his last year, he published only a scattering of poems, prose fragments, a handful of pamphlets and manifestos and three booklets of poems in English. In 1915 came the first, and only, two editions of the review *Orpheu* through which Pessoa and his friends had a dramatic influence on twentieth-century literature. José Sobral de Almada Negreiros regarded their work, including that of Mário de Sá-Carneiro, a friend who killed himself in Paris in 1916, as a glorious and catastrophic break with the past.

Of course, like all modernisms, it wasn't. In 1915, Pessoa wrote to another friend, 'The patriotic idea, always present in my intentions to some extent, is now growing in me, and I can't think of creating anything without aiming to exalt the name of Portugal through whatever I am able to accomplish.' He planned to set up as an astrologer (that and his later relationship with the magus Aleister Crowley, among other things, invite comparison with W.B. Yeats). After the First World War he began works which aimed at a re-vision of Portugal, that had once been great and should be again, now in spiritual rather than political terms; the finest of them would be the multi-faceted poem *Mensagem* (Message), published in 1934, the year before his death.

There's little evidence of this positive, propagandising frame of mind in *The Book of Disquiet*. Up to now I've led you, misled you to believe that it is by Fernando Pessoa. It's not. In the end he attributed it to one Bernardo Soares, an assistant accounts clerk, 'a demi-heteronym, a literary personage...or rather a simple mutilation of my own personality.'

In 1919, at one office where he worked, Pessoa met the nineteen-year-old Ophelia Queiroz. It was a compulsive, tender, sometimes humorous affair which lasted thirteen months. During its course he moved in with his widowed mother on her return from Africa. She died in 1925 and his relationship with Ophelia revived painfully a few years later. He stayed in the house he'd shared with his mother for the rest of his life. At work:

'I approach my desk as if it were a bulwark against life...I feel love for all this, perhaps because I have nothing else to love or perhaps too, because even though nothing truly merits the love of any soul, if, out of sentiment, we must give it, I might just as well lavish it on the smallness of an inkwell as on the grand indifference of the stars. (*The Book of Disquiet* tr M J Costa)

The meditations on love in *The Book of Disquiet* are remarkable for their chill luminosity and hopeless tenderness. The pictures of Lisbon come (especially if you know the city) with the shock of the new. The folders and disorganized papers that make up Soares's book sat in a big trunk with the rest of Pessoa's life's work — 27,000-plus documents — for years until, painstakingly but still not finally collated, it was published in 1982. Three English translations were published in 1991; Richard Zenith's is the fullest, sharp and scholarly; Iain Watson's good selection reads rather stiffly; Margaret Jull Costa's prizewinning version is the one I return to because, for me, it breathes with Pessoa/Soares's breath: to read it is to overhear a man, often seeming pathetic because so courageous, and for all the costume-changes, suffering life voluptuously, nakedly.

Pessoa's guidebook, *Lisboa: What the Tourist Should See*, first published in 1992, has quite a different voice. Perhaps he never quite rediscovered the city his five-year-old self lost: he gives us an enthusiast's pedantic catalogue of monuments spiced with moments of 'poetry'. It can hardly be compared with the Lisbon of his other writing. Alvaro de Campos's town is a wharf wide open to the world, a station like an ever-beating heart. Bernardo Soares prizes the 'village' that is the city's soul.

Pessoa wants us to know how great a city Lisbon is, and was, and will be: not merely the Cultural Capital of Europe (as in 1994), but spiritual capital of the world, and head of the Fifth Empire when King Sebastian, who fell in his ill-conceived Moroccan campaign of 1578, returns like King Arthur or Christ himself to restore Portugal to greatness. This mythic metaphor is what Pessoa explores in *Mensagem's* poems: a great modernist's book that sets Portugal's prophetic heroes in an heraldic shieldscape. Like Camões's epic *Lusiads*, it seeks out Portugal's destiny. Despite the doubtful fog with which it ends, it won second prize from the Propaganda Ministry of the dictator Salazar whom Pessoa despised. It's potent, some say dangerous, stuff.

> 'At this moment I have so many fundamental thoughts, so many truly metaphysical things to say that I feel suddenly tired and decide not to write anymore, not to think anymore, but to let the fever of saying lull me to sleep whilst, with closed eyes, I gently stroke as I would a cat all the things I might have said.'
> (*The Book of Disquiet* tr. M J Costa)

But then, Soares is a humbler creature than his progenitor. If we could melt the bronze Pessoa at his cafe table, he'd order another brandy, another coffee, light maybe his seventy-sixth cigarette of the day and, if he was comfortable, snap at the world with wit and dazzle us with his sharp mind. They say he was fun to be with. He died in hospital in 1935, aged forty- seven. The previous day he'd written his very last words, in English: 'I know not what tomorrow will bring.' Perhaps the empty bronze chair beside him waits for a dutiful tourist or for any *pessoa* willing to lift an eyebrow at destiny. Or for Ophelia. Or for King Sebastian. P H

Note:The poetry of Fernando Pessoa (including Mensagem *mentioned above) has been widely if patchily translated.*

'Sadly I write in my quiet room, alone as I have always been, alone as I will always be. And I wonder if my apparently feeble voice might not embody the essence of thousands of voices, the longing for self-expression of thousands of voices, the patience of millions of souls resigned like my own to useless dreaming and clueless hoping in this quotidian destiny. In these moments my heart beats louder because I'm conscious of it. I live more because I live more grandly. I feel a religious force in my person, a species of prayer, something like an outcry. But from my mind comes its rebuttal... I see myself on the high fourth floor of Douradores Street, where I feel sleepy; I look past the half-written page at unlovely vain life and at the cheap cigarette [...] on my worn blotting-paper. Here I am on this fourth floor, interrogating life!, saying what souls feel!, inventing prose...' p11 (*The Book of Disquietude* tr. Richard Zenith)

Always Astonished

A valuable, accessible little collection of varied pieces from His Supreme Quirkiness, Fernando Pessoa. Pessoa published little in his lifetime but amassed a great pile of writings which have only recently been published in various forms. A selection like this is a valid enough way to get something of this curious genius of 'self-reflexivity' across to a wider public.

Always Astonished includes little essays by Pessoa 'explaining' his famous heteronyms (the invented alter egos he created to write different flavours of poetry and criticism), a long letter to the Italian Futurist supremo Marinetti detailing his objections and affiliations to Futurism as well as his only completed short story *The Anarchist Banker*.

The title *Always Astonished* however is taken from a collection of extracts from his journal and focuses mainly on moments of awareness and self-awakening; passages where Pessoa takes his exploration of his own individual human consciousness — and by extension that of us all — to fascinatingly observed heights; an achievement which prompts the adjective we always come to with Pessoa; *unique*. Unique, unique, unique.

R K

'Anyone who is in any way a poet knows very well how much easier it is to write a good poem (if good poems lie in the man's power) about a woman who interests him very much than about a woman he is deeply in love with. The best sort of love poem is generally written about an abstract woman.

A great emotion is too selfish; it takes into itself all the blood of the spirit, and the congestion leaves the hands too cold to write. Three sorts of emotions produce great poetry-strong but quick emotions, seized upon for art as soon as they have passed; strong and deep emotions in their remembrance a long time after; and false emotions, that is to say, emotions felt in the intellect. Not insincerity, yet a translated sincerity is the basis of all art.' p53

A Centenary Pessoa

A special and rather beautiful book, the studied tribute of many artists and writers to the unusual genius of Fernando Pessoa, based around a diverse selection of his work. Several biographical and literary essays are also included, penned by some of his most eminent interrogators; Octavio Paz and Roy Campbell amongst others. It is the Mexican Paz who points out the strong Anglo-Saxon influence on Pessoa who spoke and wrote English since his boyhood in South Africa.

Pessoa, despite his 'young fogey' dress and manners, was part of a strong modernist and avant-garde current and this is brought out in a very appealing way by the reproduction of the covers of literary magazines of the time with their advanced typographic design and Futurist graphics. There is an equally fascinating photo-essay on Pessoa, his friends and family and on the very charming-looking bars and cafés he spent half his life in.

The greatest achievement of this book though is to reflect so well, in its diversity of sources, Pessoa's notoriously fragmented artistic persona. He was a man who wrote in several distinct voices and who claimed 'to pretend is to know yourself'. He was a grand pioneer in fact of the latest stage in the human quest for a developed individuality. He was so individual that he transcended individuality itself and played with it instead; a theme explored at length in Paz's contribution to this book. Other highlights must be the twenty-two colour plates of paintings inspired by Pessoa's character and work; particularly the astonishing portraits by Pessoa's friend Almada Negreiros and by the contemporary painter José Joâo Brito.

There is a selection here of Pessoa's writing from all major areas of his work, quite a treasure-trove, as well as a useful bibliography of articles and books about him in English.

'I am nothing

I shall never be anything

I cannot wish to be anything

Apart from this I have in me all the world's dreams'

from *The Tobacco Shop* p92

José Cardoso

Ballad Of Dog's Beach [Ballada da praia dos cães]

Ballad of Dog's Beach won the 1982 Grand Prize for Fiction
of the Portuguese Writers' Association, when Cardoso Pires,
already the celebrated author of a dozen books was fifty-seven.
Why should a mere thriller gain such recognition? This mere
thriller is a fine novel, written by a marvellously mordant
novelist who was born in 1925, just prior to the birth of the
New State, the name given to the fascist-like Salazar regime,
and was present in Largo do Carmo to witness its demise on
25 April 1974.

Based on a true story of intrigue and murder under Salazar's
regime, *Ballad of Dog's Beach* begins with a chilling, because
objective, fifteen-point forensic portrait of the body of an
unknown man, followed by 'Circumstances of discovery':

'Sand removed with every precaution, and man's body found
lying on left side, much decayed. Shoes were
reversed...Woollen socks, well-worn. Wrist-watch (Tissot MM)
stopped at 05.27.41. No documents, personal effects or evidence of identity. Shreds of clothing at no great distance, torn
by dogs.'

Little more is objective. For much of the novel we (with the
narrator) are inside the head — a sympathetic and thus
profoundly disturbing interior — of Inspector Elias Santana
who lives with his pet lizard, the Reptile; Elias is a
superbly-drawn character whose presumptions, teasings-out,
blind alleys, fantasies and base instincts draw us into a murky
universe of possible motives and actions that culminated in
the squalid death of Major Dantas. For within a few pages we
know who the victim is: a soldier who escaped detention while
awaiting sentence for his part in an abortive coup. We know
who the suspects are: Mena, young, beautiful and far from
innocent; the corporal, a scared boy; the idealistic architect.
We know that all four holed up in a house. The superintendent
informs Elias — nick-named 'Graveyard' — that the PIDE,
the political police they don't trust, are involved.

'That corpse was ours when they thought we had a sex- crime,
but the theory's altered.'

'If blood starts smelling of politics,' Elias rejoined, 'even the
flies take off.'

The superintendent stroked his coat lapels.

'Graveyard,' he said, 'whether they want it or whether they don't, it's political. The flavour is *animus conspirandi*. It tends to conspiracy, and what tends to conspiracy is, need I say, the concern of the PIDE. Otherwise, what are they there for?'

He looked up, and from where Elias sat was a brown Polaroid reflection of the window-pane and an auburn moustache above a nodding cigarette. *Animus conspirandi.* Or *anus conspirandi*, what was a syllable here or there...?

In the person of its agents we outstare the psychopathology of a corrupt state, as well as the curdled idealism and paranoia of those who would overthrow it. The safe house is scene of an erotic sado-masochistic reign of terror. Lipstick, semen, blood. Elias too — with his heartburn, his thin hair, his long little fingernail — is sexually obsessed. Fear and lust complicates everything until at last it sifts and simplifies. Nothing is quite what it seems, or what it has come to seem since policemen, rather than dogs, began to dig a body out of a sand-dune.

The novel intricately reconstructs the reconstruction of the crime. 'Thus,' writes Cardoso Pires in a concluding note, 'fact and fiction, at every step, divide and come together, independent when parallel, conflicting when they meet; and no resemblance between truth and conjecture is purely coincidental.' You bet. P H

The Year Of The Death Of Ricardo Reis [O Ano da morte de Ricardo Reis]

The Stone Raft [A Jangada de Pedra]

The Chair (in 'Passport to Portugal')

Baltasar And Blimunda [Memorial do Convento]

Manual Of Painting And Calligraphy [Manual de Pintura e Caligrafia]

On 7 June 1994, the fifth centenary of the Treaty of Tordesillas, Spanish and Portuguese newspapers featured a debate between Gonzalo Torrente Ballester and José Saramago. That eminent novelists should discuss a treaty which divided the heathen world between Portugal and Castile by drawing an imaginary line from pole to pole in 1494, and that their discussion should fill a double-page spread in the daily newspaper *Público*, says a good deal about post-revolutionary, post-colonial Portuguese consciousness.

While the Spaniard proclaimed himself a man of the north, a European, Saramago defended his vision of the Iberian Peninsula drifting southwards between Africa and Latin America; an idea which angers Portuguese who are glad to turn their backs on the exhausted ocean and face Brussels where money comes from today. In Iberia, Saramago insisted, 'there is the call of the south.'

José Saramago was born in 1922. His first novel was published in 1977. He was named Portuguese Writer of the Year in 1992. Self-taught, he had worked as a mechanic and a technical designer before moving to journalism, editing, and translation. In the late sixties he published a book of poetry, followed by essays, short stories and a play. The revolution of 1974 gave him a new subject for fiction or, rather, allowed his subjects new fictive liberty and focus.

That first novel, *Manual of Painting and Calligraphy*, was at first hardly noticed but it brilliantly set out the agenda for subsequent work. His third, the grim and sumptuous *Memorial do Convento*, published in English as *Baltasar and Blimunda*, brought him widespread recognition. Some say it's his sixth for which he will be remembered, *The Gospel According to Jesus Christ*. His books have won many prizes and have been translated into more than twenty languages. He and his English language translator Giovanni Pontiero won in 1993 *The Independent's* Foreign Fiction Award for *The Year of the Death of Ricardo Reis*.

His is a mature voice of great range and power. When Saramago speaks, Portugal listens. Not that it necessarily likes what it hears. He finds it more congenial to live in Lanzarotte. But ask any Portuguese bookseller which native writer sells most copies and the answer is always Saramago. The Portuguese novelist Lídia Jorge told me that many people buy Saramago because of who he is and despite the density of his writing which, she felt, was difficult for the public at large.

It's the density of his work that I love, and its depths and heights, a spaciousness which can be compared with the best of Manueline and modern Portuguese architecture: soaring masses that excite mind and spirit combined with intricate detail — joyful, sensuous, surreal and grotesque. Saramago succeeds in focusing and developing metaphorical long shots and close-ups of souls in palpable worlds. Classical eloquence, fireside storytelling, modernist imagery and angst, postmodern playfulness and ironic self-consciousness are all at his command, a repertoire of rhetoric which enables him to shift his discourse from homespun to sophisticated, satirical to passionate, poetic to philosophic, gutsy to visionary.

One of his most famous short stories, *The Chair*, is a semantic and stylistic game, a study of the anatomy of a chair leg infested by wood-beetle, a chair in Chaplinesque slapstick, a Tom Mix parable about justice, a fierce political satire, a close examination of the skull, brain and eventual haematoma of the old man who is sitting on the chair when it falls, is falling, to the ground. The man, who does not die, has no name.

> 'His double chin trembles over the larynx and other cartilages, and his whole body accompanies the chair backwards, while on the floor the broken leg has rolled over to one side, not far away, because we are there to look on. It has scattered a dense, yellow dust, not all that much, but enough for us to delight in the image of an hour-glass with sand that consists eschatologically of the excrement of coleoptera..' p12

The man in the story has no name, but any Portuguese knows that he is Salazar, Portugal's dictator for thirty-six years, whose repressive order effectively ended in 1968 when he fell from his chair while his chiropodist was washing his hands.

'Any Portuguese knows', but can *we* understand the references and sub-texts of these fictions? Saramago himself has suggested that *The Year of the Death of Ricardo Reis* might be fully appreciated only by a Portuguese. But the iconography of Portugal's culture is itself very entertaining; I recommend Saramago's work as a seductive introduction.

Ricardo Reis was one of the names under which Fernando Pessoa (1888-1935) wrote, not just a pseudonym but a heteronym, one of the great poet's multiple personalities. In Saramago's novel Reis outlives Pessoa by nine months. The book begins with his return to Lisbon in 1935 from sixteen years' exile in Brazil. Pessoa has just died. Salazar is capitalising on the nation's insecurity in pre-war years. Reis finds a changed homeland, but stays in the Hotel Bragança, a hint of royalism (the building, no longer an hotel, is still owned by the Duke of Bragança, putative heir to the throne, who once arranged for me to look at 'Reis's' room). There he finds a suspicious staff and two lovers — the full-hearted chambermaid and the rich guest's daughter with a withered arm. There, as New Year dawns, Pessoa comes from the grave to visit him for the first time. Later, walking to the Tagus, they continue their conversation, Dr. Reis first:

'I am thinking of settling here, of establishing a practice, So you have no intention of ever going back to Brazil, why, It's difficult to explain...let's say that I'm like the insomniac who finally finds a comfortable position on the pillow and can get some sleep. If it's sleep you're after, you've come to the right country. If I accept sleep, it's to be able to dream, To dream is to be absent, to be on the other side, But life has two sides, Pessoa, at least two, we can only reach the other side through dreams, you say this to a dead man, who can tell you from his own experience that on the other side of life there is only death.'

Reis, doctor and poet, moves to an apartment in the Rua de Santa Catarina and does a little locum work while his spirit faces the issues that a man, and especially an artist, must face. Through Reis — his dialogue with Pessoa, his encounters with contrasting lovers, with agents of the state — Saramago brilliantly recreates that uneasy moment in Portuguese history and, in the frank intimacy of Reis's mind, takes on the nation's mythos, Salazar's repressive present, and the legacy of Pessoa himself.

The book starts, 'Here the sea ends and the earth begins.' It finishes, 'Here, where the sea ends and the earth awaits.' The minutiae of great minds and the magnitude of a petty world might well be wearisome, but Saramago's readers are kept full of expectancy.

Early in his next novel, *The Stone Raft*, those who believe that the dead are anything else but dead are reproved: 'if anyone ever said otherwise, or suggested, for example, that Fernando Pessoa visited Ricardo Reis...it was their foolish imagination and nothing else.' But this book is not confined to period Lisbon; its stage is the Iberian Peninsula now and, on it, five characters and a dog who find each other because all are implicated in 'magical' acts which coincide with the Pyrenees' splitting in Saramago's 'foolish imagination':

Portugal and Spain's dramatic separation from the rest of Europe.

Saramago's characters, sharply and tenderly drawn, become fellow travellers and eventually lovers, while Iberia, Europe and the world undergo degrees of social and political upheaval.

> 'For several hundred meters the dog accompanied the wagon in the rain. Then it saw that it could travel, even though on foot, sheltered by that great encumbrance...and that is how we shall see the dog for the rest of the journey...since it does not fancy acting as guide or amusing itself with all that coming and going without any apparent meaning which makes men and dogs so very much alike.'

The stone raft almost collides with the Azores, but side-steps cataclysms and slides south between Africa and Latin America...

> 'the headline which made the deepest impression was the one in a Portuguese newspaper which read The Need for a New Treaty of Tordesillas, this is truly the simplicity of genius...'

Well, you should enjoy the unfolding plot: a parable about cause and effect and cultural potency, with a deliciously written — and translated — account of the characters' geographical, philosophical and sexual pilgrimage to an unknown destination.

The book's direction is clear enough to some critics. The novelist Almeida Faria, a friend of Saramago, doesn't like its anti-European tone. 'Saramago is a communist,' he told me, 'and only communists and fascists have this idea.' The book's big metaphor *is* political, and much more. Nothing should distract you from the rich texture of a marvellous tale. Saramago does what he defines as the writer's task: to enlarge the world. P H

'Already there are cries of anticipation, and the din reaches a crescendo as the deep voice of anchored ships can be heard from the direction of the river, dinosaurs bellowing with their pehistoric rumble that makes one's stomach churn. Sirens rend the air with piercing screams like those of animals being slaughtered, the frantic hooting of cars nearby is deafening, the little bells of the trams tinkle for all they are worth, which is not much, until finally the minute hand covers the hour hand, it is midnight, the happiness of freedom. For one brief moment time has released mankind, has allowed them to live their own lives, time stands aside and looks on, ironic, benevolent, as people embrace one another, friends and strangers, men and women kissing at random. These are the best kisses of all, kisses without any future.' p61 (*Year of the Death of Ricardo Reis*)

The Gospel According to Jesus Christ [O Evangelho segundo Jesus Cristo]

This book assumes an honourable place among works of fiction exploring or using the life of Christ. It doesn't attempt the eyewitness feeling of Henryk Panas' *The Gospel According to Judas*; it lacks the visionary intensity of the account in Mikhail Bulgakov's *The Master and Margarita*; nor is it concerned with the inner or spiritual meaning of events like Michel Tournier's *The Four Wise Men*. Although there are elements of all these in Saramago's version, its substance is very different: an unflinching anatomy of religion, and Christianity in particular, as mass psychosis.

To this end, Jesus appears as a sensitive, sane and fully human man who is already questioning aspects of Judaism, especially its reliance on sacrifice, in his early life. As Saramago comments on the Temple in Jerusalem, 'Anyone witnessing the scene would have to be a saint in order to understand how God could condone this appalling carnage if He is, as He claims, the Father of all men and beasts.' (p68)

Saramago treats Jesus, and his contemporaries, tenderly and with great compassion. The account of Jesus' and Mary Magadelene's meeting and first lovemaking, for example, is simultaneously erotically charged and very moving. There are also nice touches of humour: 'Jesus told the adulteress, Go, and sin no more, but deep down he had grave doubts.' (p267)

With God, however, Saramago is merciless. His God is a psychotic despot who 'does not forgive the sins He makes us commit,' (p117) and for whom 'No salvation suffices, yet condemnation is final.'(p203) When Jesus points out that 'Being God, You must know everything, Up to a certain point, only up to a certain point, What point is that, The point where it starts to become interesting to pretend that I know nothing...' (p279)

In two momentous encounters, the first in the desert and the second years later in an offshore fog, God tricks and bullies Jesus into becoming a martyr and victim in order for Him to become not merely the god of the Jews but a universal god: (P C)

'...My son, man is a piece of wood that can be used for everything, from the moment he's born until the moment he dies, he's always ready to obey, send him there and he goes, tell him to halt and he stops, tell him to turn back and he retreats, whether in peace or in war, man, generally speaking, is the best thing that could have happened to the gods, And the wood from which I'm made, since I'm a man, what use will it be put to, since I'm Your son, You will be the spoon I shall dip into humanity and bring out laden with men who shall believe in the new god I intend to become, Laden with men You will devour, There's no need for Me to devour those who devour themselves.' p284

DE SENA
Jorge

By the Rivers of Babylon

Jorge de Sena was a leading Portuguese poet and man of letters who translated Poe, Hemingway, Faulkner, Cavafy and Brecht. A polymath, multicultural character he lived mainly in exile from Salazar's Portugal. *By the Rivers of Babylon* is a collection of his stories, varied and at times experimental. There's distinctly the manner of an artist in one medium working in another; as with Mervyn Peake (a renowned illustrator) writing the *Gormenghast Trilogy* in an intense close-grained descriptive prose obsessed with material objects — and unlike anything else of its time.

In *By the Rivers of Babylon* De Sena the poet and academic writes about his mainly intellectual and spiritual preoccupations, with a poet's sometimes lucid sometimes obscure tongue. In general the stories concern solitary, intellectual individuals existing in self-made worlds, often quite horrible in nature. There are passages of great beauty and wit and insights into De Sena's very original, reflective personality. R K

'Once in the monastery church, he was overcome with embarrassment when his old friend, Father Athelstan, upon seeing that he did not rise to hear the Gospel read, touched his habit and the habit crumpled to the floor with no-one inside. The memories came back to him: he had been distracted only momentarily, absorbed in the contemplation of all the copies of historical documents that he had received the previous day. Yet he had been perfectly able to feel the touch on his sleeve and was unaware that he was not there. The episode soon became famous and only the abbot's esteem for his scholarly disposition and incessant labours had spared him the scandalous notoriety that would have brought pilgrims and devotees to disturb the peace of mind of a soul who always wrote, always read, debated always, inquired always.' pp20-21

Requiem: A hallucination [Requiem]

Italian novelist Antonio Tabucchi wrote this story in Portuguese because, he says, a story like this could only be written in Portuguese. It was published in Lisbon (1991) before the Italian version came out (1992). But then Professor Tabucchi, foremost champion of Portuguese literature in Italy, specialises in and translates the work of Fernando Pessoa. So it's refreshing to find *Requiem* a quite unprofessorish read. After all, professors aren't supposed to have hallucinations.

> 'I thought: the bloke isn't going to turn up. And then I thought:
> I can't call him a 'bloke', he's a great poet, perhaps the greatest
> poet of the twentieth century, he died years ago, I should treat
> him with respect or, at least, with deference....'

So, right at the beginning, we think we know what we're in for, though the poet is only ever named My Guest. Some nerve, on Tabucchi's part, to have his narrator meet him so soon after José Saramago brought Pessoa back from a fresh grave in *TheYear of the Death of Ricardo Reis* (1984). Reis meets Pessoa in 1935. Tabucchi's 'I' waits for him now, and waits until the very last chapter of a book which, in contrast to Saramago's strenuous masterpiece, is very short, languid, limpid. And enchanting.

It's set in a dream of Lisbon, not the 'real' city, but hot, deserted Lisbon on the last Sunday in July.

> 'He said twelve o'clock, but perhaps he meant twelve o'clock
> at night, because that's when ghosts appear, at midnight.'

That's the plot: the narrator has twelve hours to play with and twenty-three characters to meet in his picaresque ramble, including the Lame Lottery-Ticket Seller, the Cemetery Keeper, Viriata, My Father as a Young Man, the Lighthousekeeper's Wife and the Accordionist. Tadeus, for instance, he last saw in 1965.

> 'Come in, he said, come in, don't be shy, this is the house I've
> always lived in, the house where you ate, slept, fucked, don't
> tell me you don't recognize it? It isn't that, I protested, it's just
> that there are a few matters I need to clear up, you died without
> telling me anything, and I've spent years agonising over it, now
> it's time that I knew, I'm free now, today I feel extra-ordinarily

free, look, I've even lost my Super-Ego, it just reached its expiry date, like milk in a carton, I mean it....'

Requiem is a quest and a homage to the Portuguese. Don't let its affection and blokishness fool you into thinking it simply light. By the time we are sitting with 'I' and My Guest in the post-modern restaurant/disco (the wondrous Alcântara Mar, though it's not named) near the quay after midnight, we've moved, and been deeply moved, a long way in a short time through real imagined Lisbon. After the meal (and there's a note on recipes at the end of the book), the requiem's last notes are played outside on the accordion. There is silence, and the moon. P H

nb Tabucchi's fiction written in Italian is reviewed in *The Babel Guide to Italian Fiction in Translation* (1995)

TORGA
Miguel

Tales from the Mountain[Contos da Montanha + Novos Contos da Montanha]

Torga, twice nominated for the Nobel Prize was undoubtedly one of the great writers of our century. He once said 'the universal is the local without walls' and although his short stories are set in the rugged mountains of Trás-os-Montes in the Portuguese Northland they transcend narrow geography with their subject matter —— human beings and the emotions that drive them, the love and hatred, courage and fear, the greed and (sometimes) the generosity of spirit. Read singly the stories are striking, together the effect is stunning.

Although they could be classed as part of the literature of social protest they avoid the flat, proselytizing tone associated with some Portuguese Neo-Realist works. Torga wrote that four decades of an oppressive regime had disfigured the landscape of his country, in human as much as in physical terms. As a result of his critical stance he was arrested and imprisoned and his work banned. While he undoubtedly loved his homeland and respected its people, warts and all, he was far more ambivalent about the forces of law and authority, amongst whom he included the Church, although for a writer who rejected religion he used many religious images and symbols.

These *Tales from the Mountain* are told from the point of view of an omniscient 'outside' narrator. Given Torga's own medical background, the obvious analogy is with the doctor who steps back to make a diagnosis and them comes forward with a cure. Compassion balances detachment and he doesn't hesitate to present human conduct in all its ugliness as when the villagers burn Julião alive in the story *The Leper*. Torga doesn't stand in judgment but leaves the reader to draw his own conclusions.

Much of Torga's writing has a filmic quality and in fact *The Leper* was turned into a short film. His cinemaesque technique is seen too in the opening paragraphs of *Fronteira* with the frontier village silhouetted against a twilight sky and coming to life as darkness falls. The narrator is the eye of the camera, focusing on particular characters and events just as a director would select shots, angles and lighting set-ups. Torga alternates wide pans of village and mountains with close-ups of its inhabitants — a community of smugglers setting off on their clandestine business. He even 'cuts' back and forth between different individuals to reinforce the point that the village of Fronteira (= Frontier) is a collective protagonist, where the villagers act as one.

Fronteira has all the usual Torga ingredients; birth and death — through violence rather than old age — religious symbolism, healthy sexual desire and an underlying criticism of a society that does nothing to alleviate poverty and deprivation. There is also humour as when we see Isabel the smuggler-heroine of the piece looking more like a woman off to launder a load of nappies while the trigger-happy national guardsman Robalo, first described a mastiff on the prowl, dogged and persistent falls for her like a ton of bricks and ends up joining the bad guys himself.

Torga gives his characters an authentic voice, rendering popular speech with its proverbs and archaic rural usage. His great readability comes from showing the whole community, male and female, young and old, as characters transcending the stereotypical, formed and deformed by a harsh environment but often rising above it with courage and dignity. P O

'Although Robalo was shy and aloof, on Sunday when he was off duty there was a fiesta at Fronteira, and he could not resist going near the good people of the village. There, right under his eyes, bathed by the golden light of the sun, was Isabel. Isabel! The girl took one's breath away. Twenty-two years full of joy. Such arms... such legs... such breasts were delights to behold. Well, Robalo was the same age, and not exactly made of stone, so the wick caught fire, caught so strongly that by the end of the week Robalo was a changed man. His holier-than-thou air vanished, and he began to see Fronteira with different eyes.' pp108-9

The Creation (Days One and Two)[A Criação do Mundo (Os Dois Primeiros Dias)]

This book contains the first two parts of Miguel Torga's fictionalised autobiography. The title is a multi-purpose signpost, reminding us of the biblical creation, particularly relevant given Torga's preoccupation with religion, and also indicating his profound awareness of his role as artist, as literary creator. Then again, the title could equally apply to the creation of the narrator, formed by his childhood and adolescent experiences.

Days One and Two focus on key events in the life of one fore-grounded character, a young boy undergoing the significant experiences of school, the first job, enrolling in a seminar, losing his faith and then deciding to emigrate. But *Day One* is more than just a school novel, since school is only one of various formative influences on his personality and behaviour. *Day Two* travels to a very different area both geographically and psychologically as the narrator describes the harsh physical experience of working on a plantation and the emotional cost of exile.

Day One covers the first thirteen years of a life, presented as something of a golden age, Paradise before the Fall. The boy is happy and secure, unaware of any unhappiness in store. His relationship with his parents is affectionate and trusting and schooldays are described without great rancour, despite the savage corporal punishments and the harshness of the peasant's life in general. What triumphs is his delight in learning, his pleasure in listening to the older generation with their rhymes and songs, proverbs and fairy stories, and his profound joy in reading. The emphasis is on rural tranquillity and harmony; but nothing is so straightforward in life and his village of Agarez is not the Garden of Eden; the scene where the local boys decide to put Venâncio's mule out of its misery is horribly reminiscent of certain passages in Golding's *Lord of the Flies*.

In *Day Two* he crosses the sea to his uncle's plantation in Brazil, where he is unwelcome and unappreciated by his uncle, reviled by his aunt, worked incredibly hard but eventually allowed to go back to school.

Both *Day One* and *Day Two* are, in the end, about a child's journeys, both real and symbolic where physical journeys parallel and reflect the metaphysical journey through the different stages of human experience and development. P O

BRAZIL

ANTHOLOGY
Caistor, N.(Ed.)

Faber Book of Contemporary Latin American Short Stories

This is an interesting, wide-ranging anthology of stories from all over Latin America, many by writers who are not translated in the UK (like Helio Vera) or only very poorly represented (like the marvellously witty Uruguayan writer Cristina Peri Rossi).

The two Brazilian writers represented here are João Ubaldo Ribeiro who has three books available or forthcoming in the UK and Moacyr Scliar who has been published in the USA.

Ribeiro's short story *Alaindelon de la Patrie* about a stud bull who hasn't quite got what it takes has him showing off his lightest touch; it's ironic, funny and ribald — a good introduction to its author. The Scliar story *Peace and War* printed here is probably not enough to put this interesting Brazilian-Jewish writer on the map in the UK, but it's a start. It shows the writer in his humorous science-fiction mood, although in Brazil the lines between science fiction and straight fiction are not as constricting as in the English-speaking world.

As a fairly current sampler of Latin American writing this is a good and enjoyable collection. R K

'The rooster sometimes seems to be conversing with its shadow or discussing elections or something when all of a sudden he flares up with great brilliance and begins pecking the chickens back and forth and puffing himself up in the direction of their tails, and thus he does all his work in something like five minutes, spark-like. The eggs that follow are brown, not white, fertile, not barren, and quite good for one's health, or else out come little chicks and all the chickens go on with their chickening as Our Lord wished. Thus the little lizard has two rods, one at the right, one at the left, so that any female lizard can be well provided whether she be left or right, and it should be said that the lizard only catches one lizardess at a time, not taking advantage of being able to serve two. For it is not a matter of vanity, it is a question of not wasting time, because if it is true that the lizard has many flies to eat, it is also true that there are many other creatures who want to eat the lizard, so he cannot afford to take it easy.' p27 (*Alaindelon De La Patrie* João Ubaldo Ribeiro)

Modern Brazilian Short Stories

An anthology with sixteen Brazilian authors, first published in 1967 but still worth having today because created with such authority, professionalism and passion. Published by a US-based University press it may need a bit of tracking down in the UK but it *is* available.

There are here, as well as the great and the good already well-known in the Anglo-Saxon world, some authors considered highly in Brazil but not otherwise translated. An example is Marques Rebêlo with his poignant story *The Beautiful Rabbits,* about childhood's insecurities and rivalries but with a sting of social critique in it too.

Mário de Andrade, the great man of Brazilian modernism famous for his extraordinary myth-novel *Macunaima,* is represented here with *It can hurt plenty,* an expert, moving story told, like Rebêlo's, from a child's point of view. *It can hurt plenty* is a small, casual masterpiece, as humane as Chekov, as socially-aware as Orwell.

Other major stories in the collection are *Metonomy* by Rachel de Queirós, written with great 'spring' and encapsulating very well the ironic strain in Brazilian writing; *The Thief* by Graciliano Ramos — like Rachel de Queirós another famous social novelist — is short with a sharp, filmic quality and finally there is Guimarães Rosa's *The Third Bank of the River,* a birthday present of a story, stunningly profound and resonant, a genuine touch of the spiritual. It would be worth getting the book for this story alone.

A genial part of this anthology is the provision of potted biographies at the end of each story; lives of Brazilian authors are often interesting in themselves. Altogether *Brazilian Short Stories* is a perfect starting point to explore Brazilian writing.

'She was home. But could you really call it a home? It looked like one of those road huts where the mule drivers rest. Just about as dirty. Two things that looked vaguely like chairs. One table. One bed. On the floor there was a mattress where the cockroaches lived. At night they came out and danced on the old lady's face. After all, where do all the insects of this world perform their tribal dances? On somebody's face, right?' p13 Mário de Andrade *It Can Hurt Plenty* (RK)

Dragons [Os dragões não conhecem o paraíso]

There's a strange familiarity about the stories of *Dragons*...
Not the familiarity of something we feel we've read or heard
spoken before — although the sensation of déjà-vu, the
bittersweet memory or echo of emotions felt in some other
time, somewhere else, by someone else, is experienced on
many occasions in the pages of this book, by the characters
— and by the reader. Nor am I simply talking about the 'punks,
beggars, neon lights, prostitutes and moaning synthesizers'
that float about in the night fog of the story entitled *The Sad-
dest Boy in the World*, the health freaks and wind surfers of
Blues Without Ana', the unfulfilled, slightly ageing professional
couple looking for romance second time around in a phoney

tropical holiday resort, in *Honey and Sunflowers'*. Of course all these social types help remind us that not only the physical landscapes, but the human landscapes, too, of London, New York, Tokyo and São Paulo are growing more alike as we enter the last decade of the twentieth century.

But more than these things, it's the familiarity of recognition, the recognition of experiences that have been or at least could be our own: a young boy's struggle to come to terms with his awakening adolescent sexuality; the joyful discovery of shared emotions and sensations; the pain and the anger of separation; the exhilaration and danger of freedom; the panic and grief of loneliness. They are experiences which have been moulded, made theirs and ours, by the common conditions of our global culture in the 1990s, a culture of uncertainty, decay and alienation, in which the traditional models of social, economic and family life have failed to provide happiness and security for the majority, while at the same time repressing or excluding those who have discovered alternative sexual identities and lifestyles. It's a culture, too, which continually sells us a thousand ready-made mass-produced roles and masks, offering us instant identity in an anonymous world, the identity of the cliché, the stereotype, allowing us to forget who we really are, if we ever knew. These are the lost souls who inhabit the pages of *Dragons;*

> 'the Totally Liberated But Profoundly Misunderstood Woman Who Accepted Her Inevitable Solitude, the Independent Man Who Can Do Without That Nonsense Called Love, the Psychoanalyst At Odds with the Elitism of Her Own Profession, or the Basketball Player Looking for a More Natural Life.'

This sense of familiarity or recognition, even if it is the recognition of our shared anonymity, alienation and marginalisation, is extremely important, it seems to me. Important, particularly when our perceptions of Latin America and Latin Americans have been largely shaped by a literature which emphasizes their difference from us, their uniqueness and the impossibility of understanding their world. With one or two exceptions, European and North American publishers have until recently preferred to publish those Latin American (and occasionally Brazilian) authors whose work confirms the image of an exotic, alien, incomprehensible culture, whose essence lies in its magical 'primitiveness', its pre-industrial, pre-capitalist backwardness, its 'Third-Worldness'. The publication of this book in English contributes towards a new understanding of the experience of those living in Latin America, and Brazil in particular.

In that sense, for all the familiarity of the dramas told to us by Caio, they are also profoundly Latin American. The emotions of self-discovery, loss, bewilderment and despair have an extra intensity that has something to do with the special impact of our global crisis on the cities of Buenos Aires, Lima, São Paulo and Rio de Janeiro. The lateness, swiftness and brutality of modernisation in these places, their lack of any control over the process, and their fragility and weakness in the face of the world's major economic powers, all these things have made the lives of the newly urbanised Latin American masses especially traumatic and alienated. How many of Caio's characters are found drifting in a limbo between the provincial towns of their childhood and the faceless metropolis? Like the narrator of *A Little White Sandy Beach, Down by the Gully* who says:

'...that's what happens when you leave a little town that's stopped being yours and go and live in another town that hasn't started being yours yet. You always start feeling a bit weird when you think you don't really want to stay but you don't want to — or can't — go back either. You feel just like one of those guys in the circus who walks the tightrope and suddenly the wire breaks, snap! and you're just hanging there, suspended in mid-air, empty space below your feet. With nowhere in the world to go, do you know what I mean?'

If the masks and roles we take on are already borrowed ready-made from the fictional world of advertising or the soap opera, then the illusion becomes a double-deception for a culture whose role models are imported from Dallas or Hollywood. How much more difficult it is to sustain the dream of True Love in one of the biggest AIDS capitals of the world, where state health care is virtually non-existent, and, as the young kid in *The Queen of the Night* hears, the telly tells you 'love kills love kills love kills'?

It's all the more moving and inspiring, then, to witness Caio's characters struggling, against all these odds, to find love, to peer through the fog, reach out and touch, and even, occasionally to celebrate the innocence of a shared moment of warmth and communication recovered from a filthy, corrupted world. Sometimes all that is possible in a fragmented, atomised society such as this, is the continuity and meaning offered by the mystical language of astral coincidences, Chinese horoscopes or the symbolism of candomblé. At other times, the characters have nothing to cling to but the dependable, eternal image of a matinée idol, or the dream of an invisible dragon. It is these courageous struggles that we have the privilege of witnessing when we read the stories of Caio Fernando Abreu, stories which invite, not just sympathy or comprehension but recognition and solidarity. D T

'When Ana left me, I stood for a long time in the living room of the apartment with her note in my hands. It was around eight o'clock in the evening. The clocks were on summer time and through the open living-room window it was still possible to make out, in that eight o'clock in the evening light, a few traces of gold and red left by the sun going down behind the buildings over towards Pinheiros. I stood there a long time, in the middle of the living room, Ana's last note in my hands, looking out of the window at the reds and golds in the sky. And I remember thinking, 'now the phone's going to ring': it might have been Lucinha ringing from the agency or Paulo from the film club or Nelson from Paris or my mother from the South, inviting me to dinner, to snort some coke, to see Nastassia Kinski in the nude, asking what the weather was like or something like that, but it didn't ring so after some time in which it hadn't rung I thought, 'now someone's going to ring the doorbell'. It might be the janitor delivering some mail, the neighbour from upstairs looking for her Persian cat that liked to escape down the stairs... But the doorbell didn't ring either, and I stood there for a good while longer without any means of salvation, in the middle of the room which was beginning to turn a bluish colour as the evening drew on, like the inside of a fish tank, Ana's note in my hands, doing absolutely nothing except breathe.' pp30-31

AMADO
Jorge

Dona Flor and her Two Husbands [Dona Flor e seus Dois Maridos]

Here is Amado's book of Bahian cuisine, with its African, tropical and coastal elements celebrated throughout Brazil. See for instance ; what to serve at a wake (p1), Dona Flor's recipe for marinated crabs (p14), stewed turtle and other unusual dishes (p221) and the culinary likes and dislikes of deities (p421).

The reader will not find a complete cookery book in this, one of Amado's most famous works but might enjoy his recipe for an international bestseller. The story of the beautiful Dona Flor is set in the lush tropics of Bahia (on the North-East coast of Brazil). Flor marries Vadinho — gambler, bohemian, womaniser. Make him die, still young and charming, during the celebration of Carnival. Bring the story to a simmer in the tears of Dona Flor the widow, suffering from the tongues of the local gossips and from her own memories of pleasure and impossible desire. Add a new husband — with a degree, a pharmacy, some money, and complete devotion to his lovely new wife. When the narrative is about to fall into the boring rut of middle-class marriage, add the supernatural element that will give an exquisite flavour to the dish.

Undoubtedly, only Jorge Amado could season this every-day plot and turn it into a special dish of Bahian cuisine composed of humour, love, sex, friendship, bohemian life, social analysis and unforgettable characters. All of them are present in Amado's pages and in the streets of Bahia, in the 'fearsome battle between spirit and matter'. M D

'I am the husband of the poor Dona Flor, the one who comes to stir up your longing and provoke your desire, hidden in the depths of your being, your modesty. He is the husband of Madame Dona Flor, who protects your virtue, your honour, your respect among people. He is your outward face, I your inner, the lover whom you don't know how and can't bear to evade. We are your two husbands, your two faces, your yes, your no. To be happy you need both of us.' p535

Home is the Sailor [A Completa Verdade sobre as Discutidas Aventuras do Comandante Vasco Moscoso de Aragão, Capitão de Longo Curso]

The portrait of a hero, the famous sailor who travelled the seven seas and has wonderful stories to entertain the bored folk of Periperi, a suburb of Salvador (Bahia), makes up the first part of this novel. And that might have been the only part — a simple account of adventure and bravery — were it not for the envy of the ex-customs inspector Chico Pacheco and the attempt and interest of the narrator in offering us 'the *whole* truth concerning the redoubtable adventures of Captain Vasco Moscoso de Aragão, Master Mariner'.

We get a more realistic account, none the less adventurous or intriguing though, set in the licentious, friendly and hypocritical society of the port. In the final part, the narrator gives the noted sailor the chance of proving the truth about his own life, and the readers the hints from which to draw their own conclusions. Given both the thesis and the antithesis as it were, the reader can take on the challenge of finding out the truth or just enjoy this light-hearted combination of adventure novel, love (of all kinds) story and social chronicle of Bahia at the beginning of the 20th century. M D

'When he reached the top, he stood there, his arms folded across his breast, gazing out at the waters. In that silent pose, his face to the sun, his hair fluttering in the wind (that gentle, perpetual breeze of Periperi), he resembled a soldier standing at attention, or, in view of his impressiveness, the bronze statue of a general. He wore an odd coat, not unlike a military tunic, of heavy blue cloth with a broad collar. Only Zequinha Curvelo, a tireless reader of adventure stories, grasped the fact that there before them, in the flesh, was a sea dog, a man whose element was ships and storms. He whispered his discovery to the others: on the cover of a novel about the sea, the story of a little sailing vessel lashed by tempests on the Sargasso Sea, there was a sailor wearing a coat like that.' p10

The War of the Saints [O Sumiço da Santa]

The writer amused himself with *The War of the Saints*, as he says in the preface: 'It's been fun to write; if someone else has fun reading it, I'll consider myself satisfied'. It's hard not to enjoy reading this breathless narration of the events which took place — at the height of the military dictatorship in Brazil and of revolutionary fervour around the world — during forty-eight hours sometime in the late 60s or early 70s in Bahia .

The disappearance of the sculpture of Saint Barbara, in transit to an exhibition of sacred art, doesn't provide the reader with a detective story — we know from the beginning who is responsible for the theft — but with entangled stories of love, religion and politics.

In a very relaxed way Jorge Amado writes about the famous Brazilian 'syncretism'; the blending of Roman Catholicism with African religions, about high art and popular art, national politics and local 'arrangements', about deep-rooted prejudices and familiar racial intermingling, blending his fictional characters with real celebrities of Bahian society and real history with a well-written plot that joins together reality, invention and the supernatural. M D

'The land of Bahia, where fate had led him to live and work, a land where everything is intermixed and commingled, where no one can separate virtue from sin, or distinguish the certain from the absurd, or draw the line between truth and trickery, between reality and dream. In this land of Bahia, saints and enchanted ones make miracles and sorcery, and not even Marxist ethnologists are surprised to see a carving from a Catholic altar turn into a bewitching mulatto woman at the hour of dusk.' pp23-4

The Violent Land [Terras do sem-fim]

The land in the title is the tropical forest of Bahia (in North-Eastern Brazil) cleared for cocoa production at around the turn of the century; it was apparently a kind of Very Wild West, with riverboats, gamblers, gunmen and adventurers and adventuresses of every stripe. The whole greedy onslaught on tropical nature was masterminded by gangsterish Cocoa Barons, adept at persuading others to do the gruelling ground-clearing and planting, then stepping in to swipe the resultant crop of 'brown gold'.

This is the *early* Jorge Amado, the social novelist, so he has tales of exploitation to tell strong enough to make you choke on your chocolate bar; but this is also *Jorge Amado* social realism so there's plenty of sex and sensuality too; this is Brazil not Soviet Russia. The Bahian cocoa zone was Amado's birthplace and early environment so there's a real wish to convince, a heartfeltness in the writing; the little plantation towns under the moon are made intensely, almost absurdly romantic. There's the lyrical evocation of the rain-forest running side by side with the story of how the Cocoa Barons accumulated their fortunes through violence and institutionalized corruption. This Brazil is a land where law and redress under the law belong only to the rich and powerful.

The Violent Land is a real chronicle of a period and place, with fascinating layers of social detail about the 'conquest of the cocoa lands' and it's the big, bad, bold story that established Jorge Amado as the best known of Brazil's writers. R K

'The forest lay sleeping in its never interrupted sleep. Over it passed the days and the nights. The summer sun shone above it, the winter rains fell upon it. Its trees were centuries old, an unending green overrunning the mountain, invading the plain, lost in the infinite. It was like a sea that had never been explored, locked in its own mystery. It was like a virgin whose flesh had never known the call of passion. Like a virgin, it was lovely, radiant, young, despite those century-old trunks. Mysterious as the body of a woman that has not yet been possessed, it too was now ardently desired.' p33

Tent of Miracles [Tenda dos milagres]

Set in the city of Bahia, Brazil's black capital, this novel brings together themes explored in Amado's earlier work: the social mobility of blacks in Brazil and the struggle against racial discrimination, and the emergence of Afro-Brazilian religious and musical culture onto the national stage, from a situation of obscurity and police persecution.

It is a split-level novel. We follow the life story of the book's black hero, Pedro Archanjo, from the turn of the century through to his death in the 1940s. Archanjo lives these years to the full. He is a leading figure of the Bahia's bohemian dockside life, lover of many women, labour agitator in the

1920s, samba composer, popular scholar of Bahian customs, whose fight against discrimination and injustice reflects the wider struggle of Black Brazilians for equality during the first half of the 20th century. Intercalated between the episodes of Archanjo's epic life are the experiences of a North American university professor, who has written a book about Archanjo, and who is visiting Bahia to take part in the carnival celebration of the local figure at the end of the 1960's. This provides Amado with an opportunity to point up the differences in cultural attitudes between North and South Americans.

Typical of Amado's writing, it is a colourful, atmospheric novel, with an emphasis on action, and a wide array of popular characters. Amado's sympathies are, as ever, with the underdogs, who are seen as the true inheritors and preservers of Bahia's unique African-American culture. The price of mobility into the 'whitened' bourgeoisie seems to be to sacrifice these cultural roots, but if we are to understand the book's message, the situation is less dire now than it was fifty years ago. The struggle of men like Archanjo has not been in vain.
D B

'From the stonemason/corporal Pedro Archanjo inherited the intelligence and bravery cited in the war bulletins, and from Noca, his gentle features and his stubbornness. Stubbornly she reared her child, saw that he had a home and enough to eat, and put him through school, all without a man's support or help. She would never have anyone else, never again indulged in even a passing affair, although there were no lack of followers who hung around her doorstep coaxing her and making offers. From that hard, meagre life with his mother, the child learned to endure and never to give up, but to keep right on going.

Archanjo often thought of her during the fruitful decade of hard work. She had died still young, when the seeds of yellow fever planted in the manure of the city streets grew and put forth deadly blossoms. It was a good year for yellow fever: the disease reaped an abundant harvest, taking corpses even from the houses of the rich, and Noca de Logunedê was carried off with first batch. Not even Omolú could save her. Noca's strength melted into sores, her youthful grace rotted in the alleys among pools of pus. Whenever Archanjo's strength flagged he would think of his mother, laboring to exhaustion from morning to night, locked in a circle of longing, unyielding in her determination to wear mourning forever and to earn the keep of her child with the strength of her own fragile arms.' p219

Macunaima [Macunaíma]

In July 1928, Mário de Andrade, poet, critic and unofficial artistic leader of his generation, introduced Brazil's reading public to what was to become one of the best known and loved figures in the country's literary, theatrical, and cinematic history- Macunaima: the characterless hero.

For much of the nineteenth century, newly independent Brazil had enjoyed a reassuringly heroic and liberal self-image in the Romantic figure of the Indian warrior. This image legitimized the semi-colonial world of the plantation-owners and slaves through his combination of aristocratic pride, freedom-loving defiance and fraternal loyalty to the white man. In 1889 a Republic was declared in the name of 'Order and Progress', a slogan inspired by Auguste Comte's evolutionist philosophy of Positivism. This motto still appears on the Brazilian national flag. The period from the end of the nineteenth century right through to the accession to power of dictator Getulio Vargas in 1930 was one of rapid change. While the coffee export sector was still important, society and economy were being transformed with large-scale European immigration, the growth of urban centres like São Paulo and the beginning of industrialization. All this was shifting influence away from the 'coffee oligarchy' and towards the cities. For the new urban classes and the military élite the Indian, black and mestizo peasant seemed to offer only negative models of national identity, rooted in a semi-feudal, rural past and, according to the racial theories of the time, in a biological and psychological degeneracy.

To those who looked towards the Classical traditions and the industrial technology of Europe as a means of fitting Brazil into the 'universal' history of European civilization, Andrade's *Macunaima* posed a disturbing challenge. For here was an anti-hero, an enemy of order, a failure of progress, a 'characterless' psychological and cultural chameleon. Indian, black, and white all at once Macunaima is an overgrown child, infuriatingly selfish and irresponsible, lazy and oversexed, disloyal and destructive; yet by the same token, irresistibly subversive, irrepressibly mercurial, capable of defeating or escaping his enemies through his infinite adaptability and magical powers of self-transformation.

At the same time, Andrade's prose 'rhapsody' exposed his middle-class city audience to a dazzlingly rich cultural world which had remained until then virtually invisible in the country's literature. This was the world of popular traditions, celebrations, rituals and religious practices through which Brazil's rural and urban masses gave meaning to their experience of life in the first quarter of the twentieth century.

With Brazil beginning to follow the model of European and North American development, the pre-industrial, non-Western communities in the countryside with their fragile ways of life were faced with a dilemma.

Macunaima can be seen as a dramatic reconstruction of that dilemma, as he proceeds on his fantastic journey through that pre-industrial cultural universe. The hero leaves his Amazonian village for the city of São Paulo, in a quest to recover the sacred talisman left to him by the Empress of the forest. Ironically, though, in the course of confronting and eventually defeating his arch-enemy, the cannibalistic business tycoon Piaimã/Venceslau Pietro Pietra, he adapts so effectively to the commercial, technological culture of the city that his entire identity is undermined, and the betrayal of his origins leads inexorably to his self-destruction. D T

'While Macunaíma was going about his business he came across the very tall tree known as Voloman. Sitting on a branch was a bright green pepper shrike with red brows. On catching sight of the hero, it cleared its throat and sang, "Look who's coming down the road! Look who's coming down the road!" Macunaíma looked up intending to thank it and noticed that the tree, Voloman, the Tree of Life, was heavy with fruit. The hero had gone hungry for many hours and his belly balked at the sight of all the oranges and lemons, the sapotes and simatoos, the grapes and grenadillas, pineapples and pomegranates, mangoes and mombins, sweetsop and sour-sop, all kinds of fruit hanging from its branches.

"Voloman, give me some of your fruit!" begged Macunaíma. The tree refused to give him any. Then Macunaíma shouted this spell, twice over, *"Boiôiô! Boiôiô! Quinzama quizu!"*

All the fruit fell from the tree and the hero stuffed himself till he was gorged. This annoyed Voloman so much that it grabbed the hero by the feet and dragged him far away, to the other side of the Guanabara Bay, to a desert isle which had been inhabited in the olden days by Alamoa, a nymph who came with the Dutch. Macunaima was so tired that he just hung there asleep during the flight. Still asleep, he was landed underneath a very smelly bitter coconut palm at the top of which perched a vulture.

At that very moment this bird felt the need to perform its daily duties and covered the hero with its filthy droppings.' pp60-61

AZEVEDO
Aluizio de

The Mulatto [O Mulato]

Azevedo was an important early Brazilian writer, an exponent of the Zola-esque 'naturalist' style. This is the story of the struggle of a mixed-race man (or 'mulatto') to make his way in a provincial society dominated by a white elite still looking to Portugal, the colonial Mother Country, as the source of all goodness. Brazil in contrast was seen by this highly conservative sector as an inherently corrupting environment, full of corrupt human 'types', particularly people with African or Amerindian roots.

Although strongly influenced by Eça de Queirós and Émile Zola, Azevedo doesn't show Eça's light and sure step as a writer. In compensation though his raw material is both very interesting and very Brazilian. Azevedo is an authentic witness of his times (he lived 1857–1913) and delivers a detailed exploration of mentality and daily life in the formative years of modern Brazil.

There's an awful fascination too in the constant stream of racist ideas and fantasies about Black/mixed-race people that Azevedo puts in the mouths of his white characters. Although these characters live cheek-by-jowl with non-white people it makes no difference to their views, so powerful is the simplistic categorisation of racial thinking. *The Mulatto* must be a useful document for understanding the theories of racial superiority which have been so popular and damaging in the last 100 years, in Brazil and elesewhere.

Like his model Eça de Queirós, Azevedo enjoyed laying into the powerful Catholic clergy of the time and the respectable, narrow-minded provincial merchants and officials who were their greatest admirers. Azevedo's anti-clerical attack encapsulated in the character of Canon Diogo resulted in his having to move out of the town of Maranhão where *The Mulatto* is set; the book did however contribute to the movement for the total abolition of slavery active at that time and which finally ended the scandal of Brazil as the world's last slave state. R K

'The canon came to life again.

"A priest?!"

"That's what José, his father wanted."

"What nonsense!" retorted Diogo, getting brusquely out of the chair. "There are already too many dark-skinned priests in these parts!"

"But compadre, look here, it's not that..."

'What do you mean, my good man? Imagine — becoming priests! Imagine! And you can see what's happening. Why soon there'll be prelates blacker than our cooking women! You think that's proper? The government should take some serious action in regard to this problem! It should ban nonwhites from certain occupations."

"But compadre..."

"I say put them in their place!"

And the canon grew heated with indignation.' pp47–48

Turbulence [Estorvo]

This is Chico Buarque's first novel but one sees straightway it's not his first piece of writing — he is of course world famous as a composer and performer of songs of love and protest, with a career reaching back to the years of military dictatorship in Brazil (1964-1985). In *Turbulence* there's the same acute eye at work as in his best songs.

The novel has something of a *bossa nova* rhythm in its strange but satisfying leaps of focus, starting off for example with the world observed through the spy-hole in the narrator's front door. When its protagonist leaves his flat he restlessly drags the reader with him through the streets, buildings and suburbs of an often chaotic, sometimes violent city. The book is an up-to-date picture of Rio de Janeiro where, however confusing the trajectory, it's always possible to recognise the lifestyles and thought-patterns of the last two decades — concrete architecture fighting luxuriant nature, high consumerism, electronic gadgetry and the invasion of violence into public and private life. At the centre of its drama is the social apartheid that Rio de Janeiro epitomises so starkly — the paranoia and tension running between the high-rise condominiums of the rich, with their electric fences and security guards, and the gang warfares and narco-trafficking that govern the lives of their shanty-town 'neighbours'.

The characters are not given names but are nonetheless recognisable figures from Brazil's street corners and gossip columns and, although the 'turbulent' flow of the narration is as discontinuous as a dream, it very effectively captures the reality of contemporary Brazil, alive, disparate, scandalous and surprising. M D & R K

'She twitches her eyebrows in my direction, then looking down again so her hair falls over her face, absorbed in the photos she is sifting into small heaps. They set out a place for me opposite her, some distance away, and she doesn't look up as she passes me photos where there are no people, only parks, streets, snow, repeated landscapes I dispatch in half a minute. They must be photos from the beginning of her trip, when she was lonely and emotionally drained; though she's studied photography, her framing is uneven, she under- or over-exposed, as if she was in rush to finish the film. In the photos she's piling up out of my reach I imagine her now with a fresh complexion, perhaps she's opening her arms on a bridge, having shown a stranger how to handle the camera. And in the more recent photos she's standing behind the milk jug, I expect there are the friends she keeps making, and the friends of friends, and artists and public figures, and the lights of the boat during the farewell dinner.' p10

COELHO
Paulo

The Alchemist [O Alquimista]

Something like Kahlil Gilbran's *The Prophet* but less mystical in its language, this is a book of 'lessons for living', in the form of a young man's journey from initial poverty and ignorance to the acquiring, after many tests and trials, of a degree of wisdom, experience and contentment. The principal theme is of discovering and staying true to one's *destiny*. It is directed at those determined to break out of an inherited niche in the world and who want somehow to excel and achieve more than the acceptable, mediocre minimum in life.

It is a thoughtful and thought-out book full of genuinely wise points; for example that 'every blessing ignored becomes a curse' and that intuition is 'immersion in the universal current of life'. Coelho wants us to understand how to connect to landscapes, real and metaphorical ('one must love the desert, but never trust it completely. Because the desert tests all men; it challenges every step and kills those who become distracted'), and to people ('there was a language in the world that everyone understood... the language of enthusiasm, of things accomplished with love and purpose.').

An authentically inspirational book; if you need inspiration or are setting out on a new tack, *The Alchemist* could be a great support, with its truths and its warnings. R K

'They crossed the desert for another two days in silence. The alchemist had become much more cautious, because they were approaching the area where the most violent battles were being waged. As they moved along the boy tried to listen to his heart.

It was not easy to do; in earlier times, his heart had always been ready to tell its story, but lately that wasn't true. There had been times when his heart spent hours telling of its sadness, and at other times it became so emotional over the desert sunrise that the boy had to hide his tears. His heart beat fastest when it spoke to the boy of treasure, and more slowly when the boy stared entranced at the endless horizons of the desert. But his heart was never quiet, even when the boy and the alchemist had fallen into silence.

"Why do we have to listen to our hearts?" the boy asked. when they had made camp that day.

"Because wherever your heart is that is where you'll find your treasure."

"But my heart is agitated," the boy said. "It has its dreams,. it gets emotional. and it's become passionate over a woman of the desert. It asks things of me, and it keeps me from sleeping many nights, when I'm thinking about her."

"Well, that's good. Your heart is alive. Keep listening to what it has to say." pp134-5

CUNHA
Helena Parente

Woman between Mirrors [Mulher no Espelho]

Woman between Mirrors is a work of dialogue/inner dialogue about, primarily, the feminine personality and about challenging and exploring female identity. Helena Parente Cunha is a Brazilian writer from Bahia and this intense, experimental work full of revelatory flashes and irony at the very least helps to show that Bahia is not just the land of dusky beauties Jorge Amado, the most famous writer on Bahia, popularised in books like *Gabriella, Cinnamon and Cloves*. Cunha does however use images from Afro-Brazilian myth in *Woman between Mirrors*. Brazil, so caught between different traditions: antique Portugal, avant-garde Europe, the mass culture of the US and African religions, is perhaps a uniquely interesting situation to look at in search of the 20th century personality This is essentially the undertaking of *Woman between Mirrors* and of Clarice Lispector's related if more accessible writing. R K

'When you were little, you still reacted to things. At least a little. Today you don't react any more. Paralyzed, apathetic, alienated, indifferent.

I'm patient. Being soft but ready to act. I give consent if I'm given consent, I can be patient about accepting people, including the woman who writes me. When I was little, I still hadn't developed very much patience, and I paid for it more than once. Hence the intense fear and panic I felt, that came from my not being able to adjust to my father's temperament.

By giving up the things I want, I can live the life I want. Not a bad way to cut down on walls. At peace with my husband and sons.

What you call peace is your ability to efface yourself.

The woman who writes me is continually getting into fights because of her egotism, her vanity. She's always insisted on having her own way, whatever the cost. Little by little I stopped making decisions about things. I want what my husband wants. Being soft but ready to act. So simple. There are the windows of my former house. If my father wouldn't let me stand at the window watching the street and the people going by, often I'd start crying, and get punished for it. If I had spontaneously given up my window, I wouldn't have suffered the fear of punishment or felt so terribly sorry. The windows of my former house are shut up.'

DOURADO
Autran

Pattern for a Tapestry [O risco do bordado]

Small town life, in the archetypal imaginary town of 'Duas Pontes' ('Two Bridges') in the archetypal but real province of

Minas Gerais. Against the backdrop of the 1930s and 40s in a quiet backwater, stories of burning youthful passions, for love, for knowledge, for a wider world. There are some extraordinary set pieces; 'the brothel', 'the dying man' as well as episodes of the violent frontier period but what sticks in the mind is the strange magic of youthful emotion Dourado captures so well.

At the other end of youthfulness the haunting image of Aunt Margarida, in her late thirties, the story of an unmarried woman forced to renounce her sexuality and live in emotional solitude; a classic case of painful provincial manners being imposed on the spirit of each new generation.

Even if a quarter century after first publication sometimes Dourado's tone seems slightly sentimental or picturesque, it's clear the reader is in the safe hands of a skilled and self-confident writer, who brings a suggestive picture of a distinct part of the world to life. R K

'Loveless, of uncertain age, in appearance older than her years, her eyes sharp or sometimes vacant, floating in distant mists, she was a milky shadow drifting quietly along the corridors, through the bedrooms, the living-rooms, through life. If she would at least devote herself to church work, become one of those altar mice, those camels on which God crosses the desert, she would have an occupation, someone to devote herself to, someone to whom she could give a placid, carefully hoarded love. But curiously Aunt Margarida struggled against that surrender, that destiny which awaited the maiden ladies of Duas Pontes. She wasn't even religious, did no more than go to church with her mother on Sundays. In church her lips were never seen to move even in prayer: her face was opaque, tranquil, vacant in the gilded half light. As if she were not there.' p119

FONSECA
Rubem

High Art [A Grande Arte]

High Art is not a literary novel but a detective story set in Rio with some political and historical touches involving rich old Brazilian families and right-wing loonies. The male protagonists take plenty of time out for sexual adventures, usually with prostitutes, while the narrative marches on via murders, intrigues and mysteries. There are some very atmospheric bits and pieces, sandwiched between the detectivery and debauchery, which capture the unique combination of squalor and wealth, power and powerlessness that is Brazil.

Within the frenetic and abbreviated irrealism of the detective story lies some acid social comment; seeing the decor of a designer flat — smoked glass, giant aquarium, built-in wardrobes — the cynical private eye describes it as 'Playtime for parvenus in an underdeveloped country'. R K

'Homicide was located in a dilapidated building on Avenida Presidente Vargas. From the window in Raul's office you could see the endless line of cars filling the wide avenue that linked the Zona Norte to downtown. The building's walls were dirty and full of holes. Frayed emergency electrical wiring snaked across the floor. The foyer door had broken hinges and looked about ready to fall off. In the corner, on a piece of newspaper, sat a wooden box of ashes, cigarette butts, and dried spittle. The floor Raul worked on was divided by partitions that formed small cubicles where clerks took depositions from defendants and witnesses. The cops wore cheap, informal sports clothes.' p103

GALVÃO
Patrícia

Industrial Park [Parque Industrial]

Patrícia Galvão's 1933 'proletarian novel' Industrial Park records a crucial moment in working class life in the São Paulo of the early 1930s, and so adjusts the rural bias that has dominated impressions of the fiction of that time. *Industrial Park* also reveals the unique perspective of one of Modernism's more fascinating but neglected female figures.

In his useful and informative 'afterword' translator K. David Jackson reminds us that Galvão, or 'Pagu' as she was known, was censured by and expelled from the Communist Party in 1930, for her 'individualism and sensationalist agitation', and was forced to adopt a pseudonym, Mara Lobo, for the book's publication. This novel however demonstrates her 'agitational' commitment to transforming the complex and contradictory reality of class struggle into literature.

It is a very different approach from the socialist 'realism' of Jorge Amado, with its unproblematic narratives of feudal decline and capitalist modernisation. Here rather is the disturbingly chaotic maelstrom of social life — the novel's title in fact was taken from a contemporary advertising billboard, whose triumphant celebration of the new capitalist order of things is the object of her satirical critique.

What we are given, rather than an evolving narrative, is a fragmented series of vignettes, juxtaposing the cynical self-indulgence of São Paulo's rich with the daily struggle for existence of the workers, particularly the women, of the immigrant industrial quarter, Braz, on whom they prey. Alongside the exposure of racism, poverty, the exploitation of the textile factories in both its petty and most brutal forms, and the repression of a young trade union movement, it is perhaps Galvão's particular insight into the sexual lives of her characters which, without sensationalism, voyeurism or sentimentality, manages to dramatise the precariousness of their existence. Sexual vitality and sexual vulnerability, that ambivalence encapsulates the optimism and energy of this new social class, its determination to imagine and snatch glimpses of love and solidarity inside and outside the sordid world of factory and slum, yet its all-too easy victimisation in the brothel or the workhouse for single mothers. The novel ends, not with an easy victory for the socialist ideals which the characters struggle to sustain, but with a chance encounter between two of the novel's fleeting figures who, 'clinging together, victims of the same unawareness, cast on the same shore of capitalist ventures, carry salted popcorn to the same bed'.

The novel's style, which its translator describes as having a 'primitive' rawness of rapid-fire, truncated language descends partly from the 'telegraphic' style Oswald de Andrade had explored in his *Manifestos da Poesia Pau-Brasil* and *Antropofágico* (Pagu participated in the Movimiento Antropofágico of the late 1920s and was married to Oswald for a time). Like Galvão's fragmented narrative technique, this corresponded to the movement's commitment to deconstruct or explode the illusory and repressive unity of perspective and narrative which had held together Brazil's pre-Modernist self-image.

This style does succeed in conveying the dynamism of the novel's social milieu and usually accommodates the vigorous blend of colloquial and political language which, in another context, might sound like crude sloganeering. D T

'Sampson Street moves full in the direction of the factories. It seems like the worn paving stones are going to break apart.

Coloured slippers drag along still sleepy and unhurried on Monday. Wanting to stay behind. Seizing the last small bit of freedom.

The girls tell about the previous evening's dates, squeezing lunches wrapped in brown and green paper.

'I'll only marry a worker!'

'Knock on wood! One poor person is enough. Spend my whole life in this shit!'

'You think the rich date us seriously? Only to fool around.'

'I told Bralio that if it's a fling, I'll tear him apart.'

'There's Pedro!'

'Is he waiting for you? Then I'll get lost!'

The powerful cry of the smokestack envelops the borough. The laggards fly, skirting the factory wall, gritty, long crowned with spikes. They pant like tired dogs so as not to lose the day's pay. A small red slipper without a sole is abandoned in the gutter. A shoeless foot is cut on the slivers of a milk bottle. A dark girl goes hopping and crying to reach the black door.

The last kick at a rag ball.

The whistle ends in a blast. The machines shake in desperation. The street is sad and deserted. Banana peels. The residue of black vapours vanishing. Blood mixed with milk.' pp8-9

The Besieged City [A Cidade Sitiada]

One of Clarice Lispector's early novels but newly translated into English, *The Besieged City* chronicles the life and development of a small town, São Geraldo and of a young woman, Lucretia Neves; as São Geraldo changes over the years so does she.

Lucretia seems carefree, something of a dreamer. She lives in her hometown with a kind of disgust for it, always wishing to be somewhere else. She satisfies her desire to leave for a more comfortable life by dreaming of a different world. She dreams by day and by night. She dreams of a world where objects are alive, where the external world is one with her rather than against her. She lives inside herself.

She sees only one solution to her predicament: to marry a man who can offer her wealth, jewels — who can offer her a life in a big city with hotels, cafés and theatres. For Lucretia a husband would be a saviour. Mateus Correia, a lawyer, offers her all that she wishes for and marrying him she leaves São Geraldo for the big city.

Now that she has left what she considers to be a backward town and lifestyle, she is still dissatisfied. The *bourgeois* life she has entered is not all that magical and soon tires her. She has to fake her happiness and appreciation. She starts to long for what she was dying to leave: São Geraldo.

The Besieged City is a story of the *internal* struggle of a human being trying to adjust to her predicament. Lucretia is estranged from her own life and never finds what she longs for — does she know what it is she so desires or is she a dreamer with fuzzy dreams? Her only way is to adapt to where she is: in São Geraldo she is a young girl, a dreamer, an idealist; married and in the big city a young bourgeois wife, a materialist. She is a prisoner of her dreams, a prisoner of her thought-processes that never allow her to reach internal peace.

In this novel full of rich imagery of light, darkness, mirrors, water and Nature, Lispector takes a sceptical look at dreams and desire. She looks at marriage with a critical eye as never seeming to provide what one imagines. She writes about a woman who does not fit anywhere, always struggling with what she wants and what she has or can have. Written with irony, it is about a woman incapable of freeing herself from her own ideas, from the desire for a safe and settled lifestyle, but who never takes her life in her own hands. M C-L

'But the portrait became increasingly different from the sitter and Lucretia Neves considered it the perfect image. The face on the wall, so swollen and signified, carried the mark of destiny in that dazed expression, while she herself....Perhaps she had fallen into the routine of things and the portrait was the unattainable surface, the higher order of solitude — her own history captured for posterity by the photographer without her even noticing.'

Discovering the World [A Descoberta do Mundo]
Near to the Wild Heart [Perto do coracao selvagem]

'I am so mysterious that I do not understand myself' CL

Clarice Lispector is universally recognised as being the most original and influential Brazilian woman writer of her time. In feminist circles she is revered as an intensely feminine writer who articulates the needs and concerns of every woman in pursuit of self-awareness. Critics worldwide have found much to admire in her introspective writings, both fictional and non-fiction. Her obsessive questioning of human relationships and the social constraints which threaten rather than foster meaningful communication bring her to the conclusion that the problem of existence is that of language itself.

In 1984, seven years after she died of cancer, Lispector's son edited and published the so-called *Crônicas* or chronicles she had written for the Saturday edition of Rio's leading newspaper, the *Jornal do Brasil*, from August 1967 until December 1973. The book comprises a miscellaneous collection of aphorisms, diary entries, reminiscences, travel notes, interviews, serialised stories, and essays, somewhat loosely defined as 'chronicles': a genre peculiar to Brazil which allows poets and writers to address a wider readership on a vast range of topics and themes. The general tone is one of greater freedom and intimacy than one finds in comparable articles or weekly columns in the European press.

Lispector, the severe and impassioned novelist, confided that she did not find it easy to adapt to the freedom and intimacy of the weekly column. She asked; 'Is the chronicle a story? a conversation? the revelation of one's inner thoughts?' She questioned the wisdom of tackling a genre which to some extent was alien to her introspective nature. Summing up her disquiet, she commented: 'I am apprehensive. Writing too much and too often can contaminate the word' or as Fernando Pessoa, once said: 'Speaking is the easiest way of becoming unknown'. Weighing up the contrasting demands of journalism and creative fiction, she shied from the stereotyped role of the garrulous agony aunt and frequently ignored the expectations of her readers with arbitrary forays into other genres. To her surprise, readers reacted positively to her unpredictable contributions and she was soon freely adapting the chronicle to suit her own idiosyncrasies.

The wide range of genres assembled in *Discovering the World* allows the reader to piece together the life and career of this singular personality. The material registers contrasting moods, one moment whimsical, the next grave and questioning, but whatever the topic, the chronicles are disarmingly frank.

Marriage to a fellow-student, Maury Gurgel Valente, coincided with the publication of her first novel *Near to the Wild Heart*. Lispector was in her early twenties and unknown, but the unusual form and searing effect of this unsparing account of marriage and betrayal attracted the attention of several important literary critics. Sérgio Milliet and Antônio Cândido recognized at once that a promising new writer had made her début. Their reviews spoke of a 'sudden break' with established criteria and of a radically different concept of fiction, which opened up new possibilities. Her début was timely.

Marriage to a diplomat meant foreign postings, for some sixteen years Lispector was to be separated from her beloved Brazil, apart from brief return visits which only intensified her sense of exile and homesickness. She found many of the social obligations required of a diplomat's wife extremely - tedious. Writing became increasingly important for her spiritual survival and synonymous with a more meaningful form of existence, and only her work and children kept her sane during those years in alien surroundings. In 1959, she finally separated from her husband and returned to Rio with her children. Despite her Ukrainian ancestry, Lispector identified completely with Brazil and, most of all, with north-eastern Brazil. Memories of her childhood, especially in Recife, evoked the authentic Brazil where traditions and folklore had been preserved. A slight speech defect made her sound like a foreigner, but she was adamant that she had forged her soul and innermost thoughts with the Portuguese language, 'a difficult language', which she was to transform and even re-invent by means of conceptual refinements, subtle nuances and bold experiments with syntax.

Brazil's other great writer of this century, João Guimarães Rosa, once told her: 'Clarice, I don't read you just for the literature, but in order to learn about life.' Most readers would agree. Her dramatic insights can surprise and shock, amuse and distress. Such is the intensity and vehemence of her prose that it unleashes everything which is gentle and violent in this world of ours. And as she herself confided: 'Everything affects me... I see too much, hear too much, everything demands too much of me.'

The intimate revelations of *Discovering the World* take us through the various stages of womanhood from childhood innocence to awakening perceptions of good and evil. The transition from adolescence to maturity is re-enacted in solemn rites, at once delicate and perilous. The lurking fear of 'ambush', both physical and emotional, is central to many of the narratives. Lispector stalked the uncertainties of life in fear and trepidation, yet anxious and determined to unravel the mystery of existence. She dubbed herself 'an audacious coward' and persisted in confronting life on those terms.

In all her work there is relentless self-questioning. Aware that she was speaking on behalf of all mankind, she was wont to say: 'I am so mysterious that I do not understand myself.' She saw the human condition as flawed, fragmentary and incomplete; the darker side of our nature as being compounded of fear, revulsion, cruelty and hatred. But once having recognised the inherent contradictions, she set about trying to reconcile freedom with restraint, humility with pride, solitude with the need to communicate. Strength had to be drawn from weakness, human reversals transformed into salvation.

The sense of wounded innocence and cruel deception is a constant theme in Lispector's stories and chronicles. She is nevertheless convinced that 'generosity (akin to love) is the very core of our humanity' and that 'wrath and hatred are the sorrow of not being able to love'. For her, 'a world without love is lost', and like most of her women characters she confessed to 'an enormous capacity for love'. Strong convictions, alas, are no guarantee of painless achievement. She understood that love could elevate the spirit but that it could also be deceptive. 'Love', she observed, 'can never be a bad thing. But it often turns out to be hatred in disguise.' Her characters invariably discover that love, whatever its nature, exacts some measure of self-abnegation. As she herself confided: 'I often tire of people. Then it passes and I once more become curious and attentive.' For Lispector, it was most essential that love should never become obtrusive. In one of her chronicles she describes the perfect companion: 'Someone who will not stare too much and cause embarrassment. Someone who will know when to speak and when to be silent, someone who will adore me with discretion and accept both my virtues and faults.'

This might explain why she enjoyed most of all the company of children and her pet animals. Her conversations with young children provide some of the most engaging dialogues in *Discovering the World*. Lispector excels in expressing a child's sense of things. Her maternal instincts were strong and she never tired of observing, guiding, questioning her own sons, but, above all, of listening to them and analysing their responses to the world around them. She insisted: 'One must be gentle, very gentle when dealing with children.' She associated children with spontaneity and a refreshing candour.

The constant presence of some pet animal gave her the same sense of compatibility and mutual understanding. As a child, her family nicknamed her 'The Protector of Animals', and she brought up her own children to love and care for domestic pets. The various species in her narratives and chronicles arouse a wide range of emotions: compassion, fear, amusement and horror, but in general terms she firmly believed that the beasts of the earth enjoy greater freedom and adapt more readily to 'the grace of existence'. She explained: 'An animal never substitutes one thing for another, never sublimates things as we humans are obliged to sublimate them.' Pets offered the loyalty and integrity she often found lacking in human beings.

The haunting fear and mistrust of her own inner nature intrigued Lispector as she struggled to unravel the mysteries of life and death and the ultimate meaning of existence. The nature of God, matter, spirit, and human misery is explored time and time again throughout her work. She asks: 'What is anguish?' then gives her own answer. 'This search of mine for meaning is in itself a kind of anguish. This is something which starts with life, for when they cut the umbilical cord there is pain and separation'. Like the man who came close to suicide in one of her chronicles, we can only survive by finding a register mid-way between pianissimo and fortissimo. The temptation to abdicate was often overwhelming. But in the end, Lispector saw life as a mandate. Death held no fears for her, only its prelude.

Guided by inner rather than external voices, solitude and silence were an essential part of her spiritual armour. She agreed with Thomas Merton that 'true solitude separates a human being from others so that he or she might develop all that is good in their heart and soul'. She astutely observed that 'the solitude of others saves us from solitude, just as self-imposed solitude can save us from being submerged by the excessive love of others'. An habitual insomniac, she learned how to value silence and converse with the night. In her own words: 'There is a great silence inside me. And this silence has been the fount of my words. And from this same silence has come the most precious thing of all, namely, silence itself.'

Solitude and silence were conducive to 'a state of grace' (another of her favourite phrases), which she was careful to differentiate from inspiration or that spiritual state often attributed to saints. The 'state of grace' to which she referred was that enjoyed by ordinary people who suddenly become totally real, because they are ordinary, human and recognisable, 'an experience capable of redeeming the human condition even while emphasising its cruel limitations.' The spiritual world Lispector inhabited, like that of her fiction, was woven from fragments of experience and intuition. Her search for a faceless god was also a search for 'lost essence', a search for unassailable integrity and wholeness.

Fleeting references throughout *Discovering the World* identify the writers at home and abroad who made most impact (she preferred the word impact to influence) on her. Critics have suggested links with Kafka, Joyce, Virginia Woolf, Camus and Faulkner. She herself singled out the names of D.H.Lawrence, whom she described as 'pure fire', and of Hermann Hesse, whose seminal work, *Steppenwolf* left her spellbound. She defines the book in one of her chronicles as a 'spiritual voyage' and classifies Hesse's novel as a genuine landmark. Lispector clearly interpreted this book as Hesse himself intended: as 'a tale of griefs and needs; still not a book of a man despairing, but of a man believing.'

Her links with the philosophers and writers of the so-called Existentialist Movement have been exhaustively researched and sometimes over-stated. Echoes of Kierkegaard, Heidegger and Sartre can be found in many of her narratives and essays. She shared their anguished awareness of nothingness and encroaching absurdity which renders life intolerable and meaningless. She experienced the same frustration and nausea in the face of life's contradictions and the uncertain nature of human freedom. Endless confrontations with human weakness — her own as well as that of others — when confronted by the enormity of life, led her to conclude: We can use our defects as crutches just as easily as our qualities' and continuous errors helped her find new paths.

Inevitably Lispector is compared with Virginia Woolf. Both women were concerned with the inner life of feelings and thoughts and forged a language of their own to describe the fragility of existence and its dark, enigmatic forces. Emotionally they were both prone to alternating moods of elation and depression, of expansiveness and withdrawal. In both writers there are the same intensive perceptions of sound, sight, touch, the same irresistible urge 'to brush, scrape and kindle ...' And most important of all, they shared a belief that plots do not matter, what goes on inside the characters' minds does. Lispector dismissed any direct influence. She claimed only to have read Virginia Woolf's novels some years after the publication of her own first novel *Near to the Wild Heart.*

Lispector's prose, like that of the New Zealand writer Katherine Mansfield whose work she deeply appreciated, appears to flow easily and naturally, governed by feeling and observation rather than by any apparent calculation of its effect. Both built their narratives on fragments of memory and experience with single-minded intensity. Both writers excelled in shorter narrative forms, their eye focused on the moment, the instantaneous, fleeting impressions amidst cross-currents of fear and hope.

Both imposed their own shape on the seemingly intractable realities of life in the shared belief that art is not an attempt on the part of the artist to reconcile existence with his or her vision: it is an attempt to create his or her world within this world.

The enemy of creative lies, she was anxious to enlighten rather than to mystify her readers. Like Mansfield, she was labelled both witch and mystic, but neither of these descriptions does her justice. If she could be stark and pessimistic, she could also be droll and witty. Her sharp eye misses nothing of the human foibles and absurdities around her. The chronicles include amusing encounters with society women, loquacious taxi-drivers, the business-like madam of a brothel, beggars with their own code of honour, unpredictable housemaids who can be formidable and wreak havoc, and an envious nanny whose social ambitions outstrip those of her mistress.

The chronicles also confirm that Lispector was by no means indifferent to political and social problems. The temptation to see her as a tragic muse has misled some critics and readers. The image is not merely false but a travesty of her true nature. Lispector was an astute observer of human concerns. The economic plight and social divisions in her native Brazil were never far from her thoughts. As a child, she had seen the most degrading poverty in the North-eastern provinces, causing her 'to tremble with impotent rage'; in Rio, the starving poor pricked her conscience, and the future of the Brazilian Indians concerned her as deeply as the exploitation of the indigenous population in Portugal's African colonies. She wrote: 'Frankly, I feel socially committed. Everything I write is tied, at least in my mind, to the real world in which we live. Perhaps this aspect of my writing will become stronger one day.' She wrote those words in December 1967, and this social concern had indeed become stronger by the time she came to write her penultimate novel *The Hour of The Star* some ten years later. The plight of her heroine, the ugly, illiterate, impoverished Macabea, who has made her way from Alagoas to the slums of Rio, sums up the Brazilian social drama: the same drama which perplexed and disturbed Lispector as a child in Recife and later influenced her decision to study law in the hope that she might help to reform the country's penal system. When pressed to comment on the question of literature and commitment, she replied: 'It would indeed be strange if I were to remain indifferent to life in my own country. I may not write about social problems but I live them intensely.' Even in her stories for children there is a gentle plea for racial tolerance and social equality. And her mistrust of politicians and their abuse of power is quite unambiguous in two chronicles: 'The Leader's Dream' and 'In Memory of the Man who Stood Down'.

Her political voice may have been understated, her note of censure discreet, but her solidarity on behalf of justice and human dignity was beyond question. She needed no convincing that charity is a futile substitute for social justice and firmly believed that hunger spiritualises no one. Her sentiments echoed those of Carlos Drummond de Andrade, Brazil's most politically-committed poet this century, when he declared: 'Time is my concern, time now, men now, life now.'

First and foremost, however, was her commitment to writing. In a television interview, she confessed: 'When I am not writing, I am dead.' She believed that writing could turn a human being into a divinity. And when the words flowed in harmony with thought and feeling, she experienced something akin to ecstasy. She staunchly defended her individual freedom as a writer and insisted: 'If there exists such a thing as expression, then let it emanate from what I am.' Appropriately enough, the last item in this collection leaves us with the question which was to haunt her all her life: 'Could it be that the person who sees most, feels and suffers most?' That was the price she paid for the rare insights she so memorably expressed. G P

Family Ties [Laços de Família]

Family Ties is a compilation of thirteen short stories, all linked by one theme: *love*. There is love and how it binds family members together, love and how it imprisons, love and love's cruelty, love and how it liberates or should liberate us.

Writing of love for Lispector is to write about the human condition. Each story is a profound journey into the psychology of her mainly female characters. Strong women, weak women, old women and young girls. Some men too; strong and weak; old and young. All of them seem to be on the verge of experiencing something new; plodding through their daily and often boring routines, set in their habits and habituated to the superficiality that surrounds them. But whether it is a blind man chewing gum, or a dead dog found in the streets, or a buffalo in a zoo, or the smallest woman on Earth in Equatorial Africa, these men and women are all susceptible to experiencing a breaking point in their consciousness.

Lispector brings the external world into the inner reality of each human being she encounters in her writings. And with words that so transparently transmit emotions she relates the intensity of this inner world when questioned, when shattered.

Thus the fifteen year old girl in *Preciousness* who is subjected to the sexual gaze of two young men in the street feels a huge change has occurred, something has been taken from her. The woman of *The Imitation of the Rose* focuses on a bunch of flowers and feels an intensity she has not known before. Should she give away these roses in their unbelievable beauty, or does she want to keep them for herself? The three young men of *Mystery in São Cristóvão*, on their way to a party, stop in a garden to break off a stem of hyacinth, but a white face behind the window stops them, scares them, makes them run away and a great mystery settles on this house.

Writing of love, Clarice Lispector draws us into another's inner self and so draws us into our own inner self. She does it by showing us that love, at the core of the human being and what links us one to the other, however strong it is, very rarely manages to deliver the spiritual liberty we expect of it. And families, as in the story *Happy Birthday,* end up being linked more by superficiality than by love.

In these short stories Clarice Lispector creates worlds that could be ours, worlds and existences that seem totally normal and yet are totally absurd, life that is real and surreal at the same time. She seems to be able write outside the usual social and political constraints with great feeling, wisdom, scepticism and warmth She writes about what is most real and what is kept furthest away from daily life. She questions, she shatters and she (re)creates. M C - L

'And she considered the cruel necessity of loving. She considered the malignity of our desire to be happy. She considered the ferocity with which we want to play. And the number of times when we murder for love. She then looked at her mischievous son, as if she was looking at a dangerous stranger. And she was horrified at her own soul, which, more than her body, had engendered that being so apt for life and happiness. And thus she looked at him attentively and with uneasy pride, her child already without two front teeth, his evolution, his evolution under way, his teeth falling out to make room for those which bite best.' p92 (*The smallest woman in the world*)

The Foreign Legion [A Legião Estrangeira: Contos e Crônica]

The Foreign Legion is a compilation of short stories and 'chronicles' (a Brazilian literary speciality; short pieces originally published in newspapers, reflections on all and everything, on daily life) from two lines to 20 pages long. They are parcels of thoughts and feelings from Clarice Lispector, as writer, as woman, as human being in society, there are pieces on various subjects — yet all on the same theme: the attempt to reach the essence of life. Whether autobiographical accounts or social commentaries, they embody moments of discovery of a kind of truth, finally or spontaneously attained. There is a connection in this to Sartre's existentialism as embodied in his astonishing *Nausea*. Thus, a 'truth' is discovered: in the darkness of a night (*A Night in February*), in the brightness of the day when two people separate (*The Message*), in the shape of an egg (*The Egg and the Chicken*), in the architecture of a city (*Five Days in Brasilia*), in a rainy day (*An Angel's Disquiet*), in the acute and unexpected intelligence of a young girl (*The Misfortunes of Sophia*) and in the lies we tell others and ourselves (*Without any warning*).

Clarice Lispector's stories are moments in suspension where one sees through the unnecessary and distracting decorations of life. We see beyond the superficiality of the conversations of two people who love each other but cannot communicate (*A Sincere Friendship*). The title of the story *A Bottom Drawer* is the perfect metaphorical expression of the content of the stories, as well as of the manner in which Clarice Lispector writes. With her writing she gets to the bottom of the drawer. She empties out all its contents and lets it be full of its own emptiness, letting what is at the very bottom come up, in precisely chosen words.

As in her book *Family Ties* Clarice Lispector speaks of love, of the courageous or the cowardly choices we make in life, of honesty towards ourselves, of our never ending search. She takes us on a journey to try to understand ourselves knowing pertinently that it is (almost) impossible — so that we remain a *Foreign Legion* to ourselves and to others, with maybe our only valid hope: to conquer our own freedom. M C-L

'Did I understand? No. Nor do I know what I understood at the time. But just as far as one brief moment I had seen with horrified fascination the world is my teacher — and to this day I do not know what I saw — so I understand us, even though I shall never know whom I understood. I shall never know what I understand. Whatever I understood in the park was, with the shock of extreme sweetness, understood by my ignorance. An ignorance which stood there — in the same numbed solitude as the surrounding trees — an ignorance which I fully recovered with its incomprehensible truth. There I stood, the girl who was too knowing by far, and beheld how all that was unworthy in me served both God and man. All that was unworthy about me, was also my treasure.' pp26-27 (*The Disasters of Sophia*)

      'But do they understand each other? They have never thought of understanding each other. They have brought themselves as their only banner.' p200 (*Mute Singing, Mute Dancing*)

The Passion according to G.H. [A Paixão segundo G.H.]

The Passion according to G.H. is a novel that somehow feels like a series of short stories, for each chapter starts with a sentence that gives it a theme.

The overall theme is the same as in the compilations *The Foreign Legion* and *Family Ties;* getting to the bottom of the drawer, coming to an understanding of oneself and the essence of life, embodied, essentially and symbolically, in the notions of love, honesty, truth.

In *The Passion according to G.H.* a woman is questioned existentially about her life but the questions find no answers. It speaks of the self-discovery of a human being, in this case the almost anonymous G.H., as she questions, criticises and wonders. It examines the processes G.H. goes through to arrive at a greater understanding of what her life is about, of what *life* is about. The crucial moment is the premeditated killing of a cockroach in the door of a wardrobe.

Before this pivotal event, G.H. is the one others see and perceive; she is her name. A name that we only know as G.H., her initials as engraved on her suitcase. Even though she is a questioning being she lives in ignorance of her own self. Something is amiss but it eludes her. She tries to grasp it but only distances the possibility of understanding by talking too much, by delaying the silence that could reveal what she is searching for. She defines herself by all her possible external extensions, never being truly honest — she fears what honesty may reveal.

There is one prerequisite for change: that the deadly safe routine should be broken. Killing the cockroach is more about killing than about what she kills; about what she kills in herself and the effect that has on her life from that moment on. It is about her starting to be truthful with herself and leaving the fears that immobilise behind her, replacing them with a new courage that will set her free, that will give her the necessary space to undergo her mystical experience of the self.

In a story where all seems to fall apart, chapters are symbolically linked by the last sentence of the previous chapter becoming the first sentence of the next one, as if this sentence were a unique point of reference to hold onto, for everything else is being questioned, dismantled, thrown away. The 'I' of the protagonist is fused with the 'I' of the author in a way that allows any reader to fully identify with G.H. and 'become' her.

This is a world where external and internal realities rarely meet, or coincide, but when they meet, an explosion takes place. She tries to bring into her meaningless life of routine the dimension of the spiritual embodied in rituals, here the killing of a cockroach and what follows it; the 'eating' of the cockroach. The 'moment of truth' in itself becomes crucial. In this moment, everything else disappears so that G.H. can make sense of what this killing means to her, of how it changes her. M C-L

'But are the discoveries of infancy like those made in a laboratory, where one finds what one will? Was it when, only when I became an adult that I started to fear and grew the third leg? Can I, as an adult, have the childlike courage to love myself? to lose oneself is to go looking with no sense of what to do with what you might find. The two walking feet minus that extra third one that holds a person down. And I want to be held down. I don't know what to do with the horrifying freedom that can destroy me. But while I was held down, was I happy? Or was there — and there was — an uncanny restless something in my happy prison routine? Or was there — and there was — that throbbing something to which I was accustomed that I thought throbbing was the same as being a person? Isn't that it? Yes, that too... that too...' pp5-6

Hour of the Star [A Hora da Estrella]

The great Clarice Lispector's last book, published in the year of her death in early middle age. Her respected translator Giovanni Pontiero said she 'narrates from within'; a way of suggesting her astonishing ability to create intimacy with her readers, not through the gossipy divulgation of real or faked personal trivia, but an intimacy based on mastery of what she is saying combined with *heart*. Heart that is not just that engaging *Brazilian* humanness but, in her tenderness for children, animals, hurt souls there is something of her Ukrainian Jewish background too.

Hour of the Star, the story of poor Macabea, a girl with no real talents, accomplishments or gifts — except her ability to accept humility and humiliation as if they were entirely natural things — is Clarice's testament for many reasons. Partly because it hits that fundamental question in Brazil and elsewhere; Do you care? Also because in it she succeeds so well with her ideas about writing and her ideas about life, about women's lives, about Brazil. In Macabea, immortalized in a brilliant film version directed by Suzana Amaral, she has created a character whose life was a kind of opposite to her own — Lispector herself was a successful writer and the beautiful, cosmopolitan wife of a diplomat — and she has used her sympathy and writerly talent in a marvellous piece of observation and creation.

Hour of the Star begins with a dialogue with the reader so that when the 'facts of the case' (as Macabea's life and past is revealed) become known, the trust previously created makes them rebound in the reader's thoughts. Clarice does not write from a great distance but whispers in your ear and Macabea, who is at one extreme of the human condition where 'sadness was a luxury' reaches us as all the more human for that.

Reading the book is not a sad experience as it is often appallingly funny; all Macabea's conversational tidbits and world-view are supplied by 'Radio Clock', a downmarket FM station that intersperses a constant stream of time announcements with the kind of desperate 'interesting facts' only Radio DJs know. *Hour of the Star* is quite possibly the best Brazilian book ever translated into English, appalling, delightful, accessible but radical and brilliantly accomplished. R K

'When she realized that her remark about the animals displeased Olímpico, she tried to change the topic of conversation:

"On Radio Clock they used a word that worried me: mimetism."

Olímpico eyed her disapprovingly:

"That's not a nice word for a virgin to be using. Why do you have to keep on asking questions about things that don't concern you? The brothels in the Mangue are full of women who asked far too many questions."

"Is the Mangue a district?"

"It's an evil place frequented only by men. This won't sink in, but I'm going to tell you something. A chap can still get a woman on the cheap. You've only cost me a coffee so far. That's your lot. I won't be wasting any more money buying you things. Is that clear."

Macabéa thought to herself: he's right. I don't deserve anything from him because I've wet my knickers.' p55

LUFT
Lya

Island of the Dead [O Quarto Fechado]

Lya Luft is from Brazil's extreme South, the city of Porto Alegre in the state of Rio Grande do Sul, a zone of Northern European immigration, famous for its German colonies. Luft's writing seems to reflect the teutonic element and all her characters seem to be enveloped by a gloomy northern fog of nameless unhappiness.

However *Island of the Dead,* despite the gloom, is a concise minor masterpiece. The title refers to a copy of the famous painting 'Island of the Dead' by Arnold Böcklin which comes to dominate the thoughts of the main character, Renata. She is a woman who has arrived at a savage vision of marriage — she followed the emotional impulse to marry and have children but her marriage has turned into passionate hatred for her husband and herself. She has also emotionally rejected her children. Renata is a woman who has absolutely made the wrong move in marrying, violating her own nature which is artistic and solitary.

This is a fascinating and fairly unusual theme and Luft has the courage as a writer to confront it unsparingly. Apart from the relationship of man and woman in marriage there is an exploration of other intimacies; that of brother and sister in a pair of twins who try to absorb each other absolutely; thereby experiencing a kind of ideal closeness, but it is an intimacy, a union of twin souls that is bought at the expense of everything else. Outside their symbiotic emotional affinity no real contact with any other reality is possible for them.

Overhanging the various kinds of failed relationships is a variety of 'deaths' that these failures of love have engendered; the husband Martin is emotionally dead, Clara, an elder daughter, is sexually dead, poisoned by a perverse liaison at the awakening of her sexuality, the twins are socially dead, another daughter Ella is mentally dead after an accident and one of the twins Camilo becomes actually dead.

Luft says here 'all human relationships involve suffering'; an unfortunate truth everyone has to face sooner or later; Luft's book is a brilliant, valid exploration of how and why that is true, in its way very life-affirming, warning us to steer towards achievable goals in our lives, rather than (ultimately poisonous) over-idealisations of *love*. R K

'She had lived with him, slept with him, for many years and had made him suffer. With him she had gone from ecstasy to alienation, from passion to hatred, and with him she had seen disintegrate what they had built to last forever. But an interior gulf had never been overcome. Ardour and sweetness had turned to impatience, after being lovers they had become strangers. Whose fault was it?

A successful pianist, Renata had come down from the concert stage to Martin's world, a matter-of-fact world of strength and rationality. But old enough to have her habits already ingrained. she hadn't been able to change. She had tried to substitute her domestic life for her art, but very soon found her new surroundings vulgar. Until then she had concentrated on herself, she could not share herself with another. With so many demands on her now, she felt impotent.

No, love had not been enough. They had gone through all the stages of a slow, painful separation. They rarely saw each other; actually they avoided each other, fearing new scenes.

Years ago she had said, "I'm nor the type to get married," seeing women her age surrounded by children. After marriage, too late, she realized that she had been right. Even though it could be lonely, difficult, and sterile, her art was less complex for her than human love.' p7

The Red House [Exílio]

We don't entirely discover where the Red House is but it certainly isn't in that stereotypical Brazil of sinuous Mulattas, coffee beans and carnival. Here instead are the themes and images of contemporary European fiction and yet — not exactly.

This is a book about the tides of affectionate connection in women's lives and simultaneously it is about the damage caused by the lack or the destruction of those connections. To an extent there's the caring narrative presence, maternal in a way, one recognises from Clarice Lispector's work. Lya Luft though is more sombre, more obsessional and gets at emotional truth in a different way. In *The Red House* she examines the states of mind of a daughter abandoned by her mother. The narrative is driven by the desire of this woman from a disrupted family for stability and fixity in her own adult life. The strength of her need, unsurprisingly, destroys the possibility of achieving it.

Lya Luft has worked a great deal as a literary translator and translated Virginia Woolf amongst others. There is some Woolf in this book — the attempt to go below the surface by looking very hard at the surface of things. So while the days of the nameless 'abandoned daughter' pass in apparently prosaic, cloistered circumstances, we gradually absorb the psychic picture of an individual's feelings and patterns.

Luft writes very well; 'People from the provinces who spoke in whispers and wore a permanent expression of alarm', and although the book is the troubling account of a troubled individual, in a place suffused with that South American, Deep South gloom that never lifts, many readers will find it finally therapeutic and connecting. R K

'It is already evening when I return from work. I shut myself away in my room; the same hovering disquiet as I sit there anxiously waiting. Waiting for whom? Whom am I expecting?

Today it finally dawned on me. This was the hour when Lucas came home from school. Notwithstanding the long hours I had to spend at work, Lucas's existence had been the compass which quietly governed mine: the time he left for school, the time he arrived home, the time for his bath and his meals. Despite my busy life and demanding job, I constantly had to reassure myself: Lucas is all right, he is in good hands and perfectly safe.

Without him I was like a deserted house, doors wide open, the floorboards eaten away once the rats moved in.

My heart tells me: Lucas should be home now.' pp98-99

MACHADO DE ASSIS
Joaquim Maria

Dom Casmurro [Dom Casmurro]

Dom Casmurro is Machado's most famous novel and is apparently read by every Brazilian schoolchild, though perhaps not for the right reasons. On the surface, it's a sort of *Bildungsroman*, ('novel of achieving maturity') a personal account of the narrator's coming of age in mid-nineteenth century Rio de Janeiro, a time when the Monarchy, the landowning élite and slavery seemed most unassailable. Bentinho ('little Bento'), the cosseted successor to the family fortune seems to epitomize this stifling world of privileged security, as well as its darker underbelly of vulnerabilities and suspicions.

Before his birth, Bentinho's mother made a pact with God: if He gave her a son, she would bring him up to be a priest. Bentinho has other ideas: he's in love with his next-door neighbour and childhood playmate Capitu Pádua. Too young to assert their own will or to elope, the two children hatch a long-term plan to secure their future happiness. They succeed, but then the adult Bento's growing certainty that he has been the victim of an explicable infidelity robs them of everything they've fought for, including the shared joy of raising their own son together. The novel is Bento's account of this betrayal, reconstituted out of affectionate reminiscences and bitterly ironic insinuations in the twilight solitude of his life.

What, though, if our lawyer-narrator has abused his position in order to construct an incontrovertible case for the prosecution? What if his narrative is the meticulously elaborated character assassination of an upstart wife, more intelligent than her husband, intended to rationalise his irrational insecurities and suspicions and restore some meaning to the life that he himself has wrecked? Once we accept that possibility, that we may have become the willing accomplices to some ingenious manipulation, then this wistful

recollection is dramatically turned on its head. We are faced instead with the disturbing portrait of infantile paranoia, class resentments and snobbery, and projected guilt, all based on Bentinho's preference for the world of his imagination rather than that of an unsettling reality. His own thoughts and desires are revealed to him like epiphanies: he realises he's in love with Capitu only when he overhears an adult insinuating it;

he runs next door and finds her absent-mindedly scratching his name on her garden wall, and they face each other in astonished silence, struck by a realisation that's jumped out at them, taken them by surprise.

A character in Thomas Pynchon's *The Crying of Lot 49* describes miracles as collisions between cosmic pool-balls, the intrusion of another universe into our own. In *Dom Casmurro* this idea is raised into the principle of Bento's entire existence, except that the miracle is too great for his ego to bear. One such moment occurs when Bentinho, obsessed by Capitu, sees the body of a neglected friend, a poor young neighbour who has died of leprosy. Bentinho's cosily amorous thoughts are annoyingly disturbed by this inconvenient reminder of a less privileged world — as he puts it, people's individual consciousnesses are like separate galaxies, one 'poking its nose' into another from time to time. T M & D T

'Of the furniture only the sofa seemed to have understood our situation, offering its services with such insistence that we accepted and sat down. My own particular opinion concerning sofas dates from that moment. They unite intimacy with decorum, revealing the whole house without us having to leave the drawing-room. Two men sitting on one can discuss the destiny of an empire, and two women the cut of a frock; but only by some aberration of nature will a man and a woman talk about anything other than themselves. That was what we did, Capitu and I.' pp129-30

The Devil's Church [A Igreja do Diabo]

Were it not for the strange unease the reader will feel and find hard to identify, these short stories could be taken as pure entertainment; the amazing results of an attempt by the Devil to establish his own church; the useful and profitable findings of a sage in an exotic place; the disappointment and frustration of a man who claims to have come back from the dead; various incidents and accidents in affairs of the heart, updated versions of ancient fables and brief biographies of curious characters.

When, however, the reader starts to appreciate all the richness of details, which are never merely details but convey the meaning of many things which cannot be presented in such short, concise texts; when the uncomfortable complicity created by the narrator with the reader is detected; when the ironical veil is lifted and the sharp critique is revealed, then there are some fascinating meditations on ethics, society and human behaviour.

At the end of the 19th century de Assis provides us with a witty depiction of Brazilian bourgeois values and behaviour; but a deeper reading makes us reflect on the relativity of values and virtues, the vanity of knowledge, the doubtful motivation of philanthropy and the emptiness of rhetoric.

Machado's writing career brought him from the lower social classes to the heights of intellectual eminence but he never lost the acute awareness of a society based on exploitation and hypocrisy. The pleasure of reading him is in appreciating his mastery of style and continually finding fresh layers of meaning. M D

'He proclaimed that the accepted virtues ought to be replaced by others which were the natural, legitimate ones. Vanity, lust and sloth were reinstated, as was avarice, which he declared was only the mother of economy, the difference between the two being that the mother was robust and the daughter skin and bones. Anger had its best justification in the existence of Homer — without Achilles' fury there would have been no *Iliad*: "Muse, sing the wrath of Achilles, son of Peleus..."'p.39

Epitaph of a Small Winner [Memórias póstumas de Brás Cubas]

Brás Cubas, the 'small winner' whose epitaph this novel writes, is an unremarkable man. A well-to-do citizen of Rio de Janeiro, he tries his hand at politics, journalism and romance, conducting a long and much talked-about affair with an acquaintance's wife. What is remarkable about the novel is its style. After a long illness in 1879 Assis, who had till then been tentatively exploring the relations between Brazil's different social groups, but within the constraints of Romantic convention, turned to a more subjective, psychological form, the model for which he found in Lawrence Sterne's *Tristram Shandy*.

Like *Tristram Shandy*, *Epitaph of a Small Winner* advances not in a straight line but in fits and starts, loops and cutbacks. There is even a 'chapter which I shall not write,' a trick taken directly from Sterne. Where *Epitaph of a Small Winner* differs from *Tristram Shandy*, though, is in the status of its narrator. Bras Cubas, as he writes, is dead, and his autobiography begins not with his conception but with his demise and burial. This unusual set-up gives the narrative a limitlessness that Assis' later novel *Dom Casmurro*, also its main character's autobiography, lacks. Bras Cubas takes a ride on a hippopotamus to the beginning of the ages and speaks to Nature or Pandora herself, standing beyond all the boundaries of the world he writes about. This limitlessness allows him a cynical relativism, thinly disguised as honest sincerity. within which he can accommodate every cruelty, every hypocrisy with chilling bonhomie. All-encompassing religious or philosophical systems that justify a brutally competitive status quo are mercilessly parodied in Cubas's grim sophistry, a variation on Pangloss's 'all's for the best in the best of all possible worlds'. At the end of life's sordid game he has neither gained nor lost anything much (though, as a good child of the slave owning élite, he has been spared the humiliation of working for a living), so he decides that as he hasn't transmitted his legacy of misery to any descendants, he's come out a 'small winner'. T M & D T

'How glorious to throw away your cloak, to dump your spangles in a ditch, to unfold yourself, to strip off all your paint and ornaments, to confess plainly what you were and what you failed to be! For, after all, you have no neighbours, no friends, no enemies, no acquaintances, no strangers, no audience at all. The sharp and judicial eye of public opinion loses its power as soon as we enter the territory of death. I do not deny that it sometimes glances this way and examines and judges us, but we dead folk are not concerned about its judgement. You who still live, believe me, there is nothing in the world so monstrously vast as our indifference.' p75

Machado & Modernism, Machado & Gender

Fernando Pessoa, the voice of Modernism in the Portuguese-speaking world, wrote in a famous poem that 'the poet is a feigner./ So completely does he feign/ that the pain he truly suffers/ he even feigns as pain.'(translated by J R. Longland in *Fernando Pessoa: A Galaxy of Poets*.) Yet many of the preoccupations that were the intellectual daily bread of the European Modernists (including the question of the possibility of truth, aesthetic and otherwise) had been rehearsed by Machado de Assis in Brazil forty to fifty years before, a fact all the more remarkable, given Brazil's situation on the periphery of Europe's rapidly shifting intellectual panorama.

Born in 1839 and dead by 1908, Machado de Assis' literary development is all the more extraordinarily pioneering given its beginnings in the last stages of Brazilian Romanticism. Machado, although an admirer of a key figure of the latter movement, José de Alencar, must nevertheless take the credit for the final ousting of the Romantics and for pioneering in Brazil some principal aspects of the 'Idéia Nova' or 'New Idea,' which had by the early 1870s established itself as the main literary style in Portugal after similar developments elsewhere in Europe, particularly in France.

But as an intellectual maverick Machado also engaged in undoing what he saw as some of the fallacies of the movement he had helped introduce to the Brazilian literary scene. Thus, his scepticism concerning the 'Naturalist documentary method' and his aversion to the excesses of description and detail upheld by that school in the name of truth and objectivity emerge unambiguously from pages of criticism and fiction in which he considers, dissects and subsequently dismisses the arch-goal of the Realists/Positivists, namely 'the Truth'. While the Positivist influenced Realist or Naturalist movement believed in the need to classify and describe reality objectively as a sine qua non of social reform, Machado, remained sceptical about the possibility of discovering and promoting this transcendental 'Truth', despite being equally or more more aware of social injustice through personal experience.

Machado shared with authors like Eça de Queiroz in Portugal the belief that irony, bordering sometimes on farce, was an effective vehicle for social criticism. Yet his hilarity is always tinged with a profoundly serious intent and a sombreness which suggest he felt that collective and individual moral improvement might not be attainable after all. *Epitaph of a Small Winner* and *Quincas Borba, Philosopher or Dog?* offer delightfully funny parodies of concepts dear to the Realists, such as Darwinism and natural selection which he caricatures as the philosophy of 'Humanitismo',' the product of a sick mind whose followers are crooks'. But the humour in every debate on 'Humanitismo' reveals a darker side and the author's (if not his narrator's) deeply felt conviction that to appeal to a so-called law of nature, unrestrained by any collective or individual responsibility, as an apology for humanity's savagery, is nothing short of pernicious. The appalling prospect of humanity excusing itself from social responsibility and from discarded notions of altruism by reference to a Darwinian notion of survival of the fittest is central to Machado's vision. While showing him to be a 'a man of his epoch and of his country,' and involved in its debates, it also removes him from the local and the particular to the universal, rendering many of his preoccupations as pertinent here and now as he was in his own time and place.

The importance he gave to the portrayal of women and the nature of women's existence within the family, marriage, state and religion, already apparent in his earlier novels such as *Helena* and *Yaya Garcia*, becomes more explicit in the later works. Through his portrayal of the plight of silenced, dependent and slandered female protagonists, who often end up suffering a real or metaphorical death at the hands of their male nearest and dearest, Machado ressurrects classic themes from Greek tragedy such as matricide, incest, betrayal and retribution. At the same time he anticipates the political and literary debates of feminism and the women's movement, just then beginning to stir but not yet raging in Brazilian urban society. By framing his approach to these issues in the context of narratives which questioned an established (male, patriarchal, middle-class) discourse claiming to be unideological truth, he challenged that idea of scientifically-validated truth which then seemed impregnable. In doing so, he also paved the way for the Modernist and Post-Modernist scepticism about transcendental truths anchored in 'pure' reality, and raised, for the first time within Brazilian literature less abstract issues which remain pertinent to us today, namely the intricacies and traps of love and marriage and the struggle for power in the relations between the sexes. M-M L

Machado & Slavery

Scepticism, politely devastating irony, a preference for the disturbingly unreliable first-person narrator, and a sensitivity to the disempowerment of women — why should these qualities have been so central to the work of the greatest writer of late nineteenth-century Brazil?

The impact of slavery has long since been recognised as fundamental to the country's economic and social development — it was, after all, almost the exclusive source of profit during the four centuries of Brazil's colonial and Imperial history. But its effect on the mental life of the nation, especially that of its landowning, slave owning élite, has only recently been understood. Most crucially, in the century of Liberalism and Progress, when Brazil's independence (1822) and its First Republic (1889) were declared in the name of the principles of Liberty, Equality and Fraternity, how could the country's rulers confidently claim membership of a modern, enlightened international brotherhood when their prosperity, cultural well-being and power depended on the systematic denial of such rights to the majority of its citizens?

As the mulatto son of poor parents, dependent on the arbitrary exercise of ruling-class patronage for his education and access to the world of privilege, it is perhaps not surprising that Machado should have developed an acute perception of the strategies used to live with this lie, to veil the barbarism of slavery in the cloak of civilisation, to rationalise and justify the unjustifiable through apparently value-free, objective systems of 'scientific' analysis, and to turn the voices of doubt and dissent into ambitious conspirators and traitors.

Machado's mastery was to incorporate those same mechanisms into the very structure of his narratives. Invisible to those of his readers who 'innocently' identified with the Truth of the authorial voice, they suddenly and devastatingly reveal themselves to us once we dare, consciously, to tread the precarious, shifting terrain of Machado's own ironic scepticism. D T

Yayá Garcia [Yayá Garcia]

A beautiful tribute to the talents, perceptiveness and intelligence of young women who may lack experience but have a precious kind of optimism and energy, Machado slowly builds up a picture of the attractive young Yayá, a charming and affectionate girl, still at school when we meet her.

To begin with we think we're going to read a rather romantic and rose-coloured love story; expecting of course that there might be a few tricks of fate to twist the path of true love — but no reader could ever guess the actual course of events. After his sugary start Machado plunges Yayá and three other contenders in the mating rite into the most extraordinary thwarted situation of mutual dissimulation, manipulation and betrayal.

It is widely agreed that in this early work Machado first demonstrates his genius as a writer and the book's climax in a mad incestual mêlée of jealousy and rivalry is simply very startling. A very deceiving book to begin with that finishes in a narrative whirl. R K

'Of the various qualities needed in chess Yayá possessed two of the most essential: quick apprehension and a benedictine patience — qualities equally precious in life, which with its problems and conflicts is itself a game of chess, some games being won, others lost, others drawn.' p138

MIRANDA
Ana

Bay of All Saints and Every Conceivable Sin [Boca do Inferno]

An evocation of the seventeenth century city of Bahia more officially known as 'Saint Salvador of all the Saints', then the capital of Brazil, with its wealth based on sugar cane, Bahia has always been an important city in Brazil and the heartland of the African element in her cultural life.

Ana Miranda's book is a colourful historical novel, following the lives of certain leading players in the courtly and ecclesiastical politics of the age, focusing on actual personalities such as the reforming Jesuit Father Antonio Vieira, an important early figure in Brazilian letters and the poet Gregorio de Matos.

Gregorio is a Villonesque character who is as at home in Bahia's brothels as on the heights of Poetic Parnassus. In fact one of Ana Miranda's themes seems to be that large-scale prostitution, like political corruption, has a long tradition in Brazil, reaching right back into the period of Portuguese rule.

Father Vieira, the foil to the enlightened libertine poet de Matos, represents a more sombre social and moral critique of the world around him, including the mistreatment of the American Indian population at that time being kidnapped for forced labour.

Inside this quite extensive book is a wealth of material about life and culture in the Bahia of those days and for the

Brazilians, who made it into a bestseller, this is a 'Roots' book, showing the background to much of their history. R K

"'Brazil is bring torn apart by the sharp claws of those who govern her," said Padre Vieira. "Brazil's problem is that any unjust or arbitrary act carried out here never reaches the right ears in Portugal. Even the thieving doesn't seem to be noticed back in the metropolis. So the people struggle on in the greatest misery. And Brazil is no more than the image and reflection of Portugal, a hotbed of vice and corruption, of infinite extravagance without any financial resources and riddled with all the other contradictions of human nature."' p57

OLINTO
Antonio

The Water House [A Casa de Água]

In *The Water House* and its sequel book *King of Ketu*, Olinto tackles the Afro-Brazilian experience, particularly exploring the connections of Black Brazilians with West Africa, where many originated and from where they were carried to Brazil to be plantation slaves.

The Water House is the story of a freed slave making the journey back to Nigeria to find relatives left behind and their original homeland. It makes it a Brazilian 'Roots' book written years before Alex Hailey's *Roots* which followed the story of a contemporary African-American tracing his family line back to an African ancestor.

Different from *Roots* is that Olinto tries to stay close to the forms of African speech and oral literature, 'the voices of the people' to tell the story, making it a more poetic, more difficult but also more unique literary work. R K

'I do not know how she spent her last days, I cannot find anything in her memories which sets aside these days from others, each the same as the next, going down to the river, milk and salt corn-cake in the morning, black beans and cabbage at midday, now and then dried salt meat and black beans, conversations about things that hid themselves in the cellar, the mula-sem-cabeça, the priest's mistress who, when she was dead, turned into a mule without a head and came out of the cemetery in the middle of the night, dead people who came back to tell you what heaven was like, or hell or purgatory, the little girls playing ring games, here comes Margarida, Olé Olé Olà, I am poor, poor, poor, the night fell suddenly and the stars twinkled with happiness, when everything was dark the talking in the kitchen went on until very late, the stove crackling, the lamp lighting the way along the passage full of mystery. But yes, she does remember the last day, or rather not the whole day, but the moment of departure, four horses, her mother, her grandmother, her brother and sister herself and a man who was going to look after them, from early morning...'p7

RAMOS
Graciliano

Barren Lives [Vidas Secas]

Dating back to 1938 this is one of the all time great novels of rural existence in Brazil, telling of the life of a small family (and their dog) in the harsh social and ecological conditions of the drought-plagued state of Alagoas. In an elementally sparse ranching landscape of scrubland and marginal pastures Ramos studies his family in separate chapters, one by one, from the leathery, ignorant father down to the most sympathetic member the family dog, chapters which somehow seem to be exactly the right length. We share the realities of their lives, including a brush with the law, the experience of winter, huddling around the fireplace and then the overwhelming impact of a town on the two little boys visiting it for the first time, kids who have never seen other people before.

Ramos writes with a satisfying simplicity that seems to reflect perfectly the stripped-down lifestyle of his characters, semi-nomadic hired hands who have to live with the bare minimum of things and aspirations.

The final fate of this family, poised between the drought that begins the book and the one that ends it is to continue their trek out of the countryside and into the big city, following in the footsteps of so many other poor Brazilians. *Barren Lives* is a moving and deeply sympathetic short book, with a sweet wry touch; an undoubted and enjoyable classic. R K

'Indignant at the injustice, the boy left the house, crossed the yard and took refuge under the dry catingueira trees beside the empty pond.

The dog was his companion in that hour of trial. She had been stretched out beside the stones on which Vitória did the cooking, drowsing in the heat, waiting for a bone. In all probability she wouldn't get one, but she believed in bones and she found the state of torpor enjoyable. She stirred a bit from time to time, raising to her mistress black eyes shining with confidence. Having accepted the idea that there might be a bone in the kettle, she was not going to let anybody or anything disturb her modest hopes. She got an occasional kick for no reason at all. The kicks were to be expected and did nothing to dispel the vision of the bone.' p56

RIBEIRO
Darcy

Maira [Maíra]

Published in Brazil in 1976, the appearance of Maíra in an English translation came not a moment too soon, as an awareness abroad of Brazilian indigenous problems becomes daily more necessary.

Ribeiro is well qualified to write about the Brazilian Indians; during almost forty years of a distinguished career as an anthropologist, he has researched among and written on numerous tribal groups in Brazil. In 1970 he published *The Indians and Civilization*, a masterfully comprehensive work originally commissioned by UNESCO to assess, in the words of the book's subtitle 'the integration of the indigenous populations into modern Brazil'. What in fact emerged was an account of the failure of any such assimilation, and it is that failure which lies at the heart of *Maira*.

The story of the central character Isaías Avá is based on the real case of a Bororo Indian from Matto Grosso who in 1910, at the age of twelve, was removed from his community by Salesian missionaries and eventually sent to Rome and Paris to become a priest. On attempting to resume his tribal role as hunter and farmer by marrying a Bororo woman, he discovered that he had been alienated from the society of his birth. For the rest of his life he occupied a cultural and psychological limbo between two worlds.

The real achievement of *Maira*, though, is its location of this individual struggle for personal self-integration within a complex yet skillfully constructed picture of Amazonian society and of the political, economic and cultural forces trying to transform it. The voices of the principal characters in the drama each contribute their own perspective: the voice of tribal tradition, recounting the story of the creation of the world, and the beautiful funeral ritual of the Mairun chief; the voice of the river trader Juca, himself a detribalised Indian determined to seduce the remainder of his people into the economic slavery to which the local population is condemned; the voice of the police inspector sent to investigate the mysterious death of a white woman, and who in the process reveals the negligent role played by FUNAI (the Brazilian government organization that deals with Amerindians) as intermediary between the Indians and white society; and the voice of Isaías himself, resigned to the eventual disappearance of the Mairuns as the conclusion of an inexorable process of contact with white culture.

The chapters devoted to the Mairun culture and mythology are the most memorable, not least due to the painful irony which they bring to the whole question of the survival of the tribal communities. For the strength of the Indians' highly sophisticated systems of kinship, social organisation and cosmology, their self-containment and self-sufficiency, also contain the seeds of their vulnerability. The duality which divides the Mairuns into two clans, and thereafter penetrates every aspect of tribal life, must necessarily include the duality of within/without, here/there, Indian/white. Most significantly, it extends to the book's title, whose several related meanings — Maira the universal creator hero of Tupi mythology; Maira the 'transformer'; Maira the bringer of civilization; Maira the foreigner; Maira the white man — attest to the Indians' innocently high expectations of a society which has not proved itself worthy of them. D T

'But soon the heavier rains fall, raining for many days, weeks, and months. The world then seemed to dissolve under the mantle of widespread water. Black clouds darken the horizons; as they break, rain pours in white curtains on to the thatch of roofs, mud unto the dancing ground. The people, consumed by sadness, huddling around little fires, now are eating dry cassava bread or roast or boiled potatoes, almost always without meat or fish, and are drinking nothing but plain cassava beer. Mosquitoes come out and multiply. Fierce midges, gnats, and punkies sting, annoy. They are the lords of the world. The beaches disappear, inundated by the cold and turbid water of the paraná. With them fish, birds, and large and small game also disappear.

So it was for months until little by little the joyfulness of summer began to return. This year the first to arrive were the spotless white ibis and the dusky herons, serene in flight, perching on the crowns of trees, afraid of dirtying their feet. Then came the toucans and their cousins, the toucanets and, finally, flocks of macaws and parrots. All life renews itself. At last clear blue days, blue waters, blue skies, open and luminous, return, infinite beaches are reborn.' pp269-270

RIBEIRO
João Ubaldo

Sergeant Getulio [Sargento Getúlio]

Sergeant Getulio is a man with a mission — to escort a left-wing political prisoner across the wild, hostile backlands of Brazil's North-East and deliver him, alive, to the coastal town of Aracaju, where he awaits his trial and probable execution. Whether or not Getulio completes this mission becomes a dramatic test of his own survival, as the personification of an entire culture of brutally *machista* individualism and uncompromising order. For he is beset by pressures that seem intent on undermining his purpose and role — the vacillations of government, which announces half-way through the journey that the prisoner must be released, pursuing Getulio as a criminal deserter when he refuses to comply; the urge to anticipate the court's judgement and execute his own sentence of justice on the man who comes to symbolise all his loathing and contempt for the values of the wider world; and the power of the desert itself, inspiring both love and hatred in Getulio, reminding him of his encroaching old age and mortality, with its twin options: voluntary retirement with a wife and family, or a sudden, violent death at the head of some apocalyptic army of latter-day bandits.

Sergeant Getulio stands in the best tradition of North-Eastern fiction — punctuated by Graciliano Ramos's *Barren Lives* and Guimarães Rosa's *The Devil to Pay in the Backlands* — in its exploration of the culture and mentality of the rural interior through the medium of its own oral language, at once primitive and severe, rich and lyrical. The only voice is that of Getulio's rambling monologue, heard by his literally captive audience and by the few companions on his mission, living and dead. In this near seamless monologue he reveals the social, psychological and emotional anatomy of a people struggling to assert its identity as its traditional world is eroded and collapses about it. Like the excellent film based on it, this book poses an unforgettable challenge — to recognise a humanity in Getulio's cruel rage, in his violent refusal to surrender to anonymity and oblivion. D T

'All houses look like platefuls of food even if it is manioc flour mush. This Hudson, when it broke down for lack of gasoline, I gave it a good look and thought it was quite a monarch of a thing , because it necessitated the putting of gasoline in it by us and we used up all the cans and I wonder where the hell we are in this world. To tell the truth, I do know, but I see that walking is the thing that must be done and the junk opens his mouth and says that he cannot walk. And I say, yes, you can walk. Otherwise I will do the worst things to you, don't get fresh. But I really wouldn't do anything, with all this tiredness and even my jacket I took off because it weighed on me, I can barely carry my weapon and Amaro his, he actually likes it very much, he does everything short of kissing it, in fact I think he does, at night when no one is watching he gives it a few kisses. I know he polishes it with the cloth he got from the car. I stood looking at this car, which is new but has long become old, and I remained looking at it, all cold. It stood there, dead. Amaro still lifted the hood and looked inside, a heap of parts it had inside, all still; even Hudsons die. Then what is left for Amaro is the little two-barrelled thing, which he strokes and polishes and sniffs and when he leans it against something he pulls back and makes it stand on its butt and takes to gazing at it like a father gazes at a daughter.' pp93-94

An Invincible Memory [Viva o povo brasileiro]

João Ubaldo Ribeiro's *An Invincible Memory* seems to promise us something that contemporary Brazilian fiction has tended to shy away from, but which is nevertheless an endeavour worth defending: the construction of a coherent and meaningful vision of his country's historical experience 'from below', challenging the 'Great Men' theory of Brazilian history 'as it was taught to me in school' (to quote the dust jacket). Indeed, the novel's moral weight undoubtedly derives from its identification with the oppressed of Brazil and its insistent call for their liberation.

Yet in reality, far from offering the Brazilian people a way out of their oppression, *An Invincible Memory* condemns them instead to an eternal search for a mysterious national consciousness whose discovery is forever postponed. As one of the book's heroes, General Patrício, reveals in the closing pages: 'You'll only be able to be anything after you are you!'. It is not surprising that Ribeiro's characters make little progress in their striving for a sense of identity, given the contradictory, ambiguous and ultimately indeterminate nature of the notion on which the entire novel rests. 'Long live the Brazilian People!' is the ubiquitous slogan which the plot's two entangled dynasties of masters and slaves struggle to interpret for themselves. But who is the Brazilian People if, as Ribeiro rightly suggests, the ruling, Europhile elite of sugar-planters and slave-owners has no legitimate claim to the title? For the visionary militia commander, Maria da Fé, the descendent of an Indian *mestiça* ('mixed race' individual), a Dutch soldier, an emancipated slave and a tyrannical baron, the Brazilian People is 'the dispossessed, the oppressed and the wronged' or, in a rare moment of precision, all the 'workers' of nineteenth century society: the artisans, tradesmen, farmers, millers, innkeepers and musicians.

However, as the blood of one dynasty contaminates that of the other, and individuals even renounce family loyalties to fight alongside the rebels, it becomes clear that Ribeiro cannot and does not want to make up his mind: blurring the boundaries between class and nation, his notion of the spirit of the people is less a matter of social identity and more an attitude of mind, a belief in freedom. Thus the members of the mysterious Brotherhood are only recognisable by an intuitive sixth sense: 'There was something in certain people, the way they walked, the way they talked, their type of voice'. The strengths and weaknesses of the author's translation have much to do with this abstract, mystical notion of the popular consciousness.

Meanwhile, by reducing a complex history of class, ideological and ethnic antagonisms to a single idealistic struggle for national identity, Ribeiro has effectively exchanged one set of myths, those of racial degeneracy and pathological underdevelopment, for another — Gilberto Freyre's myth of *mestiçagem*. The *mestiça* heroine, Maria da Fé, embodies the spirit of a permanent struggle for social and racial democracy, in which contradiction, plurality and difference are the vitalising ingredients of a dynamic, but essentially integrated, harmonious society. Outright elitism is exchanged for a more subtle, and sinister, populism, whose exhortation to freedom becomes an end in itself, because there is no real end.

This is the dispiriting message of a novel that, for all its wealth of material, carefully dated chapter titles and panoramic sweep of Brazilian history, is in essence profoundly anti-historical. It is not by chance that seventeen of the book's twenty chapters are concerned solely with events from the nineteenth century. Besides marking the independence and consolidation of the Brazilian nation-state, this is the period in which the notion of a Brazilian 'people', let alone a working class, with distinct common interests, is most problematic, given the dominant centrality of slavery to the country's economy and society. Da Fé's list of 'workers' corresponds much more closely to a pre-industrial petite bourgeoisie, straddling an uncertain, ambiguous terrain between the slaves, whose material oppression they often shared, and the masters, on whose patronage they were socially dependent.

Ribeiro's version of the 'people's' democratic struggle therefore remains, for the most part, conveniently distant from the new and complex social reality of twentieth century industrial Brazil, which merits only two chapters.

Not acknowledging the reemergence of popular and working class movements during the last decade or more, the book instead retreats to the safety of a mythical Golden age and place, the nineteenth century North-east, which stands for a timeless national-popular consciousness. A succession of slave rebellions, Liberal revolts, regional uprisings and messianic movements is subsumed, often by means of contrived circumstantial connections, into the history of the (Bahian) Brazilian people's search for its identity, losing in the process their specific social and political character. Most important of all, in Ribeiro's essentially Hegelian view of the struggle between oppressor and oppressed, it is only the people's consciousness which is ever transformed. Moments before his death, General Patricio speaks of the Spirit of Man, which 'yearns for perfection, that is to say, Good'.

'Souls do not learn anything, but they dream uncontrollably', we read in the first chapter of *An Invincible Memory*, as the spirit of the Brazilian people resumes its journey of self-realisation, a journey evidently still far from completed. D T

'Lord in heaven, who was that statue of glory, beautiful in countenance and speech, if not the warrior Maria da Fé, bursting forth through incomprehensible arts, emerging from the clothes of a mean looking captain like an obscure worm turning into a triumphant butterfly, shining like a sun amid all the rain, coming to unleash the pride that had been rotting away in their fearful hearts? Here she is in flesh and bone, not a legend but a truth you could touch, not distant but near, leading not soldiers but a squad of militiamen — the Militia of the People, whom so many had heard of and so few had seen.' p288

TORRES
Antonio

The Land [Essa Terra]

Blues for a lost childhood [Balada da infância perdida]

After twenty years' absence in the city of São Paulo, Nelo makes an unexpected homecoming to the moribund farming community of Junco, in the interior of the North East. Within days he is inexplicably found hanged. Must this be the fate, too, of the big-city journalist Calunga, who drinks 'as a form of (peaceful!) resistance against the froth of daily life', and eventually returns, a broken man, to the arms of his mother in his native Bahia?

The mystery of suicide and the mist of alcohol — the twin filters through which Antonio Torres's characters view the nightmarish confusion of a world in flux around them. That world is a familiar one — Brazil caught in the relentless slide from rural stagnation to urban chaos — but in Torres's vision it is shorn of the epic dimensions, or the sense of tragic destiny that veils much of the preceding literature on the theme. As Totonhim, the lost, orphaned heir to the Cruz family of *The Land* is told: 'Your life hangs by a thread of pure chance. And you are the child of that chance... You will not die from shock, a stray bullet or sinful living, Totonhim. You will sink in a swamp of problems, the sweet inheritance they have left you... Wretchedness comes from wretchedness born of wretchedness.'

The Land and *Blues for a lost childhood* lie at opposite ends of this thread of chance, the thread of dreams, migrations and memories, which both binds the chaotic modernity of the southern metropolis to the decadent backlands left behind, yet also reveals all the pain and distance between them. In *The Land*, Nelo's homecoming and suicide force the rest of his family to contemplate the course of their own disintegration — a disintegration stemming from the magnetism of the big city, its promise of self-realisation and its bewildering destruction of rural certainties. A conversation between father and son encapsulates this mix of attraction and disruption:

'When he was a boy my son Nelo used to say: "the earth is round like an orange. What I want to do is turn it."

And I said: "nobody can say that. Nobody knows what the world is like."

My son Nelo used to say:

"A man needs to be smart."

And I would say, "Well, now. Aren't we all smart enough? I'm smart."

He said, "you need to be smart to stay alive."

He said:

"The world is an oxcart that goes rolling forward, groaning on its axle."

I said, "the world doesn't have an axle. It's held steady by the hands of God."

He said: "the earth turns."

I said: "if the earth turned, we'd all fall off."

He said: "the earth turns very fast, that's why we don't fall off."

I said: "if the earth turned, we would all get dizzy."' (from *The Land*)

By the time we join Calunga and his cousin in *Blues for a lost childhood*, the world has inexorably started turning. The dizziness is that of the military dictatorship and its Economic Miracle, a 'Nobel Prize afternoon' of 'traffic jams, tunnels, overpasses, sirens, barracks, tortured and torturers, and the dog-shit on the sidewalks.' The childhood language of prayer and ritual, lullabies, romantic poetry memorised at school, rural ballads reciting murder and myth, remains as both a haunting and comforting reminder of another universe, populated too by the processions of blue 'angels' coffins, the tragedy of infant mortality. But it is rapidly submerging beneath a new language, that of journalism and advertising, television and popular song, state propaganda and revolutionary protest, where any perspective of depth and truth has disappeared. The apocalyptic mysticism of a culture of tradition and religiosity has been exchanged for the apocalyptic mysticism of consumerist capitalism, with its un-fulfilled promises and superficiality.

In the limbo between these two cultures, where there is no longer any centre to hold, and where there is no possible return, then perhaps suicide, alcoholism or madness are understandable options. As Nelo puts it in *The Land*, 'Probably it's because the earth turns that there are so many crazy people.' D T

"'This item is urgent. Urgent, urgent, URGENT. Everything is urgent... No, no. It's not the news of the end of the world, not yet. The late Antonio Conselheiro, the one who dragged all that horde into the Canudos war, in the country of God and the Devil in the Land of the Sun, on the Bahian border, in days when nothing was urgent, said that this old world won't get past the year 2000, but we haven't got there yet, what got here was merely the urgent task of publicising a new (fantabulous!) sandwich bar which is due to open tomorrow in Ipanema, Rio de Janeiro.'" (from *Blues for a lost childhood*)

VEIGA
José J.

The Three Trials of Manirema [A Hora dos Ruminantes]

A beautiful, flowing story of small-town life in a kind of Brazilian Wild West. As in Macondo, the town in Colombian Gabriel García Márquez's masterwork *One Hundred Years of Solitude,* Manirema is afflicted with various slightly humorous plagues; in Macondo butterflies and the loss of words so that the inhabitants have to write 'door' on the door and 'window' on the window while in Manirema there is a mass invasion of first stray dogs, then of oxen that crowd the streets so thickly that children are sent as messengers to walk over their backs. Finally, and again reminiscent of García Márquez's book, there is the arrival of mysterious and threatening 'Outsiders' who leave as suddenly as they came.

Veiga has a delicious way with words as he creates the characters and conflicts of a small-town; the dispensing of folksy wisdom and the enacting of chronic feuds over the barrels of pork and chicken feed in the provisions store.

But amongst the young love and the Jabotica bushes is a modernist, sometimes Kafkaesque, edge too, that makes *Manirema* a punchy 20th century work. R K

'Strange dogs snoozing in doorways were treated with more consideration than children or old folks; people tip-toed to avoid disturbing them, some went as far as to enter their houses through the windows or the back door to keep from stepping on the animals. Many a tender meatball, fried in good fat, was served to them on the best china, the way an honoured guest would be treated. The whole town was virtually at the service of the animals; all other activity stopped or was postponed, relegated, forgotten. So long as it was a stranger, any flea-ridden, filthy, mangy dog could find someone to extol in it qualities that none could see but all confirmed. Being a strange dog in Manirema was a very advantageous thing.' p57

AFRICA

Voices made night [Vozes anitecidas]

Every man is a race [Cada homem é uma raça + Cronicando]

These two collections of stories from Mozambique are set mainly in the post-independence period, some of them reflecting directly the war which assailed the country between 1978 and 1991. While a few of the stories focus on city life, Couto's favourite setting is the rural or semi-rural environment of the suburbs, where traditional African culture meets and seeks to adapt to modern urban values. The most tangible result of this cultural encounter is found in Couto's unorthodox use of language, which derives its inspiration from the way the language of the Portuguese colonialists has been transformed in the mouths of Mozambicans.

One of the constant themes which runs through all Couto's tales is the way the human imagination is fueled by adversity. Fantasy is at once a destructive force, capable of tragic and cruel consequences, but it can also be a source of beauty, and poetry. Man's ability to explain mythically the events which affect him in his daily life, is the stuff of which Couto's stories are made. Another important feature of Couto's work is the way women are portrayed as bearers of values such as constancy, stoicism and compassion, which make of them morally stronger characters than men. In many of his tales, Couto demonstrates great sadness at the plight of his characters, and the attempted solutions to their problems, but he never fails to show understanding and solidarity with them, often extracting humour from their situation.

On the other hand, his pen is more sharply ironic in its depiction of the excesses of petty bureaucracy, the abuse of power by officials, and the empty use of revolutionary political slogans by those who either do not understand their meaning, or unashamedly quote them while cynically pursuing their own ends. D B

'"Each man's boat is in his own heart" (Makua proverb from Northern Mozambique)

We live far from ourselves , in distant make-believe. We vanish into concealment. Why do we prefer to live in this inner darkness? Maybe because the dark joins things, sews together the threads of separation. In the warm embrace of night, the impossible wins us to suppose we can see it. Our fantasies come to rest in such illusion.' p51 Every Man is a Race

HONWANA
Luis Bernardo

We killed Mangy-dog & other stories [Nós Matamos O Cão-Tinhoso]

These are stories from Mozambique, where Portuguese is still an important language of literature and administration. Set in the colonial era — extended until 1975 by the Salazar regime's refusal to accept political independence — they reflect some of the harsh ways of that time. In *Dina*, apart from the shocking cruelty, with its echoes of slavery, in the life of field labourers under a brutal white overseer, there is something else; the marvellous smell of Africa, its rich soil and the hours of intense heat.

Honwana is a gifted writer delivering authentic fragments of a time and place. Written while he was still in his twenties he demonstrates a kind of wise authorial detachment unusual at that age; in the story *Hands of the Blacks* he gives us a funny, unbitter record of the everyday racism of colonial society. Nevertheless he doesn't pander either to a sentimental vision of 'traditional Africa' but deals with the lives of mineworkers returned from years in the Republic of South Africa; hardened men who play cards in bars, fight, drink and fornicate.

Disturbing, well-written, truthful stories, where you hear the true voices of the people of Mozambique. R K

'A wide veil of mist covered the lands of the chief Goana. The finest threads of vapour surrounded the trees, the houses and the animals in a blue halo without, however, leaving any signs of humidity on the surface. From above the tree tops the mist was pierced by the first rays of the sun, and turned to gold before dissolving in the heat. Greeting the day, the sounds of the bush, like harsh, strident yawns, zigzagged lazily from leaf to leaf, and echoed dully until they lost themselves in the depths of the veil of the mist. A strong smell of clay rose from the earth, mingled with the acrid vapours of the swamp and the fragrances of the forest, then attached itself to the droplets of the blue veil and dissolved up above, in the air now intensely golden in the rising sun.' pp66-67

Dumba nengue: run for your life. Peasant tales of tragedy in Mozambique [Dumba Nengue. Histórias trágicas do banditismo]

Mozambique achieved independence from Portugal in 1975. The promise of its first years of statehood under Samora Machel's socialist Frelimo (Front for the Liberation of Mozambique) government did not last long. Armed 'bandits', glorified by the name of the Mozambique National Resistance and sponsored by Rhodesia and South Africa, soon began their predations on a defenceless peasant population. The suffering, destruction and destabilization that has since been inflicted on Mozambique is barely imaginable.

Dumba nengue is, according to the translator's introduction, a Mozambican proverb meaning 'you have to trust your feet'.

It is also a name given to an area surrounding the country's main highway. This once prosperous region was targeted by the bandits and the peasants fled. The twenty-two short sketches which make up the book *Dumba nengue* tell of atrocities of barely credible sadism and brutality. They are not fictional. As a writer, Magaia faces a considerable challenge in dealing with such shocking material. She wisely chooses to tell the peasants' stories in simple language. Free of embellishments the events seem to speak louder.

Since the publication of this book international negotiations have brought rapprochement between the MNR and Frelimo and refugees have been returning. Sadly, the stories will have continuing relevance. The peasants captured by the bandits were themselves forced to participate in the slaughter of their own families. What homecoming can there be for Julieta's young brother, in 'How Julieta's brother was "baptized"':

"Julieta's husband was writhing. The bandit chief took out a knife and pointed it at Julieta's brother. He ordered that the brother be given the axe and use it to put an end to his brother-in-law's torment.

Julieta's husband was gripped by the legs by two bandits and his head was held in the curve carved on the wooden mortar. Her brother raised the axe and delivered the fatal blow. Her husband's neck was severed on the two sides of the mortar, and he died.

Julieta's seven children clung tightly to their mother, unable even to shed their tears of terror and horror.

The bandit chief said to Julieta's brother, "Now you're one of us. You've been baptized. You can come with us."

He and all the kidnapped people went off at gunpoint into the bush." p33-34

The traumatization and brutalization of the children kidnapped by the bandits will be a continuing problem for Mozambique. Girls between eight and fourteen years of age were routinely raped. Boys became killers. In 'A young killer' a woman described one young bandit whom she saw on the night she was kidnapped:

"'Chief, chief, let me kill someone. I want to. I want to kill one of them, let me.' And he trembled as if possessed, or drugged. He was crying.

'I've already told you that I don't want to see any blood today.'

It was very dark, and there was bush all around. Some people managed to escape in this confusion. Others continued their forced march.

She had felt herself very close to death. 'I can't stop thinking about the woman who gave birth to that bandit. What must she be like? What would she think if she saw her son now? What did the bandits do to him to make him end up like that?'" (p. 44)

> In *'An armed bandit: an unfinished portrait'* Magaia raises, but
> cannot bring herself to answer, the question that must occur
> to every reader of her book. She is watching a captured ban-
> dit describe his activities: (C S)

'The smile he gave as he spoke was an insult to the human race. I suspect he took a mad delight in talking of the blood that poured onto him from the victims and from the blades he used to draw it. I have never seen so much cynicism in one human being.

And the same revulsion and cringing I have when I see a snake made my flesh come out in goose pimples and a shiver run down my spine.

Can this be a man?' p102

PEPETELA

Mayombe

> Mayombe is the forest home of a group of MPLA (People's
> Movement for the Liberation of Angola) guerrillas fighting
> the Portuguese in the early 1970s for Angolan independence.
> The Portuguese are the least of the guerrillas' problems
> however: tribalism, political differences and a beautiful woman
> over the border in the Congo all create divisions between the
> men.
>
> The incident of a theft after a mission to mobilize the Fiote
> people of Cabinda reveals the depth of tribal suspicions (see
> quotation below). In fact hindsight colours the story with
> tragedy: it is a prescient foreshadowing of the terrible
> consequences of tribal divisions suffered by post-independence
> Angola.
>
> If one thing alone placed this novel in its era it would be its
> optimistic discussion of the construction of a new society. In
> their camp the guerrillas earnestly debate Marxist theory. Back
> at headquarters Ondine and her sexual relationships with
> Fearless, Andre, and the Commissar symbolize the freedom
> that is to come to the new generation of Angolans.
>
> Striding through the novel is the charismatic figure of
> Commander Fearless. He is the epitome of the tragic hero: a
> leader of men, lover of women, a loner, a man who will never

fit into the society he is sacrificing himself to create. Fearless is an intellectual, but anti-dogmatic, a man who only finds himself in action.

Pepetela, the pen-name of Artur Carlos Maurício Pestana dos Santos, was born in Angola in 1941. In 1969 he joined the MPLA and served in the Cabinda region of Angola. *Mayombe* was written around 1971-72 although it wasn't published in Portuguese until 1980, five years after Angola achieved independence. C S

'See how the Commander was so concerned about the hundred escudos of that Cabinda traitor? Didn't you ask why, didn't you wonder? Well I'll explain. The Commander is Kikongo: although he went to Luanda as an infant, the truth is that his family comes from Uije. Now, Fiote and Kikongo are relatives, and basically the same people. That is why he was so angry at a theft from one of his cousins. That is why he protects Struggle, another traitor. Did you see his rage when he grabbed Ungrateful? Why? Ungrateful is Kimbundu, there you have the whole story.' pp28-29

VIEIRA
José Luandino

Luuanda

Three stories make up *Luuanda*, 'Grandma Xíxi and her grandson Zeca Santos', 'The tale of the thief and the parrot' and 'The tale of the hen and the egg'. The characters who inhabit these stories all reflect the precariousness of life in the shanty towns of Luanda. Hunger reduces Grandma Xíxi to eating dahlia bulbs. An accident leads a former railway switchman to drug use. Young women become prostitutes. An old man and a crippled boy end up in jail for stealing ducks.

The shanty towns have little in common with the city's commercial centre or its affluent white suburbs. Europeans are barely even given off-stage roles. They are commented on as policemen, or unknown fathers of mulatto children, or the shadowy criminal mastermind in 'The tale of the thief and the parrot' known as *Kabulu*, a Kimbundu name for the rabbit hero of many folk tales:

'"That whiteman had his own magic, no one ever caught him, even if his name was given.

"*Ach*! Magic? Shit! Maybe, but it's his cousin!"

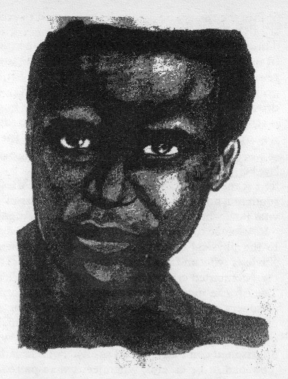

"Sure, but even with a cousin in the police they could've grabbed him to pay the fine and nothing like that's ever happened."'p40

The Kimbundu language and its oral culture are an integral part of this book. 'The tale of the hen and the egg' in particular has the feel of a traditional story, complete with a moral at the end. A woman is disputing the ownership of an egg which her hen has laid in her neighbour's backyard. A series of characters are called upon to try and resolve the problem. The shopkeeper, the seminary student, the landlord, the notary's former assistant and the soldier all fail to offer a satisfactory answer. But, through a trick carried out by two little boys, the affair is settled in a spirit of general good will. The voice of the storyteller concludes the tale: (C S)

'My tale.

If it's pretty, if it's ugly, only you know. But I swear I didn't tell a lie and that these affairs happened in this our land of Luanda.' p109

The real life of Domingos Xavier

This novel of the struggle for Angolan independence, written in 1961, was not published in Portugal until after the revolution of 1974. It could, on the face of it, be simply a grim piece of socialist realism — Domingos Xavier is a tractor driver, working on the construction site of a huge dam, who is arrested, brought to a police station in Luanda, and brutally tortured. He dies, still refusing to betray his friends:

'The face was awful to see, bleeding, nearly featureless but an obstinate smile played on the lips.' p68

The scenes of irrational rage and brutality in the interrogation room are, however, bleak islands in the midst of the vivid and vital flow which is the novel's depiction of Angolan life.

Resistance to opression takes many forms and is not limited to the physical courage of young working men. Domingos Xavier's wife and baby son search for him across the city: their combined cries tell the shanty-town dwellers of his fate. The African nationalists are supplied with information about prisoners by the unlikely duo of intelligence agents made up of old 'One-Bum' Petelo and his urchin grandson Xito. The novel ends with a clandestine party to pay homage to imprisoned compatriots and as an act of resistance, although: 'One had to be careful, when jeeps were patrolling the huts, trying to stamp out the people's stubborn joy.' p77

Angola itself is a physical presence of near overwhelming power. Its rain storms, fresh breezes and the smell of its red sand even manage to reach and sooth Domingos Xavier in his cell. The river Kuanza becomes a symbol of the history of the Angolan people: where it has been dammed and diverted it rages and smashes itself on the new walls: (C S)

'But very soon amid trees and grass, the mosses and the familiar sounds, trickles of water moved the old colossus to pity: the memory returned of the course followed through the long stretch of the green plateau of Huambo, of the friends received in its bed, and so the voice softened, the roar disappeared, in front of Dondo it only purred, and then it wore a smile on its face further on towards Muxima in the direction of the sea.' p63

The World of 'Mestre' Tamoda [Discursos de 'Mestre' Tamoda]

Set in and around Luanda, the Angolan capital, during colonial times the book centres on the antics of 'Mestre' Tamoda, bush lawyer, small time orator and self-taught speaker of Portuguese — a language he has picked up working as an office boy in a city law firm.

Through Tamoda's comic adventures, Xitu satirizes race relations in the old Portuguese empire, while suggesting in the romance of the black boy, Maraja with the white girl Arlette, a reconciliation and compromise relevant to the war-torn Angola of today.

Like other African writers, he also focuses on the rural/urban divide, and the inter-relationship between the colonial language and the local people's African language. There is a strong taste of traditional oral culture both in the lively storytelling itself and in its digressions.

The figure mainly reflecting the split between rural, traditional, and modern, urban Angola, is Tamoda himself who lives in both worlds: in his village he competes for the hearts and attention of the school children against the prim white school mistress; in the city he is in demand among the racially mixed Luanda bourgeoisie at wedding receptions and other festive occasions. On the one hand, he is a slave of the bookish, pedantic Portuguese he has picked up in the town, on the other like the African 'griot' (storyteller/keeper of clan traditions), he is seen by his community as possessing mastery of the spoken word. It is this creative, anarchic side to Tamoda's character that makes him so outrageous, and potentially subversive to a colonial order determined to keep the majority illiterate. D B

'The boys started to use Tamoda's vocabulary in their quarrels, both at home and outside, which got them into a lot of trouble because their parents and elder brothers, not knowing the meaning of the words, assumed they were wicked and deserved a beating. Take an example. One day as Tamoda was coming out of the bathing-pool, two kids asked him a question:

"Tamoda, friend, what is the feminine of 'youth' ?" Tamoda replied: "The feminine of 'youth' is maiden, in Portuguese 'muchachala'". He spoke with great assurance, happy to clear up any difficulties. The two boys, Kidi and Kuzela, sped off to add the new word to those already in circulation, such as lackey, lickspittle, dumbfounded, scoundrel, captious, pudenda, exacerbate, namby-pamby, hoity-toity, jocose, rigor mortis, zoomorphous, sylvan, hoi-polloi, buffoon, block-head, pilferer, ruffian, nincompoop, jackanapes, willy-nilly...' pp3-4

Contributors

Ray Keenoy
is founder and editor of the Babel Guides series
David Treece
heads the Centre for the Study of Brazilian
Culture & Society at King's College London
Paul Hyland
is an author and broadcaster
David Brookshaw
lectures at the University of Bristol
Marina Coriolano-Lykourezos
works in the publishing industry
Maria-Amelia Dalsenter
is a postgraduate at Oxford Brookes University
Maria-Manuela Lisboa
lectures at the University of Cambridge
Tom MacCarthy
is an author
Carmo Ponte
is a research associate at King's College London
Giovanni Pontiero
is the leading translator of Portuguese &
Brazilian fiction
Pat Odber
lectures at the University of Birmingham
Caroline Shaw
is a postgraduate at King's College London

Illustrations
Jackie Wrout

Portuguese Titles Reviewed

Brazilian Titles Reviewed

Angolan Titles Reviewed

Mozambiquan Titles Reviewed

Portuguese

Antunes, António Lobo
Queirós, Eça de
Garrett, Almeida
Pessoa, Fernando
Pires, José Cardoso
Saramago, José
De Sena, Jorge
Tabucchi, Antonio
Torga, Miguel

Brazilian

Abreu, Caio Fernando
Amado, Jorge
Andrade, Mário De
Azevedo, Aluizio De
Buarque, Chico
Coelho, Paulo
Cunha, Helena Parente
Dourado, Autran
Fonseca, Rubem
Galvão, Patrícia
Lispector, Clarice
Luft, Lya
Machado de Assis, Joaquim Maria
Miranda, Ana
Olinto, Antonio
Ramos, Graciliano
Ribeiro, Darcy
Ribeiro, João Ubaldo
Torres, Antonio
Veiga, José J.

Angolan

Pepetela
Vieira, José Luandino
Xitu, Uanhenga

Mozambiquan

Couto, Mia
Honwana, Luis Bernardo
Magaia, Lina

Database of fiction from Brazil, Portugal, Angola and Mozambique translated in UK

This database is for anyone who wants to read writers from these countries in English. Its main goal is to let you know what's available. The reviews section of the guide emphasizes books that are currently in print and that you can find or order at your bookshop now but this section includes *all* the contemporary (written after 1900) fiction we could trace.

Please note the price and availability of books changes from day to day as publishers withdraw, re-price and reprint. This database is a handy guide but for the latest information on a particular book ask your bookseller or librarian. Remember your bookseller can order you any in-print book and that public libraries can get you any current or out-of-print title, often at no charge.

Abbreviations:
HB = hard cover edition
PB = paperback edition
O/P = out of print (this means your bookshop can only sell you a copy if they have one in stock already. The publisher may reprint it though, so check later.)

PORTUGAL

ANTUNES
António Lobo

Act of the Damned
1993
Auto dos danados
1985
Zenith, Richard
SECKER
PB
246
8.99

Explanation of the Birds, An
1992
Explicacao dos passaros
1981
Zenith, Richard
SECKER
PB
251
7.99

South of Nowhere
Cus de Judas, Os
Lowe, Elizabeth
CHATTO
HB
144
O/P

BARRENO ET AL
Maria Isabel

New Portuguese Letters
1994
Novas Cartas Portuguesas
1972
Lane, Helen R & Gillespie, Faith
READERS INTERNATIONAL
HB
326
12.95

New Portuguese Letters
1994
Novas Cartas Portuguesas
1972
Lane, Helen R & Gillespie, Faith
READERS INTERNATIONAL
PB
326
6.99

BARTES
A.R.

Portugal through her literature; an anthology of prose & verse
1972
WALTON P: GLASTONBURY
185
O/P

CAMOES
Luis de

Epic and Lyric
1989
Bosley, K
CARCANET
PB
9.95

Luisiads
1975
Lusiades, Os
Atkinson, William C.
PENGUIN
PB
6.99

Luisiads
1975
Lusiades, Os
Fanshawe, Sir R.
CENTAUR P
38.00

CONSIGLIERE-PEDROSO
Zophimo (ed.)

Portuguese Folk-Tales
1882
Monteiro, Henriquetta
FOLK LORE SOC. LONDO
124
O/P

FERREIRA DE CASTRO
José Maria

Emigrants
1964
Emigrantes, Os

1928
Bell, D
MACMILLAN: NY, LONDON
284
O/P

Jungle. A tale of the Amazon
rubber-tappers
1964
Selva, A
1930
Duff, C
LOVAT DICKSON: LONDON
340
O/P

Mission, The
1963
Missão, A
1954
Stevens, Ann
H.HAMILTON
126
O/P

GARRETT
Almeida
Travels in my Homeland
1987
Viagens na minha terra
1843
Parker, John
OWEN
HB
256
12.95

GERRARD,M & MACCARTHY,T
(Ed.s)
Passport to Portugal
1994
PASSPORT: SERPENT'S TAIL DIST
PB
155
6.99

LISBOA
Eugénio (Ed.)
Portuguese Short Fiction. An
Antholgy. Vol. 1
1995
n/a
Various
CARCANET
HB
16.95

Portuguese Short Fiction.An
Antholgy. Vol. 2
1996
n/a
Various
CARCANET
HB
16.95

LISBOA, E & MACEDO, H (ED.S)
Dedalus Book of Portuguese
Fantasy
1994
Costa, MJ
DEDALUS
PB
356
8.99

MIGUÉIS
José Rodrigues
Happy Easter
1995
Páscoa Feliz
1932
Byrne, John
CARCANET
PB
8.95

MONTEIRO
Luiz de
Rules of the game, The
1964
Angustia para o jantar
1961
Stevens, Ann

PORTUGAL

PUTNAM
O/P

NAMORA
Fernando

Mountain Doctor
1956
Retalhos da vida de um médico
1953
Ball, D
WILLIAM KIMBER: LONDON
200
O/P

PESSOA
Fernando

Always Astonished: Selected Prose
1989
Honig, E
CITY LIGHTS
PB
7.99

Book of Disquiet, The
1991
Livro do Desassossego por Bernardo Soares
1982
Costa, Margaret Jull
SERPENTS' TAIL
PB
262
9.99

Book of Disquiet, The
1991
Livro do desassossego por Bernardo Soares
1982
Watson, I
QUARTET
PB
196
5.95

Book of Disquietude, The
1991
Livro do Desassossego por Bernardo Soares
1982

Zenith, R
CARCANET
HB
323
18.95

Centenary Pessoa
1995
Bosley, K, McGuirk, B et al.
CARCANET
HB
335
25.00

Fernando Pessoa Poems
1989
ECCO P
234
7.50

Message
1992
1934
MENARD P
9.00

Selected Poems
1996 (1974, 1988)
Griffin, Johnathan
PENGUIN INTERNATIONAL POETS
PB
6.99

Selected Poems
1971
Rickard, Peter
EDINBURGH UP
PB
201
O/P

Surprise of Being
ANGEL: DIST. AIRLIFT
PB
5.50

Surprise of Being. 25 Poems
ANGEL: DIST. AIRLIFT
HB
8.95

PINTO
Fernao Mendes
  Peregrination, The (A Selection)
  1992
  Peregrinaçam
  Lowery, Michael
  CARCANET
  HB
  14.95

  Travels of Mendes Pinto, Fernao
  Mendes Pinto
  1989
  Peregrinaçam
  Catz, Rebecca D
  CHICAGO UP
  HB
  663

PIRES
Jose Cardoso
  Ballad of Dogs' Beach
  1986
  Ballada da Praia dos Caes
  Fitton, Mary
  DENT: LONDON
  181
  4.50

  O/P

  Ballad of Dogs' Beach
  1986
  Ballada da Praia dos Caes
  Fitton, Mary
  DENT
  4.50

  O/P

QUEIROS
Eça de
  Alves and Co.
  1989
  Alves & Cia.
  Fedorchek, Robert M.
  UNIV P OF AMERICA
  HB
  33.50

  Alves and Co.

  1989
  Alves & Cia.
  Fedorchek, Robert M
  UNIV P OF AMERICA
  PB
  15.50

  City & the Mountains, The
  1994 (1955)
  Cidade e as Serras, As
  Campbell, Roy
  CARCANET
  HB
  218
  14.95

  Cousin Bazilio
  1992 (1953)
  Primo Bazilio, O
  Campbell, Roy
  CARCANET
  HB
  295
  14.95

  Illustrious House of Ramires
  1993
  Illustre Casa de Ramires, A
  Stevens, Anne
  QUARTET
  PB
  309
  7.95

  Illustrious House of Ramires
  1992
  Illustre Casa de Ramires, A
  Stevens, Anne
  CARCANET
  HB
  309
  14.95

  Letters from England
  1970
  Cartas de Inglaterra
  Stevens, Anne
  BODLEY HEAD
  192
  O/P

  Maias; The

PORTUGAL

1986
Maias, Os
1888
McGowan, P.& Stevens, A.
DENT
633
O/P

Maias, The
1993
Maias, Os
1888
McGowan, P.& Stevens, A.
CARCANET
HB
633
14.95

Mandarin, The
1992
1880
DEDALUS
PB
6.99

Perfection. (Illustrated by John Austen)
1923
Marriot, Charles
SELWYN & BLOUNT: LONDON
43
O/P

Relic, The
1994
Reliquia, A
1887
Costa, MJ
DEDALUS
8.99

Reliquary, The
1954
1887
Bell, Aubrey
REINHARDT
231
O/P

Sin of Father Amaro, The
1994
Crime do Padre Amaro, O

1874
Flanagan, Nan
CARCANET
HB
352
14.95

Sweet Miracle
1905
Suave Milagre, O (from 'Contos')
Prestage, E
DAVID NUTT: LONDON
36
O/P

To the Capital
1995
Capital, A
1925
Veitch, John
CARCANET
HB
293
18.95

Yellow Sofa and Other Stories
1993
Vetch, J.
CARCANET
HB
181
14.95

RIBEIRO
Aquilino
When the wolves howl
1963
Quando os lobos uivam
1958
Pinheiro, Patricia McGowan
CAPE
O/P

SA-CARNEIRO
Mario de
Lucio's Confession
1994
Confisão de Lucio
1913
Costa, MJ

PORTUGAL

DENT
PB
3.95

O/P

Rivers of Babylon and Other
Stories, The
1989
POLYGON
PB
155
7.95

O/P

TABUCCHI
Antonio
Requiem
1994
Requiem
1991
Costa, M J
HARVILL
HB
112
14.99

Requiem
1994
Requiem
1991
Costa, M J
HARVILL
PB
112
7.99

TORGA
Miguel de
Creation, The (Days One and Two)
1996
*Criacão do Mundo, A (Os Dois
Primeiros Dias)*
1937
Carlsen, Ivana
CARCANET
PB
8.95

Tales from the Mountain
1995
*Contos da Montanha & Novos Contos da
Montanha*
1982, 1986
Carlsen, Ivana
CARCANET
PB
9.95

BRAZIL

ABREU
Caio Fernando
  Dragons
  1990
  Os Dragoes nao conhecem o Paraiso
  1988
  Treece, David
  BOULEVARD: DIST. CENTRAL BOOKS
  PB
  148
  5.95

ALENCAR
Jose Martiniano
  Senhora: Profile of a woman
  1994
  Senhora
  1875
  Edinger, Catarina Feldmann
  TEXAS UP: AUSTIN
  HB
  198
  O/P

ALMEIDA
Jose Americo de
  Trash, a novel
  1978
  Bagaceira, A
  1928
  Scott-Buccleuch, R.L.
  OWEN
  160
  O/P

AMADO
Jorge
  Dona Flor and Her Two Husbands
  1986
  Dona Flor e seus dois maridos
  1966
  Onis, Harriet de
  SERPENT'S TAIL
  PB
  553
  9.99

  Dona Flor and Her Two Husbands
  1969
  Dona Flor e seus dois maridos
  1966
  Onis, Harriet de
  WEDENFELD
  HB
  O/P

  Gabriela, Clove and Cinnamon
  1983
  Gabriela, Cravo e Canela
  1958
  Taylor, James L. & Grossman, W.L.
  SOUVENIR
  HB
  O/P

  Gabriela, Clove and Cinnamon
  1984
  Gabriela, Cravo e Canela
  1958
  Taylor, James L. & Grossman, W.L.
  ABACUS
  PB
  O/P

  Home is the Sailor
  1990
  Completa Verdade sobre... Com, V.M. de Aragao
  1961
  Onis, Harriet de
  HARVILL
  PB
  256
  7.95

  Pen, Sword, Camisole
  1986
  Farda, Fardao, Camisola de Dormir
  1979?
  Lane, Helen
  AVON
  PB
  3.95

  O/P

  Shepherds in the Night
  1989
  Pastores da noite, Os
  1966

148

Onis, Harriet de
HARVILL
PB
384
6.95

Showdown
1988
Tocaia Grande
1985?
Rabassa, Gregory
BANTAM
422
12.95

O/P

Tent of Miracles
1989
Tenda dos milagres
Shelby, Barbara
HARVILL
PB
392
6.95

Teresa Batista: Home from the Wars
1982
Teresa Batista, cansada de guerra
Merello, Barbara Shelby
SOUVENIR P (CONDORBOOKS)
HB
14.95

Teresa Batista: Home from the Wars
1983
Teresa Batista, cansada de guerra
Merello, Barbara Shelby
ABACUS
PB
576
O/P

Tieta the Goat Girl
1981
Tieta do Agreste
1977?
Merollo, Barbara Shelby
SOUVENIR
HB
671
14.95

Tieta the Goat Girl
1982
Tieta do Agreste
1977?
Merollo, Barbara Shelby
ABACUS
PB
671

Violent Land
1989
Terras do sem-fim
1942
Putnam, Samuel
HARVILL
PB
320
6.95

War of the Saints
1994
Sumiço da Santa, O
Rabassa, G
SERPENTS TAIL
PB
357
9.99

ANDRADE
Mario de
Macunaima
1988
Macunaima, o herói sem nenhum caráter
1928
Goodland, E
QUARTET
HB
170
10.95

Macunaima
1988
Macunaima, o herói sem nenhum caráter
1928
Goodland, E.A.
QUARTET
PB
170
5.95

ARANHA
Jose Pereira da Graca
  Canaa
  1921
  Canaa
  1902
  Lorente, Joaquim Mariano
  ALLEN & UNWIN
  O/P

AZEVEDO
Aluizio de
  Brazilian Tenement, A
  1928
  Cortico, O
  1890
  Brown, Harry R.
  CASSELL: LONDON
  O/P

  Mulatto
  1990
  Mulato, O
  1881
  Murray, Graeme MacNicoll
  ASSOCIATED UPs: LONDON
  298
  33.00

BARRETO
Alfonso Henriques Lima
  Patriot, The
  1978
  Triste Fim de Policarpo Quaresma
  1915
  Buccleuch, Robert Scott
  REX COLLINGS
  HB
  226
  7.50

BUARQUE DE HOLLANDA
Chico
  Turbulence
  1992
  Estorvo
  1991
  Macadam, A

BLOOMSBURY
224
13.99

CAISTOR
Nick (Ed.)
  Contemporary Latin American
  Short Stories, Faber Book of
  1989
  Various
  FABER
  HB
  188
  11.99

  Contemporary Latin American
  Short Stories, Faber Book of
  1990
  Various
  FABER
  PB
  5.99

COELHO
Paulo
  Alchemist, The
  1993
  Alquimista, O
  Clarke, Alan R.
  HARPER SAN FRANCISCO
  PB
  177
  5.99

  Alchemist, The
  1993
  Alquimista, O
  Clarke, Alan R.
  HARPER SAN FRANCISCO
  HB
  177

COHEN
J.M.
  Latin American Writing Today
  1967
  Various
  PENGUIN
  PB

BRAZIL

267
O/P

CORCAO
Gustavo
My neighbour as myself
1957
Descoberta da outro, A
1944
Wilson, Clotilde
LONGMANS GREEN: LONDON
O/P

CUNHA
Euclydes da
Rebellion in the Backlands
1947
Sertoes, Os
Putnam, Samuel
GOLLANCZ
347
O/P

CUNHA
Helena Parente
Woman Between Mirrors.
1990
Mulher no Espelho
Ellison, F.P. & Lindstrom, N.
POLYGON
PB
132
8.95

DOURADO
Autran
Bells of Agony
1988
Sinos da agonia, Os
1974
Parker, John
OWEN
HB
224
12.95

Pattern for a Tapestry
1984

Risco do bordado, O
1970
Parker, John
OWEN
HB
169
11.95

Pattern for a Tapestry
1986
Risco do bordado, O
1970
Parker, John
PENGUIN
PB
169
O/P

Voices of the Dead
1980
Opera dos mortos
1967
Parker, John
OWEN
HB
248
11.95

FELINTO
Marilene
Women of Tijucopapo, The
1994
1982
Matthews, I
Nebraska UP; AUPG dist.
HB
132
28.50

Women of Tijucopapo, The
1994
1982
Matthews, I
Nebraska UP; AUPG dist.
PB
132
9.95

FONSECA
Rubem
  High Art
  1987
  Grande Arte, A
  1983
  Watson, Ellen
  COLLINS
  PB
  345
  O/P

GALVAO
Patricia (Pagu)
  Industrial Park
  1993
  Parque Industrial
  1933
  Jackson, Eliz. & K. David
  NEBRASKA UP
  HB
  153
  19.95

  Industrial Park
  1993
  Parque Industrial
  1933
  Jackson, Eliz. & K. David
  NEBRASKA UP
  PB
  153
  8.95

GOLDBERG
Isaac
  Brazilian Tales
  1963 (1924)
  BRANDON PUBLISHERS (US)
  149
  4.50

GROSSMAN
William (ed.)
  Modern Brazilian Short Stories
  1974
  GROSSMAN, William
  CALIFORNIA UP: BERKELEY

PB
2.50

IVO
Lêdo
  Snakes' Nest
  1989
  Ninho de cobras
  Krapohl, Ken
  OWEN
  HB
  136
  O/P

LISPECTOR
Clarice
  Apple in the Dark, The
  1985
  Maca no escuro, A
  1961
  Rabassa, Gregory
  VIRAGO
  PB
  378
  O/P

  Besieged City, The
  1995
  Cidade Sitiada
  Pontiero, Giovanni
  CARCANET
  HB
  160
  14.95

  Discovering the World
  1992
  Descoberta do mundo, A
  CARCANET
  HB
  400
  18.95

  Family Ties
  1985
  Lacos de familia
  1960
  Pontiero, G
  CARCANET
  HB

BRAZIL

156
12.95

Family Ties
1985
Lacos de familia
1960
Pontiero, G
CARCANET
PB
156
O/P

Foreign Legion, The
1986
Legiao estrangeira, A
1964?
Pontiero, Giovanni
CARCANET
HB
219
12.95

Foreign Legion, The
1986
Legiao estrangeira, A
1964?
Pontiero, Giovanni
CARCANET
PB
219
O/P

Hour of the Star
1987
Hora da estrela, A
1977?
Pontiero, Giovanni
PALADIN
PB
96
O/P

Hour of the Star
1992
Hora da estrela, A
1977?
Pontiero, Giovanni
CARCANET
PB
96

O/P

Hour of the Star, The
1986
Hora da estrela, A
1977?
Pontiero, Giovanni
CARCANET
HB
96
O/P

Hour of the Star, The
1993
Hora da estrela, A
1977?
Pontiero, Giovanni
CARCANET BLACK & WHITE
PB
96
5.95

Near to the Wild Heart
1990
Perto do coracao selvagem
1943?
Pontiero, Giovanni
CARCANET
HB
192
12.95

LUFT
Lya
Island of the Dead
1986
McLendon, CC & Craige, BJ
GEORGIA UP
HB
10.95

Red House, The
1994
Exilio
1987
Pontiero, Giovanni
CARCANET
HB
182
14.95

MACHADO DE ASSIS

Joaquim

Brazilian Tales
BRANDON
PB
3.25

O/P

Counselor Ayres' memorial
1973
Memorial de Ayres
1908
Caldwell, Helen
CALIFORNIA U.P.
PB
6.50

Devil's Church & Other Stories, The
1985
CARCANET
HB
O/P

Devil's Church & Other Stories, The
1987
Igreja do Diabo, A
Schmidt, J. & Ishimatsu, L.
GRAFTON
PB
166
O/P

Don Casmurro
1953
Don Casmurro
1900
Caldwell, Helen
W.H.ALLEN
O/P

Don Casmurro
1992
Don Casmurro
1900
Scott-Buccleugh, R.L.
OWEN
HB
216
14.95

Epitaph of a Small Winner
1985
Memorias postumas de Bras cubas
1881
Grossman, William
HOGARTH PRESS
HB
O/P

Epitaph of a Small Winner
1991
Memorias postumas de Bras cubas
1881
Grossman, William
VINTAGE
PB
4.99

Esau and Jacob
1966
Esau e Jaco
1904
Caldwell, Helen
OWEN
14.95

Helena
1984
Helena
1876
Caldwell, Helen
CALIFORNIA UP
HB
197
28.00

Helena
1984
Helena
1876
Caldwell, Helen
CALIFORNIA UP
PB
197
7.95

Philosopher or Dog?
1954
Quincas Borba
1891
Wilson, Clotilde

BRAZIL

W.H.ALLEN
PB
288
O/P

Psychiatrist and other stories, The
1963
Grossman, W. & Caldwell, H.
OWEN
O/P

Yaya Garcia
1976
Yaya Garcia
1878
Scott-Buccleuch, R.L.
OWEN
HB
220
14.95

Wager: Aires' Journal
1990
Memorial de Aires
1908
Scott-Buccleuch, R.L.
OWEN
HB
165
14.95

MANGUEL
Albert (Ed.)
Other Fires: Short Fiction by Latin
American Women
1986
PAN
PB
222
O/P

MIRANDA
Ana
Bay of All Saints and Every
Conceivable Sin
1992
Boca do Inferno
1989
Pontiero, Giovanni
HARVILL

HB
305
14.99

Bay of All Saints and Every
Conceivable Sin
1992
Boca do Inferno
1989
Pontiero, Giovanni
HARVILL
PB
7.99

MONTELLO
Jose
Coronation Quay
1975
Cais da Sagracao
1971
Henderson, Myriam
REX COLLINGS
PB
266
5.00

OLINTO
Antonio
King of Ketu, The
1987
Rei de Keto, O
Chappell, Richard
REX COLLINGS
281
10.50

Water House, The
1970
Casa de Agua, A
1969
Heapy, Dorothy
REX COLLINGS
410
7.50

QUEIROZ
Dinah Silveira de
Christ's Memorial
1978

BRAZIL

1991
Viva o povo brasileiro
1984
Author
FABER
HB
504
O/P

Sergeant Getulio
1994
Sargento Getulio
1971
Author
DEUTSCH
PB
146
7.99

Lizard's Smile, The
1995
1989
DEUTSCH
HB
355
15.99

Sergeant Getulio
1986
Sargento Getulio
1971
Author
FABER: LONDON
146
O/P

SABINO
Fernando
Time to meet, A
1967
Encontro marcado, O
1956
Procter, John
SOUVENIR
HB
O/P

Time to meet, A
1967
Encontro marcado, O

1956
Procter, John
PANTHER
PB
319
O/P

SALES
Herbert
Fruit of thy Womb, The
1976
Fruto do vosso ventre, O
1976
Fody, Michael
WYVERN: BRINGSTY, WORCS.
185

Werewolf and other stories, The
1978
Lobisomem e outros contos folcloricos
1970
Goddard, Richard
REX COLLINGS
112
7.00

SANTIAGO
Silviano
Stella Manhattan
1995
Stella Manhattan
1985
Yudice, G
DUKE UP: DIST. AUPG
HB
212
43.50

Stella Manhattan
1995
Stella Manhattan
1985
Yudice, G
DUKE UP: DIST. AUPG
PB
212
13.95

SARNEY
Jose
Tales of Rain & Sunlight
1986
Noites das Aguas
1969
Hallam, Vera
WYVERN: BRINGSTY, WORCS.
143
O/P

SOUZA
Mario de
Emperor of the Amazon
1982
Galvez, Imperador do Acre
1976
Colchie, Thomas
SPHERE
PB
189
O/P

TAUNAY
Viscount A d'E
Inocencia
1921
Inocencia
1872
?
HEATH: LONDON
O/P

TORRES
Antonio
Blues for a Lost Childhood
1989
Balada da infancia perdida
READERS' INTERNATIONAL
HB
202
10.95

Blues for a Lost Childhood
1989
Balada da infancia perdida
READERS' INTERNATIONAL
PB
5.95

Land, The
1987

Essa Terra
Neves, M.A.
READERS' INTERNATIONAL
PB
3.95

Land, The
1987
Essa Terra
1976
READERS' INTERNATIONAL
HB
136
8.95

VASCONCELOS
Jose Mauro de
My sweet-orange tree
1971
Meu pe de laranja lima
1968
Miller, Edgar H. (Jr.)
M. JOSEPH: LONDON
O/P

My sweet-orange tree
1983
Meu pe de laranja lima
1968
Miller, Edgar H. (Jr.)
HUTCHINSON: LONDON
166

VEIGA
Jose
Three Trials of Manirema, The
1979
Hora dos ruminantes, A
1966
Bird, Pamela G.
OWEN
154
10.95

VERISSIMO
Erico
Consider the Lilies of the Field
1969
Olhai os lirios do campo
1938

BRAZIL

Karnoff, Jean
GREENWOOD?: NY
32.50

Crossroads and destinies
1956
Caminhos cruzados
1935
Kaplan, L.C.
ARCO: LONDON
O/P

Night
1956
Noite
1954
Barrett, Linton L.
ARCO: LONDON
166
O/P

Rest is Silence, The
1956
Resto e Silencio, O
1953
Kaplan, L.C.
ARCO: LONDON
O/P

Time and the Wind
1954
Tempo e o vento, O
1949
Barrett, Linton L.
ARCO: LONDON
624

ANGOLAN

PEPETELA
Mayombe
  Pepetela
  1983
  Mayombe
  Wolfers, Michael
  HEINEMANN AFRICAN W
  PB
  269
  O/P

VIEIRA
Jose Luandino
  Luuanda
  1980
  Bender, Tamara & Hill, D
  HEINEMANN
  PB
  128
  O/P

  Real Life of Domingos Xavier
  1978
  Wolfers, Michael
  HEINEMAN EDUCATIONAL
  84
  O/P

XITU
Uanhenga
  World of 'Mestre' Tamoda
  1988
  Discursos de 'Mestre' Tamoda
  1977
  McDermott, Annella
  READERS' INTERNATIONAL
  HB
  158
  9.95

  World of 'Mestre' Tamoda
  1988
  Discursos de 'Mestre' Tamoda
  1977
  McDermott, Annella
  READERS' INTERNATIONAL
  PB
  200
  4.95

MOZAMBIQUAN

COUTO
Mia

Everyman is a race
1994
Cada homem e uma raca + Cronicando
1990,1989
Brookshaw, David
HEINEMANN AFRICAN WRITERS
PB
118
4.99

Voices Made Night
1990
Vozes anitecidas
1986
Brookshaw, David
HEINEMANN AFRICAN WRITERS
PB
115
4.99?

HONWANA
Luis Bernardo

We killed Mangy-dog & other stories
1969
Nós Matamos O Cão-Tinhoso
Guedes, Dorothy
HEINEMANN AFRICAN WRITERS
117
4.99

MAGAIA
Lina

Dumba Nengue, Run for your life
1989
Dumba Nengue. Histórias trágicas do banditismo
1987
Wolfers, Michael
KARNAK HOUSE
PB
118
4.50

Babel Guides on Disk:

This Fiction in English Translation Database is available to bona fide Researchers and Libraries on 3½ inch diskettes in DOS.txt or DBF format, £50 post free. Regular updates to include titles and reviews entered since publication date can be provided to subscribers.

Babel Guide to
FRENCH
fiction in translation

A unique guide to novels and short
stories by French writers of the 20th
Century translated into English.
All the best books are reviewed with
additional feature pieces on writers.

Use the listings and reviews to choose
books to read available in your
bookshop or library and put a new
world of writing at your fingertips.

➢ Original reviews & features
➢ Covers books 1945–1996
➢ 45 illustrations
➢ c.2500 books and editions listed

224 pages   £8.95
ISBN 1899460 10 1 Spring 1996

Babel Guide to

ITALIAN

fiction in translation

A unique guide to novels and short
stories by Italian writers of the 20th
Century translated into English.
All the best books are reviewed with
additional feature pieces on writers.

'Excellent reviews, well written and adroitly edited'
– The Observer
'Recommended'
– The Independent
'Accessible and fun'
– British Centre for Literary Translation

➢ 150 full-length reviews & features
➢ Covers books 1945–1996
➢ 25 illustrations
➢ 650 books and editions listed

192 pages £7.95
ISBN 1899460 004

for the traveller with literary inclinations...

The Babel Guides are a new series of illustrated guides in a lively, accessible style to *world fiction available in English*. Each Guide has over 150 reviews of novels or short story collections and each review is an enjoyable 'trailer' for the book, with a long quote as a taster. As well as reviews there is a unique *database* with the original titles and current prices of ALL the 20th Century fiction from the country published in the UK since 1945.

'Absolutely wonderful, accessible and fun'
British Centre for Literary Translation
'A brilliant idea'
BBC Radio 3
'A novel way to travel'
The Observer
'Recommended'
The Independent
'Cheap and portable'
The European

Babel Guide to Italian Fiction in Translation
ISBN 1899460004 £7.95/$12.00
Babel Guide to the Fiction of Portugal, Brazil & Africa in Translation
ISBN 1899460055 £7.95/$12.00
Babel Guide to French Fiction in Translation
ISBN 1899460101 £8.95/$14.00
Babel Guide to German Fiction in Translation
ISBN 1899460209 £7.95/$12.00
Babel Guide to Latin American Fiction in Translation
ISBN 1899460152 £8.95/$14.00

Available in bookshops or from the publisher, post and packing free in the European Union or USA, elsewhere please add 10%, US$ or UK£ cheques/eurocheques accepted.

Boulevard Books 8 Aldbourne Road London W12 OLN UK
Tel/Fax 0181 743 5278
US Agent: J. Gallagher 49 Huron Circle Dorchester
MA 02124 USA

the toy catalogue

by Sandra Petrignani

The *Toy Catalogue* is a compendium of childhood passions — the smell of plasticine, the lickability of play-nails and the comforting hug of your rag doll. A genial Gulliverian hand picks you up and lets you fall into the deepest seas of childhood.
Guaranteed to take you back to the delicious intensities of childhood, on a wonderful and healing journey.

Winner of the Bergamo Prize in 1989.

'An enchanting exercise in playfulness'
Ian McEwan

Boulevard Italians

128p £5.95

Portugal 600

Promoting the arts and culture of Portugal

*PORTUGAL 600 IS PLEASED TO SUPPORT THE
PUBLICATION OF THIS BOOK*

PALINGSWICK HOUSE, 241 KING STREET, LONDON W6 9LP
PHONE 00 44 (0)181 748 0884 FAX 00 44 (0)181 748 4187

Portugal 600 is a registered charity

TRAVELLER'S LITERARY COMPANION TO SOUTH AND CENTRAL AMERICA

Jason Wilson

The perfect travel guide for lovers of South American literature

'I suspect the publication of this inaugural book might prove to be a landmark as significant as the original *South American Handbook*.'
Daily Telegraph

'a mine of literary information'
Times Literary Supplement

'like taking a whole library with you on holiday'
Classic FM Travel Programme

The *Traveller's Literary Companion* series is specially designed to emphasize the relationship between writer and place, and to introduce the reader to fiction, poetry and travel writing from and about the regions concerned. The *South and Central America* volume includes, for example, passages by García Márquez on Colombia, Graham Greene on Mexico and Vargas Llosa on Peru, among over 250 extracts. In addition the book contains short biographies of all the writers extracted, invaluable bibliographic information, and a lively and informative introduction to the literature of each of the 21 countries covered. 472 pp.

Other titles in the *Traveller's Literary Companion* series include *Africa, Eastern and Central Europe, Indian Subcontinent, Japan,* and *South-east Asia.*

Available from good bookshops or directly from the publisher.

Published in the UK at £13.95 by In Print Publishing Ltd, 9 Beaufort Terrace, Brighton BN2 2SU, UK. Tel: (01273) 682836. Fax: (01273) 620958. (Orders from outside the UK please add £4.00 for postage and packing.) ISBN 1 873047 65 7.

Published in the USA at $17.95 by Passport Books, NTC Publishing Group, 4255 West Tuohy Avenue, Lincolnwood (Chicago), IL 60646-1975, USA. Tel: 708 679-5500. Fax: 708 679-6375. ISBN 0-8442-9673-6.

DEPARTMENT OF PORTUGUESE AND BRAZILIAN STUDIES
KING'S COLLEGE LONDON

The only department in the UK devoted exclusively to the study of the language, literature, culture and history of the Portuguese-speaking world.

Teaching and research expertise covering all the inter-related cultures of Portugal, Brazil and the five African countries which have adopted Portuguese as their official language: Angola, Mozambique, Guinea-Bissau, Cape Verde, São Tomé e Principe

Course options include; Creole Literature and West African Oral Tradition; Camões and the Portuguese Renaissance; Faces of Women in the Medieval Galician-Portuguese Lyric; the Indian in Brazilian literature and culture; history and politics of modern Portuguese-speaking Africa; the place of the Portuguese 'Discoveries' and ideas of Nation in Portuguese history and culture; Brazilian Poetry and Popular Music; literature and politics before and after the Portuguese Revolution of 1974

Undergraduate BA degrees

No previous knowledge of Portuguese necessary

High level of language proficiency, including specialist courses in Translation, Composition and Linguistics

Over twenty specific course options to choose from, to suit individual thematic, geographical and historical interests

Many combinations possible with other disciplines

Postgraduate degrees

Two specialised taught **Masters Degrees, the MA in Portuguese Studies and MA in Romance Languages and Literatures (Portuguese)**

Concentrate and deepen investigation of two or more geographical areas

Independently researched dissertation on a theme chosen by the student

Unique range of supervisory expertise for postgraduate students wishing to embark on a programme of research leading to the **MPhil** or **PhD degree**

Further information and applications;-
Department of Portuguese and Brazilian Studies, King's College London, Strand, London, WC2R 2LS.
Head of Department and Postgraduate Admissions Tutor *Professor Patrick Chabal* (Tel 0171 873 2507)
Undergraduate Admissions Tutor *Dr Juliet Perkins* (Tel 0171 836 5454 ext 3532)

KING'S
College
LONDON
Founded 1829

University of London

PORTUGUESE STUDIES

An annual journal devoted to the literature, culture and history of Portugal, Brazil and the Portuguese-speaking countries of Africa.

CELJ 'Best New Journal' Award 1987

"...the coming of age of Portuguese studies in this country"
— *Times Higher Education Supplement*

"...a melhor revista do mundo lusófono"
— *Jornal de Letras*, (Lisbon)

Published by Modern Humanities Research Association.
Editor, Professor Helder Macedo.
Obtainable from the Hon. Treasurer, MHRA, King's College London, Strand, London WC2R 2LS. Inclusive price (non members):
UK/EU £32.00; overseas £38.50; USA $77.00.
MHRA membership (including volume 11 of Portuguese Studies); £33.00; $66.00.

CENTRE FOR THE STUDY OF BRAZILIAN CULTURE AND SOCIETY
KING'S COLLEGE LONDON

Established in the 1995-96 academic year, the Centre for the Study of Brazilian Culture and Society at King's College London is the only such centre of its kind in the UK and Europe, dedicated to the promotion of postgraduate teaching, research, scholarship and dissemination in the field of Brazilian cultural studies, literature and history.

Activities will include:

— research programme on **Brazilian Popular Music**, including the development of an Archive of Brazilian Popular Music, seminars and publications

— **translation programme** for the promotion of Brazilian fiction in English, including a rolling series of translations co-published with Boulevard Books, and a practical translation seminar.

— seminars, lecture series, conferences and publications on aspects of Brazilian culture, literature, history and society

MA in Brazilian Studies

Register at King's College London for a new specialist Masters Degree in Brazilian Studies administered by the University of London's Institute of Latin American Studies.

Drawing from the range of expertise on Brazil across the University of London, the MA is the first multidisciplinary degree of its kind in Europe. It offers students a unique opportunity to combine study of the country's history, politics, economy, culture and environmental issues in recognition of Brazil's growing importance as a regional and world power.

For further information, contact *Dr David Treece*, Director of the Centre for the Study of Brazilian Culture and Society, and Coordinator of the MA in Brazilian Studies: King's College London, Strand, London WC2R 2LS (Tel 0171 836 5454)

TURNAROUND DISTRIBUTION

TURNAROUND IS PROUD TO DISTRIBUTE A WIDE RANGE OF HIGH QUALITY LISTS FROM A VARIETY OF UK, IRISH AND US PUBLISHERS. SUBJECTS INCLUDE FICTION, LITERARY FICTION, LITERARY CRITICISM, FICTION IN TRANSLATION AND MANY MORE. PHONE OR WRITE TO BE INCLUDED ON OUR LISTS FOR CATALOGUES OF THESE ESSENTIAL BUT SOMETIMES HARD TO FIND TITLES.

PUBLISHERS DISTRIBUTED BY US INCLUDE:

AFRICA WORLD PRESS

BASEMENT PRESS

BAY PRESS

BLAST BOOKS

BRANDON BOOKS

CATBIRD PRESS

DALKEY ARCHIVE PRESS

EXACT CHANGE

FICTION TWO COLLECTIVE

FOUR WALLS EIGHT WINDOWS

GORSE

HANUMAN PRESS

MARLBORO PRESS

THE OVERLOOK PRESS

THE PARIS REVIEW

RICHARD KASAK BOOKS

TRAFIKA

TURTLE POINT PRESS

TURNAROUND DISTRIBUTION
27 HORSELL ROAD, LONDON, N51XL
TEL: 0171 609 7836 FAX: 0171 700 1205

Elizabet   ault crime
fiction, c   d an inter-
nationally bestselling author. She lives on Whidbey Island in
the state of Washington and that is one of the inspirations
for *The Edge of Nowhere* series, which marks an exciting
departure for this talented novelist. Visit Elizabeth's website
at www.elizabethgeorgeonline.com.

Praise for Elizabeth George
and THE EDGE OF NOWHERE:

'Action-packed, mysterious, and somewhat creepy . . . A
combination of great characters and relationships have this
novel raising the bar when it comes to today's YA fiction.'
Suspense Magazine

'In combining her skills in crime writing with an obvious
flair for the supernatural, this award-winning author creates
a wonderful tale.' *My Weekly*

'Presses all the buttons to make us hoover her stuff up.'
Daily Telegraph

'The author writes brilliantly and has an incredible ability
to set a scene and create characters you want to know more
about.' *Sun*

ELIZABETH GEORGE

The Edge of the Light

HODDER

First published in Great Britain in 2016 by Hodder & Stoughton
An Hachette UK company

First published in paperback in 2017

I

A CIP catalogue record for this title is available from the British Library

B format ISBN: 978 1 444 72013 6
A format ISBN: 978 1 444 72012 9

Typeset in Plantin Light by Palimpsest Book Production Ltd,
Falkirk, Stirlingshire

Printed and bound by CPI Group (UK) Ltd, Croydon, CR0 4YY

Hodder & Stoughton policy is to use papers that are natural, renewable
and recyclable products and made from wood grown in sustainable forests.
The logging and manufacturing processes are expected to conform to
the environmental regulations of the country of origin.

Hodder & Stoughton Ltd
Carmelite House
50 Victoria Embankment
London EC4Y 0DZ

www.hodder.co.uk

In loving memory of GA

But this swift business
I must uneasy make, lest too light winning
Make the prize light.

William Shakespeare,
The Tempest

I

Hospitals were bad, but rehab centers were worse. In a hospital, rotten stuff that happened to people at least got dealt with pronto and you ended up knowing what the outcome was going to be. You had a car wreck, you got carted to Emergency, you got patched up or operated on, you lived, or you died. It all took time, but the time ended. In a rehab center, though, everything went on and on. Especially if you had a stroke.

That was what Seth Darrow was thinking as he watched his grandfather in one of the physical therapy rooms at Penn Cove Care, which was situated on a leafy side street in the old Victorian town of Coupeville on Whidbey Island. Seth and his dad had just engaged in a depressing meeting with the head of PT, a woman who'd spent twenty-five years in the military and who had a way of speaking that pretty much showed it. The news they'd been given had matched the weather outside, which was wintertime bleak with a sky pouring down a fifteenth straight day of steady rain accompanied by the occasional wind gust that was taking down aged alders and lofty Douglas firs across the island.

"Mr. Darrow still isn't working with us," she announced to Seth and his dad ten seconds after they'd sat in front of her desk. Her name plate called her G. H. FIELDSTONE, and she'd introduced herself as George. Then she'd added *doctor* in front of it, just in case they'd considered getting friendly. "This has to change," she said. "This is a rehab facility, with the accent on *rehab*. If Mr. Darrow doesn't make more progress . . ." She did one of those lifting of the fingers routines, which meant they were to fill in the blanks. She looked severely at Seth's dad, Rich. It seemed she thought he was thick as a board because she added, "This isn't a permanent living facility. You understand."

She then suggested that they have a look for themselves from the hallway outside of the PT room where Ralph Darrow was working with the occupational therapist. That was what they were doing at the moment, and Seth's heart thudded painfully as he watched his grandfather.

It had been more than four weeks since the stroke that had robbed Ralph Darrow of speech and the ability to use his right arm. His right leg had been affected, too, but not as badly as his arm. He'd more or less got back the use of the leg, which was the good news, although he was still unsteady. But when it came to the arm, he was toast. The damage was done, the arm was finito, and what he had to do was learn how to be left handed. He also had to learn how to use his left hand to exercise his right arm so that he didn't develop something called contractures. If that happened, his right arm's muscles would totally freeze up as the muscles thickened.

So once he got steadier on his feet, Ralph had PT sessions for his arm several times a day. He also had speech therapy sessions twice a day to handle the loss of language. The situation Ralph was in would've been a bummer for anyone, but for Seth's grandfather, who for the last fifty-two of his seventy-three years had been a carpenter, a gardener, and a forester who maintained well over one hundred acres of woodland, it was like a death blow.

Seth's insides ached as he watched his granddad. He shot a look at his father and saw that Rich Darrow felt the same. The occupational therapist was presenting Ralph with exercises that involved using his left hand to lift his useless right hand to the height of his shoulder, but once the therapist did it for him in demonstration, Ralph did nothing to show that he understood.

Seth's father said, "He's not even trying," as his cell phone rang. He pulled it from his pocket, gave it a look, said, "It's your mom" to Seth and then into the phone, "Hi, sweetheart. You doing okay?" Rich listened for a moment and, for his part, Seth strained to hear. His mom said something to which his dad replied, "You don't need to go so long without a pill, Amy. It's not like you're going to get addicted. . . . What're you going to do with them, sell them? . . . Don't be stubborn. Take a pill, get some rest, and we'll be home soon. . . . No. It's not looking good. We'll talk when Seth and I get back." He listened for a second, said, "Will do. Love you," and ended the call. He said to Seth, "Your mom loves you, she said."

"Back at her." Seth nodded at his granddad, who was still sitting lifelessly in front of the therapist. "What do we do now?"

Rich settled his shoulders. "We talk to him."

"But if he doesn't understand . . . ?"

"Oh, you can bet he understands," Rich said. "Underneath it all, he's still Ralph Darrow. I guarantee you, he understands."

Seth wasn't sure. It seemed to him that if his granddad understood that the key to getting back home was showing everyone that he was capable of reacquiring speech and also capable of learning to use his left hand and arm in place of his right one, then Ralph would throw himself into these tasks. He wouldn't spend weeks just *sitting* there.

The speech therapist would show him picture cards representing words like cat, hat, bat. She would say the words that went with the cards. But all that came from Ralph in return was a dull-eyed look at what was being flashed in front of him.

The occupational therapist would present him with blocks of various shapes to manipulate into holes by means of his left hand, and he'd just let his left hand fall to his lap. Seth had said more than once that his granddad wasn't *like* this man who slumped in a chair and did not respond. Grand was filled with life and joy and wisdom, and right now he just didn't understand what was going on. Somehow none of the medical people had made a breakthrough with him.

Seth followed his father into the PT room. They stood out of Ralph's line of vision until the end of the session with the occupational therapist. At that point, the therapist stood and said – as cheerfully as possible, considering the lack of cooperation from the patient – "That's enough for today. Let's get you back to your room." That was when Rich and Seth stepped forward.

Rich said to the therapist, "We'll take him from here, if that's okay," and the tone that he used communicated something more than just helping her out.

She said to Ralph, "Mr. Darrow, I'm leaving you in the hands of your son and grandson," which got Ralph's attention. He turned his head and, in doing so, confirmed what Rich had been declaring: When Ralph wanted to understand something, he understood completely. The therapist patted Ralph's shoulder, said to him, "Don't you get into trouble," and she left them.

Rich went around to the front of Ralph's wheelchair. He set the brake and said to his father, "Let's see how you're doing with walking back to your room. Seth, you take the chair. Dad, I'm helping you up."

Ralph stiffened. Rich said to his father, "You know what's

going on, and it's time to stop pretending you don't. Here's the deal, Dad: If you don't improve, Brenda wins. So what you've got to ask yourself is whether you want that to happen."

Brenda was Brenda Sloan. She was Seth's aunt and Rich Darrow's older sister, and she had buckets of money and the will to use it. She lived in the upscale community of Medina east of Seattle and across Lake Washington, where her husband made megabucks dealing in high end real estate and Brenda had a successful business staging homes prior to putting them on the market. That is, she staged homes when she *wasn't* getting involved in Ralph Darrow's health and welfare, which had become her primary obsession about twenty-four hours after Ralph's stroke.

That was when she'd shown up on the island and made the declaration that Ralph "obviously" could no longer live on his own. The fact that he'd had a stroke while alone and had not been discovered till some hours later indicated to her that he was destined for assisted living.

That Ralph Darrow did not live alone was something that didn't impress Brenda Sloan. For he shared his house with a teenaged girl who traded housecleaning and cooking for her room and board. This *child*, Brenda announced, hadn't been present when the stroke occurred. *That* indicated what the future would be if Ralph was allowed to return to his home.

"He'll have another stroke, she won't be there, and he'll die," was Brenda's repeated refrain. "Do you *want* that, Rich?"

No one wanted that, but no one aside from Brenda wanted Ralph to have to leave his home.

2

In Deception Pass State Park, the weather was milder. While the rain had been coming down in great waving sheets in Coupeville at the center of Whidbey, in the north part of the island the day was wet, but not wet enough to cancel a hike.

No one worth his salt in the Pacific Northwest would have been put off by rain, anyway. A change of gear was all it took, along with using more care on the park's trails. But on one particular trail, hikers were largely protected from the weather. For despite the elevation gain, most of the path carved its way beneath some of the greatest trees of the park: hemlocks that loomed like skyscrapers, Douglas firs that shed small cones everywhere, fragrant cedars, madrones gracefully stretching their bark-peeling branches above the forest floor. All of these formed a canopy through which only the most severe rainfall could pierce. True, there were boulders for hikers to contend with along the way, and they could be slick, but the three individuals on the trail weren't bothered by this.

Becca King – sixteen years old – was one of the hikers. The second was her boyfriend Derric. The third was fifteen-year-old Rejoice Ayoka, and Becca had sensed from the moment when she and Derric had picked the girl up for this hike that Rejoice wasn't happy. Before this, eighteen-year-old Derric had always driven to La Conner alone to see Rejoice, which was no problem as far as Becca was concerned. For although she and Derric were a couple, he shared a past and a heritage with the younger girl: they were both Ugandan, and they had both been adopted out of the same orphanage in Kampala. There were other parts of the Derric-and-Rejoice relationship, too. But Derric had not yet mentioned them to Rejoice, and Becca wasn't about to say a word in reference to them, either.

Now they were approaching the final section of the trail. The going was trickier, with a sharp descent down a bluff followed by a jump onto a path that edged a raindrop-speckled and winter-bleak expanse of water called Cornet Bay. Derric went first to break the fall should either of the girls slip, and when he reached the bottom and made the leap onto the path below, he turned to help the girls.

Becca was cautious. She'd been concentrating on more than just her footwork. She'd also been working hard to keep her mind as perfect a blank as possible. *Empty of all there is* was a mantra she was using to achieve this blank. She'd been repeating it silently since leaving Derric's car, and only when there was conversation among them had she allowed anything else to enter her head.

Becca was full of the mantra when she heard Derric saying, "Hey, don't do it that way, Rejoice!" in a tone of alarm. She roused herself to see that the other girl was poised to jump down to the lower path, arms extended behind her, as if she intended to fly.

"He's right," Becca said to the fifteen-year-old. "Don't, Rejoice!"

But Rejoice didn't appear interested in either of their warnings because she laughed and called out, "Catch me, Derric!" and flung herself off her perch in his direction.

Derric scrambled, saying, "That's a dumb-ass thing to—" but he managed to catch her, although both of them ended up on their butts in the mud. Rejoice laughed as Derric began struggling onto his feet.

"I knew you could do it!" She clapped, as if applauding the boy's heroics on her behalf.

Derric looked at Becca, and she heard him perfectly. *What she thinks about it* came to her as clearly as if he'd spoken although he'd not said a single word.

She wanted to reply. She told herself what she *would* have said had Derric only known that she could hear what was going on in his head: "It's not what I think. It's what Rejoice is thinking. You better watch out." But she said nothing. Instead, she smiled at him as he came back over to the final jump and helped her down.

"Ooooh, Becca was too scared to jump," Rejoice said airily.

Derric replied with, "Becca was too *smart* to jump. You, on the other hand, could've broken a leg."

"No way," Rejoice countered. "I knew you'd take care of me."

Although the path was now virtually flat as it skirted Cornet Bay and led in the direction of the Deception Pass Bridge and the roiling waters beneath it, Rejoice appeared to have considerable trouble staying upright. "Way too slippery!" was how she explained it as she grabbed for Derric's support time and again. "Can you help me, Derric?" became a constant refrain.

Derric maintained his cool. He was, as far as Becca was concerned, the personification of patience with the younger girl. It had been a number of weeks since Becca had taken him to La Conner to meet Rejoice, and it was obvious that he considered it too early to do anything more than just hang with her when he was able to make the drive. Talking to her honestly did not seem to be something that was going to happen any time soon.

The trouble with this was how Rejoice was interpreting Derric's visits. Becca had had her suspicions about this when the girl's calls to Derric's cell phone began to come more than three times a day. So when Derric had invited Becca to join them on this particular hike, Becca had said "sure," because she wanted to be exactly that: sure about what was happening with Rejoice.

Back at Derric's car, they stowed their gear and the remains of the snacks they'd taken with them. Rejoice called out, "Shotgun!" and over her shoulder said to Becca, "It *is* my regular place, you know," and clambered inside the car.

Derric muttered, "Sorry, babe," as he shut the cargo area of the Forester.

"No problem," she said, and added, "but we should probably talk, you and me."

He didn't reply. She'd gone back to *Empty of all there is* for the remainder of their walk, so she didn't hear anything else from him. She climbed into the car and told herself that the prospect of studying the back of Derric's dark, shaven skull wasn't so bad anyway. He had gorgeous skin the color of bitter chocolate, and from her angle behind the passenger seat, she could see the smooth curve of his cheek and the muscle in his jaw that moved when he was feeling something he hoped not to reveal.

As they took off, Rejoice declared, "Next time I'll make sandwiches to bring with us. What kind of sandwich d'you like best, Derric? PBJ? Roast beef? Ham?"

"Anything but bologna," he replied, and with a glance over his shoulder at Becca, "What about you, babe?"

"I wasn't *asking* Becca," Rejoice said.

"No prob," Derric told her. "I was."

Rejoice settled her shoulders in girl fuming mode. She shot a look at Derric before saying, "Okay. What *about* you,

Becca? Do you even eat sandwiches? I bet you think they'll make you fat. I bet you exist on celery."

Becca smiled to herself at this. When she'd first come to the island almost sixteen months previously, *fat* certainly would have been one of the words to describe her, although *chunky* had been her mom's word of choice as she'd monitored every morsel that had passed Becca's lips. But thinking about her mom was too scary a thing, so instead Becca said, "I go for tuna mostly. But it's got to have a ton of mayo and relish. And I like whole wheat bread."

"*Course* you do," Rejoice muttered. "It's more *healthy*."

A little silence settled among them. Derric's gaze met Becca's in the rear view mirror. She gave him a look that was meant to tell him that there were things he couldn't put off much longer, but she kept in her head *Empty of all there is* because she didn't want to hear what he was thinking. On the other hand, she wouldn't have minded hearing what was going on in Rejoice's head, but to loosen her hold on the mantra would mean to give Derric's thoughts admittance as well as Rejoice's, and she'd long ago realized that the only way she could even the playing field between herself and her boyfriend was to give him the privacy of his own thoughts. She pretty much always learned them eventually anyway.

Such was the case now. Derric said to Rejoice, "Can I ask you a question?"

"Depends," Rejoice told him. "Mom's not letting me date till I'm sixteen, you know. I mean a *real* date, like at night going to the movies or something."

"I know that."

"Oh." She sounded disappointed. "Then what d'you want to ask me?"

"Why you do white girl hair."

Becca winced. Very *bad* idea for a topic of conversation.

Girls and their hair . . . ? Guys should just stay away from it. In the case of Rejoice's hair, Derric would have been wiser to run in the opposite direction. And calling it white girl hair? Dumb, dumb, dumb.

So she was unsurprised when Rejoice demanded, "What's *wrong* with my hair?"

"Straight and stiff like that? It looks . . . I dunno. Unnatural, I guess."

Becca wanted to say, "Don't!" to Derric. She also wanted to say, "Are you an idiot?" But instead she waited for Rejoice's reply, which was fast enough in coming.

"So what am I s'posed to do exactly? Shave my head like *you*?"

He shrugged. "No one in Kampala had hair like yours. Don't you remember?"

"I didn't even *have* hair," she told him. "And alls I remember is getting my head shaved. What did I have? Lice or something?"

"Everyone had their heads shaved. Or they wore hair super short so they didn't have to comb it and break it."

"My hair doesn't break," Rejoice said.

"That's because of all the gunk you smear on it. What is it anyway?"

"Uh, Derric . . . ?" When he glanced at the mirror, Becca shot him a don't-go-there look.

"I *like* my hair this way," Rejoice said. "I had frizz bombs all over my head and then my mom found this and I *like* it."

Becca could feel the girl's hurt, and she touched Rejoice's shoulder. "Rejoice, he's a guy. He doesn't get it."

Rejoice flinched to shake Becca off. Derric said, "Whatever," in that universal male way of ending a discussion.

But Rejoice continued with, "What would make my hair better, then?"

For you went unspoken, but it was as if Rejoice had said it anyway. Derric had to have known that, Becca thought, but instead of reassuring Rejoice that, really, her hair was just fine and he'd been having a moment of male insanity, Derric said, "Wear it short or shave it all off. It'd make you look cool. It'd make you look African."

What Becca thought was, It'd make you look like Derric, and she couldn't believe he didn't know that. On the other hand, maybe that was how he was going to clue Rejoice in to the truth. Head shaved and smiling, Rejoice would virtually be Derric's twin.

"I'm not African," Rejoice was saying. "I'm American."

"Your style might be American," he replied. "But your blood is African, just like mine."

Rejoice squirmed in her seat, as if she wanted to disappear into the Forester's fabric. She set her face and crossed her arms. It wasn't until they'd finally reached her family's farm outside of the town of La Conner that she spoke again. Then it was only to say, "You're really mean, Derric. And *not* just about my hair." Before he could reply to this, she jumped out of the Forester and ran to the house.

Becca moved from the back seat to the front. She looked at Derric. He looked at her. He said, "I blew it."

"Ya think? When did you get so dumb?"

"I was trying to help her out. Her hair—"

"That was seriously uncool." Becca fastened her seat belt as he backed the car away from the pristine white farmhouse where Rejoice lived with her parents – Jeff and Darla Vickland – and her four siblings. "No girl wants some guy criticizing her hair. *Or* her body. *Or* her clothes."

"I was only trying to help," he protested. "Her hair looks bad. It's like . . . grisly. She needs to know it. What else am I supposed to do? I'm her brother, for God's sake."

"And you've *got* to tell her that. She's *into* you, Derric."

"No way. She knows I'm just a friend."

"Don't be a sponge brain."

. . . probably feeling jealous of what we have only what we have isn't anything because I'm not going there no way . . .

Becca was defeated by this sudden jumble of Derric's thoughts. Even the mantra didn't help her. She grabbed her backpack from the back seat and began to riffle through it to find what she needed. This was an earbud connected to what looked like – but was not – an iPod. Instead, it was what she'd learned to call an AUD box, a device that obscured the thoughts of others with static so that Becca herself could concentrate.

She said, "Here's the deal: You can't control her feelings. She's into you, and you better tell her who you are. Plus if she shaves her head, she's going to look like a female you, and how the heck do you explain *that* one?"

"What you really mean is how the hell do I plan to explain that I'm the brother who left her behind in Kampala because I never bothered to tell anyone that she was my sister?"

"I'm *not* saying that. I don't know how you're going to tell her, but you're going to have to. And you better do it soon because if you wait much longer, it's going to go down super bad. Like I said, she's *into* you. And before you say I'm jealous or something, what I say is just open your eyes."

They were at the end of the farm's long driveway. Derric stopped the car, his gaze on the road. He looked out at the fields across the street and then at Becca.

"What?" she asked him.

"I know," he replied. "It's why I wanted you to come this time. I figured if she saw you and me together, she'd see how things are between us."

"Not if she doesn't want to," Becca said.

★

Darkness came early to the Pacific Northwest in the winter, so when Derric and Becca drove through the rainfall into the village of Langley at the south end of the island, lights were blinking in the cottages and houses that spread out before them. They drove down Third Street, a bumpy lane that descended into the heart of the village and ended at a small, white steepled Methodist church.

Becca had begun her time on Whidbey Island in this old village, which had been born late in the nineteenth century. Then it was a spot from which downed fir trees were shipped to support the growing metropolis of Seattle some thirty miles to the south of where Whidbey lay among the other islands of Puget Sound. Now, however, it was a struggling little place of ancient storefronts and early-twentieth-century cottages. It was set in a landscape filled with visual artists, writers, weavers, glass blowers, sculptors, and retirees. In the summer it boomed with tourists who came by car or by boats that were docked in the town's natural marina: a watery horseshoe at the base of a tall bluff. In the winter, it was nearly a ghost town, and the business people fought like starving dogs to survive.

One of these business people owned a motel on the far edge of the village, and it was to this motel that Derric drove. Here lived Derric's official Little Brother. He was called Josh Grieder, and along with his sister Chloe, he was cared for by their grandmother. Here also Becca had stayed during the first few months of her time on Whidbey Island.

When they reached the motel, Derric didn't pull into the parking lot. Instead, he slowed, pulled to the side of the road, and said to Becca, "You sure you don't want to come with us? It's just what you like: comic book action heroes fighting bad guys, lots of explosions, huge car crashes, and a token female in a skimpy costume. And . . . oh yeah, she'll have big boobs. They always have big boobs."

Becca pretended to consider this. He was describing the film that was playing in the village movie theater. Going to see this constituted his date with his Little Brother. Josh, she knew, would generously welcome her to join them because that was who the boy was. But his private time with Derric was a treasure to him. She said, "Damn . . . you make it sound *so* tempting."

"It was the big boobs that got you," he said. "Admit it."

"Oh for sure. I'm excessively into looking at big boobs on a thirty-foot screen."

"Pizza afterward," he added.

She gave a sigh meant to convey her intense disappointment at having to decline. "Got to say no. Mrs. Kinsale's expecting me."

"You'll regret it."

"I'll try to survive. It'll be tough, but I'm made of steel."

He laughed and drove on past the motel. He would, she knew, take her to her destination. He did question it, though, saying, "You've been going over there a lot, babe."

"To Diana's? Yeah. She's my friend."

"She's sort of old to be a friend, don't you think? What is she, like . . . seventy or something?"

Becca lifted one shoulder in a halfway shrug. "What difference does that make?"

They coursed to the edge of the village, on a road that took them past an old brick middle school and the tiny fairgrounds beyond it. Before heading out of town entirely, Derric made a turn onto a narrow road that dipped into and out of more forest and passed houses half-hidden among the trees. This ultimately deposited them on a Z-turn that became the lane where Diana Kinsale's large gray house overlooked a tumble of beach cottages down on the water as well as the fast moving currents of Saratoga Passage.

When he pulled into the driveway and stopped the

Forester, Derric turned to Becca. He said, "What d'you guys do?"

"Me and Mrs. Kinsale? Nothing much. Talk mostly. Or we play with her dogs."

He frowned. "It's sort of strange, you ask me."

"I like her, Der. I can learn from her." She saw his expression shift, and she knew at once what worried him. She added, "I've never told her. Or anyone else."

"What?" ·

"You know. You. Rejoice. And," she added hastily, because she knew very well that he didn't want to go there a second time in one day, "if I bring it up with you, it's only because I think you're going to be bummed out until you make everything right."

"By doing what?"

"By telling the truth."

He looked at Diana's house for a long moment and then back at her. She could sense tension in him, but the AUD box prevented her from hearing his thoughts. He said with his dark eyes grown even darker, "That works for everyone, don't you think, Becca?"

Indeed it did. She held her own secrets close. She left them unspoken to nearly everyone, including to Derric, whom she loved. She knew there should only be truth between them, but she'd told herself since the day she'd met him that it was because she wanted to protect Derric Mathieson that she did not tell him what had brought her to Whidbey.

Becca gave Derric a final wave as he reversed the Forester and then drove back to town. She would, she'd told him, take the island bus to get home. Easy peasy to do that, she'd said. He replied with "Nothing's easy, Becca," but he'd kissed her, fondly touched her cheek, and kissed her again.

She went to Diana Kinsale's front door, removing the AUD box's earbud from her ear and removing the box itself from her waist. The device would not be necessary.

She saw that lights were on in the house, and when she rang the bell, Diana's dogs began barking. Through the window, Becca saw four of them charge from the sunroom through the living room and into the entry. They were followed by a stately black poodle who, as ever, did not join in their raucous greeting. From somewhere within, Becca heard Diana's voice calling out. The barking dogs fell silent. Diana, she realized, had been working with them.

She tried the door. It was unlocked, as usual. She called out, "It's me," and was immediately surrounded by the canine pack. They pressed their noses to her pockets. She dug out the treats that she usually carried when she came to Diana's, and these they devoured with considerable joy. Even the poodle seemed interested. Oscar approached, deigned to be patted on his curly head, and accepted a treat.

Diana's voice came from the doorway to the kitchen. "Hello, Becca. I had no idea it was time already."

Becca looked up and immediately felt a quiver of concern. Diana appeared tired, which wasn't strange. But she also looked ragged. Her posture wasn't its usual military stance, and the skin beneath her eyes seemed loose. Becca said to her, "You okay, Mrs. Kinsale?"

"I've been strolling down memory lane." She indicated the direction she'd come from. "Basement," she told Becca. "I've finally started on it. Thirty years of living in this house and the basement is crammed. That's the trouble with basements. Why throw something out when you can just toss it down the stairs and tell yourself you'll get to it later?"

"What about these guys?" Becca indicated the dogs. Not Oscar, but the rest of the gang. They'd long been far too

ungovernable as a group to come into the house. "How
come they're not in their run?"

"They're in training. Watch." Diana turned to the dogs.
"All dogs come," she said, and they obeyed her. "All dogs
sit," she said, and again they obeyed. "Of course, I haven't
tried it when there's a rabbit on the lawn," she admitted.
"All dogs sunroom," she said to the animals. Off they went.

"Impressive," Becca said.

"They're coming along." Diana wiped her hands on the
tail of her flannel shirt. It was overlarge and looked like one
of her long dead husband's. If Diana still had it these nearly
thirty years since his death, Becca thought, then her basement was indeed bursting with long forgotten goods.

"Want some help down there?" Becca asked. "We could
do that instead of the practice."

"The practice is far more important," Diana told her.
"Come along. Let's get started." She led the way up the
stairs and along a corridor painted in the warm colors of a
sunset. They did their practicing in Diana's bedroom, where
an alcove offered two comfortable armchairs, a fireplace,
and a view that took in tiny Hat Island and, beyond it at a
distance across the water, the city of Everett. This was
Diana's retreat, where she read, relaxed, and meditated.
Becca was there to learn a variation of the last: something
that was not quite meditation but was instead a way to
control what otherwise bombarded her every waking
moment.

She walked to the large bay window. From the start, it
had been her preference to sit with the view spreading out
before her: Hat Island, Camano Head, the energetic water,
houses, distant city lights, the occasional boat. But Diana
had not allowed this, instructing her instead to sit with her
chair facing the fireplace. Above this, the only distraction
was a large pastel of a stairway climbing the side of a

barn-red building. Becca knew this place quite well. It was called the Dog House, a tavern that stood on the bluff within Langley village.

She turned from the window. "Can I try facing the view this time?"

Diana bent to switch on the gas in the fireplace. She said over her shoulder, "I don't think you're ready for that yet. Too many distractions, and at this point you need as few as possible."

"I want to try it," Becca said.

"Impatient as always." But Diana softened the criticism with a smile. "Overcoming impatience is at the core of this process, Becca. Your mind still moves toward *rushing* instead of *being*. Being is the key to unlocking the power."

Becca narrowed her eyes. "You're getting *way* too close to Yoda again, Mrs. Kinsale."

Diana laughed. "I hope I'm more attractive. All right, try it if you must."

Becca pumped her fist and swung her chair to face the window. She plopped down. "Ready when you are," she told Diana.

"Settle first," Diana said. "Breathe. Go deep. Feel the blood coursing. Feel the heart beating." She waited more than a minute before saying quietly, "Now. Find something in the view to concentrate on."

Becca settled her gaze on Hat Island, on one of the houses that winked light into the late afternoon darkness. She murmured, "Got it," and Diana said softly, "There is no world. There is only this. The moment itself, the single point on which your eyes are resting. Begin with the mantra, then slowly let it go."

Empty of all there is, there is. Empty of all there is.
Empty of all there is, there is. Empty of all there is.

Into the stillness came the unmistakable cry of an eagle. Following hard upon it came the raucous calling of crows. It was a mass of them from the sound of it. And what was a mass of crows called? You had a gaggle of geese, a pride of lions, a congress of . . . something? Not crows, though. Not a congress of—

"*Damn,*" Becca muttered.

"What is it?"

"I *hate* it when you're right." She shoved herself out of the chair and turned it to face the fireplace. "I got caught up in the crows. What's it called when there's a bunch of them, anyway?"

Diana, sitting in the other chair, smiled. "A murder."

"A murder of crows?" Becca plopped back down, this time with her gaze on the flames of the gas fire. "I would've gone a long time without figuring that one out."

"Shall we start again?"

And so they did. Back to the blood coursing, back to the breathing, back to the mantra.

There was nothing else. Absolutely nothing beyond the mantra came into Becca's mind. After a few minutes, she heard Diana murmur, "Now let it go," which was the signal to cease the mantra. Still, there was nothing.

This wasn't unusual. Diana Kinsale was the only person whose thoughts Becca had never been able to hear in the form of what she'd long ago learned to call whispers. At first, Becca had believed it was because Diana possessed an unearthly ability far beyond her own. But she'd learned it was simply because Diana was able to control her thoughts when she wasn't speaking, and because her thoughts exactly matched her words when she did speak.

In this practice that the two of them engaged in, however, Diana allowed her mind to wander, and it was Becca's job to learn to block Diana's thoughts without the aid of the AUD box. At first they'd used the mantra to do this. Now they were moving on to the ability to empty the mind first and to lock it off from invasion second.

Becca breathed deeply and maintained control. The moments passed. Each second ticked off an entire eternity and then, *down to my soul here Clarence comes* was as loud as the crows had been.

"Damn it!" Becca cried. "This is hopeless. What was it, five seconds?"

Diana rose. Her warm hand came down on Becca's shoulder. "What did you hear?"

"*I* don't know. Something about my soul and Clarence."

"That's all?"

"Is it another mantra? Not that it matters because it invaded my brain in like . . . I don't know . . . like I said, five seconds."

"You went nearly two minutes if you heard nothing else," Diana said. "'Dive, thoughts, down to my soul. Here Clarence comes.'"

"Yeah. That's it. I held it off for a while but then . . . there it was."

"Did you hear more?"

"*Was* there more?"

Diana came around to the front of Becca's chair. She crossed her arms and observed Becca solemnly. "There was indeed. I was thinking the opening soliloquy of *Richard the Third*. It's two pages long."

"Richard the who?"

"Shakespeare," Diana said. "A very fine play. You must read it sometime."

"Shakespeare?" Becca groused. "No wonder I couldn't hold it off."

Diana shook her head. "I don't believe you understand.

As I said, the soliloquy is two pages long. You held it off until the last line."

"So you were thinking, like, the *whole* soliloquy?"

"From the moment you let the mantra go. It might have seemed like five seconds to you, my dear. But the soliloquy – done well – takes more than a minute and closer to two."

Becca's eyes widened as she took this in, along with its implications. Nearly two minutes of holding a mental barrier against the invasion of people's thoughts? It felt like a miracle to her.

3

Holy Redeemer Pentecostal Church had no windows. The reason for this was that it had long ago been decided that nothing from the external world should distract the church's congregants from worship. So the windows that *had* existed in the storefront where services took place every Sunday and Bible study occurred every Wednesday night had been boarded up with plywood. The look at first had suggested a hurricane was imminent, and because of this, a committee with marginal talent had painted scenes from the Old Testament upon the wood. Jenn McDaniels thought the place looked like a preschool now, one where the finger painting had gotten badly out of control.

She was inside, along with her mom. Her little brothers were in the children's group that met in an airless walled-off section of the former shop. It had once been a hair salon, and the kids' section was within the storage and color-mixing part of the place. Jenn remembered it only too well. She'd spent her formative years there learning Bible stories while outside in the regular church, the congregation sang, listened to Mr. Sawyer banging the pulpit and preaching his head off, and waited for the Holy Spirit to descend upon them and gift them with tongues.

Her mom had already received this gift. Nearly every Sunday, her eyes rolled back in her head, and she began to babble. It didn't matter which part of the service was going on, either. Mr. Sawyer could work himself into a lather about Samson, Delilah, and the scissors, and what all that meant (like get a regular haircut, Jenn thought), and Kate McDaniels would rise, sway, and begin using nonsense words that came out as a murmur and then as a moan and finally a loud exclamation. To Jenn, it was an excruciating spectacle, and when people fell into silent awe, Jenn wanted to sink into the ground and disappear. She had never been able to figure out why anyone would want the Holy Spirit to "bless" them this way. It was her intention never to come *close* to having Him or Her or It anywhere near her.

Kate's ambition for Jenn was the opposite. Having tongues was the pinnacle. She meant Jenn to reach it. So she'd started her out as a five-year-old in the storage and color room of the former salon where Jenn learned that the earth was not billions of years old but rather a creation that took God six days: from the dinosaurs right to Adam and Eve. She'd believed this at first because as a five-year-old that was what you did: you believed adults. She got over that when she went to school and sat in the science class that first mentioned Charles Darwin.

Now, she squirmed in her seat. Right outside on the island highway, traffic from over town was coming off the ferry. She could hear the grinding of gears from a big tractor trailer climbing the steep slope through the little commercial area that was Clinton. She wished she was on it. Or in one of the cars. In fact, she wished she was anywhere but in this airless room where, she knew, at any moment her mom was going to demonstrate just what the Holy Spirit could do for *you* if you only waited and prayed enough.

Kate's lips had started to move. Her body had started to sway. Liftoff had begun to occur, and there was no way Jenn wanted to witness another display of her mom's religious fervor.

So she rose from her chair. She could tell that the people

closest to her thought that she was about to declare herself for Jesus. She heard murmurs of "Praise Him" and the like, and she knew that if she didn't get out of there ASAP, she would be surrounded by the joyful who believed their prayers on her behalf had been answered.

She stepped over legs. She excused herself. She tromped on two purses and nearly tripped on a stack of hymnals. Behind her, she sensed that her mom was on her feet, and she thought that Kate was coming after her. But when she heard the sound of a deep-throated moan, she knew that she didn't have to worry.

Jenn whispered, "Sorry, sorry. Need a bathroom," and hoped that would be enough. The faithful allowed her to pass to the aisle and from there to dash to the door. She burst outside just as someone behind her shouted, "Come unto *me*, I pray you." Jenn shut the door. She breathed in relief. Another Sunday and she'd made her escape.

It was raining outside. At this time of year, it was usually raining. Or it was gray with clouds or soupy with fog. Sometimes it was white with snow, but that wasn't often. Mostly it was damp and cold and you had to get used to it or you'd off yourself sometime in the middle of January.

Jenn was used to it. She'd lived all her life on Whidbey Island, and although her ambition was to live the rest of her life *off* Whidbey Island, she wasn't going to be able to do that unless and until she managed a college scholarship that got her far away from this dismal place. But that was more than two years in the future, and in the meantime she had to put up with Holy Redeemer, her mom's religious fervor, and a degree of poverty that sent the family to the thrift store for clothes and to the food bank for meals.

It didn't have to be this way, she told herself. If she had a father with a normal job and a mother who made money doing *anything* other than driving the Whidbey Island taxi, they wouldn't have to live at the edge of the water, selling bait to fishermen during the season and illegally selling growlers to the local beer lovers the rest of the time. They would live in one of the three towns at the south end of the island: Freeland, which spread out along enormous Holmes Harbor; Langley, which sat above the waters of Saratoga Passage; or even Clinton, where she stood now in front of one of the strip of shops and empty storefronts and bars that defined the place.

She wanted a cigarette. She wished she hadn't given them up. She knew she'd needed to, because of soccer, but at the moment it would have felt so good to be lighting up. Part of the good feeling would have been the satisfaction of a need. The other part would have been the statement that she'd be making, a fine moment of rebellion that she wanted people to see as they came out of the Sunday service.

But she had no cigarettes and there was no place close by to purchase them. There was just the rain. That and the cars coming off the ferry with their headlights piercing the gloom. They were heading north without stopping, which was poor Clinton's curse. People opened businesses here and then closed them after a year or two. No one slowed long enough to glance at the windows of the few shops that managed to stay in business. It was a miracle, Jenn thought, that there was anything left in the place at all.

Behind her she heard voices swelling in song, accompanied by piano music that tried to keep up with them. The piano was played by Reverend Sawyer's twelve-year-old daughter. She had no talent, but she'd been given tongues when she was eight, so she was much admired.

"Just *look* at her, Jennifer," Kate McDaniels would whisper when the girl made her way to the folding chair that served as piano stool. "Think how deeply God loves her to have sent His Holy Spirit."

Jenn would look at her dutifully. The poor kid had absolutely no ankles. Her legs dropped down from her knees like vertical tree limbs, and the knee socks she wore in winter made them look like poles decorated by the anonymous knitters who went around Langley putting sweaters on the street lights.

Now the girl was pounding the piano enthusiastically. When she missed a note, no one cared.

At the conclusion of this, Jenn readied herself to face her mom. Kate was going to be furious with her for ducking out.

Her brothers managed to get out first. Petey was carrying a picture he'd drawn. Andy was carrying three crayons that he'd stolen. Petey's picture was a stick figure with a sword held high over his head. Andy's crayons were red, black, and green.

"It's Abraham," Petey announced, holding the picture up proudly. "See, he's going to kill his kid only the angel'll stop 'im just before he chops his head off."

Jenn examined it. "Where's the angel?"

"Not there yet," Petey said.

"Where's the kid?"

"He was too smart. He ran away."

Jenn guffawed, saying, "Don't tell Mom that. And, Andy, put away the crayons if you got hopes of keeping 'em. Shove 'em in your pocket or something."

"But I wanted to show you—" he began.

She cut him off with, "If you want to keep 'em, you do what I say. Else Mom sees and someone's gonna get a swat on the butt."

"'Kay," Andy said, and the crayons went into his pocket.

The congregation began piling out of the church. Jenn was glad that Mr. Sawyer wasn't the type of preacher who had to greet every single person at the door as they left.

Along with her mom, he'd have had something to say about Jenn's ducking out. For she'd caught his expression as she'd made her way down the row of chairs to the aisle, and he hadn't looked like someone who thought she was on her way to the nearest toilet.

"Let's go," were Kate McDaniels's first words. Her tone told Jenn that she wasn't going to believe any excuse Jenn came up with. "Get in the car," she said to the boys. "Back seat, please. Jenn and I need to have words in the front."

Jenn plodded behind her mother's slim back to the island taxi. Kate acknowledged the greetings of her fellow congregants and pressed her hand to her chest to receive their awed respect. She *was* truly humble, and Jenn admired this in her mom. With other people, she never made a big deal about the level of her relationship with God. It was only with Jenn that she became fire, brimstone, and determination.

They drove up the highway. Kate said nothing till they made the left turn at Deer Lake Road, which would take them in the direction of Possession Point. She said patiently, "Jennifer, this has to stop. You're not an adult yet, free to make your own decisions. You're going to have to get with the program as I define it."

Jenn looked out the window. They were cruising past farmland that the rain had made into a succession of ponds. "What about Dad?" she protested. "He doesn't go to church."

"Your father is an adult," Kate said. "His relationship with God is in his own hands. *Your* relationship with God is not."

"I don't want—"

"Don't say you don't want a relationship with God. You can't allow that thought in your head. It's a simple thing for the devil to possess someone your age, and this is how is all begins. Stubborn refusal first and then derision."

"Why don't you ever listen to me?" Jenn fumed.

"Because your words don't come from *you*. They come from the temptations of the outer world and it's the inner world that matters. That's the world sanctified by the Holy Spirit."

"Mom, I got no intention of *ever* babbling a bunch of dumb words in front of a crowd of people," Jenn said. "If that's what the Holy Spirit has to offer, then no thank you. I really mean it."

Kate's hand was swift. It didn't hit her. It grasped her by the back of the neck, though, and her grip was so firm that Jenn shouted, "Ow!" although more dramatically than was completely necessary.

Kate held on, never taking her eyes off the road. She said, "Do *not* speak of tongues in that way. You have no idea what you're talking about."

"Do *you*?" Jenn demanded. "Mom, you're hurting me!"

"How much hurt do you think you'll feel if you go to hell?" Kate countered.

"So if I learn how to moan and shout *oohba gooba ully watsie yango doobie doo*, I go to heaven? Do you really believe that?"

"What I believe is that the condition of your soul is my responsibility until you leave my house and are out on your own. So you *will* obey me on Sunday and every other day of the week."

Kate released her grip. Jenn rubbed her neck. She said, "You don't get me at all, do you?"

Kate said, "It's not important that I 'get' you. It's important that I save you. Do you understand?"

Jenn understood, all right. But the difference between herself and her mother was that while Jenn wanted to save herself, too, the way she had in mind to accomplish this had nothing to do with religion.

4

It was nearly a week after monitoring what went for his grandfather's recovery progress that Seth and his father, Rich, stood on the front porch of Ralph Darrow's house along with Becca King. The house was cedar shingled in the manner of the Pacific Northwest, and like many homes and cabins in the area, it was unpainted and had been allowed to weather naturally. Small but perfectly constructed by Ralph's own hands, the house sat at the base of and behind a modest hill up which the driveway ran from Newman Road. A lawn and a prize-winning garden of specimen trees and massive rhododendrons fronted it. To one side at a distance, a pond spread out. Behind this and behind the house itself, a great forest loomed.

Seth, his dad, and Becca were examining Ralph's garden from the porch. The distance allowed them to take it all in. The distance also allowed them to take in the enormous amount of work that needed to be done. Winter in the Pacific Northwest involved a mind-boggling exercise in raking, digging, dividing, transplanting, pruning, hauling, and mulching. And that was just in the garden. The forest needed to be seen to as well. Storms downed trees that required removal, and trails that wound through Ralph's acreage had to be maintained. Left to their own devices, the trails would be overgrown within a few months as spring brought a burgeoning in the greenery that made it akin to a woods in a fairy tale. Creepers creeped, holly shot up, and yellow archangel and English ivy did their best to choke the daylights out of everything. Winter blow-down from strong storm winds cluttered the landscape. It was a job for a team and not for anyone who didn't know exactly what to do and how to do it.

None of them were gardeners. None of them were foresters. Yet something had to be done to maintain the place, and Seth was the one to voice the problem with a mere two words. "It's epic."

"I've got no idea how he's managed to do it," was his father's reply.

"It's his passion," Becca noted.

A movement from near the pond caught their attention. Seth's golden lab came bounding toward them. Gus had dived into the forest the moment Seth had opened the car door upon his arrival with his father. Some critter, Seth decided, had caught the dog's attention, and when Gus's attention was caught, everything related to obedience training went out the window. Now he was feet-to-dog-elbows in mud as he happily loped toward them.

Becca went for a wooden box on the porch. She brought out one of the bones Ralph kept there for the dog. She threw it, Gus's eyes went bonkers with thrill, and he crashed through several priceless rhodies to get it.

"Sorry," Becca said. "Bad aim."

"No worries," Seth replied. "Maybe he'll prune 'em for us."

A voice called hello from the top of the small hill. There, just out of sight, the parking area for the property formed a rough trapezoid fashioned from grass, gravel, mud, and ruts. The owner of the voice was a broad-beamed woman in jeans, tall rubber boots, and a down jacket with a repair made of a long strip of duct tape on its sleeve. She wore massive gloves that made her look like a cartoon character, and when she finally reached them, Seth could see that she also sported a rather alarming mustache that made him uncertain where to look.

This was the home health care specialist, and it was because of a visit from her that Seth and his dad had come to Ralph's place. For her part, Becca lived in the house. She'd joined Ralph as his cook and house cleaner in exchange for a room after a spate of living in a treehouse deep within the man's forest.

"Be careful coming down," Rich Darrow called in greeting to the home health care specialist. "It's wet. Don't slip."

"Hmmm, yes, I see," she said, and her tone told Seth she was evaluating what his dad had said. Next to him, he saw Becca remove the earbud from the AUD box.

"Could use a handrail here," the health care specialist called out.

"Right." Rich went to meet her.

She made it down safely, came through the arbor that marked the entrance to the garden, and negotiated the stone steps, taking care with the winter moss that grew upon them. Next to him Seth heard Becca murmur, "That's another problem."

But there were problems everywhere when it came to the house, the property, and Ralph's ability to return to either. The place wasn't built to accommodate someone who wasn't able bodied. They didn't need a home health care specialist to tell them that. So before Ralph would be allowed to return – *if* he would be allowed to return – the place had to be looked over by an expert. Recommendations had to be made by this expert. Those recommendations had to be followed to the letter and inspected when they were completed. None of this was going to be easy.

"Steph Vanderslip," the woman said by way of introducing herself. "You must be Seth. And you are . . . ?" to Becca.

Rich Darrow was the one to introduce Becca. "Seth's friend and Ralph's boarder," was how he put it.

"Beck does the house stuff. And she cooks for Grand," Seth said. "They get along great," he added. "Huh, Beck?"

"Long as I don't have to play chess with him." She added, so that Ms. Vanderslip would understand, "He always wins. I think he cheats."

"Wouldn't surprise me," Rich Darrow said.

Steph Vanderslip said, "You ask me, the older they get, the wilier they become. Say, let's start outside here so I can keep my boots on for a while."

Thus began the evaluation of Ralph Darrow's property, and Steph Vanderslip was thorough. She began with the four front steps that led up to the porch, pointing out that their slick and unprotected condition could and would lead to broken legs if something wasn't done to protect the surface against the persistent rain of the Pacific Northwest. In fact, she said, Ralph Darrow would be better served by the removal of the steps altogether and the installation of a galvanized steel ramp of the sort used in boating marinas. No moss, algae, lichen, or anything else grew on galvanized steel, she pointed out. The expense was greater than a wooden ramp but the upkeep was marginal. If the cost was too much for them, then they could go with a wooden ramp, as long as it was weatherproofed with rubber matting, chicken wire, or thick tar paper. Or they could keep the steps – which she didn't recommend – and protect them in the same manner. If they chose to do that, though, stronger handrails would be needed: one on each side and another down the middle. But even then . . . a ramp would be better.

Sheesh, Seth thought. This was only the beginning.

Becca gazed at him. Her look was sympathetic. She was probably figuring things were going to get worse.

Steph Vanderslip walked them all back up the hill to the parking area. There she asked pointedly, "How's he going to get down to the house? Obviously, from the road to here can be done by car. But from here to the house . . . ? From the house to here when he has an appointment . . . What's the plan?"

"I can help him," Seth said. "So can Beck. Dad can—"

"Nope," Ms Vanderslip said. "He needs to be brought down to the house by vehicle and you currently have no vehicular access."

That was true, Seth thought. You arrived at the garden and the house via the trail that encircled and descended the hill. But they could carry Grand down there, and once they had him in the house, how often would he realistically have to leave the place? Once a week? Twice a month?

"He'd get pretty depressed if he couldn't get out," Becca said quietly. "I bet there's a way, though."

Rich Darrow walked over to the side of the hill opposite the side that accommodated the path leading down to Ralph's garden. Here the land was treed but not heavily forested and it sloped gradually in the direction of the house. "It's simple enough," he said to the home health care specialist, "we'll put in a driveway to the back of the house."

Simple wasn't how Seth would have put it, but when he joined his father, he saw that Rich had a point. Trees would need to come down, but most of them could be sold for lumber, and the profits could pay for the rest of the work to grade the land so that it could accommodate a vehicle.

Steph Vanderslip gave a we'll-see-about-that *hmph*, but she also agreed that a modestly sloping driveway down to the house would solve the problem. Then she led them back down to the house again, pointing out that no handrail existed along the path and Ralph Darrow was lucky no one had slipped, fallen, broken an arm, and sued him. If Ralph became mobile enough, she said, they would definitely need a handrail for him unless they planned to confine him to the house, allowing him to leave only by vehicle.

Seth wondered at the entire idea of anyone thinking they could "allow" Grand to do something. Grand did what he wanted to do.

Steph Vanderslip nearly went down as she marched them along the path. She caught herself and shot a look at Seth's dad that said, See what I mean?

From there, it was one room at a time. Handrails down the corridor, handrails in the downstairs shower, a seat in the shower as well, handrails on either side of the toilet, a thick bumper around the fireplace hearth to protect Ralph Darrow should he take a fall. As for his easy chair, they would need one simpler for him to get out of, and she recommended the sort with a seat that automatically tilted at the touch of—

The front door opened, allowing a rush of frigid air to enter the place. They all swung at the sound of, "Ah. Here you are."

It was Seth's aunt, and his first thought when he saw her was *Crap. We're in for it now.* He saw Becca give him a puzzled glance. She wouldn't know who Aunt Brenda was, because so far she'd only heard about Rich Darrow's sister but had never met her. She'd be surprised when she got introduced.

Brenda looked *nothing* like someone from Whidbey Island. She didn't really look Pacific Northwest at all. She showed off her money with designer jeans, handmade Italian boots, a cashmere Burberry scarf, a leather jacket, and a ring with a diamond the size of New Jersey. Her hair was blonde and perfect. So was her makeup. So was everything about her, right down to the Lexus SUV that, Seth figured, was parked up above, standing spotlessly clean on the other side of the hill.

Seth's dad was the one to introduce Aunt Brenda to Becca and to Steph Vanderslip. He didn't mention to his sister what they were all doing there. This didn't matter, because Steph Vanderslip offered her hand in a shake and said, "We're just going over what needs to be done to your dad's house before he comes home."

To this Brenda said to Seth's dad, "D'you want to tell me what's going on?" Before Rich could reply, Brenda went on to Steph Vanderslip with, "He's not coming home."

Rich said, "Nothing's been decided, Bren."

"Nothing needs to be decided. There's no decision because there's only one point that needs to be considered and it's obvious: He can't live on his own."

Seth said, "He's not living on his own. Becca lives here."

"And what *about* the fact that Becca lives here?" Brenda asked, giving Becca a dismissive glance. "She's what . . . fourteen years old?" She turned to Rich Darrow and demanded, "You're planning to put Dad's welfare into the hands of a child? Have you lost your mind?"

"Beck's sixteen," Seth offered.

"Oh wonderful!" Brenda hooted. "That makes all the difference. Is she a health care worker? Doesn't she go to school? Or is she some kind of freeloading dropout that Dad took pity on?"

He saw Becca wince, sort of as if she'd been smacked in the face. She put her earbud back in her ear at that point. Seth couldn't work this one out, since he figured it would have been smarter to do the reverse. Without it, she couldn't hear his aunt that well. With it, she could hear her perfectly.

And what Brenda was saying was pretty mean, as if Becca was an idiot or something.

Rich said, "Bren, this isn't the time. . . ." And to Steph Vanderslip, "Seth works in construction. He's a fine carpenter, so any work that needs to be done isn't a problem."

"Don't tell me this isn't the time!" Brenda's voice went up. "Mike's coming over to evaluate the property."

"No way!" Seth said hotly. "You two don't have *any* right to—"

"Don't you speak to me like that!"

"I'll talk to you how I feel like talking. This is my grandfather!"

"This is my father!"

Through this, Steph Vanderslip had been like someone watching a tennis match. She finally said, "You know, I think I'll be on my way. Obviously, there are family issues that need to be resolved here. But . . ." She looked a little regretful. "One way or another arrangements are going to have to be made for Mr. Darrow." Saying this, she took herself out of the house, which left the rest of them with Brenda.

Seth saw Becca ease the earbud out of her ear again as Brenda said in a hiss to Rich Darrow, "You always think you're so clever. You arranged to have this meeting without me because you knew I'd object. He needs full-time care and he's *not* going to get it here."

"Not that you're volunteering to take care of him," Seth put in.

She swung on him. "Don't you dare—"

"Seth, let me handle this," Rich said. "Why don't you and Becca wait outside?"

Seth didn't want this. He was too scared that his aunt would strong-arm his dad. Because Brenda had money, Brenda had power. Rich was a glass blower lucky enough to make ends meet. But Seth said, "Come on, Beck," and he went outside to the porch. On the lawn, Gus looked up from the bone he was working on, and his tail wagged happily. Seth went over to him and patted the Lab's head.

He said with some determination to Becca, "He's *not* going anywhere but home, Beck."

"I know it's important," she replied. "It's what he'd want."

"We got to get him here fast. If we don't, my uncle's going to come over with his polished shoes and his sports jacket and his razor cut hair and believe me he's going to have a calculator in his pocket. You ask me, he'll be looking at the house to sell it and then we'll be done for, especially if Grand isn't sitting on the front porch when he shows up."

5

The work on Ralph Darrow's house was going to take two weekends. Becca and Seth had first assumed one weekend would do it. But when they had all the supplies gathered and when they stood together outside Ralph's house, having a look at the scope of the work they'd taken on, they had to admit it couldn't be accomplished in the two and a third days they had blocked out for it. There was too much to be done, and a lot of it had to be accomplished out-of-doors, where daylight in January was in short supply.

"Sheesh," had been Seth's reaction, and although his thoughts were fuller, they made the same point. *No way José* had been foremost in his mind, followed by . . . *I don't do this and he ends up getting booted because that's what she'll do to him depend on it.*

Becca was pleased by the amount of whispering she picked up from Seth as they stood together. Time was that she'd only heard fragments. Working with Diana Kinsale to block out people's whispers when she didn't want to hear them was also improving her ability to hear them when she wished to do so.

"We can make a serious dent in it, can't we?" she asked Seth.

"S'pose," he said.

"Then what's left, you and I can do next weekend. Prynne'll come back, I bet."

Prynne was Seth's girlfriend: Hester Prynne Haring. She

was one of Seth's fellow musicians, and she'd grown up west of Whidbey Island in the vicinity of the Hood Canal, which stretched its length between the Kitsap and Olympic peninsulas. She and Seth had been together for several months now, and from what Becca had picked up from whispers, things were pretty serious. At least that was the case on Seth's part. On Prynne's part . . . Becca wasn't so sure.

Prynne came out of the house, followed by Jenn McDaniels and Squat Cooper. Squat was wearing a BOB THE BUILDER baseball cap over his thick, rust-colored hair, and somewhere he'd found a pair of workman's overalls to go with it. He'd scored tools from his mom's garage as well, leftovers from before his dad had deserted the family for his receptionist. Despite his appearance as a worker, Squat represented the brains of the group. The rest of them represented the brawn.

That included Derric, who was up above on the area where the driveway would go in. The trees there had been felled and hauled off by professionals. The profits from selling the downed wood to a lumber mill were being used to buy what they needed to fix Ralph's house. Two trees, however, had been left where they'd fallen. Seth's plan was that they would be turned into firewood for his grandfather. They needed to be sawed into manageable lengths, chopped into fireplace logs, and set in covered stacks to dry. Derric had asked for this project. Becca could tell from the roaring of the chainsaw that he was deep into it as the rest of them gathered on the front porch of the house.

It was a frigid day. Seth's words came out in puffs of vapor as he assigned them their tasks.

"Jenn and Squat," he said, "you're with me on the ramp. Beck and Prynne, you're doing all the rails for the house. They're already cut but they need to be stained. The brackets are ready, too. We got stainless steel for the shower, and those're in the downstairs bathroom ready to mount. Everything else is in Grand's shop. Everyone okay with that?"

"We live to serve," was how Squat put it. He extended his arm to Jenn, adding, "Shall we, dearest?"

"Don't make me hurl," she replied with a roll of her eyes.

Becca and Prynne headed for Ralph Darrow's shop, which stood at the foot of the hill down which the new driveway would descend. Overhung with a winter-bare wisteria, the shop wasn't a large building, but it had served Ralph well. It was the first structure he'd put onto his property, and from it he'd built the entire house in which he and wife had lived.

Inside, Becca and Prynne found the rails that the house needed. They were stacked along one wall in varying sizes, and on them was taped the location of their installation. Brackets to hold them sat on the workbench. These were wrought iron: simple, without ornament, and made by one of the island blacksmiths.

Prynne looked at the scope of their work and said to Becca, "We got the better deal. Sometimes it's useful to have only one eye. Otherwise, I'd be outside pounding a hammer, I bet."

Becca was switching on the two portable heaters. It seemed even colder in the building than it was outside. She turned to see Prynne popping out her false eye and pulling from the pocket of her long wool skirt a small box and the piratical patch she wore when she didn't have the glass eye in her empty socket. She stored the glass eye inside the box, positioned the eye patch where it belonged, and fastened the band that held it in place.

"Don't want to get sawdust in the old socket," she said in answer to Becca's unasked question.

"You're nice to help us," Becca told her.

"Well, Seth's my guy," Prynne said.

Becca nodded, but the truth was, she wasn't so sure. Earlier, when Seth and Prynne had entered Ralph's house in advance of Derric, Jenn, and Squat, she'd hugged hello to both of them. When her hands touched Prynne, she'd had a flash of an image. It had lasted two seconds, perhaps a little longer. But it was enough for her to see a bearded and bony guy looking up from a cluttered table, his eyebrows raised and a smile on his face. Sly, the smile seemed. Knowing as well. Becca felt uneasy when she saw him. She had glanced between Seth and Prynne, and she'd tried to read the level of comfort and trust they had in each other. But that was an impossibility. She might be able to hear their whispers, and she might be able to see through their eyes a previous moment they'd lived through. But that was it.

Now, she and Prynne set out to do their assigned task. There were two cans of stain to make the railing match the woodwork in the house. Becca opened one of them as Prynne brought two of the rails to the workbench. They worked in silence for a couple of minutes, a silence broken by the periodic roar of the chainsaw and Seth's voice outside Ralph's shop, telling Squat and Jenn what they needed to do to help him build the ramp. Since he'd already put the posts in, they heard him say, they had to frame out the structure. Grand would have to be able to walk up and down it and he'd also have to be able to be pushed in a wheelchair on occasion, so the degree of the slope . . .

"He sure loves that guy," Prynne murmured. "Working all week on construction and then coming here to do more? He's tough."

"He wants Grand home," Becca said.

Prynne dipped her rag into the stain and began applying

it. "I didn't get to meet him before . . . you know . . . before the stroke."

"He's great."

"Got to be. Nice that you get to stay here, too. I mean, nice that he lets you. Lots of old people . . . that'd sort of be the last thing they'd want, taking in some teenager they don't really know. How'd it happen?"

Becca had replaced her earbud when Prynne and the other two kids had come out of the house. That many people in her immediate vicinity still proved too much for her to block out. But now she eased the earbud from her ear, the better to pick up what Prynne might be thinking about Becca King and her advent on the island.

Becca went with a slight variation of her original story: She'd come north from San Luis Obispo in California to live with her "aunt Debbie" at the Cliff Motel in Langley because her relationship with her mom wasn't so hot. But things hadn't worked out with her aunt, and she'd ended up here at Ralph's because she knew Seth from his job at the Star Store grocery in town. "Where he used to work before construction," she told Prynne. "He pretty much rescued me."

"I know a *lot* about things not working out with relatives, that's for sure," Prynne said frankly when she'd heard the story. She confided that she'd moved out of her parents' home for just that reason. Port Gamble, she said, had to be the *worst* place on the planet to grow up. "You ever been there?" she asked Becca. When Becca shook her head, Prynne said, "It's Nowheresville. There's *nothing* nearby. I do not lie. I hate it there." *If I'd never lived there I wouldn't be no way I'm not thinking about that today.*

Becca gave her a curious look. Thinking about what? was what she wondered. What she said was "Bummer," and she tried to hear more. She even tried her luck touching

Prynne's arm when she told Prynne she was going to the house to make the sandwiches for lunch after nearly three hours of staining. But nothing else came from Prynne except a brief moment of her fiddle music.

Becca was assembling sandwiches for everyone when the roar of the chainsaw up on the new driveway stopped. She figured Derric was breaking for lunch, and Squat's and Jenn's entry to the house followed by Seth and Prynne seemed to support this. Seth went to the fridge and brought out the pasta salad while Jenn and Squat did what they usually did, which was spar verbally. In this case, the sparring had to do with Jenn's calf muscles. Squat pointed out to her the dangers of becoming too studly. Jenn pointed out to him how little she cared. She strode to the window as the others began loading the table with chips, cookies, fruit, and drinks.

She said, "There's some woman coming down the trail, Seth. Wow, that's seriously dumb footwear. She's going to . . . Whoops. Ooooh. That's hard on the ass."

Dumb footwear equated to one person, and it wasn't long before they heard the staccato sound of Brenda Sloan's boot heels on the front steps over which the ramp was in the process of being built. She marched across the porch and flung open the door. She took in all of them, and Becca thought the course of wisdom was to remove her earbud. She did so as Brenda Sloan said, "What the hell is going on? And who is that black kid up in the forest?"

The atmosphere was suddenly rife with whispers. *Man what a bitch . . . who's she think . . . when Mike sees this he's going to understand why . . . better call Dad . . .* were just some of them. Diana Kinsale would have called this the perfect opportunity to practice *Empty of all there is,* but Becca didn't think that would be the most useful route to take.

Seth was saying, "That 'black kid in the forest' is the undersheriff's son."

"Don't try to impress me," Brenda said. "*Or* intimidate me. Now who *are* you people and what are you doing in my father's house?"

"It's pretty obvious," Seth replied. "We're getting it ready for Grand."

"How dare you even think you can go ahead when nothing's been decided. A twenty-year-old doesn't get to determine what happens to *my* father."

"Grand is Dad's father, too, and Dad says Grand stays here." *Or he will* came after that, which told Becca volumes. She learned less from the rest flying around the room: *Bitch on wheels . . . trespassing . . . all I need after not making money anyway . . . lying to me* and *maybe back to Port Townsend now.*

"We'll see about *that*," Brenda said.

The door's flying open stopped Seth from replying. A well-dressed man walked in, and he had Derric by the arm in a way that suggested he'd dragged him down from the driveway. He said, "D'you want to tell me who the *hell* this thug is and what he's doing ripping off Ralph's trees?"

It was a jaw-dropping moment. Everyone went silent. Becca shoved her earbud back into her ear. She didn't want anything more to come at her. Derric's face was enough. His expression. His eyes.

Seth said acidly, "He's our friend, Uncle Mike. And Sheriff Mathieson's son."

Mike dropped Derric's arm like a branch on fire. "Why the hell didn't you tell me when I asked you?" he demanded of Derric.

Becca didn't need to be without the AUD box to understand what Derric was thinking. *Because I'm black* was on his face. *Because of what you thought because I'm black.*

Mike Sloan looked around. He seemed to take in the markings on the wall that indicated where the handrails were going to be placed. Obviously, he'd already seen the early stages of the ramp to the porch. He said, "You're completely reducing the value of this place. Trees going down, turning this into a house for the handicapped. D'you have *any* idea what that does to its sale price?"

"Doesn't matter," Seth said. "Grand's not selling."

6

Seth put his arm around Prynne to keep her warm. They were at the dock, outside of the waiting area, having left it when the ferry from Port Townsend made its turn around the mass of Admiralty Head and began crawling through the near waters of Admiralty Bay. All lights were blazing welcomingly upon it. Prynne said, "Finally." She sounded relieved. But Seth didn't want her to leave the island.

He said, "Still wish you'd spend the night."

She pulled her knitted cap down over her mass of hair, giving him a smile and scooting even closer for warmth. "Your parents would really love that," she told him.

"They'd be cool with it," he said. "They like you. Plus they already *know* me and you. . . . You know. . . . Whatever. They wouldn't care."

"You mean they wouldn't care if we slept together."

Seth felt his skin get hot with a blush that went from up his chest and onto his neck and his cheeks. "Well, yeah. No big deal to them."

"Parents can be less cool than you think, especially when it comes to kids hooking up right under their noses."

"Yeah, but like I said, they *know* about me and you."

"And like *I* said, you better check it out with them. Anyway, who wants the pressure?"

Seth was watching the ferry maneuver slowly into the dock. Other walk-on passengers came out of the warmth of the waiting room and into the dark and frigid air. The wind had died down and the sky was clear, heavy gusts having blown away the cloud cover. But without the cloud cover, the temperature had dropped further. With the least precipitation, there would be snow. He said, "What pressure?"

"Pressure at breakfast. Like, I'm not exactly ready to face your mom and dad over the granola, you know? Anyway, I got to get home to my peeps. I told them I'd be back."

Prynne's peeps were her three roommates: musicians like her. They were also all guys. Seth didn't like this, but he coped with the fact of it as best he could. He also coped with the fact that in the last month Prynne had moved from her family's home to Port Townsend without even telling him. He felt odd about this and odder still that she'd not yet invited him over to her place. Because of this and because he'd still not met her housemates – not to mention her parents – he said, "When do I get to meet these guys? It sucks, you know."

"That my roommates are guys? The only sucky part is the smell. *What* is it about guys' shoes? I have to burn scented candles so the house doesn't reek. And the idea of doing laundry? Totally a foreign concept to them."

"I still want to meet them," Seth told her. "Wouldn't mind meeting your parents either."

"I'll try to get them to come to Port Townsend, but I got to tell you: they hardly ever go anywhere. I got no clue why they stay in Port Gamble. I mean, there's peace and tranquility, and there's living in a total backwater."

The cars began to roll off the ferry. More cars waited on the Whidbey side to make the journey across Admiralty Inlet. Weekend night, and people wanted to head to the Olympic Peninsula for a few days. It was storm watching season, and a popular activity was to book into a cabin along the Pacific Ocean, where waves could rise to twenty feet or more.

"I could come over with you right now," Seth offered. "I could even spend the night."

"What about Gus? You'd just leave him in the VW wondering where you went?"

"I'd go get him. He could go, too. Why d'you have to go back tonight anyway? If we're working on Grand's house, I need you here."

"I'll be back tomorrow. As for tonight . . . Look, I just need to get home and so do you. We both need to relax for a while. This thing with your aunt and her husband . . . It's too intense for me. I bet you they're going to be at your dad's house when you get there."

Seth homed in on the word *relax*. When Prynne said that, he knew it was just another way of saying that she wanted to get high. That didn't bother him. Weed was legal in the state. She was close to being the right age to buy it, too. But that she couldn't figure out another way to relax . . . That *was* a big deal to him, although he wasn't sure why. He lied about it, though, saying, "You can do weed at my place, you know. Mom and Dad won't care. They wouldn't want it in the house, but outside, it'd be okay."

"I'm not going to freeze my ass off smoking outside, bud. And anyway, how okay would it be with you?"

Truth was, Seth didn't like her stoned. He didn't smoke weed himself because it made his learning disabilities worse: causing him more difficulty with reading, writing, or even being able to add or subtract. So early on, he'd learned that weed wasn't right for him. He didn't do it, and he had to admit that despite saying he could go back to Port Townsend with Prynne, he didn't really want to be there when she and her roommates were toking up.

"I'll handle it," he said. "And Gus'll be all right. He'll just sleep. Compromise, okay?"

The cars in the waiting lot began to start their engines. The waiting walk-ons stirred as one of the dock workers moved into position to allow them onto the ferry. Prynne said, "You wouldn't like it at my place, Seth. These guys . . . they do it pretty heavy. Anway I'll be back tomorrow, like I said. I'll come as early as I can."

Seth had to be okay with that. He drew her to him, kissed her goodbye, made sure the kiss showed her he would miss her. He felt her fingers play with his ponytail. She tugged on it playfully, whispered goodbye against his lips, and then was gone with a wave as the line of walk-ons moved forward.

He watched her go. He had a feeling that there was something not quite right about their conversation, but he couldn't put his finger on what it was. So he told himself he was being a dumbnut, he was smothering her, and he needed to back off. But he wasn't able to reach a point of believing that. Even saying Prynne was just being Prynne didn't do much good.

He waited till the ferry moved away from the dock before he went back to his old VW. Gus greeted him like a long-lost litter mate, his tail thumping in anticipation. Seth reached for the glove compartment and its contents: dog bones the size of shoes. He gave one to the Lab. Gus crunched it happily.

There was little traffic on the drive south to Seth's parents' house. It was over twenty miles, but with only two traffic lights and an eye on the speed limit, it didn't take Seth long to get there. He kept on alert for deer and other critters. All was still, though, and he made it without incident to an intersection where the highway ran west to east and a road called Coles ran north and south.

He turned onto the south branch. A wetland to the right created a good-sized pond edged with winter-dead grasses and reeds. To the left, a strip of forest formed a curtain of Douglas firs, alders, and branch-drooping cedars that created a barrier between him and the broad fertile bowl of Maxwelton Valley. His parents lived at the very end of this road, in a house that Rich Darrow had built many years ago. It stood on two acres, and the land also accommodated a refurbished barn, where Rich did his glass blowing, and a small studio, where Amy Darrow did her weaving, her knitting, and her flat-surface design projects. These two buildings adjoined each other and were separated from the house by the goat pen, the vegetable garden, and a wide strip of land where a Lexus SUV was parked.

Seth knew what it meant that his aunt and uncle were inside his parents' house. So he was going to need a moment to center himself before facing what was probably going to be a family firestorm.

He parked behind the SUV, let Gus out, and followed the Lab to his usual spot for sniffing, peeing, and all the rest. This vantage point on his father's property looked out in the darkness at the lights from the scattering of buildings – farmhouses and barns – that formed an enclave across the valley called Midvale Corner. Between where he stood and that tiny community lay a placid shield of water that was Miller Lake. It wasn't large, but it reflected the wind-cleared sky, and so it looked in the night like a miniature, earthbound Milky Way.

Gus snuffled. Seth waited. He imagined he could hear raised voices from within his parents' house.

When the dog had done all he intended to do and was unable to scare up a rabbit to chase, Seth told him to come. Gus hesitated, but when Seth said his name sharply, the Lab seemed to decide that obedience might serve him well.

He loped back to join Seth, and they went to the house. They entered into the middle of an argument, just as Seth had figured they would. Gus sought his bed. Seth couldn't blame him. He wished he could have done the same.

Everything was as it usually was when his aunt came to call. The house was small; all rooms save the bedrooms opened onto each other. So Seth could take everything in with a glance. Mike Sloan was sitting on the sofa, which he'd probably brushed free of cat fur before depositing his well-dressed butt on it. Seth's dad, Rich, was sitting backward on one of the dining chairs, his arms resting on its back. Seth's mom, Amy, was leaning against a counter in the kitchen, looking seriously pale. Brenda was pacing and waving her arms. No surprise there, Seth thought. It was what Aunt Brenda did.

Seth's immediate concern was for his mom. She'd had emergency surgery just two weeks earlier, when her bowel had become bizarrely twisted, leaving her a weeping lump of pain on her bedroom floor at 2:00 a.m. Seth didn't know how that kind of thing happened to someone, and he didn't care. He just wanted his mom to get better. So did his dad. She needed to concentrate on healing, and anything that took her mind away from that was something that Rich and Seth didn't want in the house.

Like Aunt Brenda and Uncle Mike, Seth thought. Like Aunt Brenda doing what she was doing at the moment, which was loudly demanding, "And who exactly is supposed to take care of him when he gets home? Are you going to do it, because it can't be Amy. She can barely move. She won't be able to lift a thing for months, so how d'you expect—"

"Amy's not involved in this," Rich Darrow said.

"Then who is? You? Seth? You can't take care of him, and he needs taking care of. We saw him today. He's not making progress. The light's completely gone from his eyes. He knows he's not going to get any better than he is right now."

"He will if he knows he's going home," Seth put in.

Brenda ignored him and said to her brother, "You're holding that out like a carrot on a stick: telling him he'll be able to go home when you know he can't. That's cruel. To lie like that to Dad . . . Plus to allow your son to carry on this . . . this project or whatever it is on Dad's house . . . I don't agree to it. I *never* agreed to it."

"He needs to go home, Bren," Rich Darrow said wearily. "And there are aides who'll be trained to help him."

"And who intends to monitor these aides? Who's planning to be there to make sure they aren't . . . You *know* what those people can be like. They worm their way into a sick person's life and pretty soon he's signed everything over to them!"

"You're getting carried away," Rich said.

"Oh really? When was the last time you saw him?" Brenda demanded. "Do you know how bad things have gotten? D'you have any clue how vulnerable he is?"

Amy stirred. She looked exhausted. "That's not fair, Brenda. Rich is there at least four times a week. If he can't go, Seth goes. Even when Rich *can* go, Seth goes."

"And what they do is fill his head with pipe dreams." She turned to Rich and said, "Have you tried to see if he understands what's going on? Mike and I were there for an hour today, and we got nothing from him."

"Grand knows who everyone is," Seth told her. "He knows me and he knows Dad. He knows Mom had surgery. He knows why she hasn't been there to see him. So maybe he just doesn't want to know *you*."

Mike Sloan said, "That mouth of yours is going to get you into real trouble, Seth."

Rich cut in quickly with, "Let me handle this, Seth."

Seth said, "She wants to sell the place, Dad. That's the *only* reason she came to the island. They don't want Grand home no matter what kind of care he has when he gets there. They went to see him to make sure he won't understand what they're up to and—"

Mike Sloan surged to his feet. Brenda said, "Mike . . ." and he said to Seth, "I'll advise you to shut up until you know what you're talking about."

But Seth went on. "They were there to check everything out, Dad, so they could come up with a price. Only they didn't expect to find me there working."

"You have no idea why we were there. And you have no permission to alter my father's house." Brenda swung on Rich. "Are you behind what he's doing? Have you seen what he's doing?"

Rich rose but it wasn't in anger. He said reasonably, "Bren, we're not going to end up on the same page about this, so we need to let it go for now. And yes, I know what Seth's doing to the house: exactly what the health care specialist told us to do." He extended his hands, palm up, in one of those help-me-understand-this gestures. He said, "You *knew* this was going to happen, so I don't get all the drama."

"He can't live alone," Brenda said. "You damn well know it."

"He won't be living alone," Seth said. "Becca's there. She lives there, too. And if you're so freaked out about a home aide person getting too friendly with Grand, Becca can—"

"Oh yes, Becca," Brenda scoffed. "Your *sixteen-year-old* friend. She's going to keep an eye on things, is she? How is she supposed to do that?" She turned to Rich. "Dad needs to be moved to a place where he can be taken care of, and where there's no chance that someone is going to take advantage of him."

"He's going to be taken care of," Seth insisted. "And no one's going to be able to take advantage of him."

"He'll have to be bathed and fed and dressed and undressed and taken to the bathroom," Brenda went on, as if Seth hadn't spoken. "He'll have medications he'll need to take and physical therapy he'll have to get to. He'll need nursing and a proper diet and whatever else, and assisted living will give him that. Are we going to have to go to court over this, Rich?"

"Brenda, please," Amy said. "You know we can't afford to fight this out in court."

"If that's the case," Brenda said with a smile, "maybe you ought to adjust your thinking as to what's actually good for my father."

It took Seth several days to work out how he could get Grand home and make sure he was well taken care of so that his aunt had no reason to take his father to court. The home health care aides were not a problem. The state of Washington had provisions that would help pay for that. It was the monitoring of those aides that was going to be trickier. Someone needed to do it in order to appease Brenda, and that was an expense no one in his family could afford except his aunt, who wasn't going to hand out a dime to help them.

During this time of tossing around ideas, he and his friends continued to work feverishly to get the house ready. The weather cooperated, so the ramp went up quickly. Inside the house, all of the handrails got securely placed. Ralph's belongings got moved from his bedroom above to Becca's below, and Becca's got moved up into his. All that was left was the completion of the driveway, and one of

Seth's fellow construction workers had signed on to do that, in exchange for Seth's paying for materials and gas. From the sale of the downed trees, there was money enough, so the driveway got professionally graded and a porous surface of stone was applied, which would harden over time. No one could accuse it of being anything less than perfect for getting Grand down to his house.

Having someone there twenty-four hours a day to make sure the home health aides didn't "take advantage" of Grand was trickier, naturally. Seth couldn't do it because he worked. His mom couldn't do it because she had six months of healing in front of her. His dad had to keep up with his glass blowing. Options, thus, were limited. But Seth saw a way, and after work one day, he caught the ferry to Port Townsend to begin the process of making it all happen.

Prynne didn't know he was coming. Seth figured he could kill two birds with one stone that way. He could not only spell out the plan to her, but he could also meet her roommates at last. Trouble was, he didn't have her address, only the knowledge that she now lived somewhere in the upper town, where Victorian homes, fishing bungalows, and getaway houses of Seattleites filled the streets. And there were many of those streets. He knew he couldn't drive up and down them in his VW, hoping to find the house Prynne lived in. But once he called her from the ferry dock, what was she going to do?

It turned out that what she wasn't going to do was invite him over. What she said when he announced that he was in the parking lot of the sporting goods store right next to the ferry dock was, "Here? I wish you'd let me know you were coming over, Seth. This isn't a good time. Why didn't you call me before you got on the ferry?"

He'd expected surprise, followed by delight. The surprise

was there, but not the other. He said, "I need to talk to you and I wanted it to be in person. There a problem with that?"

"Only that the guys are totally obliterated here. They can't even talk."

"That's okay, since I don't want to talk to them."

"You wouldn't like it. Two of them are practically comatose. Look, I'll meet you downtown."

"I don't get why—"

"Seth, I just told you. The guys are loaded. Why don't we meet at the coffeehouse? I can be there in less than ten minutes."

He knew which coffeehouse she meant. Although this was the land of coffeehouses, and although in most towns in Washington you couldn't walk half a block without running into two of them, in Port Townsend there was only one. Several places sold espresso, of course. But when it came to a real coffeehouse . . . It was where he'd first heard Prynne playing her fiddle.

He said okay. If she didn't give him her address there was no other way he was going to see her. So he rumbled out of the parking lot, telling Gus that a wait in the car was in store for him. The Lab did his tail-thumping bit. He'd just spent the entire day dashing around the construction site where Seth was working. He'd had the companionship of two other dogs. He was ready for a nap.

The coffeehouse was practically at the end of Port Townsend's main street of old brick buildings housing boutiques, antiques shops, and art galleries. It took up space in one of the ancient warehouses not far from the dock where fishing boats still went into Puget Sound. It was exactly what a coffeehouse should be: furnished with slouching sofas and tattered easy chairs, heated by a wood-pellet stove, dimly lit. Its walls were painted oxblood and

its floor was beaten-up reclaimed lumber. Posters covered
it, commemorating ancient rock bands and advertising
appearances of newcomers.

When Seth walked in, there was music playing, sort of
an aimless strumming on a guitar. It was, he saw, coming
from a guy with tattoos covering his neck and his hands.
When he looked up at the rush of cold air, Seth saw he'd
also had himself inked with kiss me across his forehead. He
was completely stoned.

Looking around, Seth picked up on the fact that other
stoners were in the coffeehouse. Even the barista looked
halfway gone. He wondered why he'd not noticed any of
this the only other time he'd been in the place. But Prynne,
he decided, was the answer to that. He'd been there to hear
her play, and once he'd caught sight of her, he hadn't noticed
another thing.

He ordered a drip coffee for himself and a decaf skinny
latte for Prynne. He was sitting at a table with these and a
bran muffin when she breezed in the door. Before he could
stand or say hi, two of the stoners called out, "Prynne, hey"
and "Here comes trouble," this with a laugh. Prynne gave
them a smile and a raised-eyebrow nod before she walked
over to Seth and put her arms around him. She kissed him
and said, "My dude, my man. You look banged up. Hard
day at work?"

She stepped back and eyed the small table with its offering
of muffin and latte. She dropped into a chair and said,
"Sorry for being such a pig on the phone. It's just that the
guys . . . It wouldn't've been a good scene."

She picked up her latte and saluted him with it. He picked
up his coffee to do the same. She winked at him and he
wanted to smile at her. But he could tell that she, too, was
stoned.

He decided to ignore it. There was something more

important than telling her she probably shouldn't get on her Vespa if she'd just done weed.

His face must have given him away, though, because Prynne said, "Seth. Come on. You know I smoke weed. Just because you don't, it doesn't mean—"

"Weed whacks me out. I can't even read when I do it."

"Well, that's not the case for me, okay? And since I don't do it in front of you, you need to ease off if you just show up, without telling me you're coming, and I'm stoned."

He said, "Yeah. Okay, okay," but the truth was that she reeked of weed. It was like she'd taken a bath in it. He said, "You been doping all day?"

"Seth, *you* came *here*. I didn't invite you. I smoke with the guys and it's no big deal."

"What's that mean anyway? 'With the guys.' And why don't you want me to meet them?"

Prynne set down her latte. She observed him with her good eye. She said, "Is that what we're going to talk about? 'Cause if it is, I'm out of here. I love you, and I don't want to fight with you."

She was right. Going in that direction was stupid, and it wasn't why he'd come. He said, "Sorry. I'm blowing it." He went on to tell her the plan.

He had a proposition for her, he said. It had to do with the care of his grandfather. Grand was coming home, no doubt of that. There would be home health care aides to help him out. But his family wanted someone to be there to make sure they treated Grand right because sometimes when someone was old and vulnerable and not able to talk right . . . Prynne got that, huh?

"Sure," Prynne said, although she cocked her head and Seth could tell she was wondering where this was leading.

Becca was there to make sure everything was okay from her after-school hours until the next morning, Seth told her. He himself could be there to make sure everything was okay on weekends. But on weekdays . . . from seven in the morning till Becca returned after school, someone else had to be there. Seth hoped it would be Prynne.

She said, "You mean to go back and forth from here to Whidbey every day? I can't afford that, Seth. I don't have money for the gas, not to mention for the ferry."

"That's not what I'm thinking," he told her.

"Then what? You planning to pick me up every day and cart me to your grandfather's place and then bring me back? How're you going to do that and still work?"

Seth pointed out to her that she didn't have a regular job and that she currently relied on her gigs with the fiddle to make money. He said to her, "What if we paid you? It would only be minimum wage, but you wouldn't have expenses because you could stay right on Whidbey at my parents' place."

"Where? On that sleeping porch?"

"In my bedroom. We'll share it. You'd get room and board and minimum wage and all you have to do is keep an eye on how things're going with Grand during the day. You'd just watch out for him. Sort of make sure the home care person's doing the job. You could take him to PT, too, and help him practice whatever they tell him that he's s'posed to practice. You could make him lunch if the aide's doing something else, but that's it. Really, Prynne, it's no big deal."

"Uh . . . how am I supposed to get him to PT, Seth? On the back of the Vespa?"

"You can use his truck."

"And how am I supposed to get him inside the truck?"

Seth considered this. To this problem, there was a simple solution. "We'll trade. You take Sammy—"

Prynne smiled. "Wait! You'll let me drive your V-dub?

Your perfectly restored, pristine, polished, always washed 1965 V-dub?"

He smiled back. "Hard to resist, huh? Yeah, you can drive Sammy and I'll take Grand's truck."

She cocked her head. "Do your parents know about all this? Me moving into their house, showing up for meals, sharing a bedroom with you? How are they going to feel about that?"

"Sheesh, Prynne. They didn't even get married till after I was born, and my sister's *older* than me, okay? Figure that one out. And besides . . ." He reached for her hand, although his own was rough with work. But she didn't seem to mind and she laced their fingers together. "I want you to be on Whidbey," Seth told her.

She seemed to be studying their joined hands, and at first Seth thought she wasn't going to reply. He thought he'd misread her somehow, that her feelings for him weren't as strong as his were for her. When she said "Can I have a couple of days to decide?" he was disappointed, and he knew his face showed it. He said, "Why? Don't you want to be with me?"

"I don't know how it'd all work out. I mean, such as it is, I have a life here."

"You'd have one on Whidbey, too. You'd have more of a life because we'd be together."

"In your parents' house," she reminded him.

"Just at first."

"I need a couple of days. And you need to go over all this with your parents."

"Okay," he said. "A couple of days."

But he felt uneasy about her hesitation.

7

The following Monday Jenn McDaniels was running the trails behind South Whidbey High School. The school backed up to a large community park: a vast area of forest that was accompanied by a concrete skateboard bowl with jumps and rails, a playground for little ones, a baseball diamond, and enormous open lawns that were used for soccer. The forested section was filled with trails, and here the various athletic teams at the high school ran. Jenn's team was girls' soccer, varsity level. She was the center midfielder, and although soccer season was finished, it was her intention to make it onto the All Island Girls' Soccer team, whose tryouts were in May this year. She'd tried out during the previous year, but she hadn't put enough effort into her prep, so she hadn't made it past the first cut. That *wasn't* going to happen this time around. The All Island team was her key to an athletic scholarship. An athletic scholarship was her key to going to college. If she didn't go to college, she'd have nothing in her future but finding a lousy job on Whidbey, living at home, fighting with her mom about religion, and listening to her read the Bible aloud, special emphasis on Sodom and Gomorrah.

She was on her eighth time around the Waterman Loop, hurtling along the north side of the upper field where a fellow member of the high school team, a girl called Cynthia Richardson, was still working on her goalie skills. She'd been there each time Jenn had run past, in the company of another girl: Lexie Ovanov. Lexie wasn't a member of the soccer team, so she was pathetic at keeping the ball away from Cynthia. It didn't seem to matter to either of them, though, since every time Jenn dashed by, they were yelling at each other and shrieking with laughter at how bad Lexie was.

Jenn wasn't sure what the point was. It wasn't like Cynthia actually needed to train. She'd made the All Island team every year since ninth grade. She was a super player. She was also tough not to notice. She was five foot ten, she was blond, she was blue eyed, and she had a perfect complexion. She'd had a 4.0 average probably since kindergarten, and for that same amount of time she'd been one of the most popular girls in South Whidbey School District. So when she was elected homecoming queen, no one batted an eye. It was, after all, expected. But what wasn't expected was Cynthia taking Lexie Ovanov as her date to the homecoming dance. That had *definitely* made a statement.

"You are totally pathetic!" Jenn heard Cynthia call out to Lexie on a burst of laugher. "*Kick* the ball, dummy. This isn't bowling."

"Kiss my butt," was Lexie's reply.

"Bring it over here," Cynthia called out.

Jenn ran on, past the field, into the woods, down the slope, under the trees. She came out at the top parking lot where Becca King was waiting for her, a stopwatch in one hand and a clipboard in the other. Becca clicked the stopwatch and made a note. Jenn stumbled to a stop, breathing hard.

"Better," Becca said.

"How much?"

Becca examined the clipboard and did the math. "Two point five seconds."

"That sucks."

"Isn't the point to keep shaving off seconds?"

"The point is not to be wrecked at the end of eight laps."

Becca scratched her cheek and observed Jenn thoughtfully. "Well, it's not like I didn't tell you to give up smoking."

"I gave it up!"

"When? Last week?"

"Very funny." Jenn walked to a bench and plopped down. From there, she examined her friend. "You and my mom would get along great," she told Becca. "You're both holier than holy."

Becca walked over to join her. "You mean I get into heaven just 'cause I don't smoke? How cool is that!" She laughed. "Does it mean that otherwise I c'n be as bad as I want to be? 'Cause if it does, I'm signing up."

"Great. Speaking in tongues will be your future," Jenn told her.

"I'd sort of prefer to use my tongue for other stuff."

"You, girl, are *very* bad." Jenn bent to retie her shoes. They were old and filthy, a score from Good Cheer Thrift Store down in Langley. She'd tried to clean them up about six times but had given up the effort. She knew she needed to replace them, but as always, she lacked the funds.

Becca seemed to know what she was thinking. She said, "How's the job hunt going?"

"It's not. I'd become a streetwalker if someone was actually out on the streets after five p.m. around here. What about you?"

"Nothing. There might be something with Mr. Darrow, but I don't know yet."

"You still alone at Mr. Darrow's house?" Jenn sat back up, saw Becca nod, and said, "Ooohhh, that must be nice for you and Derric." Jenn laughed when she saw the color sweep into Becca's cheeks. "So?" she encouraged her.

"So . . . what?"

"Come on. You're in a dream situation. You guys doing it?"

Becca's eyes widened. "Jenn!"

"What? Not my business? It's always the business of the BFF to know what the other BFF is up to. Come on. Give. Your secrets are totally safe with me."

"Don't you have a shower to take?" Becca gestured vaguely in the direction of the high school, which sat beyond two baseball diamonds, the skateboard area, and the children's playground.

"That must mean yes."

"No. It doesn't. I'm not ready."

"To spill?"

"To have sex with Derric. Not the whole thing, I mean."

Jenn rose from the bench. She stretched. As she did, she said to Becca, "Aren't you worried he'll do it with someone else? I mean, he's a guy. He's . . . What is he anyway? Seventeen?"

"Eighteen."

"Eighteen? Geez, in some cultures he'd already be married. *Aren't* you worried?"

"About him doing it with someone else?" Becca hooked up her ear thingy. She fiddled with the connection to the iPod on her waist. "He already did."

Jenn felt her eyes bug out. "No way."

"Way."

"But he's, like, supremely into you. Now you *have* to put out. Are you . . . I mean . . . Are you doing anything at all?"

Becca became red to the roots of her hair. She said, "Jenn!"

"Okay. Okay. Just tell me this: naked or not."

"Sometimes. And that's all I'm saying. I don't bug you about your love life."

Jenn guffawed and slapped Becca on the back. "Like I have one?" was her response.

They parted ways back at the school. Becca headed for her bike in the stands in front; Jenn made her way to the girls' locker room. Inside, she heard the showers running and over the sound of the water, singing. The choice of tune was "I Will Survive," and Cynthia and Lexie were belting it out, with interruptions of "That's not how it goes!" "Is too!" "Is not!" And then laughter and laughter. Those two were very big on laughter.

Jenn went to her locker. She grabbed her towel and headed toward the showers herself. When she got there, it was to see Cynthia and Lexie soaping each other's bodies, though. She stopped dead because they'd also fallen silent. Before she could turn away and make tracks out of there, they stopped soaping and they started kissing. Jenn beat a retreat as fast as she could.

At this hour, the only way to get home was the island transit bus. Once Jenn had her backpack of homework, she plodded across the school's front parking lot and out to the shelter along Maxwelton Road. She was waiting there when a silver Honda with Seahawks stickers all over the driver's door came out of the parking lot and rolled her way.

Cynthia was driving. Lexie was in the passenger seat. Cynthia lowered her window and called out, "Jenn! You need a ride?"

The last thing Jenn wanted – aside from being naked with those two – was to be in a car with them. She said, "Nah. It's okay. The bus'll be here in a couple of minutes."

"You sure?"

"Yep. Thanks, though."

"We saw you on the trail," Cynthia called back. "Looking good. Bye!"

Then she was gone and Jenn could breathe again. The two girls drove off in the opposite direction, toward Langley. It was just as well, Jenn thought, that she hadn't accepted Cynthia's offer because it would have taken the girl way the hell out of her way.

Jenn had to ride two different bus routes to get home from the high school. This meant a wait in the wind and in the rain that had begun to spit from the sky when she alighted from the first bus, hung around for a bus from another route, and then alighted once again at a triangle of rough, cabin-like buildings that formed a hobbit-sized commercial area called Bailey's Corner. She could have ridden the second bus farther at that point, in order to end up closer to her home, but she wanted to talk to the proprietor of the small market that was the main feature of the Corner, and she knew from experience that he would be there till seven o'clock when he shut down for the night.

So she dodged through the rain and, with her backpack of homework slung over one shoulder, she dashed to the market. The door banged closed behind her.

Tiny Holiday was behind the counter, and he was neither. The size of a Jeep, he possessed a funereal air that had long suggested to his customers a serious lack of vacation time on sun-drenched beaches or in snowy ski resorts. He was hunched over a magazine when Jenn entered the premises, and he hid this reading material beneath the counter in a furtive move that suggested the publication's questionable nature.

"Say what, Jenn?" was his greeting. "Whatcha need?"

"A job," she told him. "You been thinking any more about my proposal?"

"Big storm coming," was his reply, with a look directed outside into the darkness. Both of them could hear the wind howling, and a howling wind meant trees crashing onto the island roads and through people's roofs. "Your parents know you're out in this?"

"Course they know," Jenn told him, a marginal falsehood. Since she wasn't yet home from school, they knew she was *somewhere*. "So I'm wondering if you've thought about the job? See, I could do 'bout anything for you, only it has to be in the morning because I got soccer after school. Or I could come here *after* soccer and close up the place for you, and that way you could go home and have dinner with your family. You'd get home around six or even five-thirty if I get lucky with the buses. What d'you say?"

"Too dangerous," Tiny Holiday told her.

"What's too dangerous? Eating with your family? Why? Do they throw knives or something?"

He har-harred appreciatively but then said, "Too dangerous having a teenager here to close the place is what I mean. There's been break-ins all over South Whidbey and two armed robberies at the Wells Fargo over in Clinton. We got druggies living in the woods and coming out only when they need to score, and the only way they *can* score is with someone else's money. So the answer is still no."

Jenn was not about to be deterred. "What about early morning?" she said. "Druggies don't like to get up early."

Tiny rolled his eyes. "I'm not about to open this place any earlier than seven, girl."

"But there'd be customers. People on the way to the ferry. They'd buy coffee. They'd buy doughnuts. We could try it and see how it goes. I could open up for you at five. Or even four because of the early ferry."

He shook his head. "Not enough business, Jenn. I'd be paying you more than I'd be taking in." He raised his head as a loud *crack* indicated a heavy branch coming down nearby. He said, "You get home now. You can use the phone to call your dad to come pick you up if you'd like."

She didn't want that. She wanted a job. She shook her head and left the place after telling Tiny Holiday that she'd be fine. Her parents would be too busy anyway to have to come up from Possession Point.

Just outside the little market, Jenn dug inside her backpack for her flashlight. There were no street lights on the island roads, and once she left Bailey's Corner for the long walk to Possession Road, she'd be in complete darkness with only the wind and rain as companions.

She set off into a frenzy of storm gusts. It was long way home, and she wanted to kick her own butt for having gotten off the bus in order to talk to Tiny Holiday again.

She needed a job. Now. Yesterday. Whenever. She had to come up with the fee for the All Island team, and she also had to grab funds somewhere in order to purchase better shoes and decent equipment, none of which was going to be on sale at any of the thrift stores on the island.

It took forty minutes for her to make the walk home, but at last she reached the pockmarked driveway that led to her family's ramshackle house. It was on a property that had seen its heyday at least sixty years previously, and the features of this place were now piles of junk like old toilets and fishing nets and orange road cones, along with a single wide dump of a trailer that had been briefly occupied the previous year but was now as empty as her family's bank account.

Lights from a car came jostling toward her from the house. That would be her mom, Jenn figured. She stepped to one side, but her mom didn't pass. Instead, she halted the car, rolled down her window, and gave Jenn a look that took in her bedraggled appearance.

"Where on earth . . . ?" she began.

"Soccer practice, the island bus, and talking to Mr. Holiday about a job."

"Again? Jenn, honey, no means no."

"Sometimes it means ask me later."

"Not in this case, I'm afraid." Kate tapped her fingers on the steering wheel and frowned into the storm. She said, "I just got a call, so you'll need to help your father finish making dinner. It's easy enough. Hot dogs cut up, put into baked beans. You know your dad, though. Mr. Secret Ingredient. There's bread and canned corn, too."

"What about you? Coming back for dinner?"

Her mother shook her head. "Bible study tonight."

"Aren't you having anything to eat, then?"

"The Lord has other plans for me. I trust in Him and in His ways. For He is—"

"Yeah, yeah," Jenn said. "See you later."

She started to trudge off, but her mom went on with, "It wouldn't hurt you to become familiar with the Bible, Jennie."

Jenn ticked a salute at her. "It's on my to-do list."

Before her mother could make any further comment, Jenn headed in the direction of Possession Sound. Out of the darkness, lights began to emerge. They came from across the water, in the windows of the more expensive houses in the town of Mukilteo. They also came from the nearby shabby old building that was the house where Jenn had grown up.

Its special features were a listing front porch, sheets hung at the windows and inexpertly made into curtains, and siding with great splintered patches where the weather had worn completely through the paint. Near the house, Jenn's dad had his brew shed. Its lights were on, so she figured he hadn't gotten around to beginning the dinner yet. Typical of Bruce McDaniels, she thought. Between beer and baked beans, he'd always choose beer. Besides, this was yet another source of income for the family. His brews were popular, so he had to keep up with demand.

But when she opened the door, her father wasn't inside the shed. She sighed, switched off the light, and fastened the padlock on the door.

She found her dad where he was supposed to be. He stood in the kitchen with a completely unnecessary apron wrapped around him. He was doing something with a loaf of bread while Jenn's little brothers wrestled on the living room floor. They were in a dispute over the television remote, she saw. Pretty dumb, as they didn't have cable and had to rely on a completely inadequate antenna to pick up the two channels that they actually were able to watch.

Her father turned from the counter on which he was fashioning his creation. He said, "Jenn o' my heart! Home at last!" and his slurred voice suggested he'd been sampling brew again. He waved around himself in an expansive gesture that took in the kitchen. "Are you here to assist or just to admire?"

She walked over to see what he was doing, which was using cookie cutters shaped like whales and maple leaves to make fanciful shapes out of the bread. A lot of it was, however, going to waste. He also had the habanero sauce out along with a bag of hardened brown sugar. She sighed and said, "Want me to take over? Might be faster and those guys—" She jerked her head at her brothers. "They're not going to settle down till they eat."

"An answer to my prayers," Bruce said. "I shall advise your brothers that table setting might be in order."

Good luck with that, was what Jenn thought. She found the canned corn her mom had told her about. She stirred the baked beans with their chopped-up hot dogs. It was a meager enough meal, but sometimes they didn't even have this much. Then it would be pancakes for dinner. Syrup, no butter.

She hated her life.

8

When Becca looked out the window the following Sunday morning, what she saw was a mass of gray so thick that her field of vision ended at the poles holding up Ralph Darrow's front porch. There had been fog before during her time on Whidbey Island, but she'd not yet seen fog like this. Becca didn't even notice Derric till he was on the porch itself. He wore a heavy winter parka and a blue and lime-green ski cap with seahawks printed on the front of it. He wore gloves and boots as well. From this Becca understood that it was not only foggy outside. It was also bitterly cold.

Usually she attended church with Derric and his family, something she'd been doing since Christmas. After the service, their habit was to head to a coffee roaster deep in the woods where they enjoyed bantering over breakfast. But today Derric had claimed that he and Becca wanted instead to go over town, taking the ferry that would allow them to catch a movie in nearby Lynnwood. This wasn't the actual case, but there was no way that Derric would consider telling Dave and Rhonda Mathieson the truth.

Becca didn't like lying to them. But anything less than lying, Derric had argued, was going to make his parents suspicious. For the reality was that he had been invited to La Conner for Sunday lunch, and if he told them that, he would have to tell them who Jeff and Darla Vickland were. That would lead to him having to tell them how he'd become acquainted with a family all the way up in La Conner, which would lead to him having to bring up Rejoice.

He *could* have done this, naturally. But the problem was he'd already pointed out a different and older girl in a photograph of his days in an African orphanage, and he'd told his parents *she* was Rejoice, the object of a childhood crush. For Dave had come across a slew of unsent letters Derric had written to someone called Rejoice. His curiosity had been piqued by these letters, and he'd started to ask questions to which Derric had manufactured answers.

To Becca, the moment when Derric's parents started to ask him about Rejoice represented the moment he could have explained that he had a sister, that as a little boy of five years old, he'd not known to tell Children's Hope of Kampala that one of the mass of abandoned and orphaned children they'd picked up from an alley in the city was his sister. But whenever Becca brought this up, he countered with the fact that he *should* have told Children's Hope that the two-year-old girl was his sister. And since he hadn't, he didn't want to wreck the way his parents looked at him: both as their son and as a person.

"I was a selfish rat" was how he put it.

Her reply of "You were *five years old* when you first met Rhonda. There's no such thing as a five-year-old rat" never made any difference.

So today she just said that she didn't like lying to Dave and Rhonda. Derric's reply as they climbed into his Forester was, "I've been lying to them for the past nine years and even before that. Another lie isn't going to kill them *or* me. Don't you ever lie when it's the only thing to do?"

Becca didn't reply as she fastened her seat belt. The only response she could have made was the one she also couldn't make: Her entire life on Whidbey Island was a lie.

They rumbled from Newman onto Double Bluff Road

where the fog was so dense that they couldn't see the one hundred yards to the island highway. They crawled along, and Becca worried about what it was going to be like for Derric, driving all the way to La Conner, where the fog was probably going to be worse. He was planning to take the freeway to get there instead of driving up the island and crossing Deception Pass Bridge. He figured there would be less fog this way, and Becca could only hope he was right. He was also dropping Becca in Langley. She had work to do in the library there, using the library's Internet for a project in her graphic design class. At least, that was what she'd told Derric. It was, she explained, way too complicated to go any further into it than that.

Derric had said, "Why doesn't Mr. Darrow have Internet at his house? He could even do it through his phone, for God's sake."

To this she'd replied, "Because that would mean moving into the twenty-first century, and he's barely made it into the twentieth. I'm lucky he even *has* a phone, Der. He doesn't have a television."

"How're you feeling about Seth's plan?" he asked. "I got to say I don't like it much."

"We'll still be able to see each other," she pointed out. "Seth and Prynne'll come over when we have a date. And we can have study dates at Ralph's place, too. I think it'll work out okay."

Despite her words, Becca was uneasy. When Seth had phoned her to explain the scheme and to inform her that Prynne had agreed to come over to Whidbey in order to stay with Grand from seven till three every weekday, Becca had heard the pleasure in his voice. He wanted Prynne close to him, and now he had that. But this understanding had prompted Becca's recall of that quick vision she'd had from Prynne, the one that clearly showed another man who was part of her life. That smile of his . . . Becca remembered it all too well. It was knowing and pleased and something else, although she couldn't put a name to what that was.

At the library in Langley, the fog was so thick that Camano Island – just two miles across Saratoga Passage – was completely invisible, but you could make out the curve of First Street as well as the street that descended to a small marina at the bottom of the bluff upon which Langley sat. Derric pulled Becca's bike from the back of the car and set it on the pavement. He looked around, saying, "Maybe you should come with me. I don't like that you have to ride around in the fog."

"It'll be fine," she assured him. "Anyway, I wasn't invited."

"What're they going to do if I show up with you and say 'Oh hey, wasn't Becca invited, too?'"

"No worries, Der. If it gets worse, I can go over to the motel and wait it out. I'll play pirates with Josh and Barbies with Chloe."

"Doesn't *that* sound great?" he teased. He kissed her goodbye and Becca watched him drive off before she rolled her bike to a spot near the little city hall where she could safely lock it.

What she'd said to Derric about her need for the library's Internet had been completely true. But the reason for her need of the Internet? From start to finish, once again she had lied to him.

Becca knew she ought to feel guilty about her lies, since she kept preaching to Derric about lying to his parents. But she couldn't take the chance of telling him the truth. So for the past sixteen months she'd lived in a no man's land between the two poles of truth and falsehood, and she'd constantly reassured herself that revealing nothing to Derric about her life as Hannah Armstrong in San Diego protected him at the same time as it protected her.

There was no graphic design project. What there was, instead, was Becca's need to use one of the library's computers in order to log on to the Internet for a private reason.

Sunday morning was the perfect time, because Whidbey Island was thick with churches, and much of the population on the south end of the island attended them. There were three churches in the village alone, and within five miles of Langley, there had to be at least four more. Because of this, Sunday mornings rendered the village a ghost town. Only the village coffee roaster was open, along with the sole café that offered breakfast. Sidewalks were empty, and there was no one in the library except a middle-aged female librarian with pink-tipped pigtails working behind the desk.

Once seated at the computer farthest from this woman, Becca logged on to Google. She typed into this search engine the name of the person most responsible for her flight from San Diego: Jeff Corrie. He was her mom's fifth husband, the man to whom Laurel Armstrong had so dumbly revealed her daughter Hannah's ability to hear the broken-up thoughts of others. Why Laurel had done this when she'd never told any of her other four husbands was a question she had never answered. But her weakness throughout life had always been men – what else could five stepfathers possibly indicate? – and somehow her greatest weakness had been the last one she'd married, Jeff Corrie.

Hearing the thoughts of others equated reading minds. That was how Jeff Corrie had seen it, and this dubious skill of Hannah Armstrong's had been too much for him to resist. He had an investment firm that specialized in financial opportunities for senior citizens, and once he learned what his stepdaughter could do, he figured there was no better method to get those senior citizens to hand over their pensions than to know from the first what was on their minds. In this way, he could reassure them with facts, figures, and opportunities that looked to be surefire winners.

That was where his stepdaughter Hannah Armstrong had come in. Coffee maker, tea maker, mineral water provider, cookie deliverer, sandwich girl . . . She came in and out of the conference room where either Jeff or his partner, Connor, or both of them had met with their potential clients, and afterward she faithfully reported on what she'd heard in those clients' broken-up thoughts. She did this for three years as Jeff Corrie and his partner moved money here, there, and everywhere and made it next to impossible for the elderly to understand what was actually happening to their funds. Hannah Armstrong had not known about this part of the enterprise. She only knew she was helping old people to be less anxious about investing.

Then things fell apart one afternoon when Hannah heard among Jeff Corrie's whispers what she believed was his responsibility for the death of his partner. At that point, she'd told her mother the truth. At that point, she and Laurel had fled with a plan to drop Hannah off with a new identity on Whidbey Island where she would be in the care of Laurel's old friend Carol Quinn. With Hannah – now Becca King – safely tucked away, Laurel would lay a false trail to Nelson, BC, until it was safe and Jeff Corrie was himself also tucked away: in prison where he belonged.

It had all sounded so good, so easy, and so absolutely perfect. Indeed, the trip from San Diego to Washington State had all gone like a dream. But once on Whidbey Island, the newly born Becca King discovered that her mom's friend Carol had dropped dead of a heart attack minutes before she was supposed to leave her house to meet the ferry on which Becca was sailing. Laurel herself was, at that point, out of range of the throwaway cell phone she'd purchased for Becca, and she had remained out of range to this day. Thus Becca had been imprisoned on Whidbey Island for sixteen months, which included the day that she had discovered to her horror she'd misunderstood Jeff Corrie's whispers, for his partner Connor West was not dead at all.

A long list of newspaper articles posted to the Internet existed on the topic of Jeff Corrie and Connor West. These articles began with the disappearance of Connor West, gone without a trace in a situation that was highly suspicious: with a BLT half made on the countertop in his condo's kitchen, with the water running in the sink and a coffee carafe broken upon the floor. That had been the start of Jeff Corrie's troubles, which had only increased when a neighbor of his mentioned to the San Diego police that she hadn't seen Corrie's stepdaughter or his wife in a number of weeks.

Once Connor West had been found very much alive on a boat in Mexico, the focus of the stories altered. First they'd concentrated on the finger pointing that Jeff and Connor were doing at each other about their embezzling, which was fine with Becca, since it kept the papers' interest off her and her mom. But now as she scrolled through the stories she'd already read to collect new information on where matters stood, she saw that things had undergone a significant change in San Diego. Connor West had given an interview to a reporter, and what he'd said was paraphrased in the midst of the newspaper article:

According to Mr. West, the stepdaughter of his partner Jeff Corrie was also involved in what went on at Corrie-West investments. His claim is that without the girl's participation, nothing would have come of Corrie's scheme to embezzle money that was placed into their hands. West also suggests that the girl's mother, Laurel Armstrong, had from the first known what was going on and it is this that prompted her to flee with her then fourteen-year-old daughter when the scheme began to fall apart.

The reporter had then, it seemed, spoken to Jeff Corrie about the assertions his former partner had made, for Jeff was quoted as saying, "That's so ridiculous a claim that I'm not even going to comment." But then he'd gone on anyway, and what he'd told the reporter was paraphrased in the same manner as Connor West's words had been:

> When it was pointed out to Corrie that his wife and stepdaughter's disappearance suggests they were indeed involved, Corrie's claim was that he'd come home one day from work and they were gone. He revealed that the only clue he'd ever had as to their whereabouts was a single telephone call from the sheriff's department on Whidbey Island in Washington State.

Becca's blood went to ice when she saw this last part. The only thing she could think of doing was to look into the identity of the reporter who'd uncovered this information.

There was, luckily, a byline with the story. It had been written by one Olivia Bolding. Becca searched her out as she'd searched out the stories on Jeff Corrie. What came up was a slew of articles written by her along with links to her blog, to her website, to her Facebook page, and to Wikipedia.

Becca chose the last option. In short order she learned that Olivia Bolding was twenty-nine years old and that she had already been nominated twice for a Pulitzer Prize in journalism. These nominations had been, Becca read, for a story about a twelve-year-old Detroit boy's descent into heroin addiction and for another story about Mexican girls being smuggled into the United States and sold into sex slavery. Becca wanted desperately to believe that, compared to these stories, she was far beneath the notice of a reporter. But she had a feeling that if Olivia Bolding became intrigued by something, she didn't let go of it.

It seemed to Becca once again that her only hope was going to come from finding her mom. So she logged on to an e-mail account that only a single individual on the planet even knew existed.

9

There were families out and about when Becca left the library. People were beginning to crowd Cascade Street, not only the main route into the village but also usually the best place from which one could observe the Cascade Mountains – topped with snow – in the far distance. Today, though, beyond the gray veil of fog, there was little visible in the waters of Possession Sound. This fog would make biking to her next destination risky. But she felt she had little choice in the matter. She needed to recapture some kind of tranquility, and there seemed to be only one way to do this.

She headed out of Langley on her bike. Although she passed churchgoers, she could hear nothing of their whispers. This was just as well. The freedom inside her head allowed her to consider what she'd learned from her e-mail.

Her correspondent was Parker Natalia, a talented fiddle player whom she'd come to know the previous autumn. A native of British Columbia, he'd been in town for Langley's yearly gypsy jazz festival, and for a time he'd played with Seth and his group. She'd learned first that Parker was Canadian. In short order, she'd also learned that he'd come to Langley from the very same town that Laurel had fled to: Nelson. When he'd made his return to British Columbia, then, Becca had maintained a secret contact with him. He'd been doing his best to locate for her a woman she'd explained was her cousin. Laurel Armstrong had immigrated to Nelson a few years ago, had been Becca's claim, and the family had lost contact with her. A town of ten thousand people, Nelson wasn't a huge haystack from which a single needle had to be drawn. But so far nothing Parker had done was sufficient to unearth Becca's "cousin."

He'd accepted Becca's claim that the situation was urgent. Thus, he'd put ads in the local paper and had posted have-you-seen-this-woman flyers throughout Nelson's small downtown and inside a mall that stood a short distance from an arm of Lake Kootenay. He'd also posted flyers out on the docks in the lake on which Nelson sat, where people came and went from their boats, even in winter. He'd crossed over the lake to the other part of town and fixed posters to light poles there. But if Laurel Armstrong was indeed in Nelson, she wasn't responding to his efforts to find her.

Parker had pointed out in his last e-mail to Becca that she might want to expand her search to Castlegar and to Trail. And in this most current e-mail that he'd sent to her reply of "Parker, I know she's in Nelson," he offered a different possibility. Maybe, he wrote, her "cousin" Laurel had never actually immigrated to Canada. He pointed out that the nearest border crossing to Nelson was north of Spokane. Becca's "cousin" could have decided that Spokane was a better situation for her, Parker wrote. "It's a bigger city, there's more action, and she wouldn't have had to go through the hassle of trying to get Canadian residency."

On the other hand, he went on to tell her, one of the regular customers at his family's restaurant in Nelson was a cop. He'd see if that cop would contact Canadian immigration because, if Laurel *had* actually entered Canada at any one of the border crossings in the state of Washington, there was going to be a record of that.

Throughout all of this, Parker Natalia hadn't questioned why Becca was so determined to find an individual whom, she claimed, she hadn't seen in years. From a large and closely knit Italian family, when it came to wanting to contact your relatives, Parker understood.

Now more than ever, Becca needed to find her mom. With the reporter Olivia Bolding on the case, Becca ran the risk of being tracked down. She might need to leave Whidbey in a rush, and she didn't want to do that, because Laurel would have no way of knowing where she'd gone.

Becca headed out of town. The fog made her cautious. It increased the time it took her to reach the end of Sandy Point Road and its zigzag of streets that took her to Diana's house. When she finally got there, she was wet from the damp and cold to her bones.

She rang the bell. A chorus of barking followed. As before, all of Diana's dogs came storming from the direction of the sunroom save for Oscar. He merely paced, and over the bouncing and bobbing heads of his comrades, he looked gravely at Becca through one of two windows that sided Diana's front door. Diana herself was nowhere to be seen. Becca frowned when the woman made no appearance as she waited.

It was odd. Diana wouldn't go off and leave the dogs inside her house. And she wouldn't go off and leave Oscar behind. He was her constant companion, and even if Diana had for some reason gone somewhere without him, he and the other dogs would be in the run.

Becca tried the door and found it locked, also highly unusual for Diana if she was home. She went around to the side of the house to try the door to the mudroom, and she found the same. From there, she hurried to look through the sunroom windows. But nowhere was Diana in evidence.

Becca felt the first twinge of panic when she saw Diana's slippers and her robe next to the chaise where she sometimes rested in the sunroom. She had the distinct sensation of something being wrong, and she decided to go to the nearest neighbor. Diana lived alone. Diana could be ill. Diana could even be dead. No one would find her for days, and in that time the dogs would be in the house and they wouldn't have food and they wouldn't have water. . . . Becca forced herself to become calmer. She forced herself to walk, not run, back the way she'd come. She was on the driveway about to head to the nearest neighbor when the front door opened and Diana called her name.

"My goodness," she said, and in reference to her dogs. "I wondered what got into them. Hello, Becca. I was in the shower. Isn't it a ghastly day?"

Until tomorrow . . . time isn't right . . . came to Becca, rendering her momentarily mute. She felt a chill beyond the chills she was already feeling from the weather. Those few words represented the first time that she had heard Diana Kinsale's whispers without Diana intending her to hear them. The whispers were choppy, just as Ralph Darrow's had been in the days before he'd had his stroke.

She said, "What's wrong, Mrs. Kinsale?" and she felt the same fear she'd felt when she'd phoned her mother from outside Carol Quinn's house after learning of that woman's death.

At Becca's question, Diana inhaled so deeply that Becca knew she was attempting to align her thoughts with whatever she said next. This was, "Nothing's wrong except exhaustion from doing too much work in the garden this morning. I plant and plant every spring, and I forget that a glorious garden in summer means a pile of work to winterize everything once January rolls around. I overdid things. Sometimes I forget I'm seventy-four. Do come in, Becca."

Once inside, Becca greeted the milling dogs. They sniffed at her pockets. Diana said, "Do ignore them," then she paused on her way to the kitchen and said, "On the other hand, would you put them in their run? Not Oscar, though."

Becca called the dogs through the kitchen and the mudroom where the doorway marked the closest route to their run. They came, hopeful of treats to follow. As she hadn't intended to come to Diana's, she had nothing in her pockets, but she couldn't bear to disappoint them. She grabbed a package of freeze-dried chicken on her way out.

They crowded around her: out the door, across the lawn, and over to the dog run. She swung open its gate, and in they went after her, giving her the loopy dog smiles that were characteristic of them when they knew something special was coming. Once they were inside, she rewarded each. But she also recognized that the large run had not been cleaned in ages. The stench was overpowering.

At this, she felt a resurgence of concern, because Mrs. Kinsale was religious about keeping the dogs' run shipshape. Becca looked from the run to the house, and this allowed her to see that the lawn, too, was speckled with piles of poop. This told her that Mrs. Kinsale hadn't been walking the dogs as she usually did, nor had she been throwing the ball for them down on the beach at Sandy Point, nor had she carted them to one of the island's dog parks.

Becca hurried back to the house. Mrs. Kinsale was in the kitchen, where the Seattle newspaper was spread on the table within the nook. She was in the process of folding it up, and she turned and offered Becca a smile.

She said, "Have I forgotten that we're practicing today?" And when Becca shook her head, "Good. I thought my memory was going along with the rest of me. Would you like some hot chocolate? Doesn't that sound perfect for a day like this? Hot chocolate with marshmallows on top?"

"Sounds good to me," Becca said. "But only if you let me make it."

"All right. There's a container of African chocolate in the pantry. I think you'll like it."

As she set about it, Becca said, "I'll clean up the dog run for you, Mrs. Kinsale, if you have some mulch delivered. And there's poop on the lawn, so I'll get that, too."

Diana turned from excavating in a kitchen cupboard for a bag of marshmallows. "I can't let you do that," she said. "Dog poop? That's pushing our friendship to the limit, Becca."

"It'll be how I pay you for helping me manage the whispers." Becca returned to the kitchen with the chocolate, and she rustled in the fridge for the milk. She saw it was nonfat and she held it up in a salute. "Well, at least we only have to feel partially guilty."

She said nothing more about the purpose of her visit until they'd taken their hot chocolate to the sunroom, where Oscar was enjoying the heated floor. Diana chose the chaise longue after setting her robe and slippers to one side, while Becca sat nearby in a wicker chair. Usually, the beach cottages down on Sandy Point were visible from Diana's sunroom. But today only the environs of Diana's garden could be seen. The fog was getting thicker instead of dissipating, and Becca gave a worried thought to Derric driving to La Conner virtually blind.

Diana said, "Something tells me this isn't a social call."

"I guess it usually isn't, huh?" Becca replied.

"I've no problem with that." Diana reached for an afghan at the foot of the chaise and she spread it across her legs. "Tell me."

Becca recounted everything she'd learned from her time on the Internet in Langley's library: from Connor West's implication of her and her mom in the embezzling scheme that he and Jeff Corrie had come up with to what Parker Natalia had informed her about his failures to unearth

Laurel Armstrong. But what she stressed most was the dangers that she saw looming ahead because of the reporter Olivia Bolding. A Pulitzer Prize nominee whose specialty was investigative reporting . . . ? There wasn't going to be a single place for Becca to hide on Whidbey Island if the reporter decided that this Hannah Armstrong part of the embezzling story was intriguing.

"I got to find my mom, Mrs. Kinsale. We got to find some place better than this for me and for her."

Diana looked thoughtful. "I can see it's serious. But are you completely certain that Nelson is where your mother was going?"

"Absolutely."

"Yet people do change their minds."

"She wouldn't've." Becca adjusted her position in the chair in order to emphasize what she said next. "See, she always watched this film that was made in Nelson. It was, like, three times a year that she watched it."

"Perhaps she merely liked the film."

"No. It was like she was looking for someone among the extras. I swear that's what it was like. There's someone up there and she meant to find him."

"'Him'?"

Becca circled her hands around the mug of hot chocolate and let its warmth give her the courage to voice what she had long suspected. "I think it's my dad," she said. "I think she's gone to my dad and he's hiding her there. She's never told me who he is or where he lives or even how they got together. But this thing with her always watching that dumb film and then heading for Nelson once she left me here . . . Do you see?"

Diana set down her chocolate and extended her hand to Becca. Becca took it, knowing what would happen. It would be warmth and a lifting of her anxiety, her worry, and her pain of not knowing. As always that was what occurred. But still Becca had to ask the question that had brought her to Diana Kinsale's house in the first place, although she felt a stinging of tears when she next spoke.

"What's going to *happen*, Mrs. Kinsale?"

"I don't have the power to tell you that."

"But one time . . ." Becca felt a tear escape her right eye, and, impatient with herself for allowing her fears to get the better of her, she said, "You told me one time that Mom's safe from anyone being able to find her. You *must* know more."

"I wish I did. But that's all I've ever felt about your mother. Safe is all that I can tell you."

IO

The arrangement for Prynne to move to Whidbey Island went as close to clockwork as anything could. One of the guys she lived with drove her and her belongings down to the Port Townsend ferry, and Seth and Gus picked her up on the other side. Prynne's mode of transportation was a Vespa GTS, which had enough speed to be useful even on the island's one highway, but she would be bringing it over later. No way could she manage to cart her belongings with her on the Vespa. So it was remaining in Port Townsend until she could get back there and pick it up.

And she *would* be going to Port Townsend fairly often, she'd told Seth as they'd made their final arrangements. He understood that, didn't he? She wanted to keep her personal space for a getaway. Plus, she had a gig twice a month on Saturday afternoon and evening, and no way could she afford to give that up. It was a chance to get her music heard by people who knew that the town was a bluegrass haven.

Seth was okay with this. She was doing his family a big favor, and he told her that he would stay alone with his grandfather on those Saturdays when she had to go to Port Townsend. So everything between them had gone smoothly and well. And now here he was, trundling along the road in the evening's early winter darkness and seeing in the distance the lights from the ferry as it made its way into the bay where the dock was sheltered in a crescent of water.

Prynne came off the ferry at the head of the crowd of walk-on passengers. Seth took this as a good sign. He wanted her to be as happy about the arrangement he'd developed as he was. It meant more time together; it meant actually *living* together; it felt like they'd turned a corner in their relationship.

She wore a pack on her back. She carried her fiddle in its case, and she carted along behind her a duffel on wheels. Seth embraced her and he kissed her soundly. In the lights from the ferry dock, she seemed to sparkle.

"Hey you," she said to him with a smile. "Here's the girl, reporting for duty."

"Hope it's not *all* duty." Seth took the duffel from her as Gus bumped around them, waiting for Prynne to notice him.

She did, with half of a sugar cookie. She said to Seth, "Can I?" as Gus immediately sat and waited for the windfall. When Seth said sure, she gave the cookie to Gus and giggled as he snarfed it down in one gulp and raised his head with a hopeful expression on his face. "Nope," she told him. "That's it, you." She linked her arm with Seth's and said, "Let's get this show started. You *sure* it's okay with your parents?"

"They're cool with it."

It certainly seemed that way when they arrived at the Darrow house. Rich shouted hello from the open doors of his glass studio, where he was finishing his work for the day, and Amy turned from the stove as they walked into the house and said, "I bet you two are hungry," as if Prynne had been living there for years.

Seth led the way to his bedroom. Prynne looked concerned when she saw the bed. She said, "You didn't tell me it was only a single."

"We'll fit," he replied. "We're not big. No problem."

"Seth can always sleep on the sleeping porch if there's not enough room." Amy had come to the doorway, a wooden stirring spoon in her hand. "That's where he slept while Sarah lived at home. With the storm shutters in place and the woodstove going, it's perfectly fine."

Prynne looked at Seth and said, "I hate to put him out of his room," and when Seth said, "I'm glad to hear that," she got red in the face. She turned to his mom and blurted out, "But I got to say . . . I feel sort of weird about the situation, Mrs. Darrow."

"It's Amy, please," Seth's mom replied. "As for feeling weird, I understand. But please try not to. Seth's probably told you that Rich and I had two children before we got around to saying 'I do' to each other."

"I'm not sure if me and Seth . . . if Seth and I are going to take things *that* far," Prynne said.

Seth felt a little sinking of spirits at this, but his mom seemed to take it the way it was intended, for she said, "'Two children' or 'I do'? Don't answer that. It's fine that you're here. You're helping us with Seth's granddad, and that's what matters. Dinner in fifteen minutes, okay? I hope you like Italian food."

"Yum," Prynne said and told Seth's mom she'd be out in a second to help her. But Amy told her just to unpack, and she closed the bedroom door to let this happen with some privacy.

"Told you," Seth said. "You get the right side of the bed. Thought you might like the bedside table. I'll take the window side. It's colder there."

He lifted her duffel to the bed and showed her that he'd emptied out three of the drawers in the dresser for her use. He leaned against the bedroom door and settled in to enjoy the sight of his girlfriend unpacking. But he felt a little stirring of consternation when the first things she brought out of the duffel were a baggie crammed with weed, rolling papers, a small glass pipe, and a box of matches.

Prynne seemed to know what he was feeling. She looked over at him and said, "Seth. Come on. . . ."

He tried to sound casual. "It's okay," he told her. "Only, you got to do it outside. And . . . well . . . you can't at Grand's. I mean, it would sort of keep you from doing what you're s'posed to be doing there."

"I'm not a dummy," was her reply. And then with a sharper and closer look at him, "You *sure* you're cool with this? With me smoking weed now and then?"

"You got to do what you got to do. Lemme show you where to stow your bathroom stuff."

There was only one bathroom in the house, and it wasn't large, containing the smallest tub on the planet, a shower large enough for one person who was able to keep arms and elbows under control at all times, a toilet, a pedestal sink, and a shelf holding towels. He knew it appeared, at first glance, that there was no place for Prynne to put a thing. But he showed her how the room's single cupboard cum medicine cabinet was cleverly disguised as part of the room's knotty pine paneling. He pushed upon it at the right spot, and the cupboard opened.

"Damn. Sorry," Seth said as he took in the jumble of things inside. "I forgot to get this set up for you."

The cabinet contained everything from cleaning supplies to suppositories, with no particular sense to what went where. Seth began shoving things to one side to make a spot for Prynne. Toothpaste, mouthwash, deodorants, more towels, toilet paper, aspirin, his mom's meds, remedies for colds and cold sores and sore muscles and sore throats, holistic this and naturopathic that, extra towels of all sizes and colors . . . Seth shoved things around till a small square was clear.

"Dad hates to throw away stuff," he said.

"You think?" Prynne laughed. "I'll straighten this up for you later."

"Epic." Seth watched her for a moment. A warmth came over him that prompted him to say exactly what was on his mind. "Can I tell you something?" And when she nodded, "I'm really looking forward to bedtime."

She smiled. "Why? D'you want a bedtime story?"

"You're the story," was his reply.

It was two days later when Seth and Prynne went with Rich Darrow to Ralph's place. Becca was there, waiting for them, and together the four of them anticipated the arrival of Steph Vanderslip, who would evaluate the safety of the house as transformed by Seth and his crew. Everything she'd required was now in place: the ramp built and tightly covered with chicken wire to prevent a slick surface in the rain, handrails mounted where they were needed both inside and outside the house, a hospital bed brought in and placed in Becca's former bedroom, a stool in the shower, and a new chair in the living room that would make it easier for Ralph to rise.

If Steph Vanderslip put her stamp of approval on everything, they were in business and Ralph's return would occur within days. To enhance this possibility, Seth's dad had made contact with South Island Home Care, and during the coming week, he would be interviewing eight caregivers. From this group, he would hire two of them: one to be with Ralph from seven in the morning till three in the afternoon, and the other from three in the afternoon till eleven at night. The family had hoped for round-the-clock care for Ralph once they learned that this was a service provided by and paid for by the state of Washington. But they'd also learned that Ralph's condition didn't warrant that. They could still have round-the-clock care, naturally, but one-third of it would have to come out of the family's funds, and neither Rich nor his dad had those funds. His sister had the cash, of course. But no way was Brenda going to fork over any dough so that her dad could do exactly what she *didn't* want him to do: live at home.

When Steph Vanderslip arrived, Becca was the one who saw her first. She'd been at the window, playing around with the earbud that connected to her hearing device. In and out of her ear, like she couldn't decide if she wanted to hear what was going on. She said, "She's here," and dropped the earbud to her side. She fussed around with the box at her waist as Rich and Seth went to the door to greet the health care specialist.

The first thing Steph Vanderslip said was, "Impressive driveway," about the way she'd descended to Ralph's house. She'd come to them from the area of Ralph's shop instead of down the hillside, and she nodded in that direction, where a fan of hard surface meant that Ralph could get into and out of a car or van without having to struggle with the old hillside path.

Steph Vanderslip shook hands with both Seth and his dad. She evaluated the ramp Seth had built, testing its surface and its handrails and stepping back to examine its angle. She said, "Good work. Who did it?"

Rich said, "Seth and his friends did it all."

"You're quite a craftsman," she said to Seth. "Let's go inside."

Within, Seth introduced her to Becca and Prynne. Steph shook hands with them but was all business afterward. Seth saw that Becca's eyes got narrow as the health care specialist went from room to room, testing this and that. She squatted to look at the way the handrails had been mounted, she sat in the new chair and tested how easy it was to rise from it, she squeezed the bumpers that were fixed to the hearth to make sure their thickness was sufficient, and from there she went to Becca's former bedroom and the bathroom while the rest of them waited for her coming verdict.

"I'll be hiring two home health care aides this week," Rich told her when she at last emerged. She was writing something on a paper affixed to a clipboard she was carrying. "There'll be two shifts, ending at eleven. Becca here will be with him during the night and Prynne will be with him as a backup during the day."

Steph Vanderslip looked up from what she was writing. Her brow was furrowed. "Why?" she said. "I understand why Becca will be here at night, but why the other?"

Seth could tell his dad was trying to work out exactly what to tell the health care specialist. He went with, "Basically to reassure my sister. She's been thinking Dad would do better in assisted living with more than one person there to make sure he's okay." He didn't add the rest: that Brenda hadn't agreed to anything they were doing.

He saw Becca watching him intently. Then she looked from him to his dad to Steph Vanderslip, who was tapping her pen rapidly against the clipboard and who also didn't look too pleased to learn there was a division in the family.

She said, "I'm sorry to hear that."

"She'll come around when she sees how well Dad does at home," Rich reassured her.

"I hope so. I don't want your father walking into a family disagreement. That can make a hash of the progress he's made, and his blood pressure can't do with any spikes. He also *must* continue to make progress in speech therapy. You understand that, right?"

"That's going to happen," Rich told her. "And if it comes down to having a professional here twenty-four/seven, we'll go that route. Meantime, I'm five minutes from here. If

Becca needs me to come over in the night to help her, that won't be an issue."

Steph nodded thoughtfully. She jotted a last few items in her paperwork and said, "Let's start out with trying this for a week and see how it works, Mr. Darrow."

11

Jenn was surprised the next day when Cynthia Richardson not only stopped by the table where she and her pals were eating lunch, but also pulled out a chair and joined them. For a second she thought something had gone bad between Cynthia and Lexie Ovanov, since Lexie was with her but walked on toward their regular table against the far wall. Then Cynthia said to Lexie, "Be there in a sec," and reached over to take a carrot stick from Becca's lunch, saying, "Can I . . . ?" and "Thanks," before Becca could answer.

Squat was there, too. So was Derric, and Seth's former girlfriend Hayley Cartwright. Since Hayley was a senior like Cynthia, Jenn figured that Cynthia had come to talk to her about some brainy class they were taking together. But instead, she turned to Jenn as she removed a scrunchie that was holding her long blonde hair in a ponytail. Expertly, she fixed it back in place.

She said, "You're going for the All Island team, right? That's why you've been training after school?"

Jenn figured the other girl was about to tell her to give it up, along the lines of "You're a hopeless case," but when she nodded and told her that was the plan, Cynthia took another carrot stick from Becca and said, "Why don't you train with me? You're a good center midfielder, but you could be better. The competition's going to be from every school on the island, and it'll be tough."

"I know. I went out last year. Didn't make past the first day."

"That sucks. How did you train?"

"Mostly I didn't."

"And she smoked," Becca added. "Tell the truth, Jenn."

Jenn gave her a shut-up look. Becca laughed. Derric said, "She speaks only the truth, girl." And then he said to Cynthia, "She's been smoking since grade school."

"Have not!" Jenn said. "Seventh grade. It was stupid. I gave it up."

Cynthia said, "I did cigarettes for about five minutes in fifth grade. Down behind the Dog House in Seawall Park. Me and two girls from the Christian school."

"Figures," Squat said, under his breath.

Cynthia glanced at him. He looked impassive. He also looked completely unimpressed that the captain of the soccer team, a girl who had a scholarship to University of Virginia to play soccer, was telling Jenn she was a good center midfielder.

Cynthia said, "So d'you want to?"

Jenn had forgotten Cynthia's offer. "Want to what?"

"Train with me. I've been doing this for a long time. You're running is good, but what else're you doing to get ready?"

"Nothing."

"So . . . ?"

Jenn felt a kick under the table. She knew it was Squat. She shot him a what's-with-*you* look and said to Cynthia, "What about Lexie? I thought you trained with her."

"She'll still be there." Cynthia grinned. "Abuse motivates me."

Squat guffawed. Cynthia glanced his way. He said, "Got a picture in my mind if you know what I mean. Sorry."

Hayley said, "Isn't your sandwich calling you, Squat?"

"Something is," Derric added.

Jenn said to Cynthia, "I dunno. I sort of like training on my own."

Cynthia looked at them all, then cast a longer look at Jenn. She said, "Okay, then," as she pushed away from the table. Jenn thought that was it and she would walk off to join Lexie, but she didn't do that at once. Instead she leaned over Becca's shoulder, took a final carrot stick, said to Becca, "I owe you," and then to Jenn, "If you change your mind, let me know. It's not catching."

"What?"

"Being like me and Lexie."

Although Jenn grew hot and knew that color was climbing her neck and attacking her ears, she said, "Huh? Don't get what you're talking about."

Cynthia nodded and cast a glance at Squat before she said to Jenn, "Sure you do." She popped the carrot stick into her mouth and walked away.

At first there was a little silence at the table. Squat was the one to break it. He said, "Good decision, Jenn."

Hayley said, "She's a nice girl, Squat."

"I didn't say she wasn't nice," he countered. "But if she and the other dyke made it any more obvious they'd be doing it on the table over there."

Jenn rose at that. She grabbed up her lunch bag. "You're disgusting," she told Squat. Before he could answer, she swung around and stalked away.

The last thing she expected was that he would follow her, but that was what Squat did. She was at her locker when he came up behind her and said abruptly, "Look. I got nothing against them."

She swung around. "Got nothing against who?"

"You know. They can be what they want to be. I don't

care." His gaze darted around, as if he and Jenn were spies afraid of being caught red-handed with information they needed to pass on. "But if you start hanging with them, it looks like you're *like* them. So guys are going to wonder, and you need to ask yourself if that's what you want."

Jenn shut her locker with a little too much force. "I get it. You mean I might not get a date to the senior *prom* if I train with Cynthia Richardson. Ohhhh, that breaks my heart in two." She leaned into him so they were nose to nose. "Like I actually care?" she demanded. "You are all *over* the place, Squat, and every place you're all over is, like, completely wrong."

Squat didn't back off as she'd intended. Instead he said, "Sure, Jenn. If that's what you say. I just wanted to give you some advice. We been friends since—"

"Yeah. Right. Preschool. Got it. So *you* get this: if I want to train with the school's most out-there lesbians, I will. And if *that* means I end up with cooties and no one wants to have lunch with me, then that's how it all plays out. I guess you'll be one of them, huh?"

"One of who?"

"One of the people who decides my cooties are catching. Wow, Squat, stick around me and I might turn you trans!"

"Hey. I'm not saying—"

"I know what you're saying. Give it up. And I think it's time you trotted off to class."

Becca and Derric were coming toward her then, and Jenn figured it was going to be more of the same. She scowled, hoping to drive them off. No luck there because Derric pulled his smartphone from his pocket, frowned down at the screen, and made an adjustment to it that stopped its quacking. Becca came to join Jenn.

She'd apparently seen the action between Jenn and Squat because she said, "What's going on with Squat?"

"General asshole-ness."

"About Cynthia Richardson, I bet."

"She freaks him out. I'm surprised he didn't have a can of Raid to spray on her."

Becca made an adjustment to her iPod thingy. After a moment, she said, "I dunno, Jenn. It might be a good idea."

Jenn said, "*What?*" assuming Becca was agreeing with Squat.

But Becca said, "Training with her. If she wants to help you . . . She's got an athletic scholarship, right? She's been playing soccer since . . . when?"

"Probably since she was in her playpen."

"Then why not? What did Squat say?"

"The old what-will-the-*guys*-think."

"Really? Who cares? This's more important than what a bunch of A-holes think."

"Who's an A-hole?" Derric had come to join them. He was shoving his smartphone back into his jeans. He gave Becca a look that communicated something because she said, "Again?"

Jenn said, "Your mom bugging you?"

"Not his mom," Becca said.

"Ohhhh, that girl from Uganda? You better watch out, girlfriend," she said to Becca. "She's hot for him. You better handle it."

"They're going to arm wrestle for me," Derric said. "I want Becca to win, so we've been practicing."

Becca laughed. Derric dropped his arm around her shoulders. He told her he'd walk her to class if she was ready. Turned out that she was, but she said to Jenn before walking off, "Think about it, okay?"

Jenn nodded. She watched the two of them walk off together. Ten feet away and Becca's arm was around Derric's waist, and they disappeared around the corner. Jenn thought, seeing them, about what it would be like to have someone the way that Becca and Derric had each other.

She was waiting in the shelter for the free island bus when her day got worse. A horn honked behind her. She turned, thinking that Cynthia Richardson was going to offer her a ride home again and that she was going to have to turn her down. But it was her mom in the decrepit Whidbey Island taxi. Kate McDaniels had pulled to the side of the road. She'd just dropped someone at the language school over on Langley Road, she said. She could give Jenn a ride home.

Jenn was reluctant. The drive was long. Plenty of time for her mom to engage her on the topic of Jenn's being baptized in Deer Lake, which Kate wanted to happen just as soon as the weather made it possible for someone to be dunked without getting hypothermia. Seeing her, though, Jenn could hardly say she'd rather wait for the bus, since she *wouldn't* rather wait for the bus.

She climbed into the vehicle. She said, "Thanks. It was going to take forever."

"Happy to be of service," Kate replied. She patted Jenn's hand, said "Seat belt," and waited. As Jenn hooked it up, Kate fondly smoothed Jenn's hair. As she did this, Squat and his mom pulled out of the parking lot in the family SUV. Squat was behind the wheel. It was late for him to still be at school, Jenn thought. He'd probably been massaging his brain with trigonometry in the library.

Kate said, "That's Fergus Cooper, isn't it? He's turning into a handsome young man. Goodness, though, doesn't time fly? He's driving!"

"Looks that way."

"Why don't we see more of him, Jennie?" her mom asked. "You and he used to be such pals. I can remember—"

"We pal around at school," Jenn cut in. "He's busy

otherwise. He's in Honors Everything. Got to maintain the GPA."

"You even had play dates," Kate said wistfully.

"We can't exactly do that when we're sixteen."

"No, no. Of course not." Kate pulled into the road and they followed the Coopers' SUV toward the highway, where it would turn in the direction of Double Bluff Beach, and they would turn in the opposite direction. "Still . . . I remember him being a lovely boy. Polite, well raised . . . Is he a Christian, Jenn?"

"No clue," Jenn said. "He's probably heathen. Or maybe pagan. He could be Wiccan."

"Don't make fun," her mother said. "Christianity is our path to heaven. And God's commandments were created to get us there." She paused, as if considering something. Then she said, "Fornication is part of the sixth commandment, Jennie. It says adultery but fornication is included. You know that, don't you?"

Jenn turned to stare at her mother: upright in her seat, hands at ten and two o'clock on the wheel, gaze firmly on the road lest a deer dart out or a suicidal rabbit take the plunge. She said, "Yeah. Thanks. I know."

"And so is touching yourself. You've not been touching yourself, have you?"

Jenn gritted her teeth. Most of the time she could listen to her mom and translate it to *blah blah blah* in her head. But at the end of this day, which had seemed to pull her every which way, this was not one of those times.

"Whatever," was her final response.

She wished that she had waited for the bus.

12

When Seth drove into Coupeville after being given Steph Vanderslip's approval on the work they'd done to his grandfather's house, he had Becca and Prynne with him. They were on their way to Penn Cove Care to tell Grand how things were going to be set up, with the home health care aides seeing to his basic needs and Prynne and Becca there in the house to reassure him that he wouldn't be solely in the hands of strangers.

They also needed to make sure Grand knew that he had to do maximum work in physical therapy and he had to keep making efforts to get his language skills back once they got him home. Otherwise, they'd be into another fight with Aunt Brenda about assisted living.

At Penn Cove Care, they got out into a dazzling day. The air was frigid because there were no clouds, but they had a crystalline view of Mount Baker to the east, with its snow-capped volcanic sides reaching up into a pure blue sky. The air was sharp with scents from Penn Cove: salt water, seaweed, and shellfish. It was mussel season. The seagulls swooping down near the town's long pier seemed to be anticipating this.

Prynne looped a shopping bag over her arm, purchases that she and Seth had made at Good Cheer Thrift store and in the children's section of the bookshop on First Street in Langley. What they'd bought comprised goodies for Ralph, and part of the reason they'd come to Coupeville was to explain them to him.

Inside Penn Cove Care, they trooped to Ralph's room. Finding it empty, Seth led them to the physical therapy wing. But he wasn't there, either. Seth's first thought was a scary one: that Grand had suffered another stroke.

"Let's check at reception," Prynne suggested "Maybe they've taken a bunch of people on an outing or something."

It turned out that Ralph was on an outing, all right. But he was the only patient taking part in it. At reception they learned from a bespectacled woman with a very large mole on the side of her nose that "Mr. Darrow's daughter has taken him down to Freeland to have a look at The Cedars."

Seth knew exactly what The Cedars was: assisted living. "But the house's is approved," he said. "That lady Steph, she came to look it over. She said it was fine. She said it was safe." Seth could hear his panic, and he knew his companions heard it, too, because he felt Prynne link her hand with his. Becca's breathing became deep and steady.

The receptionist said, "Well, there appears to be some sort of miscommunication among you."

"Is she taking him there to check him in or something?" Seth demanded.

"As far as I know it's merely a visit so that he can see what it's like. If you'd like to wait . . . ? They've been gone for an hour and they'll probably return before this hour's up."

The last thing Seth wanted to do was wait. He trusted his aunt like he trusted a rattlesnake. He had to get to the car.

Prynne and Becca followed him. He punched his dad's phone number into his cell phone, and when Rich answered with, "What's up, Seth?" the words tumbled out so fast that Rich had to tell him to slow down, to start over, to make himself clear. Once Seth had done so, his father's reply was reassuring. "I'm on it," he said. "Let me handle this, Seth. I'll be in touch."

Seth knew that his dad would head directly to Freeland, where The Cedars occupied a piece of prime real estate overlooking Holmes Harbor, a huge body of water shaped like a toe-dancer's leg kicking its way south toward Mutiny Bay. He also knew that his dad considered him something of a hothead and thought that this situation called for cooler heads prevailing. But there was no way that he was going to back off. He told Prynne and Becca to get in the car, because they were going to The Cedars.

Freeland wasn't nearby. Far closer to the village of Langley than it was to Coupeville, it stood at the big toe of the dancer's foot. They had to charge south down the island's only highway to get there, passing through forest and winter-bare farmland, wetlands, and lakes. When they got to the town, Seth pressed through it and onto the road that surged up the harbor on the west side of the water. He opened up the speed here, and because of this, he nearly missed the turn through the wrought iron gates that would take them onto the grounds of The Cedars.

They piled out of the car the second Seth had it parked. No time to look for a suitable space, he just left it in the portico of The Cedars' main building, a hospital-like affair on three levels, behind which the waters of Holmes Harbor placidly gleamed. He charged inside with Prynne and Becca fast on his heels.

He'd already seen his aunt's Lexus. It was hard to miss, since she'd parked the thing overlapping two visitors' spaces so no one could mar its perfect paint job. Also in the visitors' parking was his father's pickup.

Inside, the place was all silence, hardwood floors, carefully arranged furniture, the strong scent of lavender, and a fireplace in which a phony fire flickered. Seth dimly heard someone say, "May I help you?" but he didn't need help. For the first thing he saw was a glass-windowed conference room and within that room sat his aunt, his dad, his grandfather in a wheelchair, and some lady in a business suit talking to all of them.

Seth burst in on them. He heard ". . . a compromise because a fight over guardianship can't be what you want." It was the business suit lady speaking. She started when Seth broke into the room. She said, "I beg your—"

Rich said sharply, "I told you I'd handle this, Seth."

Seth said, "She's *not* packing him into this place. He's not a discard. He's a human being."

Aunt Brenda said, "How dare you even suggest—"

"You think we don't know what you got in mind? You're pretty stupid, Aunt Brenda."

Rich stood. "You need to leave."

"Not without Grand." Seth went to his grandfather's wheelchair. Grand was slumped to one side and his good fist was clenched in a frozen position. "You guys are going to give him another stroke. I'm taking him outa here."

Brenda stood, too. "He hasn't been discharged from Penn Cove Care. You're not taking him anywhere."

"Stop me," Seth said. "Call the cops."

He went to Ralph and released the brake on the wheelchair. His father said to him, "Don't make this worse."

Seth said, "You think he likes sitting here while you guys argue over him like he's a prize steer or something? I don't think so. Come on, Grand." Seth wheeled him from the room.

He took Ralph over to the fireplace. He knew his grandfather scorned false fires, but it seemed more soothing than putting him anywhere near the conference room, from which raised voices could easily be heard.

Becca and Prynne joined him on the hearth, where he

seated himself to face his grandfather. Becca, he saw, had removed her earbud. He figured the whole deal had upset her and she pretty much didn't want to hear what was going to be said next. He couldn't blame her.

He said, "Here's what's happening, Grand. We've fixed your house so you can go home, this lady from the hospital checked it out, and Dad's hiring two health care people to be with you. But not alone, okay? Prynne'll will be with you daytimes, Becca will be with you afternoon and night-times, and me and Prynne or Dad will be with you on weekends. No one's putting you in assisted living."

Ralph's head righted itself, but his fist did not unclench. Seth put his hand over that tight ball of bones and flesh, and he felt Becca move closer to Grand.

She said to Ralph, "That okay with you, Grand? Or d'you think" – and to Seth, "I gotta ask him this, okay?" – and back to Grand, "or d'you think you might do better here?"

"No way," Seth said to her. And to his grandfather, "You got to keep up with the physical therapy and you *got* to do stuff to get better with language. These health guys, they'll take you to your appointments and we got some stuff to help you out with language, too. But here's what's happening. You probably already figured it out, but I'll say it anyway. Aunt Brenda wants to get control: of you, of your land, of where you live, of everything. Me and Dad? We're fighting her, but you got to fight her, too."

Ralph didn't move. There was no nod of understanding, nor did he make an attempt to speak.

Becca seemed to be studying his face, though, and what she apparently read on his features wasn't exactly what Seth wanted to hear. She rose to her feet and gestured Seth to walk away from the wheelchair with her. When they had some distance, she said to him quietly, "Losing everything like he has, Seth? I think . . . Well, it seems like he's not making the kind of progress everyone wants him to make because . . . I think he's waiting to die."

"No way. He's gonna get better if we take him home."

13

When Seth made the turn off Newman Road and up the incline that was Ralph Darrow's driveway, the first thing Becca saw was Derric's Forester in the parking area. As Prynne hopped out of the car so that Becca could alight, the second thing she saw was Derric himself. He'd just climbed the path that led up from the house, circling round the small hill that kept the house out of view. He smiled that two-hundred-watt smile of his when he saw them, saying, "Hey. Where've you guys been?"

"Coupeville," Seth said. "Then Freeland. Setting everything up for Grand to come home, including having an epic fight with my aunt."

"Harsh," Derric said.

Becca went to him. He pulled her into a bear hug and said over her head to Prynne, "Everything set up? You here permanently now?"

"I'm here," she told him. "I got to go back for my Vespa, though."

"That thing safe for the highway?" Derric asked as Becca put her earbud in.

"Sure. Seth says no, but if I c'n ride it around Quimper Peninsula, I c'n sure as heck ride it around here. And" – she shot an amused look at Seth – "don't you argue, buddy. I need my wheels."

Becca drew a sudden breath that stabbed. The sensation that came over her was unexpected, a brief rush of wind

that wasn't wind at all but something that quickly transformed in her vision to the image of driving a vehicle to
the side of the road in front of a small ramshackle house.
This was fronted by shrubbery long gone without pruning
and a wooden archway that tilted to one side with a heavy
growth of wisteria threatening to take it down. She had the
sensation of walking through that archway, of seeing the
house become more visible, of striding down a path that
led to the corner of the building. Then—

"You okay?"

Derric's question cut into the vision, and Becca was back
with the others. Prynne and Seth were watching her curiously. The place she'd seen must have been, she thought,
where Prynne lived. Her words had prompted it somehow.
She said to Derric, "I'm starving. I got light in the head
for a sec."

"You guys chow down," Seth said. "We gotta get going.
I'll let you know when everything's a go for Grand, Beck.
We'll rock this situation."

Becca had her doubts about that. Still, she nodded.
Prynne got back into the VW, and they took off. Becca
returned Seth's wave, and then looked at Derric. "It is *so*
good to see you," she told him.

"I was bummed when there was no one home," he
replied. "I left you a note. Sort of a poor-me-wah-wah-wah-
where-are-you-and-when're-you-getting-a-cell-phone-for-
God's-sake."

She smiled at the description. "Come on, I got some
food in the slow cooker." She led the way, saying over her
shoulder, "Did you figure I was with Seth, trying to work
on this family thing he has going on with Grand?"

"I didn't figure anything. Just that you weren't here and
I wanted to see you." As they walked up the new ramp onto
the porch, he added, "*Needed* to see you is more like it."

Becca saw his note on the door, folded into the small crack between the door and the jamb. She unfolded it, read it, and said, "I dunno. Doesn't sound like wah-wah-wah to me. But Rejoice . . . ?" She shoved the note into her pocket as she dug for her house keys. He'd said in the note that he needed to talk to her about Rejoice. *Important,* he said. *Disaster looming.*

She opened the door and shoved her shoulder against it. It was tough to open in the winter when the damp made it swell. Derric helped her, his hands reaching above her head in a way that always reminded her how much taller he was than she.

Inside, the place was cold although the air held the fragrance of a savory stew. Becca pointed out that the fire was laid in the great stone fireplace, and if Derric would light it, she'd check on what she had in the slow cooker. Lucky for her, she'd told Derric some weeks into Ralph Darrow's hospitalization and recuperation, Grand had a freezer filled with beef, chicken, and fish, as well as a root cellar at the side of the house that held enough root veggies to last her through a nuclear holocaust. So feeding herself hadn't been a problem, although she didn't much like eating alone.

When she rejoined him, Becca saw that he had a decent blaze going. He was sitting on the hearth with his back to it, but he hadn't yet removed his parka. Neither had she. The house had a heat pump, but she didn't keep it running when she wasn't there. It took a while to get the structure warm. In the meantime, the fire would do. She sat next to him, put her head on his shoulder, and twined her fingers with his.

"So what's up?" she asked.

"Oh, hell, what *isn't?*" Derric's tone suggested that Rejoice had probably taken matters another step forward in her dispute with her parents about when she was going to be allowed to do what in her life.

Derric had already told Becca that the girl was pressing her mom and dad about their dating rule: no dates on her own with a boy until she was sixteen. When Derric had eaten lunch with the Vicklands on that Sunday he'd gone to La Conner on his own, she'd announced to all present that "me and Derric need some *alone* time. It's only right. And it's not like we're gonna *do* anything, Mom." She said her parents' restrictions were "totally and absolutely unfair 'cause I can't even be alone with a boy unless we're, like, totally visible to you. Like sitting on the front porch in broad daylight. And then these guys make fun of me."

"These guys" were her siblings. They were out and about with boyfriends and girlfriends and it wasn't *fair* that she had to wait. "They had to wait, too" did not appease her.

Her dad told her at that Sunday lunch that if Derric wanted to visit, it was fine. If he wanted to take her some place, it was also fine. *But*, he'd added with a stern look that attempted to telegraph there would be no further discussion because he was tired of repeatedly laying down the law to his daughter, she could only go with Derric if someone else went along, too. "One of your sisters can go or one of your brothers," he told her. Then he added meaningfully, "Or Derric can bring his girlfriend Becca."

Rejoice had bristled at that and announced, "Becca is his *friend*, Dad, not his girlfriend," and as Derric was about to correct her, Jeff Vickland said, "She's a girl. She's his friend. Ergo, she's his girlfriend. And the topic is closed."

Derric concluded the story with, "And now there's this," as he took his iPhone from his pocket. He tapped it a few times and handed it over to Becca. She saw that it was a picture of Rejoice, a selfie she'd taken with a background of one of the family's vast tulip fields behind her, the green of the sprouting bulbs making knitted furrows that extended virtually to the horizon.

She was grinning the same grin that Derric possessed, the one that made her resemble him so much that Becca was continually amazed that Rejoice's family hadn't figured out he was her brother yet. Now, though, there was going to be little doubt about the matter. For Rejoice had shaved her head, like his, in the manner of the girls in the Kampala orphanage from which they had both been adopted.

"Looks like you've got trouble," Becca told him.

Derric said, taking the iPhone back from her, "I guess I can't hope that her mom and dad are like white people who say everyone black looks the same to them."

"I guess you can't," Becca said.

He observed the picture. "At least she's finally getting into being African," he pointed out hopefully.

"Uh, Der . . . I don't think that's what she's getting into."

Derric was quiet for a moment. The fire popped behind them. He removed his parka. She did the same. He finally said, "Well, I'm going to *pretend* that's what she's getting into. Like 'Hey, girl, now you're doing it right. Ugandans rock!' Something like that."

"And then what?" Becca asked him.

"Get her some African scarves and clothes and whatever?"

"Okay. And *then* what?"

He shoved the phone into his pocket. "Absolute hell if I know," he said.

It was two days later when Becca went into the high school library, cutting short her lunchtime in order to log on to one of the computers there. Derric's problem with Rejoice aside, she had her own issues. So she went first to her e-mail account to see if there was anything new from Parker Natalia. When she saw that there was, her heart did its usual loud thump that heralded hope.

From Parker's e-mail, she learned that he'd given the word about Laurel Armstrong to the cop he knew who had contacts in Canadian immigration. The cop, Parker said, would check things out. But then he added that it might come down to Becca traveling up to Nelson herself, maybe giving an interview about Laurel Armstrong to the paper or something like that.

Becca had to get him away from that idea fast. She had no passport, and although she did have a copy of Rebecca Dolores King's birth certificate, it was only a copy and not the original. She wondered if, in these days of terrorists, a simple copy would suffice to get someone a passport. She doubted it.

She went from her e-mail to Google, and there she typed in Jeff Corrie's name. There were no new developments, so she checked out the reporter Olivia Bolding's progress on whatever story she might be attempting to write about the missing Hannah Armstrong.

There, her anxiety spiked when she saw that Olivia Bolding wasn't about to let the Hannah Armstrong dog die. Since Becca had last been on the computer in Langley's library to see what the reporter was up to, Olivia Bolding had been to Hannah Armstrong's high school, from which she'd disappeared early in her freshman year. There, she'd interviewed Hannah's teachers, most of whom had dutifully declared Hannah to be an exemplary student. She'd also unearthed Hannah's freshman picture, which was several years more recent than the pictures Jeff Corrie had earlier supplied the newspapers. Becca stared at the picture and tried to see in it evidence of who she was now.

Hannah Armstrong had been fat. *Chubby* was only a euphemism for triple chins and thunder thighs. She'd worn her hair long but had done nothing with it, other than to fasten it with a barrette at the back of her head. It was also strawberry blond. Or strawberry blondish. It wasn't at all what it had been altered to by the time she'd arrived on Whidbey Island as Becca King.

Becca King had come to Whidbey as fat as Hannah but, through the necessity of getting around on a bike, she had eventually become slim and athletic. Her hair had been dyed hideous Goth black, but that, too, had changed along with the shedding of the weight. Now her hair was light brown, and it capped her head. And although she still wore the same phony glasses she'd had on upon her arrival on the island, she'd backed way off on the amount of makeup she'd once used. She could, she'd decided a few months earlier, only keep up the general hideousness of her appearance so long before she couldn't stand it any longer.

Now, she wanted to believe, and she *had* to believe, that she no longer resembled the Hannah Armstrong who'd disappeared from San Diego. So she decided that this was indeed the case because at the moment, what other choice did she have?

14

Jenn decided to take Becca's advice, once she learned that Lexie Ovanov, too, had acquired an athletic scholarship. For her, it was track and field. UCLA was giving her a free ride because of her performance as a distance runner. She did her own training in the early morning out on the track and on weekends with a coach from over town. Jenn hadn't known this. But when she saw Lexie running against the fastest boy on the track team just for fun and leaving him in the dust, she figured she should sign up for what Cynthia and Lexie were offering her. It sure as heck couldn't hurt her, and it sure as heck might help her make the All Island team.

Neither of the girls was put out that she'd turned Cynthia down earlier. It seemed that, for them, it was one for all and all for one and who cared what had been said in the past? Lexie said she'd work with Jenn on her running and her weight training. Cynthia said she'd take on dribbling, passing, and holding on to the ball. "It'll be good for all of us," Cynthia concluded. "Lexie's been getting lazy anyway."

"As if," was Lexie's rejoinder. "I can take you on any day of the week."

"And so you do," Cynthia said with a leer. Both of them laughed. Jenn got hot in the face.

The girls both pushed her hard. Jenn found them tough but extremely helpful. Cynthia stayed in Jenn's face whenever she tried to do anything with the ball. Lexie started her on the track, telling her that developing speed on the trails was an interesting way to look at things, but since soccer wasn't exactly played on forest trails, it made a whole lot more sense to be on a level surface where she could build up her speed and then combine it with an ability to scramble when under pressure. Lexie was there to supply the pressure. Out on the lawn, she charged Jenn like a barbarian warrior, coming at her full speed with screams and shouts. This, naturally, attracted the attention of anyone who happened to be in the vicinity. When Jenn saw other kids looking at them, she cringed a bit.

She wanted not to care that Lexie was gay. But Squat's remarks about both of the girls – Cynthia *and* Lexie – kept intruding. She shoved them away as best she could. Still they came back and especially so when Cynthia and Lexie were together.

At least they didn't do anything in the showers while she was around, Jenn told herself reassuringly. She might have accidentally witnessed them messing with each other that one day, but once she joined them in training, they kept a distance from each other. No more soaping each other up, no more shampooing each other's hair, no more kissing while naked with the water streaming around them. They still joked, slapped each other on the butt, and made comments that seemed to be private jokes between them. But that was it.

Jenn discovered almost by accident that Lexie had another girlfriend. This was on a day after training and showers when Lexie mentioned to Cynthia that Sara-Jane had found such a deal on tickets that she'd bought them at once and without asking Lexie how long she wanted to stay in Europe that summer.

Lexie's conclusion was, "I hate it when she does that."

"Yeah, but on the other hand," Cynthia pointed out reasonably, "you *want* to go to Europe together, right?"

"Course. And I know, I'm a control freak. I want to be the one to decide things for myself. For Sara-Jane, too, I guess."

From this Jenn understood that Lexie would be heading to Europe after graduation and she'd be traveling with someone other than Cynthia. At first she figured that Sara-Jane was a relative. Lexie's sister, maybe, or perhaps a cousin.

But then Lexie said, "She's also decided we have to spend time in Venice. Way too much time in Venice, if you ask me. It'll be romantic, she says. Gondolas, locking lips while some guy pushes us through the canals, plays a mandolin, and croons about love."

Cynthia laughed. "Sounds like she's getting *very* serious. Gondolas? You go straight into engagement after that. Then it's marriage, the family, and you're finished for life. I *told* you hooking up with someone so much older was going to cause problems."

"It's not like I don't love her," Lexie said. "It's just that I want to make a few of my own decisions."

Jenn was intrigued when it became clear that Lexie was talking about someone with whom she was involved outside of her relationship with Cynthia. So when Cynthia glanced in her direction – jeans in one hand and yellow cashmere sweater in the other – and said, "What? You're looking like something's on your mind," Jenn turned away hastily and started pulling her clothes out of her locker.

"Nope, nothing," Jenn said.

A little silence ensued as they put their clothes on. Then Cynthia said, "Oh. Sara-Jane, right?"

"Sara who?" Jenn asked, striving for innocence.

"I bet you think Lexie's cheating on her partner."

Jenn didn't want to say what she was really thinking, which was maybe things were different for lesbians since they weren't exactly going to get each other pregnant so maybe it didn't matter who did what and when and how. But she didn't know what she could say in *place* of that. So she went with, "I guess I don't get it."

"Get what?" Lexie had come to Jenn's locker and was leaning nearby. She'd bent and picked up one of Jenn's shoes, and for a second Jenn thought she meant to threaten her with it, although she couldn't say why Lexie would bother to do that.

Still, she did feel the other girl's presence more acutely than usual, so she said, "I thought you guys . . . you know . . . you and Cynthia . . . I thought you were a couple."

"Like in the Big Romance?" Lexie looked at Cynthia. They both laughed. "We'd kill each other in three days," Lexie told her.

"Hey! Maybe we'd last a week, Lex," Cynthia said.

"Oh." Jenn frowned. She looked in the direction of the showers. She'd seen what she'd seen, so if Lexie and Cynthia wanted to pretend they weren't involved, what was it to her?

"We're just friends," Cynthia told her.

"Right," Jenn said.

"With privileges," Lexie added.

"Oh. Right." Jenn wondered if she could come up with another word besides *right*. She felt like a dolt.

"You know what that means, don't you?" Cynthia asked.

"I'm not totally stupid," Jenn told her. "I just thought . . . You guys are always together and I've seen you and whatever. Never mind. My bad."

"Sara-Jane's in grad school," Lexie said. "Second year of a PhD program in California, at USC. We don't have strings when we're not together. If we meet someone, it's okay to mess around."

"That's what friends with privileges means," Cynthia said.

Jenn wanted to say "I *know* what it means," but more

than that, she wanted to put the conversation behind them. She found the discussion excruciating. The way they acted together, anyone would have thought the same thing: that they were exclusive. That this wasn't the case was, she told herself, No Big Deal.

She held out her hand for the shoe that Lexie was holding. She'd already put its mate in her locker.

Lexie gestured with it. "This thing's no good. It's all worn down, Jenn. You need a new pair. And this brand . . . ? Why'd you buy it?"

"It was what they had." Jenn plucked the shoe from Lexie and shoved it with the other.

"What kind of athletic store has only one brand of shoes?"

"They're what I could afford," Jenn said. There was no way she intended to tell Lexie that they were also what Good Cheer Thrift had available on the day she ducked in to see what – if anything – she could use for athletic shoes this school year.

"You got to get something better," Lexie told her. "You can't make the All Island team with these. You can't even get better at training with these."

"I'm saving up."

"Have a job?"

"Not yet. I'm working on it."

Jenn shut her locker decisively and spun the dial on the lock. She began to get the rest of her stuff together. So did the other two girls albeit more slowly.

She was out of the locker room quickly after that, but she only got as far as the school's main entrance when Lexie and Cynthia caught up with her. Lexie called out, "Idea here!" and Cynthia simultaneously called, "Wait up, Jenn."

Kids were leaving the band room after a late practice. Jenn saw it was jazz band, with Hayley Cartwright and

Derric Mathieson among them. She just thanked God Squat wasn't a member because she knew he'd give her grief if he saw her talking to Cynthia and Lexie. She waited for them. The other kids passed by. Jenn moved to one side so that Cynthia and Lexie could say whatever they needed to say away from the crowd.

It was Lexie who spoke. "Ever done restaurant work?"

"Like what? Be a waitress? No."

"Not a waitress," Lexie said. "I work at G & G's, in Freeland? Up above Holmes Harbor? We need a busboy. I know the owners, and I c'n put in a word for you. Minimum wage, but you'd get a share of the tips. You wouldn't be rolling in it 'cause they only do dinner, but you'd have enough for shoes and the rest."

"Freeland?" Jenn said. It was a stalling tactic. Working with Lexie? She didn't know. . . .

"It's a good idea," Cynthia said. "Lexie's leaving for the summer. You could train as a waitress and take over for her when she's gone."

"I dunno," Jenn said. "I don't know how I'd get there in time, after practice, I mean."

"I'll drive you." Lexie snapped her fingers to show how easy it would be.

"But it's way too far for you to take me home," Jenn said next.

"You could take the island bus home," Cynthia pointed out. "You do that after practice anyway."

"Give you time for your homework," Lexie said. "Anyway, think about it."

Jenn said she would but she knew she wouldn't. Truth was there was no way on earth she was going to spend time in a car alone with Lexie Ovanov. With her attitude toward the friends-with-privileges thing, the last thing Jenn wanted was any kind of relationship with Lexie.

15

It was one of those rotten late winter March days in the Pacific Northwest when spring remains only a wish. The wind was threatening to topple the alders that had reached the end of their life span along with all Douglas firs that possessed too shallow roots. Rain was falling in great waving sheets. It seemed that winter would go on forever.

In this weather, Ralph Darrow was returning home, traveling inside one of the island's paratransit vans with his wheelchair strapped into position. He'd worked hard to get to this point. He'd demonstrated his ability to walk, he'd made marked progress in living as a one-armed man, and with his house approved for someone in his condition, there was no reason to keep him in any care facility for another day.

Seth was with him in the van. Rich Darrow was following in his car, accompanied by Prynne. Behind them, Steph Vanderslip cruised. She would give the okay to Ralph's return once he showed her he could manage the ramp up to the porch as well as negotiate the hall, the kitchen, the living room, his bedroom, and the bathroom by using the newly installed handrails. Ralph understood that the onus was on him. At least Seth was pretty *sure* he understood, although his grandfather continued to have trouble with language.

He could tell, though, that Grand was pleased to be going home. Seth only hoped that he would approve of the changes to his house.

The transit van negotiated the rising driveway off Newman Road, and from there Seth directed the driver to the new, secondary driveway that curved off to the right of the hill that hid the house. He saw his grandfather's eyes widen when they made this turn and then proceeded down the slope. Seth had deliberately not told him that a new route had been forged to get him home easily. He'd wanted that to be a surprise.

"Pretty cool, huh?" Seth said to him. "Me and Derric did it. Some guys from work helped. We sold the trees to finance it, plus the rest of the changes in the house."

Ralph reached out with his good hand and clutched Seth's arm tightly. "Gud," he managed. "Fahv et . . ."

Seth smiled, knowing what Grand wanted to say. Ralph had called him "favorite male grandchild" for his entire life, despite the fact that he was the *only* male grandchild. Seth said to him, "This's gonna be tough because of the rain. But if you can manage it in a downpour, you can do anything."

The van came to a halt at the brick path that ran between the house and Ralph's shop. Rich and Steph Vanderslip had parked above in the older area behind the hillock, and through the back windows of the van, Seth and Ralph could see them descending the new driveway along with Prynne. The rain began to let up.

Rich opened the van doors and smiled at his father. He said, "Welcome home, old guy."

As if God was on their side, at that precise moment, the sun came out. The rain became a mist and through this mist, a rainbow shone. Prynne said, "If that's not cool, then nothing is."

Ralph was lowered from the van in his wheelchair. Seth rolled him along the brick path toward the front of the house. He could see that his grandfather was mostly concentrating on his garden at this point. It hadn't been seen to and was in desperate need of its autumn cleanup and its winter alterations.

Seth leaned over and said into Ralph's ear, "No worries, Grand. I haven't got to this part of the place yet, but I will. Promise. You'll have to tell me what to do, though. I don't want to wreck anything."

"Gud bo," Ralph said slowly.

When they reached the ramp, the front door opened. Seth was half-expecting Becca, even though it was a school day and too early for her to be back home. But instead a twentysomething guy with the body of a wide receiver came out of the house. They'd left a key for him just in case he got there while they were gone, and so he had.

He was the first of the home health care aides whom Rich Darrow had chosen. His name was Jake Burns, he was a good-looking mix of Vietnamese and Anglo, and his arms bulged with muscles that he no doubt put to good use when he worked with patients.

Seth felt a little twinge when he saw him, because this was the dude who was going to be there in the house while Prynne was there, and he wasn't sure how he felt about Prynne being alone with the guy. Jake Burns was a stud, and he was damn good-looking on top of that.

The home health care aide came down the ramp, squatted in front of the wheelchair, and extended his hand to Ralph. He said, "Mr. Darrow, it's good to meet you. I'm Jake Burns, and I'm here to make your life run smooth, sir." He already knew Rich Darrow, but he extended his hand to him and to the others as well, repeating their names as they said them to him and offering a smile that Seth figured was capable of melting hearts around the globe. "Let's get you up on your feet, sir," Jake then said to Ralph. "I know this lady here is going to want to see you do your stuff on the ramp. Need help? Steady now? Use the hand-rails, sir. Good thing the rain stopped, huh?"

It was going to be tricky, Seth saw, because Grand had only one good arm. But his walking had improved so much that Seth hoped he could manage the gentle slope of the ramp. He held his breath as Jake steadied Ralph on his feet. Ralph nodded his thanks, took a hesitant step, and then gained assurance when his good hand curved around the rail.

The chicken wire over the wood served its purpose. There was no slipping or sliding. Just a slow, sure walk up to the porch. Ralph managed it as Steph Vanderslip stood to one side and watched. When he made it after what seemed like ten minutes, she said, "Now that's what we're looking for, Mr. Darrow. Nice job. Let's get you inside and check out the rest."

Once inside the house, it seemed to Seth that his grand-father became the real Ralph Darrow again. His expression altered to that old mixture of sardonic and wise. Someone had cut his long hair during his time in the hospital and in rehab, but it was growing out now, on its way to the length he preferred, which was well below his shoulders and tied back beneath his cowboy hat that was, at the moment, hanging on its usual peg beside the front door.

Seth stood back. He worried about how Grand was going to feel not having access to his bedroom on the upper floor any longer, and he shot a concerned look at Prynne as Ralph, Steph, and Rich headed in that direction with Jake leading the way.

He felt Prynne take his hand, linking her fingers with his. She said, "It's gonna be good. No worries. And the guy – Jake? – he seems, like, perfect to be here during the day."

"That's part of my worries," Seth told her. "You and

Captain America, with lots of time to get to know each other."

Prynne stepped back to get a better look at his face. "Seriously?"

"The guy's a stud."

"He's here to do a *job*, dope. Grand has tons of work to do, with physical therapy and language. And anyway . . ." She wrinkled her brow and examined him.

"What?" he said.

"You're my guy. Don't you trust me? I don't like not being trusted, Seth."

"My deal, not yours," was what Seth told her. And it was true. At some point in his life he had to get past that less-than feeling that kept raising its ugly head. He was who he was, and that *was* good enough: for him, for his parents, for his friends, for Prynne. "I trust you, Prynne. Like I said, it's me, not you."

Ralph seemed to have approved the bedroom and the bathroom. He also appeared to understand that Becca would continue to live in the house and do the cooking and the cleaning. He nodded when it was explained that he and Becca had simply switched rooms. Rich added, "For now," although all of them knew that it wasn't likely Grand was going to be able to manage the stairs again.

"It's all looking good to me," was Steph Vanderslip's announcement when Ralph had demonstrated his ability to get around the house. "The objective, Mr. Darrow," she told him, "is to have you living on your own once again, without assistance. That could happen if you keep up the work. The language has got to improve, though."

"It . . ." Ralph seemed to search for the word. It took some time. They all waited. "Wheel," he finally managed. He pointed to his head. "Try . . . fend . . ."

Seth swallowed the lump that formed in his throat. It

wasn't only that Grand had lost words. He'd also lost the ability even to form them.

But Steph nodded, saying, "Welcome home, then," and to the rest of them, "Now you let me know if there's anything I can do to help out. Nice job," she added to Seth. "When I want some work done on my house, you're the guy I'm going to call."

And then she left them and it was time for Ralph to get to know what the routine would be, what Jake would be doing, and what Prynne would be doing. Her part – aside from keeping an eye on things – would be language skills. To that end, they'd bought flash cards, board games, and photograph books to help Ralph recapture his vocabulary.

Jake, then, suggested Ralph come into the kitchen, where he had sandwiches ready. He had Ralph lead the way, and as they went, he told Seth's granddad a bit about himself. Football, UW, and two concussions, he said. "I wanted to have enough brains left to get into nursing, sir, so that was it for me. Now I just watch. Huskies and the 'Hawks. You into football, sir?" He did his nursing course in night school, he explained. He was well on his way to earning an RN degree.

Footsteps pounded across the front porch just as Ralph was settled at the kitchen table. At first Seth figured it was Steph Vanderslip, having forgotten something. But then the door swung open, and Seth's aunt Brenda stood there.

Rich Darrow said, "He's done it all, Bren: the ramp, the house, everything. This's Jake Burns," he added as Jake's head appeared around the door to the kitchen. "My sister Brenda," Rich said to Jake.

She didn't acknowledge Jake's "Nice to meet you, ma'am." Nor did she acknowledge either Seth or Prynne. Instead, she walked to the kitchen to observe her father, said, "What kind of sandwich is that? It had better be something easy for him to chew and swallow."

"Tuna and mayo," Jake told her.

"Celery? Nuts? Seeds? What else is in it?"

"Christ, Bren, Dad can eat," Rich Darrow said.

"Dad can choke as well," she shot back at him.

"Chopped celery and relish," Jake said, and to Ralph, "You think you're okay with this, Mr. Darrow?"

"Of *course* he'll think he's okay," Brenda snapped. "Are you an idiot? He's had a stroke."

Jake said nothing in reply, and Rich went into the kitchen and suggested that Brenda come join him in the living room. A fire was laid there, and he lit it. He gestured to Ralph's new chair and chose the hearth for himself as Seth and Prynne went for the chess table that sat beneath one of the living room windows looking out into the dull winter garden.

"Here's what you need to know, Richard," Brenda said to her brother before he could make a remark. "This is just a courtesy call. I stopped at your place first. Amy told me where to find you, by the way." She said this last bit triumphantly, as if it had been some big betrayal, Seth thought: his mom revealing to Aunt Brenda where his dad had gone. "I'm on my way to Oak Harbor," Brenda continued. "I'm filing a petition for guardianship."

Seth wasn't sure what this meant, but he could tell from his dad's expression that it wasn't good. Rich said, "Come on. Don't do that. If nothing else, it gets us into a legal wrangling that could—"

"No legal wrangling at all. The judge appoints someone to evaluate Dad's circumstances. You know what I mean: his ability to care for himself, make financial decisions, and keep this place in good condition. That person will take a look at everything. He – or she, of course – will also have Dad examined by a doctor."

"Brenda—"

Brenda held up a hand to silence him, continuing with,

"The doctor will make a report. Based on that and the evaluation of Dad's circumstances, the judge will decide if guardianship is needed. It's very simple." She added with a thin smile, "Dad can have a jury trial if he wants, of course, based on what the reports say about him. But I don't encourage that, to be honest, because the cost to him – and, obviously, the cost to you – would probably get out of hand."

Prynne and Seth exchanged a look. Brenda had been talking quietly, but Seth's worry was that his grandfather might have heard. And he was going to hear if things heated up, which they definitely would if Seth's dad couldn't stay cool in the face of what his sister was planning to do.

Seth was surprised when all Rich did was sigh. He said, "I'd hoped we could resolve this easier, but I guess we can't." He then brought out of his jacket a business-size envelope and handed it to his sister. "It's durable power of attorney for health care," he told her. "Dad signed it when he turned seventy. It makes me, not you, the responsible party, Bren."

From where he was sitting, Seth could hear his aunt draw in breath like a gasp. There was no other sound aside from the popping of sap in the wood burning in the fireplace. Brenda unfolded the paperwork, which consisted of two pages. She read through them, and the rest of them waited for her reaction.

Calmly, she folded the paperwork and returned it to its envelope. "I see a signature, Rich, but it hasn't been notarized."

"It doesn't need to be notarized."

"That's not quite true," Brenda said. "So you've got yourself a bit of a problem."

Rich's eyes narrowed as he said, "What the hell are you talking about?"

"I'm talking about the fact that this doesn't look like Dad's signature to me."

"Come on, Brenda, you *know*—"

"Gosh, I know nothing at all. As far as I can tell – and anyone else, for that matter – this signature's nothing but a forgery, Richard."

16

Everything at Ralph Darrow's place trundled along. Grand did what he was supposed to do with physical therapy and language practice, and the two home health care aides showed up on time and were useful in assisting him. Prynne turned up promptly at seven in the morning to take the day shift of calming everyone's concerns. Becca got home after school as soon as she could manage it via bus and bike in order to do the same until the next morning. The only problem was Seth's aunt. But mostly Brenda remained offstage, making thunder noises by rattling pans.

Still, Becca worried about where this Aunt Brenda thing was heading. Seth told her the situation was no big deal because his dad had had Grand sign some papers about his health care a couple of years back. So Rich was the one with power, not Brenda. But Becca wasn't sure this was the case. Yet until something more happened with Brenda Sloan – like her showing up with the sheriff or something – there wasn't much Becca could do. She only wished Grand was making more progress. Physically, he was more adept. But his language skills were not improving. No one was sure why. And until he acquired the necessary language to express himself, there would always need to be someone with him in case an emergency developed.

Even his whispers had not greatly improved. They were still choppy, and although Becca could pick up his memory visions, his whispers weren't able to clarify what those visions meant.

"Hey you," was the greeting of the second home health care aide to Becca about a week later. "How's love treating you, girl? You engaged to that gorgeous hunk of yours yet? Better get on it 'cause the two of you . . . ? You're gonna make some bee-you-tee-ful, babies." She was called Celia Black, and she was a tiny birdlike thing of extraordinary strength. From Oklahoma originally, she spoke with a marked midwestern accent and the kind of small town friendliness that made her a good fit on the island.

"I figure graduating from high school might be a better goal right now," Becca told her.

Celia hooted. "Don't give me *that* one. I know kids."

"Need any help with anything?" Becca asked.

"Nope. Me and Ralphie here just about got things under control." She and Grand were seated at the chess table across the living room. She held up one of the flash cards for Ralph. A bright green tractor was pictured on it. "He's being the ornery one today, though. Come on now, Ralphie, you knew this yesterday."

Becca crossed the room to the chess table, plucking the earbud of the AUD box from her ear and removing the box itself from the waistband of her jeans. She bent to Ralph Darrow and kissed him on the cheek.

"Hey, Grand," she said. "You being ornery like Celia says?"

Ralph turned his head. He said, "Beck," in that new voice he had that struggled for sound. But what he had on his mind was more than that. *Tooper ole* came to her, as did *Tybassle.* The first she figured out fairly quickly. Grand didn't appreciate being called *Ralphie.* At seventy-plus years old, who would? *Ralphie* made him feel like a toddler. *Tooper ole* meant *two years old.* The second, though . . . Becca had to think about that one. *Tybassle*. But then it came to her. *Thai. Basil*. Near the highway, in a small area of businesses developed from a square of repurposed historic buildings called Bayview Corner, there was a Thai restaurant: the Basil Café. She went into the kitchen, looked into the fridge and then called out to Celia, "Hey, what d'you think about Thai food for dinner? If I call in an order to the Basil Café, could you pick it up? I got the cash."

Celia said to Ralph, "You want Thai food, Ralphie?" And when Ralph Darrow growled in reply, "I don't think he wants it, Becca."

"Try it by calling him Ralph, maybe. Or Mr. Darrow. That might make a difference."

"Why?"

"Just a feeling I have." Becca came to the doorway, leaned against the jamb. She held a takeaway menu in her hand.

Celia said to Ralph, "You want me to call you Ralph? Or Mr. Darrow, honey? I c'n do that easy as anything."

"Mr. Darrow might be the best," Becca said. "That's what Jake calls him, and he does anything Jake asks him to do."

"Yeah? Well, heck, then. Mr. Darrow it is. You give me that menu, Becky, hon. Me and Mr. Darrow'll decide what eats we want."

Becca cringed at *Becky* but she decided one baby step at a time would be best. She handed Celia the menu and said, "Isn't Prynne here? Did she take off already?"

"Haven't seen hide or hair," Celia told her. "She here, Ralphie? Whoops. Mr. Darrow?"

Ralph pointed at the ceiling. "No white," were the words he managed.

Becca figured he meant that Prynne was upstairs. Maybe *Not right* was what he was trying to say, she thought. If that was the case, either he didn't want her up above or something was wrong with Prynne.

Becca said to him, "I'll check on her, Grand."

She went to the stairs. In Ralph's former bedroom overlooking the garden, Prynne lay on the bed. Her arm was across her eyes in the manner of someone with a head-splitting migraine.

Becca stood quite still but got nothing at all from Prynne, which suggested she was deeply asleep. She crossed the room and touched her shoulder in a featherlike gesture against the sweater Prynne was wearing. Immediately, her vision altered and she saw the same young bearded man she'd glimpsed before. This time, though, he was with two little kids. They wore small backpacks, and one of them also carried a red lunch box with tootsie roll written in white upon it. They were climbing into an old VW van. The young man looked up. His expression marked him as deeply irritated. He gave an arm wave that clearly said "Get *out* of here," and that was it. The vision lasted less than five seconds. But it was crystal clear.

Prynne stirred. *Things get unfair when it's too much* came from her. She murmured, "Hey. Whoa," as she lowered her arm from her eyes and saw Becca. She was, Becca realized, utterly stoned.

She knew Prynne did weed. But she wasn't supposed to smoke at Ralph's, and anyway, there was no scent of weed in the air. Not that that mattered because she was there to keep on top of things, to keep an eye on what was going on with Grand, and to help out wherever it was necessary. She wasn't there to get high.

"What are you *doing*?" Becca whispered tersely. "What did you take? And don't say nothing because I'm not an idiot."

Prynne blinked twice, more an exercising of her eyelids

to see if they still functioned rather than anything else. "Damn. Sorry," she told Becca. "I just . . . I didn't think it would do anything."

"What?"

"Weed oil."

"*Weed* oil? Are you crazy? How d'you think Seth would feel if he knew that when you're here, with Grand, and everyone's depending on you . . ."

"Chill," Prynne said. "I just took a teaspoon. I didn't know how strong it was. And nothing was going on anyway except Jake helping Grand eat lunch."

"So you've been stoned since lunchtime? Oh that's just *great*, Prynne. And where'd you get weed oil anyway?"

"There's the shop . . . you know . . . over by the lumber place."

"You *bought* it? You're telling me you also have a fake ID?"

Prynne swung her legs over the side of the bed. She'd removed her eye patch but she wasn't wearing her glass eye, so Becca had her first look at what childhood cancer had done to Prynne. She wanted to feel a little bad for her, but she was so ticked off that she also wanted to smack her.

Prynne reached for the eye patch and fastened it around her head. She said, "I'm *sorry*. I just went inside to see what they had and this guy was buying some and he told me it was righteous. I sort of said I was so totally looking forward to being twenty-one and he sort of said he'd give me a sample if I wanted some."

"Wait. Are you saying that you went there *today*? While you were supposed to be here with Grand?"

"Nothing was going on here!" Prynne said hotly. "I was gone, like, twenty minutes. And Jake said I could go, okay? He and Grand were playing chess and I needed to get some tampons because it's not like Grand exactly keeps them here and I don't know where yours are. So that's what happened and I'm *sorry*. I didn't think it would affect me like this. But it's not like I committed some capital crime."

Can't do it won't do can't I knew comprised a rush of words like the wind blowing Becca's hair back. *Seth and that's it for me the best person and who am I really I screw up.*

Becca saw that Prynne was more upset with herself than she was with Becca. It was time to back off. Prynne had blown it, but she wasn't a bad person. She said, "Okay. Sorry. I freaked out. But you can't do it again. You know that, right?"

"Course." Prynne got to her feet. She swayed a little. Becca grabbed her arm.

There he was again. That guy. Youngish, bearded, smiling at her, making an *O* with his lips and then giving a grin. Then he was gone, and Prynne was there. Becca wanted to ask who he was and how he fit into Prynne's life. She wanted to know because of Seth. But there was no way that she could ask the questions. It was part of the curse of the seeing and the hearing with which she was both afflicted and blessed.

She said to Prynne, "You better not leave till you come down from that stuff. No way do you want to be on the road."

"Got it," Prynne said. She was quiet as Becca headed toward the door. Before Becca left the room altogether, she spoke again, though. "Please don't tell Seth, okay?"

17

Jenn had buried the hatchet with Squat before they saw the first of the posters that had gone up around the school during the lunch hour. They were hard to miss. Someone with a talent for drawing had created a bunch of steam punk images that were collecting a crowd at every poster: imaginative trains, outrageous flying machines, cars with parachutes attached, submarines that looked like giant squids. You just *had* to walk over to see what they were advertising.

Jenn and Squat worked their way to the front of the group standing before a poster that featured one of the flying machines. It turned out to be an announcement for something called the Rainbow Prom. Seeing this, Jenn figured at first that it was all about coming up with a dance to make it seem as if winter *was* actually going to end someday. Rain and rainbows . . .

"Don't be such a concrete head," Squat said in reply to her observation. He glanced around at the other kids and then worked his way out of the group, taking Jenn with him.

"What?" she said.

"*Rainbow*, Jenn. *Rainbow* prom."

"So?"

"It's a dance for bent twigs."

Jenn was processing this and deciding how she felt about the expression *bent twigs* when Squat went on, perhaps assuming she'd not picked up on what he meant. He said. "Those living on the other side of normal? Girls into girls? Guys into guys? Guys into *being* girls? Girls into being guys? You get my meaning?" To emphasize his point, Squat held up his hands and made a cross with them, as if to ward off vampires. "Save me!" he joked.

He got noticed. Jenn saw the smirks on some faces of kids who'd looked at the poster. She also saw the scowls on the faces of others. She was about to tell Squat to keep his opinions to himself when Becca walked up and saw the poster. She said to Jenn, "Cool! A prom! When is it?"

"You'd actually go?" Jenn asked her.

"Huh? Wouldn't you? You probably don't even need a date. But if you want one . . ." She turned to Squat. "Why don't you take Jenn to the prom?"

"You whacked out?" he demanded. "No frigging way. It might be catching."

"What might be catching?"

He pointed to the smaller print at the bottom of the sign. This indicated that the prom was being sponsored by the Gay-Straight Alliance on campus. Becca said, after reading this, "But if it's gay and *straight*, anyone can go."

Squat's reply was, "Oh sure. Anyone can go, long as they don't care if someone of the same sex puts hands on their personal parts. That, however, ain't going to be me."

Jenn found that she'd become even more irritated as he'd gone on. She said to him, "What *is* your problem, Squat? The way you act . . . It's like you're already one of them and you have to pretend that—"

"Oh right," Squat scoffed. "I'm one of them like *you're* one of them, Jenn." He gave her a shrewd look. "And maybe you are. Out there on the track every day now, aren't you?"

"You keeping *tabs* on me now?"

Jenn saw Becca fiddling with her hearing thingy, working

on the earbud as if it was dirty. She said, "Hey, you guys . . ." in the tone of someone who was trying to pour balm on a sore.

Squat, however, wasn't to be mollified. He said, "You better start thinking about what you're doing, Jenn."

To which Jenn said, "And you better stop."

She was still ticked off at him after school as she banged into the locker room to change into her training clothes. She'd thought she knew Squat better than anyone. His older brother was a creep and a half, but Squat had always been live-and-let-live and all the rest. She couldn't figure out what was happening with him.

At her locker, she dropped her backpack and went for the lock. Then she saw that beneath it stood a pair of shoes. They were identical to kind that both Cynthia and Lexie wore. She could tell they were only slightly used.

"They're mine. I thought you could wear 'em."

Jenn looked up. Lexie and Cynthia had just come around the corner into the aisle where they, too, had their lockers. Lexie was the one who'd spoken.

"Don't you need them?" Jenn asked. Shoes like this? *She* would wear them till they fell apart. Then she saw that Lexie's own shoes were new, and she realized that the other girl saw her as a charity case. The fact that she *was* one, the fact that her whole family was one . . . Jenn couldn't stand the idea that people knew about the McDaniels family's poverty. You couldn't register for the food bank, for the family support center, for Holiday House at Christmas, and for year-round free lunches without everyone knowing you were in a bad way. But Jenn didn't talk about this, and unlike Petey and Andy, she didn't take part in anything that would mark her as needy. So she said, "I don't want . . ." Only, she did. She wanted the shoes and she wanted what they might do to improve her performance.

Lexie said, "You don't have to take 'em. I get new ones every year, no matter what. I figured if you're the same size, you can use those. I'm not going to, and they're just going to end up at the thrift store."

Jenn said, "Okay. Thanks," but the thought of wearing Lexie's shoes any longer than was *absolutely* necessary prompted Jenn to bring up the busboy job that Lexie had mentioned. That job would give her what she needed: not only to pay for her place on the All Island Girls' Soccer team, should she make it, but also to buy what she needed for training. Among that stuff would be good shoes, *new* shoes so that she could return these others to Lexie.

She didn't want to consider why taking them − not to mention wearing them − was such an issue for her. She just told herself she wanted to be able to do things on her own.

In the cause of this, she said to Lexie, "I been thinking a lot about that job you told me about."

Lexie turned from her locker where she'd just pulled out her training clothes. Before she replied, she jerked her hoodie off and removed her bra. Jenn glanced away, but it was to see Cynthia watching her with a thoughtful look on her face. Jenn moved her own gaze back to Lexie who was getting into a sports bra and reaching for sweats.

Lexie said, "G & G's? The busboy job?"

"If it's still open, I sort of want to apply."

"Sure," Lexie said. "It's still open. They tried out one kid but he was a total bust. So if you want to see if you c'n do it, cool. I'm working tonight. I c'n drive you up there."

"Oh, I can take the bus," Jenn said quickly. "I'm, like, not totally sure what time I can get there. Got to talk to my mom and everything. You know?"

Lexie zipped her top. She put up the hood. She said,

"Whatever. It's up to you." And then to Cynthia, "You doing weights first?"

"Not today," Cynthia said.

"Okay." And to Jenn, "See you on the track," before she went through the far doors that led to the fields.

Jenn didn't like being left alone with Cynthia because she had the feeling that Cynthia knew more about her than she knew about herself. Which, she soon saw, Cynthia made clear enough with what she said next.

"You could have taken the ride, Jenn," she told her. "We generally don't bite unless someone asks to be bitten."

18

What Seth knew was that nobody needed any more stress, least of all his mom. She'd been ordered by her doctor to do as little as possible, all in the cause of healing. Her guts had been cut into and her whole digestive system had been more or less untangled, and she had a way to go to come back from that. She was in good condition, but even for someone in good condition, major surgery was serious. So when Seth got home from work several days later, he knew something was up the second he looked at his mom's face. When she asked him if he'd come into her bedroom, he figured it had to do with Prynne, who was in the kitchen area making tacos for dinner.

"This is very strange, Seth," was how his mom began. "I phoned the pharmacy today to renew my prescription for my pain pills, and they told me it wasn't time yet. But I had only two pills left. When I told them, they said that even if I'd been taking two each day, I should still have eight remaining."

Seth frowned. "Maybe you took more than one when you were feeling rotten. Or maybe you forgot you already took one a couple of times and you took a second when the first didn't work fast enough."

"That's not possible," Amy replied. "I was afraid I might do that, so I made a record." She went to the bedside table, and from the drawer she took a small spiral pad. She showed him how she'd divided it into days and weeks.

She showed him there were only two marks for every day since the pills had been prescribed.

Seth said, "Maybe you got up in the middle of the night a few times and took a pill and forgot to mark it."

She shook her head and her gaze seemed regretful. She said, "Seth, I don't think so."

He was forced then to ask, "What kind of pills are they, anyway?"

"OxyContin," was her reply.

Seth didn't want to have the conversation he knew he had to have with Prynne, so he stalled as long as he could. After dinner, he told her and his parents that poor ol' Gus needed a long walk, run, and ball-chasing session, and when his mom said, "In the dark?" he replied with, "You know Gus," which meant, essentially, nothing.

His parents looked surprised by this. So did Prynne when he said no to her question of, "Want me to go, too?"

He got out of there quickly. He and Gus piled into the VW. Seth drove around as long as he could. When he finally went back home, he found his dad the only one still up. Rich was loading pictures of his newest glass pieces onto his website. He said, "Everything okay, son?" and Seth claimed everything was fine.

He then went to his bedroom. He found Prynne sitting up in bed, flipping through an old *National Geographic*. She laid this aside and said to him as he closed the door, "You want to tell me what's wrong?"

"Why d'you think something's wrong?"

"Because you didn't say ten words at dinner and you never take Gus anywhere to play at night."

Seth could see no other way to go at it but directly. "You've been getting high," he said.

She seemed to be trying to read his face for what was

going on in his head before she answered with, "You know I smoke weed. I've only been doing it when you're—"

"I don't mean weed," he interrupted.

Her expression altered. He could see it get wary. She said, "Becca."

"Huh?"

"She told you."

Seth swore, which he never did in front of anyone except the guys at work. Then he said, "Becca didn't say *anything*. Are you frigging telling me you dropped Oxy over at *Grand's*?"

"You're protecting her, aren't you? That's just what I would—"

"Keep your voice down. This isn't about Becca. She didn't tell me jack. This is about my mom's pain pills. She's missing six. And she's been keeping a record of when she took them. So she knows how many she should have left. *Okay*?"

Prynne was silent for a moment before she said, "I didn't . . ." but her voice was shaky.

Seth pressed his point. "Oh right. Like I'm expected to believe you?"

She pressed her fingers to her lips. Seth said nothing else so that she would be forced to speak, which she finally did. "I ran out of weed. I can't buy it legally yet, not at the weed store, and I didn't know where else . . . I mean, I couldn't exactly ask you who's dealing, could I? So I took one of her pills. Just one."

"I said she's missing six, Prynne. The pharmacy told her she should have eight left, not just two. So tell the truth. Did you take six of her pills? Pills she needs for her frigging *pain*?"

Tears began to spill down Prynne's cheek. "I didn't think . . . It didn't seem . . ."

Seth threw his jacket onto the floor. He paced to the bed. Prynne shrank back. He hissed, "That's just *great*. So now she gets to take some completely *not* effective painkiller till she can renew her prescription. All because you just *had* to get high. Is something wrong with you? What am I missing here?"

Prynne grabbed the other pillow on the bed and held it to her stomach, as if it would somehow offer her a comfort that wasn't coming from Seth. She said, "I was an idiot. I was stupid. I saw them inside the cabinet where you told me I could put my stuff and . . . Seth, please. I'm totally sorry."

What Seth thought was that sorry wasn't going to cut it, and he was about to say that when Prynne grabbed her purse where it sat under the bedside table. She fumbled with it to get it open. "I don't know *why* I did it. I didn't think she would . . . I just wanted to see what it was like. See, I've heard of them but I've never done them and there they were and . . ." She began to sob. She brought from her purse a twisted-up tissue and shoved it at him.

He untwisted it. There were five blue pills screwed up within it. He said, "Six, *six*," because he still couldn't get his head around what she'd done to his mom by snatching the pills.

Prynne said, "I only tried one. I didn't like what it did to me. I was out of it. Becca came home and found me. I don't remember what I told her but I *think* I said I wasn't feeling good or I hadn't gotten a good night's sleep or something. But after I used that one, I forgot I even had them. If I'd remembered, I would've put them back. I swear it. I double swear it. You have to believe me."

Seth looked from the pills to Prynne's face. He'd never seen her so upset. He hesitated. She was so close to him: not only right now in this room but also in the spirit of who she was. He'd never met a girl with whom he'd had such an instant connection. He'd never even expected that out of life.

"Okay," he said. "It's okay."

"But do you . . . Seth, do you believe me? Because if you don't . . . If I've wrecked everything between us . . ."

"I believe you," he told her. "I wish you'd put the pills back, but I'm glad you didn't like what they did to you."

She said, "I was *out* of it. I don't want to feel that way again, ever."

He smoothed her wild and crinkly hair. He considered what he could do to tell his mom about what Prynne had done. When he thought he had it all straight in his head, he kissed Prynne and told her he'd be right back.

In the bathroom, he opened the cabinet. He could see that, as good as her earlier word, Prynne had organized it for the family. She'd even bought some plastic containers to help in the matter. He shifted things here and there a bit, to make it look as if he'd done a search. Then he took a bottle of Aleve and carried it, along with the five extra Oxy pills, into his mom's bedroom.

"Mystery solved," he told her. "I think you spilled six of the pills into your hand, took one, and accidentally put the rest in here." He held up the bottle of Aleve. "At least, that's where I found them."

Amy looked up from a novel she was reading. She saw the pills lying in Seth's palm. She looked from them to the bottle of Aleve. She looked from that bottle up to Seth's face. She said, "How strange. That's where you found them?"

"Yep," he told her. "You want me to put them back in the prescription bottle for you?"

She gazed at him for a very long time. He began to get hot all over. She finally said slowly, "I'd appreciate that. You go ahead and put them away for me."

19

Seth wanted to believe Prynne. But he knew people on the island who played around with everything from weed to meth, and the one thing he'd learned from knowing these people was that when it came to dopers, they'd lie about anything. And Prynne *had* lied by omission when she hadn't told him about moving to Port Townsend. He couldn't forget that.

But the thing was, he didn't *want* to think of her as a liar or a serious doper. It was true that she'd smoked weed from the time he'd met her. But she'd never done a *lot* of weed, and this had to mean something, right?

He wanted to be sure about the doper thing. If he and Prynne were going to make it together, then they had to come at things honestly. So in what he told himself was the cause of complete honesty, he decided to check up on her.

He figured he could do it through the means of her regular, twice monthly gig in Port Townsend. He needed Becca to be willing to stay with Grand, since the gig was on a Saturday afternoon and evening, but he knew she'd do it if he asked her.

Since Port Townsend was a popular destination for both Whidbey Islanders and people from over town, Seth figured the ferry would be crowded. This would be all to his benefit. He could follow Prynne in his VW at some distance from South Whidbey as she buzzed up the highway on her Vespa. If he timed everything right, she'd already be on the ferry

– at the front, where the motorcycles were placed – when he got to the dock. With the number of cars boarding after her, he'd be lost among them.

It all went as planned. He was a little surprised by the early hour at which she set off. But her explanation as she kissed him goodbye seemed completely reasonable: she wanted to go by the house so that she could tell the guys that her move to Whidbey was going to be permanent.

"If that's what you want," she said to Seth. "After the Oxy thing and all . . . You haven't said but I was hoping . . ."

"Permanent?" Seth said to her. "Like in you and me permanent?"

"Well, yeah," she said and her cheeks got red. "I love you, Seth. You've figured that out, right?"

He grabbed her, lifted her off the ground. He wanted them to be together more than anything he'd ever wanted in his life.

After that, he almost gave up the idea of seeing what was going on with her trips to Port Townsend. But since he'd made the plan and since Becca was ready to stay with Grand and since his mom was happy to keep Gus with her, he decided to go ahead. If Prynne saw him, he'd tell her that he'd intended to surprise her by showing up at her gig.

She was far ahead of him when the ferry docked across Admiralty Bay. He worried a little that he might lose her then. Parts of Port Townsend constituted a fairly vast network of streets, so if he wasn't quick to catch up with Prynne, he was going to be in trouble.

He didn't ask himself why, after her admission of love for him, he wasn't just happily heading to the coffeehouse where she was going to perform. Instead he told himself that following her was just idle curiosity. And anyway, he continued in his head, her performance was a few hours away.

He saw her veer to the left off the ferry. He knew this meant that she was taking the southeast route that would lead to the upper part of the town. He was familiar with the way, so he wasn't too concerned that he might lose her. He got a little anxious, though, when he hit the red light at the end of the ferry dock while Prynne herself zoomed out of sight.

He swore then. When traffic took off, he cranked up the speed and hoped a cop wasn't nearby.

An old clock tower marked the road that Prynne would have had to take, and he turned there as well. Along the way, a sign pointed the direction to the upper town, and he took this turn, too. The street bisected the upper part of town, running past shops and a few restaurants, with side streets perpendicular to it. Prynne wasn't in sight, so Seth knew she'd already taken a cross street somewhere. She had to have gone right or left soon after getting onto this main street, though. What he had to do was just keep an eye out.

This worked. Ten blocks along, where the businesses started to give way to the nineteenth-century mansions for which the little town was famous in the Pacific Northwest, he saw that Prynne's Vespa was parked on one of the side streets, this one narrower than the rest, populated by houses that were old like the mansions but ordinary in their architecture. Some of them were big with nothing to distinguish them, others were small with overgrown gardens.

It was in front of a house of this latter type that Prynne's Vespa was parked. Seth frowned when he got near enough to it to see what it was like. He was confused. If Prynne lived with three male roommates in a place large enough for them each to have a bedroom, the house in front of which Prynne had left the Vespa was not it.

Seth drove by slowly. He couldn't see much. There was

an untrimmed hedge in front of the place and an arbor weighed down by a massive wisteria not yet in bloom that marked the path to the front door. In a driveway shaded by a huge cherry tree in riotous pink flower, a VW van was parked. Just beyond it, Seth could see a garage. But that was it. Prynne was nowhere in sight.

He made a U-turn at the end of the block. He pulled to the side of the street and tried to decide what to do. He told himself that Prynne wasn't *up* to anything as far as he could see. But then he realized that was the point: as far as he could see. He needed to see more.

He got out of his VW and began to walk back in the direction of the small house. The fact that there was no sign of life on the outside of it suggested that Prynne had gone within. He knew that there was no way in hell that he'd be able to sneak around peering through the windows without someone catching him and raising the alarm. It seemed that his only choices were to wait out of sight or to slink down the driveway and check out the van and possibly the garage as well.

Part of him was saying that this was a very dumb move. Another part of him was saying that it was way too strange that Prynne had come to this spot instead of to a house she could have reasonably lived in with three guys. And the final part of him was saying that since Prynne had apparently not told him the truth about *why* she'd come to Port Townsend so early, it behooved him to discover the reason.

He peered into the van. In the back of it, he saw boxes of what looked like neatly stacked tiles. Handmade, they were the kind of tiles you could buy at the myriad craft fairs that sprang up around Washington with the arrival of spring. In addition to these boxes, there were two kids' seats: those booster types. A beaded necklace swung from the rear view mirror. A Mexican poncho lay across the back seat. The ashtray of the van was pulled out and filled with the butts of what looked like hand-rolled cigarettes. Seth would have decided that was indeed what they were had not a second glance at the necklace shown him that a roach clip was the pendant.

Then he knew. Prynne had come to her source for weed. Okay, he told himself. No way could he blame her. He knew that she hadn't found a source on the island, so she'd come to buy some here.

Then he heard voices: Prynne and some guy. Seth saw that the people door into the garage was open on the side of the building that faced the house. He moved closer to it to hear a guy saying, "I can't even *get* it anymore, Prynne. It's way too risky," to which Prynne responded, "You *have* to get it." To which he said, "Uh . . . no I don't."

"So what am I supposed to *do*?" she demanded, and at this her voice grew loud.

"Hey!" he said. "Lower your voice. All I need right now is Mandy coming out and seeing you here . . . or one of the kids. . . ."

"You got me started and it's your responsibility to—"

"Wait a second! Way I remember it, you came to me. I didn't go looking for you. Way I remember it, your parents threw you out, you left Port Gamble, you ended up here, and first thing you did was look for a source. You found me and now you can find someone else."

There was a silence. Then into it came words that rattled the brains in Seth's head and turned his body into an iceberg. The man spoke them. "Look. I can still sell you weed, Prynne, but nothing else. Not anymore. You're on Whidbey now, right? So find the stuff there. Everyone knows the place is crawling with dealers."

"Oh, fine. You're a real prince, Steve. I'll just take an ad out in their stupid paper."

Seth was rooted to the spot where he stood, just in front of the van. He felt frozen. He felt struck by lightning. He felt sick to his stomach. He felt sunken in quicksand. He didn't know *what* he felt.

Then Prynne came out of the garage. Then Prynne saw him. Then things got worse.

The way Seth saw it in the split second before Prynne spoke, *she* should have been the person who was embarrassed, humiliated, freaked out, upset, devastated, or any combination of those things. *She* was the one who'd lied to *him*. *She* was the one who'd come to see her dealer. *She* was the one who was doing *whatever* it was beyond marijuana, and he wasn't sure he even wanted to know what she was doping up with but he had a good idea, especially since the important bit was that she'd obviously lied to him about what her doping consisted of.

What happened next was a total surprise.

After a moment of taking him in, she strode over to him. She began swearing in a way he couldn't even have begun to imagine she was capable of. She went through every foul word she probably knew and then red in the face and shaking with rage she said, "You *followed* me! You acted like some FBI agent and you followed me. I *hate* you for that!"

Seth was struck nearly wordless. All he could think of and all he could say was, "You were the one—" before she shoved past him.

The guy in the garage came outside, and Seth took him in: bearded, bony, wearing a flannel shirt and jeans, sandals and socks on his feet. The guy said, "Hey! Shut the hell up! Damn it all, Prynne, who *is* this guy? You brought someone with you? That's just *so* fine. Get off this property before I call the cops."

Prynne then shouted, "Oh, like you're really going to do that, Steve! Like you've got *nothing* to hide."

She went to her Vespa. Seth followed her. What Steve did at that point, he neither knew nor cared. Seth said to Prynne what he'd planned to say, "I was gonna surprise you at your gig. But then you headed the wrong direction and—"

"Liar!" she shouted. "My gig's not for hours and you know it. You *followed* me because you think . . . *whatever* you think. I'm out of here and I don't want to see you again. I can't even believe what you did."

20

When Becca arrived at Diana Kinsale's house for her regular practice session, she found a note on the door. Diana's truck was in the driveway, so Becca was surprised that she wasn't at home. But the note said that she'd be back soon, that Becca was to let herself in. "You know where the key is," Diana had written.

Becca frowned. Diana's words didn't bother her, but her handwriting looked bad: skippy and scratchy, as if the pen had been faulty.

Becca read the note a second time, more thoughtfully. But she could conclude nothing, so she shoved it into her pocket and went around the house to the dog run. The extra key hung inside the dogs' shelter, a good place for it, since only a very foolish burglar would have gone inside a run housing large dogs to scout around for a house key.

She found Oscar with them, which gave her pause. He hung back from Becca with his expression suggesting offense at having been locked up with these lesser canines.

Becca eased into the run. She picked her way among the dogs and squished through the mulch to the shelter, noting once again how badly it needed to be replaced. She found the key where it was hanging on a nail. She eased back out of the run, taking Oscar with her. He seemed only too happy to leave his companions behind, since he willingly followed Becca to the back door of the house, and when she had it unlocked, he preceded her inside without a glance cast back at his run mates. They barked in protest. Becca couldn't blame them. Had she been at all confident that they would return to her when called to do so, she would have let them out into the field next to Diana's house.

In the mudroom, Oscar went to his water bowl. He lapped for a bit, turned his attention to his food dish, and began crunching on the kibble. Becca went into the kitchen. There she saw that Diana's laptop was on the table. It was plugged in and it was open. Becca decided to use the time to see if there was news from Parker Natalia.

There was not. She was beginning to think there never would be news. Her mom had been determined that Jeff Corrie would never find her, but the problem was that she'd hidden herself too well.

Becca went for Jeff Corrie next. Googling his name took her to the very latest. This consisted of Olivia Bolding and an article she'd written sometime after speaking to Connor West. It seemed that the discovery of Connor West in Mexico had prompted the police, the DA, the FBI, and the SEC to consider something Jeff Corrie had been claiming from the first about his missing wife and her daughter: that they'd headed north. For a call to the sheriff on Whidbey Island had confirmed that someone had indeed spoken to Jeff Corrie from the sheriff's office and the subject of the call had been a cell phone found on Whidbey and traced back to Laurel Armstrong sometime after her disappearance.

This detail had apparently whetted Olivia Bolding's appetite for a good story. There was, after all, a Pulitzer out there, and the story had all the elements of a win for the reporter: embezzled money, disappearances, an alleged death that turned out to be a flight into a foreign country, missing persons, accusations, possible homicides. She'd be nuts not to follow the trail, now that the sheriff had told her about the cell phone.

Becca's palms began to sweat. She felt anxiety running up and down her arms. She switched off the computer and filled a glass with water. She was drinking it down when she heard the dogs begin to yip outside.

When she went to the front door, she saw that an old hatchback had pulled into the driveway behind Diana's truck, and Diana was inside. A woman Becca recognized was just getting out of the driver's seat and coming around to the passenger door. She was Sharla Mann, and she ran a one-person hair salon out of her mudroom on the west side of Whidbey. For a while the previous year, Becca had worked for Sharla's life partner, Ivar Thorndyke. During this time, she'd come to know both of them well, but as far as she knew, Sharla and Diana were connected only because Sharla saw to Diana's hair. Yet her hair on this day was completely unchanged from the last time Becca had seen her.

Oscar eased past Becca. The dogs in the run continued to yip. Sharla helped Diana out of the car and caught sight of the poodle. She looked from him to the door, saw Becca coming toward the VW, and said, "Long time, no see. You need a haircut. What d'you think, Diana?"

"She could do with a trim," Diana said, and to Becca, "I'm so sorry I'm late."

"My fault," Sharla put in. "I talked her into a movie over town. Movie and lunch and we got caught in the ferry line."

No need to know came from one of them. Becca tried to catch more, but the dogs' racket made it impossible. So she said, "What'd you guys see?"

"That new film with Eddie Redmayne," Diana told her. "I think I'm in love."

Sharla laughed. "It's those accents of theirs. Those Brit guys make everything they say sound like genius. You okay there, old lady?" she asked Diana. "One glass of wine and since when are you done for?"

"I'm fine." Diana smiled. They exchanged a look and Sharla let loose the grip she had on Diana's arm. She returned to the driver's seat and shifted the car into reverse. It moved back about two feet only, though. Then she braked and watched as Becca came down the walk.

Diana looked *old*, Becca thought. She looked tired. She said to her, "We c'n do the practice later, if you want," but Diana's reply was, "I just need a very strong cup of tea. If you'll see to that, I'll let the dogs have a run. I made a brown Betty for us, by the way. Can you reheat it?"

Becca agreed, but she went inside reluctantly. When she was there, she watched Diana from the kitchen window as she let the dogs out and began to throw their balls for them. Her throw was weak. Her aim was bad. She leaned against the chain-link fence of the run the entire time the animals dashed about. Clearly, something was wrong, and Becca couldn't understand why Diana kept pretending this wasn't the case.

She went about making the tea. She found the brown Betty and put it into the microwave. By the time she had milk, sugar, teapot, and all the rest on the table in the nook, Diana was coming into the house and allowing the dogs to come in as well.

"This is lovely," she said when she entered the kitchen. She still wore her outdoor jacket, which she didn't remove despite the room's warmth.

"I used your laptop." Becca had left it on the table but had moved it against the wall to make room for the tea and brown Betty. "I hope that was okay."

"That's why I left it out," Diana told her. "Will you pour, Becca? I think Sharla was right. One glass of wine and I'm completely done in." She watched as Becca poured tea into their cups and cut each of them a piece of the brown Betty. "What did you learn?" she asked.

Becca told her about her belief that Olivia Bolding was probably going to come to Whidbey Island. Following the cell phone was the logical next step. "If she comes here, she's going to find me," Becca said. "I feel like I got to leave, but I don't know where to go."

Diana had forked up a tiny portion of the dessert, but she set it down. She reached across the table and settled her hand on Becca's forearm. After a moment she said, "There's more, isn't there? I sense an agitation coming from you, and it seems to have to do with more than Olivia Bolding."

Becca told her then of her other concerns: Prynne being stoned at Ralph's house, Prynne and Seth undergoing some kind of separation that Seth didn't want to talk about, Brenda Sloan trying to get control of Ralph Darrow, Jenn and Squat squabbling. . . . The only thing she didn't reveal was worry about Derric and Rejoice and where all of that was going to lead if Derric didn't give his sister the news about her *being* his sister before it was too late.

Diana nodded as she listened. Then she said, "Do you think you have power over any of these people?"

"What kind of power?"

"The power to make them behave the way you think they should behave."

"Course not. Not really, I guess."

Diana smiled as she lifted her teacup. She'd made it too full and a bit spilled into the saucer. She shook her head at this clumsiness and reached for a paper napkin to sop up the mess. "But you're not entirely certain that you *don't* have power in any of these matters, are you?"

Becca looked away from the probing gaze that Diana was giving her. She said, "I know I can't make people do what I want them to do. But it's just that I wish people could *see*—"

Diana cut in quickly at this. "Do you remember what *Seeing Beyond Sight* has told you?"

This was a small but deeply intense book that Diana had handed over to Becca some months earlier. Becca read it in bits and pieces only, because the information was so dense. She said, "It's told me a bunch, but it's hard to remember. And I don't get how anything in it applies to this."

"Then you're forgetting the quickening. This is the moment when you must begin to explore the visions instead of trying to interpret the whispers. This is why we're trying to block the whispers when they need to be blocked. We do it first with the mantra and then through the power of your will."

"And *then* what?" What Becca really wanted to know was how long this was going to take, since she didn't have all the time in the world to figure out what she was meant to do.

"Then you take action," Diana told her. "But that action, as the book tells you, must be designed 'to propel events forward to a safe, desired, or happy conclusion.' And that, Becca, has nothing to do with making people 'see' a thing."

"But if I don't do something, things're going to explode," Becca told her.

"They might," Diana admitted. "But the unfortunate truth is this: You're not ready to take any action, and you won't be ready until you're able to block the whispers fully and until you come to understand how the whispers relate to the visions, too."

21

Cynthia's remark about lesbians not biting was what made Jenn reconsider Lexie's offer of a ride to Freeland in order to apply for the busboy's job at G & G's. And Lexie, she discovered, was pretty cool. She yacked away when they were heading up the highway, and she didn't seem to have any subject that she wasn't willing to discuss.

She told her immediately that G & G's was owned and operated by two women: Gertie and Giselle. She revealed that they were somewhere in their forties, they were life partners, they had three kids between them at the Waldorf school, and they'd both once been married to men but now were married to each other. "I hope this isn't a problem for you," she said to Jenn.

Jenn found the information a little confusing. She'd always figured that if you were married to a man, you wouldn't be interested in being married to a woman. When she voiced this in a form of a question to Lexie, the other girl laughed. She said, "Lots of people think that way, but they're mostly men with big egos."

Getting the job turned out to be as easy as Lexie had predicted it would be. When they arrived at the restaurant, it was just a matter of Lexie saying to the owners, "Here she is. Ready, willing, and able," and employment was virtually hers.

It was simple work, learnable in five minutes. Gertie showed her where the supplies were: plastic bins for placing used dinnerware into, pristine white tablecloths, neatly folded and starched white napkins, black napkins for those whose clothing was dark. Giselle showed her how to remove dishes, silverware, glasses, and cups efficiently and quietly and how to replace a tablecloth without having to remove the flowers, the battery operated lamps, and the salt and pepper. She and Gertie then stood back and watched her do it. Gertie said, "You're trained," when Jenn demonstrated her skill. Giselle said, "You're hired," and they both went back to work: Gertie as executive chef, Giselle as dessert and sous chef.

At first, Jenn assumed that the restaurant was going to be the local hangout for gay people, trans people, and others of general sexual eccentricity, but this didn't turn out to be the case. G & G's was, it seemed, a high-end restaurant that attracted diners from all over the island. It sat on a hill overlooking both the small town of Freeland and Holmes Harbor beyond it, and because of the food and the view, it was the most popular dining spot from Coupeville all the way down to Clinton.

"You didn't know that?" Lexie asked her when Jenn mentioned her surprise at the number of diners who showed up every night.

Jenn didn't want to tell the other girl that she'd have no reason to know it. It wasn't like her family could afford to go out to dinner. If they scraped enough together to get slices at the pizzeria in Langley, they'd be having a terrific day.

As soon as she had the job, she told her parents. She figured that they weren't about to say she couldn't work nights at a restaurant if the whole thing was signed, sealed, and delivered. Besides, she assumed they'd be super pleased. She wouldn't be another mouth to feed at dinnertime, since she wouldn't be there, and finally she'd actually have the cash to pay for the All Island Girls' Soccer team if she made the cut. That meant there was a real possibility that she'd even be able to go to college, and Jenn knew her parents wanted that for her.

With regular employment, the world opened up to Jenn. With this *kind* of employment, she also had access to occasional leftovers, which Giselle and Gertie were perfectly happy to let her take home to shore up the meager supplies inside the McDanielses' refrigerator. It was, in short, a win-win-win. For a few weeks it actually remained that way.

Then Kate showed up. It turned out she'd had a fare from the ferry up to Freeland, and since it was nearly ten, the hour that restaurants generally closed on an island where the sidewalks rolled up at five, she had driven to G & G's to pick Jenn up. It would be far quicker than riding the island bus.

Jenn hadn't said a word to her mom about the owners of G & G's. She also hadn't said a word about the occasional bent twig – as Squat had so poetically put it – who dined there. A job was a job, and a job in a fine restaurant where she got a share of the tips was a *dream* job. It wasn't as if someone was putting hands on her butt or anywhere else when she was busing tables, Jenn thought.

When she saw her mom in the waiting area of the restaurant with its nice plush benches along the wall and its romantically dim lighting, she wasn't overly concerned. There was a large birthday party going on at the windows overlooking Holmes Harbor, and the fact that every one of the guests was female indicated very little. There were twelve of them, which meant her share of a big tip, and the tip was what Jenn was thinking about, not the nature of the women or the fact that the guest of honor and her wife were sharing a wineglass and kissing each other over it when Jenn's mom walked in.

That might have gone unremarked upon and even unnoticed by Kate had not a couple been celebrating their first anniversary at a table closer to where Kate waited for Jenn. Giselle had just brought out a special dessert for them, and when she placed it on the table, she said, "Show us some love, now, ladies," and the two women did just that.

Jenn thought later that, at least, her mom hadn't dashed across the restaurant and dragged her out of the place by her hair. But on the other hand, Kate's reaction in the taxi as she drove Jenn home afterward suggested that in her opinion, Jenn had scored a job in a house of prostitution.

Kate kept her eyes glued to the road, as if they couldn't move in their sockets if she even wanted to move them. For the first five minutes in the car, she said nothing at all. Then it was simply, "No, sweetheart."

Jenn didn't reply. She knew that saying "No what?" was an invitation to attend a concert whose music she didn't want to hear. Better to pretend she was enjoying the sight of night caressing the bowl of Maxwelton Valley. A faint glow on the land marked Miller Lake.

"Did you hear me, Jenn?" Kate asked.

Still Jenn said nothing. She adjusted her seat belt and wished she'd had the sense to pretend to be asleep. She couldn't do that now, especially when her mom glanced in her direction and said her name sharply.

"I don't get what you're talking about."

"I'm afraid you can't work in that place."

"At G & G's?" Jenn asked. It was a stall tactic. It didn't work.

"Yes, at G & G's. That *is* where you're working, isn't it?"

"It's a good job, Mom," Jenn told her. "Minimum wage *and* a share of the tips. C'n you think of anyplace else on the island where I'd get paid like that?"

Kate slowed to stop at a red light on the corner of Maxwelton Road and the highway. She took the opportunity to turn slightly so that she had a better look at Jenn. Jenn felt as if her mom was searching for evidence of something. Her skin prickled with irritation. No way, she thought, was she giving up this job.

"That's not the point," Kate said. "I understand you need the money for soccer, Jennie, but this can't be the way you earn it."

"Why not?"

"Because of who you have to associate with. Because of the people who frequent the establishment."

Kate's use of *establishment* raised Jenn's hackles. She said, "Two nice ladies own it, and people go there to eat, Mom. So I don't get what the problem is."

"The problem is sexual deviancy."

"*Huh?*"

"The problem is being exposed to sexual deviancy. I can't let that happen. When you're a mother, you'll understand."

Jenn squirmed to face her mom. The traffic light turned green. Kate had to watch the road then, so Jenn could study the side of her face. She looked perfectly at ease, as if she'd spoken her piece and that was it. The law had been laid down and Jenn was meant to follow that law. She said to her mom, "Let me get this right. You're saying I can't work in a restaurant because two lesbians own it and—"

"Please don't use that word, Jennie."

"—and because other *lesbians* eat there . . . along with all sorts of other people who, I guess, don't count. Is that what you're telling me?"

"Yes, that's what I'm telling you. I'm sorry if the money is good, but I can't allow this."

"I'm talking to Dad."

"Jennie, I'm responsible for you. I'm responsible for molding you into a woman of upright character. My telling you that you can't work at that place is no different from my telling you that you can't walk into a forest fire. Safeguarding a child's virtue until that child becomes an adult is what being a parent is all about."

Jenn took this in. She knew where it all was coming from. If the Bible didn't mention that working with lesbians was dandy, then it meant that working with lesbians was akin to Dorothy and Toto skipping along a yellow brick road to hell.

She said, "No way am I quitting that job. You'll have to tie me up and throw me into the back of the taxi to stop me, Mom."

"I'm sorry to hear you say that," was her mother's reply. "It seems we'll have to speak with Reverend Sawyer, then."

They had reached Cultus Bay Road, no great distance from Maxwelton. Had it not been so far from there to Possession Point, had it not been pitch-dark, Jenn would have insisted that her mom stop the car. She would have flung herself out and run off, although she had no clue where she could have gone. All of that being impossible, what she said was, "Reverend Sawyer? Is he hiring? Does he need someone to clean up the church after people spew on the floor in the middle of speaking in tongues, Mom? You think it's a bad idea to work around lesbians? I think it's a *rotten* idea to have anything to do with Reverend Sawyer!"

Kate pulled to the side of the road. Jenn thought she meant to throw her from the car. But it turned out that all she wanted to do was make sure Jenn heard her and heard her clearly. "We'll see about that," her mother said.

22

Seth kept trying to tell himself that he *wasn't* the person in the wrong. True, he'd followed Prynne without her knowledge. True, he'd skulked around like some incompetent private eye. But she'd stolen his mom's OxyContin, and that gave him a reason to wonder about her. And the way things turned out, he was damn right to wonder, because she was into something that she sure as hell had been hiding from him.

The only problem was how much he missed her. He'd got home from Port Townsend, looked at his bedroom door, knew he'd be spending his nights alone in there, and just wanted to disappear. The fact that Gus had been loyally waiting for him on the front porch of his parents' house didn't cheer him. Nor did the dog's immediate recognition that something had gone very wrong. Gus had risen as Seth came onto the porch, with a dog whine that asked Seth what had happened. He then followed Seth into the house and into the bedroom, where he lay at the foot of the bed with his eyes fixed mournfully on his master.

Although Seth didn't lie to his parents about where Prynne was, he did lie about the reason. "Couple of days in Port Townsend," was what he said. "She needs to clean out her room in the house so the guys can rent it out to someone else."

That voiced his hope: that Prynne would cool off and would know that what he did, he did out of love and concern for her. Of course, it was more than that. He'd also done what he'd done because he didn't trust her. She'd taken six of his mother's pills, and he was scared about what this said about her. At the same time, he loved her so much that he spent the entire night staring at the ceiling, tears pooling in his eyes and dripping onto his pillow.

He went to Grand's the next day while Becca and Derric went to Derric's church. He could see that Becca knew something was wrong. He explained as briefly as he could that Prynne was taking care of business with her Port Townsend roommates, but he could tell from her expression that Becca didn't buy this.

Once he was alone with his grandfather, he called Prynne on her cell phone. She didn't pick up. He tried three more times during that long and terrible day, each time with his grandfather's knowing eyes upon him. He'd begun on his fourth try when he heard the sound of a heavy vehicle coming down the new driveway. Ralph apparently heard it, too, because he said, "Who . . . big, Seh." Seth knew he meant that it sounded like something large. He said to Grand, "I'll check it out. Don't load the shotgun yet."

He went out onto the porch, completing the call to Prynne as he did so. He left the same message he'd been leaving all day, "I'm sorry. Prynne, I love you totally. Come on. Let's talk."

He went down the ramp and along the brick path to the new driveway. There, he saw a big truck with SOUTH WHIDBEY LAWN CARE AND GARDENING on it. Two hefty guys and a woman were climbing out. Seth only had time to say, "Hi, what's happening?" before he heard his name called from the trail that descended from the upper parking area. He turned and saw that Aunt Brenda had arrived, a three-ring binder clutched to her chest.

"Here to do the winter cleanup," the lawn care woman

said to him. She stuck out her hand and introduced herself as Daphne. The men were Bruce and Harry. They nodded and began to unload their tools.

Seth said, "On a Sunday? You guys work on Sundays?"

"Only day we had," Daphne told him. She was pulling on a pair of heavy gardening gloves as she looked around. She said to the other men, "No way can we do this in one, you guys."

They grunted. Bruce – or it could've been Harry – was unloading a wheelbarrow as Harry – or it could've been Bruce – shouldered a rake, a hoe, and a shovel. What Seth said was, "Who the heck called you?"

By that time, Brenda had reached them. She said to Seth, "The place needs to be made presentable. Daphne and her crew will be handling it. Dad's estate can absorb the cost later." To the others she said, "This is my nephew, Seth."

Seth said, "Wait a minute. Grand takes care of the garden. No way does he want a bunch of strangers touching anything. He's got specimen trees, special rhodies and—"

"*And*," his aunt finished, "the last thing he can do is take care of it."

"So what?" Seth said. "He'll tell me what to do, and I'll do it."

"I see," Brenda said. "And how do you expect him to 'tell' you, Seth. He can't even say a sentence."

"I'm calling Dad right now," was the only thing that Seth could come up with.

"You do that," Brenda said, and to the others, "You can begin. We want this place looking its best. The azaleas seemed close to blooming last time I was here. Check them out first, please. If they need fertilizing or whatever, do that."

Those directions given, she went up the ramp. As she did so, Seth saw her fish in her large purse for something. When he saw what it was, he punched his phone for his dad.

"Aunt Brenda's here," he said tersely when Rich Darrow answered. "She's got a crew working on the garden and she just took out a serious tape measure to use inside the house."

Rich said, "Five minutes," and ended the call. If Seth knew his dad, he'd make it there in three.

Seth followed his aunt. He found her kneeling in front of Grand's chair. She was speaking to him in a low, soothing voice. She was there to take a few pictures and make a few measurements, she told him. She wanted to make the house a bit more comfortable for him.

"You'll like it when I'm finished," she told him.

The last thing Seth wanted was to get into it with his aunt in front of Grand, but he knew Brenda wasn't telling the entire story. She was there to start staging the house so that Mike could put it on the market.

She got to her feet, rested her hand on Grand's shoulder, and said to Seth meaningfully, "Why don't you take Dad to his room for a while?"

"Why don't I leave him where he is," was Seth's response. "I bet he's gonna be *very* interested in all the big 'improvements' you have in mind."

Brenda shrugged. Seth could tell she thought she had the upper hand and the rest was just going to be a formality. Well, they would see about that. Seth's dad would be able to handle her.

Only . . . it turned out that Rich Darrow couldn't do a damn thing. He stormed into the house while Brenda was taking her measurements in the kitchen. He demanded to know who the hell those people were tramping around his dad's garden. And when Ralph cried out, hearing this, Brenda snapped, "Oh that's just great, Richard."

"You're upsetting the hell out of him," Rich snapped in turn. He walked to Ralph's chair.

"He wasn't upset till you got here." She made a notation

in the three-ring binder. She came out of the kitchen and started to measure the living room.

Rich said, "What the hell are you doing?"

Seth put in, "Like I said. She's getting ready to stage the house, Dad."

Ralph made a garbled noise. It wasn't language. It sounded like suffocation. He waved his good arm and managed, "Not . . . bahng."

Seth said to his aunt, "He doesn't want you doing anything to his house."

Brenda shot him a look. "Really? And that's what you got from the noise he just made?"

Things went directly south from there. Brenda announced that, as good as her word, she'd petitioned the court. Their father, she told Rich, was going to be examined and evaluated by individuals fully capable of making an objective decision about his welfare and where he ought to spend the rest of his days.

"What's wrong with you?" was how Rich countered. "He *doesn't* want to go to a rest home."

Brenda tossed her tape measure onto the sofa. "I've told you it's not a rest home. I've told you it's assisted living. I've tried to be reasonable about this whole situation. You're the one who's wearing blinders all the time. I'm sorry you don't see he can't live here any longer. You're just prolonging what has to be done."

"Which is what?" Rich demanded.

"Which is selling this house and this property so that Dad's future can be financed."

Ralph roared at this. Then he began to thrash in his chair. Rich and Brenda began to yell at each other. Threats were made. Promises were given. Things, Seth knew, were only getting worse.

23

Becca knew that, in the cause of getting control of both the visions and the whispers, she needed to practice. The trouble was how difficult she found this. It wasn't because she didn't *want* her skills to increase. She wanted that exactly. Increased skills meant it would be easier for her to figure out what the visions and the whispers meant and how they operated together. The trouble was the doing of it. It was tough to practice when she wasn't with Mrs. Kinsale because when she wasn't with Mrs. Kinsale, no one knew what she was practicing so they could offer no help. This meant that she either had to find time with just one person in order to practice without their knowledge or she had to practice when she was in a group.

She was feeling the frustration of this a week later when she went into the school library to check on her e-mail. Since it was near the end of the lunch hour, she was in a good practice area, so she spent the first few minutes with the mantra, putting her focus on the only other kid in the library with her. She allowed him in and heard *so stupid not to use a condom dumb shit* before she swept the mantra into her mind and blocked him. She released the mantra after thirty seconds, heard nothing, felt triumphant, and then *parents are going to kill me and if she wants* invaded her head. She grabbed on to the mantra another time. She blocked his thoughts. She slowly released and again there was nothing, only this time it lasted nearly forty-five seconds until a girl came into the library and made for the table where the boy was sitting and then it was *he doesn't get it* and *that's what she said it would be like* along with *big trouble over there* which appeared to be coming from the parent volunteer.

At this point, Becca returned the earbud to her ear and checked her e-mail. Parker Natalia had gotten in touch again. The subject line was *Immigration*. She clicked hastily on the message to see what it held. Her hope tanked.

Parker's friend with the police had checked into Canadian immigration. No one called Laurel Armstrong had crossed the border into Canada. This sort of thing was easy to check. Everything was in computer records. Once his friend had gotten access to them, it didn't take him long to go back through time and see that a Laurel Armstrong hadn't legally driven through or walked through any of the border crossings in Washington State. So she'd either ditched whatever car she was driving and somehow sneaked across the border on foot by creeping around the barriers in the dead of night when some of them were closed to traffic, or she wasn't in Canada at all. Or she had a new identity. But in any case, Parker said, he wasn't going to be able to find her.

Becca's body drooped. She got off the Internet and not a moment too soon. Derric walked into the library and came across toward her. At first when he said, "Not done yet?" she had no clue what he was talking about. Then he added, "Graphic design, I mean," and she recalled her previous lie to him. She said, "Almost," and added, "It's tougher than I thought."

She'd noticed earlier that something seemed to be on his mind. There had been a heaviness clinging to him for several days. He'd been to La Conner to have dinner with Rejoice and her family three nights ago. He'd been preoccupied ever since.

When he said, "Talk to you?" Becca felt relieved. When he also said, "Over there," and indicated a study carrel, she knew it was probably serious. She grabbed up her things and followed him. He pulled a second chair up to the carrel. They sat facing each other, and he reached for her hand. There it was, then: a vision of an alley and cardboard shelters and being inside one with a little girl. Kampala, she thought, where he and his sister had been found.

He said, "Okay, you were right. You're always right. Is this a girl thing, or is it just you?"

Becca frowned. "What's going on?"

"Rejoice made a play for me. I didn't expect it. Not the way it happened." He blew out a breath and ran his hand back over his smoothly shaven skull. "She did it at dinner with all of her family there."

"Did she say something, you mean?"

"No. It's what she did. They sat me next to her and she . . . under the table . . . Whew. This is hard to say, Becca. She sort of . . . She touched me. I mean like where she shouldn't have touched me. Do you get what I'm saying?"

"Yikes," Becca said. "What did you do?"

"Practically jumped out of my skin," he said. "I got away from her."

"In the middle of dinner? How'd you manage that?"

"Went to the bathroom. Splashed some water on my face. Decided I pretty much had to tell her."

Becca could see from his expression that telling Rejoice that she was his sister had not turned out the way Derric had hoped. She said, "You look like things didn't go so good."

"You think?" He gave a mirthless laugh. "She didn't believe me."

He'd told Rejoice that she was his sister just before he left La Conner that evening, he explained. Her parents always allowed her to walk out to the Forester with him because her mom could keep an eye on the action from the kitchen window. So he used that time alone with her to tell her everything: that she was his sister; that they'd been found in an alley in Kampala along with a group of other orphaned street children; that since the girls went one way and the boys another once they got to the orphanage, he hadn't said that one of the girls was his sister.

"I told her I was just freaked with the whole situation: being picked up on the street, getting carted away, starting a life at the orphanage. I told her I didn't know up from down or anything else. And when the Mathiesons came, I just went along with their belief that I was alone there."

"And she still didn't believe you?"

"She thinks I made it up."

"*Why?*"

"She thinks I'm trying to get away from her so that she and I can't be . . . well, you know. I told her to look in the mirror. We're like twins, I told her. I told her she *knows* I'm telling her the truth. I said I was sorry that I hadn't told her earlier but I just didn't know how. But all that didn't make one difference. She started to cry, she ran back to the house, and I ended up with a call from her dad later that night asking what the hell was going on."

"Did you tell him?"

"Hell no. Why tell the truth when I can mess up my life and everyone else's by making something up? I said I'd told her we needed to back off hanging around together because she was having . . . well, expectations. I said I told her that you and me . . . that we're together. I told her dad that she freaked when I said that to her. I told him I was sorry but she'd gotten the wrong idea about her and me and I needed to fix it."

Becca quirked her mouth. She wanted to say something

that she didn't say: How's lying been working out for you, Der? But instead she went with, "So what's next?"

"Man, I'm clueless. Pretty standard for me, I know."

Becca considered the state of affairs from every angle and there was only one suggestion that she could come up with. "Der, the letters. You started writing them when you were . . . what? Eight years old? She needs to see them. Every one of them is signed 'your loving brother,' and the handwriting changes as you get older. She'll *get* it then. She won't exactly be delirious over it. She's been seeing you as boyfriend material, and all of a sudden that idea has been totally wrecked. But the letters . . . ? They show her that you always thought of her, you were always connected to her, you always loved her and you love her now. Just not the way she wants you to love her."

He considered this. "I *could* take them . . ." and he shot her a look. "I guess you wouldn't give them to her for me? I mean, I drive you up there, I drop you off, I wait somewhere, then I come back and pick you up once you've given them to her?"

"Uh . . . no," Becca told him. "This is your mess, Der. Believe me, I've got my own."

"What kind of mess do you have? None. I wish I could be more like you. You've been smart enough not to lie about anything."

Except about my entire life, she thought. She wondered what was going to happen to them when she finally had to tell Derric the truth.

When she got to Ralph's after the school day had ended, Becca saw that Rich Darrow's truck was there. He'd left it in the upper parking area, and a collection of heavily made cardboard boxes suggested that he'd stopped by to see his dad on the way to making a delivery of his glass pieces to some of the galleries on the island that featured them. She rolled her bike down the new driveway. Soon it would be time for Celia Black to arrive for the late shift, but at the moment it looked like Jake was still in the house.

It turned out that everyone was more or less working on calming Ralph. Jake had apparently just taken his blood pressure, and the result had not been good. There was probably a reason for this, Becca figured, and it wasn't long before she found out what it was.

They were all gathered in the living room, at the smallish table where Grand worked on language and played games that, over time, were growing progressively more challenging. Now, though, there was paperwork on the table. It had once been folded into thirds, which suggested to Becca that it had come to Ralph or to Rich in the mail.

It seemed that Rich Darrow had been trying to explain something to his father, but either Grand wasn't getting it or he had gotten it all too clearly. In either case, he was upset and, upset, he was fast losing whatever language he'd reacquired. He was repeating the word *banks*. He was able to say *houch* as well, whatever that meant. When Becca walked toward the table, his gaze met hers and she felt the ferocity of it. She looked among them. If she removed the earbud to try to work out what was going on, there was a chance that the bombardment of everyone's thoughts was going to make her efforts useless. Still, she needed to try. She flipped it out of her ear.

Never going to . . . banks, banks, banks . . . daily thing . . . damage is going to be too . . . kill him if I can't get control . . . way too out of it . . . law is the law . . . if Brenda and Mike . . . where's a good place now . . . he doesn't know me so what does it matter . . . papers are there . . . she's not going to let up . . . banks banks . . .

Becca couldn't bear the assault. She could hardly distinguish all the words. The only thing that made sense as a direct communication from Ralph was *banks*. As for the rest, it didn't matter at the moment because Ralph was trying to get up, which he managed without help, and he came to her and grabbed on to her arm so fiercely that she yelped.

"Houch," he cried and in the contact between them she saw an exterior stairway being climbed, and she knew it had to be Ralph Darrow climbing it and there in front of him was a screened door. She saw his hand reach for it, open it, and then . . . nothing more.

Jake was saying, "Mr. Darrow, let's get you into your room. You're heading into a bad place with your blood pressure."

"Bec . . . ca," Ralph said. "Banks."

"I'll bring you some Whidbey vanilla, Grand," Becca said. "But let Jake help you to your room."

His eyes filled with tears. Becca knew he was trying to tell her something. She nodded and said, "I *promise* I'll bring you the ice cream. We'll eat it alone, you and me. Everyone'll pretend they don't know what we're up to."

He appeared to understand. He nodded in the old Grand way, with one jerk of his head, like a soldier. He wouldn't let Jake take his arm, however. He insisted upon using the handrails as help, and doing this, he made it to his room on his own. Jake followed. He would need help if he wanted the bed.

Rich Darrow watched. His face was sorrow. He sat at the table still, and when he finally moved, it was to gather up the paperwork.

If she wins this, he dies told Becca everything. She said to Seth's dad, "Has something bad happened?"

Rich was refolding the papers. He put them into an envelope. Becca could see that this had come to Rich Darrow by registered mail so that he wouldn't be able to claim later that he'd not received its contents.

Rich cleared his throat and Becca didn't need his whispers to understand how upset he was. "Brenda's been given guardianship," he said.

"But she doesn't even live on the island!"

"Doesn't matter apparently. The results of Dad's evaluation showed that he can't live on his own – which we already knew – and that he doesn't understand his financial circumstances."

"Why would they say Grand doesn't understand? You *know* he does. I know he does."

"It's the language thing. They've decided it makes him too vulnerable."

"But he's making progress. With language and with everything."

"Not enough, apparently. Physically he's improving, and that looks good. As long as he doesn't live alone."

"He's not living alone. I'm here. Celia and Jake are here. Seth's here. He's *never* alone."

He looked regretful as he said, "Unfortunately, you guys . . . everyone but Celia and Jake? To the court, you don't count. You're all too young and none of you have medical skills."

"As if we need them. That's so unfair!"

"Sort of like life," Rich pointed out. "At any rate, Brenda's got what she wanted. That's what this" – he indicated the envelope – "is all about. I wanted Dad to know before she gets here. I told him she might want to sell the house and the land, but even if she does, he's not going to assisted living. Seth and I can make changes in our place, so he can come to us. She'll go for that."

Becca looked in the direction of the bedroom. "He can't lose this place. It's his everything."

"There's not much we can do about it now."

"*Why* did he say *banks*? D'you think there's some kind of money somewhere that nobody knows about?"

"The financial guardian checked every bank on the island. He dealt with banks over town, too: in Everett, Edmonds, Mukilteo, Lynnwood. There's no special account anywhere. And no paperwork here to indicate there might be."

Jake came out of the bedroom just as the front door opened and Celia breezed into the house. She had a bakery box with her and she made an announcement of "Carrot cake all around. Who wants a piece?" but her happy invitation faded when she saw the expressions on the faces around her. "Is Mr. Darrow all right?" was her instant question.

"It depends on what you mean by all right," was Rich Darrow's reply.

24

Jenn was able to offer her mom a compromise once she figured out that her dad wasn't going to intervene in their dispute. She attended church with her without complaint, and she tried to look devout. In place of Bible study on Wednesday evening, which she couldn't attend because of her G & G's job, she accepted assignments from Kate to read various and deliberately chosen sections of the Old Testament and to write essays on them afterward. Jenn hardly had time to do this *and* her homework, but she made time whenever she had five free minutes.

She de-stressed herself by regaling her regular lunch companions with tales of the Pentecostal services. It was fire and brimstone all the way, she told them, and the last time she'd been there, one of the congregants had had a bad bizarre seizure in the middle of the aisle. Mr. Sawyer called it the Holy Spirit, but someone else wisely called it an emergency needing the paramedics. They showed up and carted the victim off to the hospital.

"Swear to God," Jenn said. "I *hate* that place. All they want to do is mess with your mind. But my mom thinks it's like having a flu shot."

"What's that about?" Squat offered his four chocolate chip cookies for the table's enjoyment. They were home baked by his mom. He said she'd been having an attack of domesticity lately because she'd met a guy on Match. com and she wanted him to think she was wife material, chocolate chip cookies seemingly the most obvious sign of this.

"It's about me not turning into a lesbian from working at G & G's," Jenn said. "If I go to church with her and study the parts of the Bible that she wants me to study, I'll be safe."

"And have you become so inclined, my friend?" Squat inquired. "Is there something in your nature that I should be aware of, since we've been engaged for something like thirteen years?"

Jenn didn't answer because Becca was saying, "Can't your dad help out?"

"No way. He likes to keep the peace and he knows that Mom will go ballistic if he says I don't have to go to church with her. It's some kind of deal they made before they got married. She wouldn't bug him about the beer brewing and he wouldn't bug her about her religion. So she doesn't have to drink his beer, and she looks away when he's selling it to people under the table. And he doesn't have to go to her church. If he brings up the rest of us having to go, she'll probably burn down the brew shed."

"Harsh," Squat said. Then he added, "On the other hand . . ." He gestured across the New Commons to where Cynthia and Lexie had just finished eating. They were going separate ways, but before they did, Lexie grabbed Cynthia and planted a smacking kiss on her mouth. "That could be in your future if you don't watch out for the company you keep."

"Don't think that's how it works," was Derric's view.

Becca's was a monitory "Squat . . ." which, Jenn knew, was meant to tell him to stay away from the subject of Lexie and Cynthia.

But Jenn found she didn't want to stay away. She said, "You know, *Fergus*," and using his real name told everyone at the table that her temper was rising, "you can actually be friends with someone without having sex with them. You can even be friends with someone who gets off on people of the same gender."

"I wouldn't be so sure of that," Squat told her.

"Why are you so freaked by them? Or are you just freaked because no one wants to have sex with *you*?"

He looked unperturbed. He reached for half of one of the cookies. "I'm saving myself for you, beloved," he said. "You'll cave in to my charms eventually." But Jenn knew that he'd felt the dig. His cheeks had grown ruddier as he was speaking.

Jenn was bothered by it all: her mom's beliefs and Squat's attitude and what it meant that they thought how they thought. She kept feeling pushed and pulled when all she really wanted to do was have a job, make some money, and get herself onto the All Island Girl's Soccer team.

She did wonder all the same, because there was something about Cynthia and Lexie's free and easy relationship that she felt drawn to. It wasn't that she wanted a relationship like theirs with another girl. It was just that she admired their openness, and she didn't find it horrifying, sickening, or anything else that they were into each other. She knew them as people first and as girls-into-other-girls second. What was the big deal?

She and Lexie were driving to G & G's after a training session when Jenn brought it up with, "Can I ask you something?"

"Can do." Lexie leaned over and opened the glove compartment. She snagged an energy bar, which she handed to Jenn. "Let's split this," she said. "You start, I'll finish."

Jenn began to unwrap it. "It's sort of dumb," she began.

"I love dumb," Lexie told her. "I deal best with dumb. Fire away."

"Okay. You and Cynthia . . . and you and Sara-Jane . . . ?"

"Yep."

"How did you know?"

"You mean that I'm into girls?" Lexie glanced in her direction. They were on the highway heading up to Freeland, so it was a quick glance only, and after that, Lexie didn't look over at her again. Jenn liked this: not only that Lexie was a careful driver but also that she herself could get red in the face or uncomfortable or anything and Lexie wouldn't be examining her. "Lemme think for a sec." Thirty seconds or more went by until Lexie finally nodded and said, "When you start liking someone – I mean liking as in more than being friends – it's because there's some kind of attraction. Maybe it's physical, maybe it's intellectual, maybe you've got the same interests . . . stuff like that. But you recognize that there's something special in this other person that you can latch onto. Get it?"

"Sure."

"So you start spending time with this person and you realize at some point it's really more than just being friends. It's loving instead. Not like loving your mom and dad and brothers and sisters. A different kind of loving that draws you to the other person and makes you want to act on it. You start to feel if you don't act on it, you're going to end up a knot of nerves. But in order to act, you've got to take a step and that step involves the other person and that other person might not feel the same way. But if they do . . . well, there you go."

Jenn considered this for a moment before she said, "But that sounds just like girls and guys," she finally said.

"Guess it is." They'd reached Bayview Corner, one of

the five traffic lights on the south end of Whidbey Island. It was red, which gave Lexie the chance to give Jenn a look that took her in from toes to head. She said, "I just think you're attracted to who you're attracted to, Jenn. For some girls, it turns out to be other girls. For some girls it turns out to be guys."

"But what about . . . See, Giselle and Gertie . . . ? Weren't they attracted to guys in the beginning?"

"Must've been or they wouldn't've married 'em."

Jenn was quiet. She handed over the rest of the energy bar, having eaten her part of it. Lexie's hand closed over hers. Reflexively, Jenn jerked away. Then she was embarrassed that she'd done so.

Lexie didn't seem bothered. She said, "You should check out the Gay Straight Alliance. We meet on Fridays. At lunch. You know Ms. Primavera?"

"The counselor. Course. Everyone knows her."

"The phony Jimmy Choos." Lexie grinned. "That's her. Anyway, she's our sponsor."

"Omigod! Is *she*—"

Lexie hooted. "It's the Gay *Straight* Alliance, Jenn. You should come to a meeting. If you show up, there's kids who'll answer your questions better 'n me."

Jenn thought that the Gay Straight Alliance meeting was just about the last place where she'd want to be seen. There was knowing and liking Cynthia and Lexie, and there was mixing and mingling with the high school freaks. But she didn't want to say that, so instead she asked Lexie if her parents knew.

"That I'm into girls? Oh, yeah. I told 'em."

"What happened?"

The light switched to green. Lexie took off. "My dad doesn't like to talk about it. My mom refuses to believe it. She keeps telling me I'm in a *stage* and as soon as I get to college and see all those buff fraternity boys, I'll be changing my colors."

"Does she know about Sara-Jane?"

"Yep. But as far as she's concerned, SJ is 'your little friend, Aleksandra. I don't quite like her. Please don't bring her by the house.'"

"That's rotten."

"I c'n cope. Anyway, you should talk to Cynthia."

Jenn wasn't sure she wanted to. There was something less approachable about Cynthia. She was beautiful, smart, confident, talented. All that gorgeous blond hair and that perfect body. She was friendly to everyone, and Jenn figured she'd be open to talking about just about anything, but still . . .

Lexie said, "Her parents practically told *her* she was a lesbian. When she came out to them, her dad said, 'Oh, we've known that for years.' And her mom was like, 'As long as you're happy, we're happy, dear.'"

"That's cool."

"Wish it was like that in my house. But it ain't, and that's life." Lexie shoved the rest of the energy bar into her mouth.

"Doesn't it bother you that your parents don't get it?"

"Truth? My mom would've only been happy if I'd turned out to be her clone. I figured that out when she wanted me to shave my legs when I was thirteen and I liked them just the way they were. You'd've thought I'd put a stiletto through her eyeball. She wouldn't talk to me for a week. My dad, though? He'll come around eventually."

"Sounds like my house. Only it's not leg shaving. It's Pentecostal Christianity."

"Ouch," Lexie said. "Now that's a tough one."

25

In Seth's final phone message to Prynne, he talked about Grand. Brenda, he told Prynne, was moving things forward in her attempt to get control of Ralph. Grand now had an attorney to fight Brenda's being given guardianship, one that Seth's parents had had to unearth, although no one knew how they were going to pay for it. That attorney had advised Seth's dad to work things out with his sister because "I've seen this sort of family thing before and it generally doesn't turn out well." That was where things stood when Seth left his message.

There would be another hearing, he told Prynne. They *thought* it looked good because the family had at least two people at the house to care for Grand, but now, of course, there were only two people when Becca was there with Celia, since Jake was on his own. Seth didn't know what the judge would make of that, he said.

He knew as he added this last part that he was trying to guilt Prynne into returning. He'd tried every other approach – I love you, I miss you, I'm sorry I followed you, We can work this out, *Please* call me back – except actually going to her, and when she didn't return *this* call about Grand's precarious position, he decided he had to appeal personally to what she'd once declared: that *she* loved *him*, Seth, too.

He waited till her next gig in Port Townsend. He was due to stay with Grand because of the weekend, but Becca said she'd do it. Derric wasn't going to be available anyway, she told him. He was spending the day up in La Conner with a fellow African from his Kampala orphanage.

In Port Townsend, Seth strode down Water Street. Early May had brought a burst of dazzling weather, so the bluebells were beginning to paint the roadsides azure, and the hillside between the lower and upper parts of the old town were ablaze with poppies, the orange of them a pleasing contrast to the wild green grass among which they grew. The spring sun had coaxed hundreds of people into the town. In the late afternoon, they were crowding the sidewalks.

The fine day lifted Seth's spirits, but he warned himself not to get cocky about the prospect of seeing Prynne. He had to make her understand how important she was to him. But he also had to realize that there was every chance he wouldn't be successful.

Her first gig started at five o'clock. He didn't want to be there when she arrived. He wanted to walk in while she was already playing because there was less chance that way that she would ask him to leave. Thus, it was five-twenty when he ducked into the coffeehouse. As usual, Prynne's appearance with her fiddle had brought in a crowd, and she was playing when Seth came through the front door.

He went to the counter, easing his way through the people. There, he ordered both an Americano and a decaf skinny vanilla latte. He bought an oatmeal raisin cookie to go with it.

There was no place to sit, but he found a space at a narrow shelf that ran along two of the walls. He stood there and listened, and looked at Prynne. Today she was 100 percent who she'd always been. She was also dressed exactly as she'd been when he'd first seen her: jeans tucked into cowboy boots, a kind of gypsy shirt, a bunch of beaded necklaces, hair wild, eye patch.

At the end of her piece, the audience hooted, applauded, and stamped their feet. Seth whistled shrilly in approval, which was when Prynne caught sight of him. He waved and tried to look like his normal self. He held up the cookie and the latte. Her lips parted, which he tried to take as a hopeful sign, but she didn't give any other indication that she was surprised or happy to see him there. She did come over to him at her break time, though.

Seth hadn't expected to be so relieved to see her. He'd known he'd missed her, but he hadn't really understood how much until she was standing in front of him in all her . . . all her Prynne-ness. What he wanted to do then was to grab her, feel her crinkly hair beneath his fingers, and tell her exactly how much they were meant to be together.

She said, "Hey," and when he handed her the latte and the cookie, she added, "Thanks. Didn't expect to see you here. Where's Gus? In the car?"

He said, "Becca's got him over at Grand's." And then nothing. Nothing from her, either. He could hardly stand this, so he burst out with, "Didn't you get my messages? Why didn't you call me back?"

She looked away from him. People were jostling as the two baristas called out completed orders. Seth knew this wasn't the right spot to have the conversation and so apparently did Prynne because she said to him, "Come with me," and she led him toward the back.

Outside, they were on the water in the vicinity of the town's docks, where fishing boats and pleasure craft bobbed. The scents of gasoline, oil, and a barbecue somewhere filled the air. In the middle of Admiralty Inlet, a ferry was making the crossing from Whidbey, accompanied by a flock of gulls. Sunset was still three hours away. Everything was brightly lit.

Seth said, "I'm sorry, Prynne. Following you like that?

It wasn't the right thing to do. I wanted to know something and I should've just asked you."

"I guess you had your reasons."

"It's just that when I saw you with that guy and when I heard what he was saying to you—"

She flashed him a quick look with, "What was he saying? I don't even remember."

"I don't either." This wasn't true. Seth remembered completely: the guy had talked about supplying her with something, not being able to get it, finding it too risky now, and all the rest. But in that moment with Prynne, Seth chose to let it all go. She was still Prynne, and he loved her. He said, "It seemed really important at the time. But alls I know now is that it doesn't matter. Nothing matters except just you and me and being together."

She still had her fiddle under her arm, and she placed it gently against the side of the building. She shoved part of her hair behind one ear and with her good eye she seemed to examine him. She said, "You mostly tore a hole in my heart, Seth. I don't know if it will ever get better."

"I want to make it better," Seth told her passionately. "I *know* that I can make it better. I was out of line. What I did . . . following you like that . . . sneaking around to check up on you . . . It's like . . . when you took that Oxy from my mom's supply, I just lost it."

"I *said* I was sorry about it. I said I only wanted to try it. When I used it once, I didn't like what it did to me but you didn't believe that, so what's different now?"

"Now I believe you," Seth told her. "I *totally* believe you. I want us to be together, and I'm telling you nothing like that's going to happen again."

"Nothing like what? Me stealing your mom's pills? How're you going to check on that one?"

"Not that," he said. "My following you and not trusting you and checking up on you. That's what."

"How'm I supposed to believe you?" Prynne asked him, and she sounded as despairing as he felt.

"By trying it with me again. That's the only way I can prove things. Oh Prynne, please. It's like you tore a hole in *my* heart, too. Not with the Oxy, I don't mean that. But with being gone from me now."

"You'll recover," she said shortly.

"I don't want to recover," Seth replied. "I want you. Whatever happened to make things bad for us, I swear it won't happen again. If you'll only give me a chance."

She looked from him to the docked boats. He hoped she looked beyond them to Whidbey Island in the distance. There was, really, nothing more for him to say. He waited in agony.

Finally, she took pity on him. "Okay. We'll try it again. I love you, Seth. But you got to trust me."

He grabbed her and kissed her. "I do," he swore.

She came back the next day. He wanted her arrival to be a forever thing. He believed the only way he could manage this was if she took the first step and gave up her escape hatch in Port Townsend: the room she still kept in that house with her fellow musicians. But now was not the time even to hint at her telling her house mates to rent the room out to someone else. He had to ease his way in that direction.

His parents seemed glad to have Prynne back. His mom's recovery from the surgery was nearly at an end and – although he hated even to think this – she'd finished up her final Oxy prescription. Seth didn't like to call those pills a temptation to Prynne, since she'd only taken one to see what it did to her. Still, not having those pills in the house removed a *minor* worry from him.

Prynne was perfect around Grand. She helped out where she was needed, she kept an eye on how Jake Burns was handling things, she worked with Grand on language and exercising, she made lunch, did laundry, and even worked in the garden. If there was *any* problem at all, it was weed. For she'd at last turned twenty-one, and it was legal for her to buy it at either of the two weed shops in the area. She took the opportunity to do this.

She smoked it some distance from the house, sitting on an old Adirondack chair that she dragged beyond the goat pen to a spot that gave her a pleasant view of Miller Lake across the undulating farmland. At first Seth's parents didn't mention the fact that Prynne smoked weed twice daily, both before and after dinner. He appreciated this and figured they might not mention it at all, since Prynne was, face it, not their kid. But finally his mom confronted him about it, on a late afternoon when he arrived home and Prynne was already outside on her chair with a thin cloud of smoke enveloping her.

His mom was at work in her studio. When Seth rumbled onto his parents' property, she came to the door. He got out and watched Gus go running in Prynne's direction. Before the Lab reached her, Amy called Seth's name.

"Got a minute?" she asked him.

He said sure, but when she shut the studio door behind him, he became uneasy. "Wha's happening?" he said.

She was direct. "You know it's not the marijuana itself. It's the amount that concerns me."

"I know Prynne's spending a lot of money," Seth said. "But that's because she's buying it legally. Black market stuff would cost her less, but she wants it to be on the up-and-up."

Amy waved him off. "This has nothing to do with the cost. We pay her for staying with your grandfather, and if she wants to spend the money on weed, she can. What concerns me, Seth, is the constant smoking and what that's going to do to her brain."

"Geez, Mom, she's twenty-one. I figure her brain is already set. And she doesn't have learning disabilities anyway."

"What I mean," his mom went on, as if he hadn't spoken, "is that I'm concerned about what this constant smoking is going to do over time. What it's going to do to her desire to strive, to her willingness to grow, to her ability to understand herself and the world around her. If she sits in a haze every afternoon and evening . . . Don't you see what this means?"

"Far as I can tell, it means she wants to relax after being at Grand's all day."

"Aren't you bothered? Is this what you want in a partner, Seth?"

He didn't reply. The question felt all wrong, but he wasn't sure why. He knew only that hearing it closed something off in him, so that a shell seemed to form around his heart.

"Have you talked to her about it?" his mom persisted. "You can't possibly want a partner who's high every day when you come home." And then when he still made no reply, "Darling, I can see you love her. I *know* you love her. We love her, too, your dad and I. But we want—"

"So just *accept* her." The words burst from him. "She is who she is and so am I."

His mom looked at him evenly and for much too long. She was like a person trying to read his mind. His mind, however, was the last place that he wanted her to be because everything she was saying was the truth and he didn't know what to do about it. He *loved* Prynne. He *wished* she didn't get high every night. He didn't *want* to come home to someone who was blitzed. But he also didn't know how to bring this about.

So he said, "I guess you want us to find some other place to live."

"Of course not!" Amy said. "Your place is here as long as you want to be here. I was just trying to bring something out into the open between us. We've always done that, you and I. I don't want to lose our willingness to speak openly to each other, honey."

Seth felt miserable. He didn't know why. But he said what he knew his mom wanted to hear. "We're not going to lose that," he declared, even though he wasn't sure he was speaking the truth.

26

When Seth saw firsthand that getting stoned had become a second nature activity in Prynne's life, he told himself that it was okay. After all, she wasn't doing anything wrong. Plus she wasn't doing anything dangerous. Plus it was legal. Plus he loved her. So he decided that the uneasiness he was beginning to feel really had to do with himself.

He'd never been a liar. Ever since he'd been a kid, anyone he tried to lie to could see on his face that he wasn't telling the truth. So he'd given up on fibs when he'd been around twelve years old, aside from small white lies like telling one of the guys in his gypsy jazz group Triple Threat that his new girlfriend was hot when really he wouldn't have given her a second look. But he'd lied to Prynne in order to get her to return to Whidbey. In his total desperation to have her back with him, he'd said he couldn't remember what that guy in Port Townsend had said to her: "I can't even *get* it anymore, Prynne. It's way too risky." And once Seth had made that declaration to Prynne – that he couldn't remember what the guy had said – he couldn't exactly start asking her what "any more of it" meant.

Not long after Prynne's return, he found himself obsessing about those words. Could Steve have been talking about weed? No matter that it was legal now, not just anyone could sell it, so if he was selling it on the sly . . . But maybe it was Oxy he'd been talking about and maybe Prynne had been lying about only trying it just that once. Or maybe it was meth, Seth thought. Maybe it was coke. It could be molly. Or K2. Geez, it could be *anything*.

He began looking at Prynne more closely when she wasn't looking at him. He started trying to gauge if her behavior was different from this day to that. Was she slurring her words? Did her eyelids droop? Was her real eye too bright? He was starting to drive himself up the wall, and the worst of it was that the only person he could really talk to about this was Grand because Grand had forever been the person in his life that Seth had turned to when he needed to sort through something.

When Prynne unexpectedly announced that she had an additional gig the next Sunday in Port Townsend, Seth decided it was time to talk to Ralph. Prynne took off too early for Seth's comfort, so he loaded Gus into the VW and headed for Newman Road.

He and the Lab piled out of the car into the sound of crows raising a ruckus above the forest trees and an eagle sounding its five-note descending cry for its mate. Grand's property was a panorama of flowers, but Seth was immune to its beauty although Gus leaped up the side of the hill and rolled in the wildflowers there.

Seth called to him, and Gus ignored him. But he did head down the hillside, and Seth followed him to where Becca and Derric were waiting on the porch.

Derric waved as Seth came into view. Gus charged toward them, barking happily. Becca turned to the front door, opened it, and said something to Grand. As Seth came up the porch steps, Derric said, "'S happening?"

"Nada," Seth told him, another lie, as Gus snuffled around the large wooden box on the porch, hoping for a bone. "Prynne's doing another gig in Port Townsend." At least that was the truth.

Becca was shrugging her way into a denim jacket. A thrift store score, Seth figured. It was way too big. "Grand's waiting for you," she told Seth. "Even set up the chessboard on his own."

"Righteous. No help?"

"He had some trouble with the pawns. Derric did those."

"Still cool, though."

"That's what we thought."

None of them said what else all of them were thinking: Nothing had changed, really. Seth had overheard his dad pleading with Aunt Brenda – a catch in his voice – about Grand's property and what it meant to him. "What's this really all about?" he'd cried. "For God's sake, Bren, let's be honest with each other." But this had achieved nothing. The only thing Seth could work out from everything Aunt Brenda had done so far was that she and Mike had big plans for the 170 acres Grand owned.

He forced a cheerful smile anyway and said to Becca and Derric, "Where you guys heading?"

"It's a Josh day," Becca told him. "We're taking him and Chloe to the Mutt Strut. God, Der, I didn't think of it," she added, turned to Derric. "We should have made a costume for Gus. The kids would've loved it."

Seth was cheered by the thought of the Lab dressed up. Josh would've gone for something like a pirate, Chloe for something like a princess. Becca was right. They would've loved it.

He waved them off, told Gus to come inside with him, and joined his grandfather. Ralph was waiting for him at the chessboard. Seth's only wish as he greeted Grand was that his language skills were what they had been. That was what he needed from him now: Grand wisdom. But Grand listening would have to do.

"Fave-rit mahl grunsho," Ralph said slowly, and the

twinkle in his eye told Seth how proud he was of coming ever closer to "favorite male grandchild."

"How's it going, Grand?" Seth asked. Gus greeted Seth's grandfather in his usual way: by sniffing around to see if Ralph had any treats. Ralph raised his hand slowly and dropped it onto the Lab's head. Gus waited patiently for the caress.

"So so," Ralph said. "Whan shess?"

"Sure," Seth said. "It's, like, the only time I'll probably ever be able to beat you." He sat and they began a game made slow by the difficulty Ralph had with the pieces. While Ralph was attempting to move a pawn, Seth said to him, "Prynne's in Port Townsend. Got an extra gig there."

"Fidduh," Ralph said.

"Yeah. She's doing her fiddle at the same place I met her, in that coffeehouse." He waited for Ralph to complete his move. He counted how long it took. Thirty seconds . . . forty-five . . . fifty. He finally said, "You having trouble, Grand?"

Ralph looked up at him and his expression said how stupid he thought the question was. Grand had never liked someone stating the obvious. He said in reply, "Mayshens."

Seth frowned. "What? Mayshens?"

"Mayshens, mayshens." Ralph gestured to the board.

"You want me to do something?" Seth said.

"*Mayshens* whan." Ralph pursed his lips. He blew out a breath that made a burble. It seemed as if what he was doing was . . . Seth wasn't sure. But he could tell his grandfather was getting upset.

He said, "Maybe we should play later. What d'you think? I sort of wanted to talk anyway."

At this, to his shock, Ralph's eyes filled with tears. Seth had *never* seen his grandfather cry. He said, "What's wrong? Grand, what's wrong?"

"T . . . t . . . talk." He spit out the word.

At first Seth thought Grand meant that he was waiting for Seth to tell him whatever he'd come to tell him. But before he could begin to go over what he'd been thinking and feeling with regard to Prynne, Ralph burst out with, "Becca banks," and with his good hand he grabbed on to Seth's arm so hard it hurt. "Houch," he said. "Seff houch . . ." and he began to flush.

Seth said, "Grand, you gotta calm down," and he looked around for the device to take his grandfather's blood pressure. He said, "Okay okay, Grand. I'll text Derric, okay? I'll tell Becca to come home, all right?"

"No!" Ralph cried. "Houch . . . banks . . ."

"Okay. No Becca. I'm calling Dad," was Seth's reply.

27

Becca wanted to help the Darrows. She wanted to figure out something that was going to end the dispute in their family. But what that something was . . . she had no clue. So because she spent the most time of everyone alone with Ralph, she used those chances she had to connect with him.

His whispers were limited mostly to *banks* and *houch*. His visions were more varied. On one occasion she'd picked up the sensation of being in a car, she'd seen Grand's hands clearly on the steering wheel, and the course he drove looked like a dirt road through forest deep with shadows thrown by mostly untrimmed cedars with lacy branches screening the way. On another occasion, she'd seen a house with cedar shingles that were blackened by the Pacific Northwest damp. On a third she'd once again walked up a stairway on the outside of a building with him, also cedar shingled. He'd gone through the screened door she'd seen once before, and there was a woman behind a desk strewn with papers. She'd looked up, smiled, made a gesture toward a chair against a window. And that was that. Who she was and why Ralph Darrow had her in his memory remained a mystery. Even when Becca told him of the vision, all Ralph would say was *banks, banks, banks*. He said it so urgently that Becca got scared she might drive him into another stroke.

There were other matters on her mind, too. When she and Derric left Ralph's place to pick up Josh and Chloe, she knew she had the opportunity to give Derric some information he wasn't going to like.

She hadn't wanted to do this on the phone. Truth be told, she needed to violate her own resolution about giving Derric the privacy of his thoughts. From what had happened to her on the previous night, it was clear that he hadn't taken her advice about the scores of letters he'd written and never mailed to his sister. As they headed along Newman Road toward the highway, she casually removed the earbud of the AUD box.

She said, "Der, I got some news for you."

He glanced at her. He was very adept at reading her, so what he said was, "When you look like that, it ain't good."

"Rejoice called me last night," she told him.

"Like I said," was his reply.

"Yeah. But it's sort of worse than her just calling me. She was, like, totally wrecked."

"*Drunk?*"

Becca hastened to clarify. "No. I mean wrecked, like in emotionally."

They were at the highway. Derric was waiting for a chance to make a left. It was obvious that the ferry had docked eight miles to the south in Clinton because the stream of traffic on the road was unbroken, which meant a wait for the traffic light down at Bayview Corner to turn red and cause a gap up here. The fine weather was bringing hordes to the island now. They would grow every weekend until, during the summer, the ferry line would be no less than two hours long.

As they waited, Derric chewed on his lip. He said, "I don't know if I want to know what she said."

"I think you got to hear it," Becca told him. "She's wrecked because you aren't calling and you're not returning her texts. She says I'm the one responsible, like I'm *making* you stay away from her." Becca didn't add the rest because there was really no point: Rejoice's tears and her accusations of Becca's refusing to put out for her boyfriend unless he stopped seeing Rejoice. The girl hadn't wanted to hear that Becca wasn't even sexual with Derric yet, not in that way. She'd shouted, "Oh right. Oh really and truly *right*, Becca! You must think I'm stupid!" and her sobs had been unnerving to hear.

Derric directed his gaze to the Forester's roof, as if there was someone up there – like God – who was going to tell him what to do next. He finally spoke once they'd managed to make the left turn onto the highway. "I've screwed this up."

"I think you just got to give her the letters," Becca said.

"And *that's* not going to freak her out?"

"It probably will for a while. She might feel hurt or whatever. But—"

Derric's head filled with swear words that he was directing at himself.

Becca said, "Seems to me, like I said before, that the one thing she's going to see – aside from the fact that you really are who you say you are, her brother – is that you love her and she's not alone. She's not on the planet without a blood relative."

True but God . . . maybe it's better because that way Mom and Dad wouldn't know . . .

Becca was pleased with the accuracy with which she heard the whisper, less pleased with how Derric was thinking about things. She said, "Course, it'd end up with a huge change in your life if she *does* believe you, since all of a sudden hello you've got a sister and then you . . . I guess then you start introducing her around. But it's sort of cool, if you think about it. Least, if I was you, I'd think it was cool, having a sibling. I wish I had one."

"In what way is it cool?" he demanded. "Hey I've got a sister I pretended wasn't my sister for the last . . . what? . . . twelve years of my life?" To this he added *selfish and what's it going to be like when everyone knows it.*

"You didn't know where she was once you got to America," Becca reminded him. "And you didn't pretend to *yourself* she wasn't your sister, since you spent all that time writing her letters. I say give her the letters. Do it in person and sit there while she reads them and see what happens."

He sighed, but he kept his eyes on the road. "You're not letting me get out of this, are you?" he said.

The Cliff Motel, sitting on its corner with the waters of Saratoga Passage glittering behind it, was aglow with spring: the ground blooming with the last of the winter pansies and freshly planted wallflowers, while Canterbury bells were sending up shoots that heralded their summer spikes of blue and white flowers. Josh and Chloe were out in front of the place, dancing with excitement as Derric and Becca drove into the parking lot.

"Yea, yea, yea!" Chloe cried as Derric and Becca got out of the car. "Grammer said I could wear a costume, Becca."

She wore a costume indeed. Debbie had fashioned her into a fairy with a castoff tulle ballerina's tutu, a pink Hello Kitty T-shirt, tennis shoes newly done up with stripes of gold glitter, and small wings of wire covered in tissue paper. For his part, Josh was having nothing to do with costumes. He was all man all the time in jeans and a flannel shirt. But he couldn't hide the thrill of seeing his Big Brother. He bounced over to Derric and they high-fived each other with "Hey man" and "Wha's happening, dude?"

Their grandmother came out of the motel office. Debbie

Grieder stood at the edge of the porch, arms akimbo. "Take these two loony birds off my hands." She directed this to Becca and Derric, but she said it with a smile. "They've been up since five."

"We got 'em covered." Derric opened the back door of the car so that Josh and Chloe could pile inside. "Okay for them to have pizza after?"

"Pizza!" Chloe shrieked.

"Cool," Josh said.

Debbie waved a yes at them before she turned and went back inside. They set off, then, with Bayview Corner in their sights. It would be crowded with costumed people and their costumed dogs, set to parade before a panel of judges.

Bayview itself was some four miles away. The route took them through the forest before it skirted several farms climbing the emerald hillsides and a thoroughbred horse ranch where three foals scooted close to their dams. It passed by Lone Lake, whose waters reflected the day's perfect sky, and ultimately it deposited them near an old 1895 school-house that was used by the island's literary arts community. Across the street from this, the buildings that had once been visited by farmers buying everything from tools to grains were now used for other purposes: arts, hair salon, taproom, wine room, restaurants, and the great red barn of a gardening center.

Some careful maneuvering got them a place to park up near the highway in a hard-packed field. Out of the car, they were at once in a stream of people heading toward the Big Event. To the joy of the kids, there were dogs every-where: all shapes and sizes, purebreds, mixed breeds, and a slew of unidentifiable, cocky mutts. They were dressed in all manner of costumes. Space dogs, princess dogs, zombie dogs, Scuba dogs, hot dogs (those would be the dachshunds, of course), pumpkin dogs, beach dogs, surfer dogs, artist dogs, gardener dogs, and everything else one could imagine. Over the sound of excited chatter all around them came the amplified voice of the master of ceremonies in the distance.

"The parade comes first." Chloe grabbed Becca's hand and began to pull her. "Come on, Becca. We don't want to miss that 'cause it's when all the doggies march with their peoples."

Becca allowed herself to be pulled. She waved goodbye to Derric and Josh, who were striding behind them.

The parade was silly and colorful and lots of fun, since both the participants and the viewers along the route became thoroughly engaged. Someone had passed out kazoos to those watching, and they were providing the music: "When the Saints Go Marching In." Becca demonstrated kazoo playing for Chloe, who picked it up pretty much as quickly as anyone picks up the use of a kazoo. With lots of giggling, they kazooed with the crowd although when the dogs came into sight, Chloe spent more time crying out "Look! Oh look!" and "I *wish* Grammer would let me have a dog."

Each person in the crowd fell into line with the parade as it passed until about two hundred people were strutting along with the costumed participants. The parade wound its way throughout Bayview Corner, into and out of the gardening center as well, and it finally came to a stop in a parking lot between the barn and the repurposed buildings, where a tiny viewing stand had been set up. Here the judges sat.

Now was the time for the costume contest. Chloe squirmed to the front so that she could see. Along with other small children, she sat in the gravel. There someone dressed like a clown was passing out balloons twisted into the shape of dogs.

Becca found a spot where she could watch the action.

Derric came to join her, and she slid her hand into his. The noise put her in the position of having to use the AUD box or ending up with a terrible headache, so she had the earbud where it belonged, and the soothing static allowed her to enjoy being among the happy crowd.

"Where's Josh?" she asked Derric but before he could answer, she saw the little boy joining the other children. He'd given in to balloons and a good view of the contest. Evidently one could participate in this and still be cool.

The contest itself involved the master of ceremonies calling forth one at a time the name of a costumed dog and the dog's costumed person. Every couple got a moment in the limelight. The rules required each costume to be hand-made, so there was much hilarity – not to mention loud applause in an attempt to sway the judges' opinions – as dog and person made their strut before the crowd.

The event was well under way when so many things became clear to Becca. The master of ceremonies announced, "Sophie and David Banks along with their grandma and her dog, Prince. What have we here? Elves and a reindeer and Mrs. Banks seems to be Mrs. Claus."

Hearing this, Becca wanted to slap herself on the fore-head. She wanted to shout "You idiot!" followed closely by "Of course, of *course*."

Grand had been telling her all along. He'd been saying it and visualizing it and doing what he could to get the message across to her, but she'd been too dim to get his point. Banks was a person, not an institution. And when she looked closely at Mrs. Claus, she recognized the woman within Grand's vision.

28

Gertie and Giselle closed G & G's for two consecutive days during the week, so on those days Jenn pushed herself in training more than usual. She could see that she was improving her skills by working with Cynthia and Lexie. Each of them was especially encouraging when it came to an area she considered her specialty. For Lexie, it was running, and when Cynthia joined them, her job was to keep Jenn moving the ball, passing it, while dodging her attempts to snatch it away. For Cynthia, it was weight training, and Lexie spotted her while Cynthia determined how much weight Jenn should be using each time they worked out. In return, Jenn kept Cynthia on her toes as a goalie, and she timed Lexie on her runs.

On these days, Jenn didn't rush home. No matter her increased liking for Cynthia and Lexie, she still didn't want them to see where she lived. They'd both offered her rides a couple more times, but Jenn had said no. There was the general dumpiness of her family's house and the property itself, but there was also her mom's attitude. She figured her mom wouldn't ever have known or guessed about Cynthia's sexual preferences, but Kate had already seen Lexie at G & G's, so Jenn assumed that her mom had probably drawn conclusions based on that. And one thing about Kate that had to be said: she wasn't a live-and-let-live sort of person.

Jenn was thinking about this as she descended Possession Road from where the island bus dropped her. The days were getting longer now as spring advanced, and filtered light reached fingers through the trees and dappled the road. It was a day of no breeze at all, so the birds were making a racket. Crows and gulls seemed to be competing with each other, and a flash of blue zipping by told her the jays were out and about. Purple martins were doing their warbling thing in the trees, and wherever Scotch broom had invaded, yellowthroats were making their *bizzing* sounds. It was a time of year that lifted people's spirits on the island, and Jenn's spirits were high as she made the turn down the gravel lane that led to her house.

Those spirits crashed when she saw that two cars were sitting between the house and the brew shed. One of them was the island taxi. The other was an old Ford Explorer with a Christian fish affixed to its bumper and those dad, mom, and kids stickers on the rear window. There was also a bumper sticker displaying a reference to the Bible merely by book, chapter, and verse. All this put into the same kettle told Jenn what was cooking inside the house: her mom was home and Mr. Sawyer was paying a visit.

Jenn swore in a way that would not have pleased the minister. She glanced at the brew shed. The Rolling Stones were singing about not always being able to get what you want. Nothing, she thought, could have been truer.

Up the front steps she went. Into the house she trudged. She figured her mom and Mr. Sawyer would be reading the Bible together or laying miracle hands on Petey and Andy to alter their generally rambunctious behavior. But it turned out that they were sitting side by side on the thread-bare flowered couch in the living room.

Jenn saw that her mom was deadly pale. With her brothers not around at this time of day, she felt a little stab of fear. "What's wrong?" she asked. "What's going on? Where's Petey and—"

Mr. Sawyer spoke as he rose from the couch, saying, "Jennifer. We've been waiting for you. Please sit with us, child."

Jenn didn't like his tone. His voice sounded like one he'd use when he thrust someone under the water to be baptized, and she especially hated his use of *child*. She went on to hate the fact that he held the Bible in one hand and extended his other hand, palm downward, as if he intended to bless the scratched-up coffee table. As soon as he started to talk, her mom started to move her lips. Jenn stayed where she was by the door. Mr. Sawyer repeated his request.

"Sit with us, child."

"I got homework and a test to—"

"Do as he says!" Kate's voice was so sharp that it made Jenn jump.

"It's the word of God, Jennifer," Mr. Sawyer said.

"Huh? God wants me to sit?"

"God wants you to walk away from sin," he replied, "and Jesus His Son wants you to shun that which exposes you to the fires of hell."

"Uh . . . okay," Jenn said. "C'n I do my homework now?"

"Don't be smart with Reverend Sawyer," Kate McDaniels said. "He's here to talk to you and after that, there are arrangements that need to be made."

To this, Jenn said nothing. She shrugged out of her backpack and put it at the foot of the stairs.

Reverend Sawyer said, "Do you know what eternity is?"

"Another word for forever?"

"And do you understand that when someone is cast into the fires of hell, it is for eternity? It's torment forever with no escape, torment after you die. Torment after the Second Coming. Torment without an *until* attached to it, stretching into infinity."

"Sort of sounds like having to be in math class," Jenn said.

Mr. Sawyer didn't smile. Kate shot eye bullets in Jenn's direction.

Mr. Sawyer said, "When individuals engage in an act against nature, they engage in that act against God, and for this they are condemned to hell. Engaging in an act against nature is worse than the sin of knowing another outside the bonds of holy matrimony for this act is so unnatural that its bestiality creates in the eyes of Our Lord and Savior, in the eyes of His Father, and in the eyes of the Holy Spirit an abhorrence so profound that no blessing can descend upon the sinner unless there is a profound repentance. Do you know what this means?"

"Which part?" Jenn asked. "You sort of just threw a lot at me."

"We begin with the word of God." He gestured with the Bible. "We move from there to your baptism."

Jenn swung to look at Kate. "I *told* you, Mom. No. Way. I said I'd go to your stupid church and I'm doing that and—"

"Don't you dare use that word to describe something you can't even begin to understand," Kate cried.

"Stupid, stupid, stupid!" Jenn repeated. "And I'm not letting anyone drag me into Deer Lake and dunk me in the frigging water. And *why* is this the big plan? Because I have a job in a restaurant owned by two married people who happen to be women? Because other women whose partners are women actually go there – OMG, showing themselves in *public* – and eat dinner sometimes? Well, so do a bunch of other people who are as straight as you are, Mom. Are they going to hell because they eat at G & G's or is it only the people who work there who're going to hell?"

"I'm trying to protect you."

"Baptism is a first step," Reverend Sawyer added. "Without baptism to wash your soul of sin, you cannot enter into God's Kingdom."

"I don't *want* to enter God's Kingdom if it means I get to hang out with people like you!" Jenn headed for the stairs. She had homework and a test and there was *no* way she was going to listen to either of them a second longer. They'd have to tie her and gag her before she'd ever submit to being baptized.

"Jennifer McDaniels, do *not* walk away," Kate said. "Reverend Sawyer is talking to you, and you need to listen. There's a class on Wednesday evenings that you will have to start attending in preparation for baptism. Once you have completed that class, you *will* be baptized."

"Like hell I will," Jenn said. "I work on Wednesday nights and I'm gonna *keep* working on Wednesday night. Got that, Mom?"

"I can't let you burn in hell!" Kate cried. "As your mother I *must* put you on the path to heaven, Jenn. You can't see that clearly, but you will someday. And in meantime, I *can* see it, and you must understand that—"

"Shut up!" Jenn shrieked. "I'm happy like I am. Why isn't that enough? Why can't that *ever* be enough?"

"Because happiness whose source is perversion is not happiness," Reverend Sawyer said.

"I'm *not* a pervert," Jenn cried. "If anyone's perverted, it's the two of you!"

All of this, Jenn thought, merely because her mom had walked into G & G's to give her a ride home. She hadn't witnessed how hard Jenn worked to earn her money, and she sure as heck hadn't bothered to meet either Giselle or Gertie to learn exactly how much effort they were putting into their restaurant. She had merely seen some ladies having a nice time celebrating someone's birthday and some other ladies having a little anniversary dinner. *That* had been enough for Kate McDaniels. No way was her precious little Jennifer going to be exposed to such sin. It was eternal damnation by association, Jenn thought. She was so furious at the end of the encounter with her mom and Mr. Sawyer that she stayed furious all night and was still furious when she got off the school bus the next morning.

Things got worse for her immediately.

There was a large newly placed banner over the front doors of South Whidbey High School. It was done in the hues of the rainbow and, like the steam punk posters, it advertised the prom. Beneath these words, RAINBOW PROM, was the relevant date. And beneath the banner itself stood Squat Cooper and two other boys.

Squat saw her as Jenn approached. He said something to the other two, and they slouched off. Jenn took note of their stupid jeans hanging low on their crotches. At least, she thought, Squat had never adopted that totally ridiculous and utterly hideous fashion statement. At least, she thought, he knew that having to look at some dude's underwear was not the thrill a girl was seeking.

"How can you stand to hang with those creeps?" Jenn asked him.

He looked startled, both at her words and her tone. "Did someone rise from the wrong side of the bed this morning?" he asked. "That's Brent and Haydn, by the way. We've been in school with them for something like thirteen years, counting preschool."

"Well, they've turned into lowlifes."

"Lowlifes with brains. Hmmm. I didn't think one qualified for lowlife-dom if one's GPA topped three point five."

"Those two don't have a *combined* GPA of three point five."

Squat seemed to study her before he said, "Have we taken to judging based on appearances?"

"I don't know, Squat, *have* we? Aren't you the person who told me I'd be judged by the company I'm keeping?"

"Since you're keeping company with me at the moment, you have nothing to fear," was his reply. "On the other hand . . ." He gave a glance at the banner above them. "I would suggest a wider berth might be in order . . . ?"

"*Would* you? Why would that be? 'Cause I like a couple of lesbians? Or 'cause unlike you, I don't judge people?"

"Didn't you just judge Brent and Haydn?" Squat asked. "Or was that someone else? Because as I recall our conversation so far—"

"Oh shut up! Stop talking like some stupid professor. Act real for once if you possibly can."

His eyes grew darker as did his face. He said, "Seriously? What's crawled up *your* butt, Jenn?"

"You, at the moment," Jenn snarled. "Do me a favor and crawl out, okay?"

She had to get away from everyone, but the only person she could realistically get away from was her mom. Both of them, she figured, needed time to cool off. Her mom, especially, needed to know that she couldn't bend Jenn to her will as long as her will involved baptism classes that took place on one of her work nights followed by some gruesome ceremony during which she was expected to wade into Deer Lake in order to have a chance of someday speaking gibberish. As long as she stayed at home, this was what she faced, though. She knew that Kate wasn't going to cease and desist until Jenn was guaranteed entrance through the Pearly Gates.

She brought this up with Becca after lunch. She began by bringing her into the picture about Mr. Sawyer's visit and about the plan he and Kate had devised to save Jenn's soul. She finished up with the only solution she could come up with to bring her mother to reason. She needed to get herself out of the house so that Kate could see how determined Jenn was not to be forced into something against her will.

She said to Becca, "C'n I stay at Mr. Darrow's place? It would just be for a few nights. Maybe only two, even. I figure if I don't go home and if my mom has to worry about where I am, maybe it'll be more important to her that I'm alive than that I'm baptized into that bizzaro church of hers."

Becca was quiet. Occasionally, she had a super unnerving way of looking at people and she was doing that now. It was like . . . Jenn wasn't sure what it was like other than that it seemed as if Becca didn't believe her.

"Can I?" she asked again. "Maybe it would be just for tonight. I won't make any noise. I won't be any bother. I can even hang around at G & G's till Mr. Darrow goes to bed and I can leave before he gets up and there won't be a reason he'd even know I was there because I wouldn't say a word."

Becca bit the side of her lip. For a horrible moment, Jenn wondered if Becca, too, was deserting her. She couldn't understand how that could possibly be. They were BFFs, and she wasn't asking for *anything* but a couch to sleep on. No food, no water, no . . . nothing.

Becca said the unbelievable then. "Can't someone from the club help you out?"

"*What* club?"

"The Gay Straight Alliance. Haven't you gone to a meeting?"

"Why would I go to a meeting?"

"I was just thinking that other kids have probably gone through this and—"

"What? Gone through what? What're you saying?"

"It's just that you're saying . . . I mean, what you're saying about your mom and everything else, like G & G's . . ."

Jenn couldn't believe her ears. Becca, too? *What* was going on in her world? She said abruptly, "Just forget it. Forget I even asked."

"But, Jenn," Becca started. "It's only that Mr. Darrow—"

"Never mind. Like I *said*, forget I asked. Forget everything while you're at it, Becca. I thought we were friends, but obviously—" Jenn was horrified to feel tears threatening. There was nothing to do but walk away.

Becca called after her. "Jenn! Wait! I was only—"

Jenn swung around, "Forget it," she cried, and she didn't care in the least that about fifty kids were nearby, heading to class, witnesses to her confrontation with Becca.

29

The solution to most every problem in Seth's life was making music. This had long been the case, and when Prynne joined the gypsy jazz group, this turned out to be doubly true. Even more than playing by himself or playing with Triple Threat, Seth discovered that with Prynne there was a complete musical understanding. There was virtually no need even to shoot a look between them to indicate who was to dominate a particular moment in what they were playing.

This was what allowed Triple Threat to shine at their next rehearsal. The group generally rehearsed in Langley at a place called South Whidbey Commons, a Second Street cottage where local kids learned how to be baristas, man a cash register, sell secondhand books, and take care of customers. South Whidbey Commons also provided a garden with seating out in front and public spaces inside for small meetings and such. It was in a room farthest in the back of the place that Triple Threat did their rehearsing of what was their specialty: the wildly complicated gypsy jazz of Django Reinhardt.

Reinhardt's music had always been a draw when they were rehearsing, and this day was no different. People had started wandering in from the front of the Commons during their first number, and more slipped into the room as they went on.

Their practice session was two hours long with all its

starts and stops. When they played their final tune, they were more than ready to call it a day. They acknowledged the applause of their listeners and were packing up their instruments when a woman unknown to any of them made her way through the departing crowd.

Her clothing said Seattle: none of it matched but it all seemed to work, from her après ski boots to her untied bow tie to her drooping dreadlock storage cap to her man's tuxedo jacket over jeans. She introduced herself as Steamer Constant, which sounded to Seth more like a drink than a name, and she went on to tell them her line of business.

She was, she said, a scout. Triple Threat exchanged looks because none of them had the first idea what she was talking about. She went on to add that she was a *talent* scout, there in Langley to attend the piano festival that was taking place at the town's art center.

"Between concerts," she said, "I've been checking out the coffeehouses. Never seen so many in a town so small. Today it was this place's turn. How long've you guys played together?"

For the original members it was four years. With Prynne, it was just over six months. When Seth told her this, Steamer Constant asked if they had representation, because her job was to look for talent.

"You an agent or something?" Jackson, the mandolin player, asked.

"Consider me an agent for the agent," Steamer replied. "Like I said a talent scout. You've heard of that, right?"

Well, they weren't exactly idiots, Seth thought.

Steamer went on to ask if they'd cut any CDs yet, if they had demos she could take with her to Seattle. They did have one, but they'd made it inside Dane the banjo player's garage, and with a look at each other, they silently agreed that they sure as hell didn't want some talent scout listening to that.

"Too expensive to do a decent one," Seth settled on telling her.

She nodded, as if this struck her as wise. She dug in a briefcase for business cards, which she handed around to all of them. She said, "C'n you get into Seattle sometime to play?"

"What, for you?" Prynne asked.

"For the agent I'm scouting for," Steamer said.

They looked at each other once again. Then they looked at her as if she were the angel Gabriel come to make his big announcement to the Virgin Mary. They all spoke at once, variations of they sure as hell could come to Seattle and play for an agent and when when when would Steamer Constant like this to occur?

"No hurry," she said. "Any time you're ready. Give me a call and we'll set it up."

That said, she was gone, leaving them holding her business card and looking from her departing back, to the card, to each other. A miracle had occurred.

After several rounds of high-fiving each other, Triple Threat split up and headed off. Seth and Prynne picked up Gus who'd been outside the Commons, attached to an exterior faucet and waiting patiently. With the dog between them, they took off up Second Street, up to the corner of Second and Anthes, where the climb out of the village began. Here Seth had parked his VW, in front of the bright white village museum.

Gus, however, was not inclined to get into the car without a little action in reward for being so patient. He pulled in the direction of the small city park across the street. Seth said to him, "Later, okay? We get back to Grand's and I'll throw your ball."

The Lab didn't look happy with this idea. Prynne said,

"Poor guy. Hey, I need some new strings and rosin, Seth. Why'n't you take him over to the park. I'll get what I need at the music store and then we can take off."

Langley Music was close, tucked inside an artful collection of shops gathered around a patio and a walkway planted with ferns and flowers. There, musical instruments and supplies were sold and lessons were given: mostly to retired baby boomers who decided now was the time to start playing guitar.

Seth said, "Good idea."

Prynne smiled and replied, "One of many, buddy," and she kissed him, slinging one arm around his neck. "I got another one, but I'll tell you later," she murmured.

"Epic." He laughed.

Contentedly he watched her walk in the direction of the music store. She was so . . . He didn't know what. She was just Prynne and he loved her and how she made him feel.

Seth said, "Come on, boy," to Gus and he could see how the dog brightened up at that. Life was *so* looking up, Seth thought. Prynne was back, Triple Threat was cooking, and now a talent scout wanted them all to come to Seattle and play for an agent.

He hadn't ever felt this happy. The future was bright. With Prynne at his side, it seemed that anything was possible.

30

When Prynne said, "But this has always been just a temporary thing. You know I'm a solo act," Seth didn't know what to think. It didn't make sense to him that someone might not *want* to play in front of a talent agent. But that was what Prynne told him when he reported to her that, a couple of days after she'd heard them play, Steamer Constant had tracked him down via South Whidbey Commons and asked Triple Threat to come into Seattle ASAP. Prynne said, "It's Triple Threat, not Quadruple Threat," when he protested that she *had* to go.

Seth figured her hesitation had to do with nerves. He was nervous, too. So were the guys. But if they didn't take this opportunity, who knew when another would come along? So despite her reluctance, Seth talked Prynne into it. On the appointed day, she stowed her fiddle in the back of Jackson's dirt-encrusted RAV4, Seth did the same with his guitar, and they took off.

Down in Clinton, there was no ferry line and they rolled right on, along with motorcycles, cars, and a school bus. Jackson and Dane stayed inside the SUV for the fifteen-minute crossing, but Prynne said she needed to go above and use the rest room. She'd been awfully quiet and she wasn't looking so great. Seth said he would go up, too, because if she was as nervous as she seemed to be, he figured she needed either moral support or someone to comfort her if she upchucked her breakfast.

The crossing was a smooth one, the waters of Possession Sound so glass-like that had anything broken the surface, you could have seen it nine hundred yards away. Seth waited at one of the windows, watching tree-studded Hat Island slide by in the distance. When Prynne joined him, she was still pale, so he bought her a sugar cookie from the cafeteria and pressed it on her. She tucked it into her shoulder bag, and they returned to the SUV.

Within five minutes of arriving in Mukilteo across the water from Whidbey, Seth knew that something was wrong. They were heading up the hill away from the water when he noticed Prynne's head had fallen forward onto her chest. He murmured, "You okay?" as the SUV hit a curve. She rocked against him and murmured something he couldn't understand. He said quietly, "Prynne, you okay?" so as not to freak out Jackson and Dane in the front of the vehicle. She didn't respond but merely smiled. She finally murmured "Sleep," scooched away from him, and then settled across the back seat with her head in his lap.

Dane glanced back and said, "She okay, man?" and Seth decided to say, "Up all night. She's totally nervous about this thing. She'll be okay, though," to which Jackson said, "Hope so," with a look into the rear view mirror.

What Seth knew was that hope was an up-in-the-air thing because Prynne was stoned out of her mind. The first thing he thought of was that she'd somehow put her hands on more Oxy. Or it was something else, but whatever it was, Prynne had taken it in the ferry bathroom. His only hope was that the effects would wear off by the time they got into Seattle.

The talent agent's office was in an area called Fremont, a quirky part of the city nudging a canal that led from Lake Union into the greater waters of Puget Sound. What characterized the place was a large statue of the Russian leader Lenin, a humongous concrete troll that sat beneath the Aurora Street Bridge, and other fanciful outdoor art. Like every other Seattle neighborhood, Fremont had its own downtown with shops offering everything from junk posing as antiques, to consignment shops, to thrift stores posing as consignment shops, to galleries offering the wares of the neighborhood's artists. From the downtown area near the canal, Fremont climbed a long hillside to a place called Phinney Ridge, and it was practically to Phinney Ridge that they had to drive before they found a parking space.

The talent agent had an office in the downtown area, above a shop called Dusty Strings, where handmade musical instruments were sold. They'd spotted this as they drove around looking for a place to park, and once they found a spot, they had a hike in front of them to get back to it.

Prynne was still out of it. No way could Seth keep claiming she was just sleeping off a bad night. Jackson opened the driver's door, got out, leaned back in, and shot a look at Prynne where she remained sprawled across Seth's lap. He said, "What the hell, Seth. What's she on?" and when Seth tried to make an excuse, Dane opened the back door of the RAV4 and grabbed Prynne's shoulder bag before Seth could protest.

He dumped its contents onto the floor of the vehicle, at Seth's feet. He pawed among them and then he swore as he grabbed up a small labeled bottle and tossed it to Jackson. "Oh great, oh too perfect, oh *hell*," Jackson said. "Weed oil, man. She's downed half the bottle."

Seth wanted to say, stupidly, that it wasn't against the law. Weed oil came in various strengths, depending on what you wanted it for, and Prynne was old enough to buy it, so what was everyone freaking out about? That's what he *wanted* to say, but he didn't because when Jackson passed the bottle to him, he saw that for some insane reason Prynne had scored the strongest of the oils and according to the label it was intended to help you sleep.

His first reaction was that he wanted to kill her. His second was to tell the two other guys that he would handle everything. They should head in the direction of the talent agent's office, he told them. He'd get Prynne straightened out and meet them there.

When Jackson's response to this was, "Get her straightened out *how*, man?" Seth told him just to leave it to him. He added, "C'n you take our instruments? We'll catch up," and when Dane said under his breath "Like that's going to do any good," Seth said, "Hey, back off."

Dane retorted with, "No way is she going to be able to play."

"She'll play. Just get going, okay?"

Once they were out of sight, Seth heaved Prynne out of the vehicle. He stood her upright, and this was enough to get her to open her eyes. He snapped at her, "What the *hell*, Prynne. Why did you *do* this?"

She squinted at him. "I tried to tell you . . ." was all she could get out.

"What?" he demanded. "That you had to get stoned because you're just so totally *nervous*? I believe that like I believe . . . I don't even know what. Like I believe anything you ever say because obviously everything you say is a lie because why would you do this?"

He started her walking in the direction of Dusty Strings. She stumbled a bit but she was able to walk. She said, "Sorry, sorry," but the words were a mumble. "I didn't know it would . . ."

"Like hell you didn't," Seth replied. "Like you couldn't have just done a little weed, huh? It had to be the oil. And not only the oil but the strongest, right? You had to have the strongest on *this* day of *all* days? I can't even believe you're real."

They came to an espresso bar. Seth ducked in quickly and bought her a double. He stood there on the sidewalk and made her drink it. Then he went inside and bought another. He didn't know if it would do any good, but he had to try something, and this was the something that came to his mind. Once she'd drunk them both, they walked on. He had nothing more to say to her. He felt like a dog she'd decided to kick.

Upstairs at Dusty Strings, they found Jackson and Dane in a reception area of the agent's office. They weren't the only ones there. A lady cellist and her guitarist partner were also waiting, and Seth recognized them from Whidbey. Steamer Constant was also in the reception area, having just come out of an inner office as Prynne and Seth entered. She frowned when she saw them and said, "Is she okay?" in reference to Prynne. He said, "She got real sick last night. She didn't want to come today, but I talked her into it."

"Will she be able to play?"

"Think so," Seth said.

"I c'n play," Prynne added.

Luckily, the cellist and the guitarist went first, so they had extra time for Prynne to recover. She walked back and forth in the reception area. Jackson and Dane wouldn't look at her.

She began to tune her fiddle as the others saw to their own instruments. She had some trouble with the bow and with the tuning keys and when she finally said, "That's close enough," Dane rolled his eyes and Jackson swore under his breath. The cellist and guitarist continued to play energetically inside the agent's office.

When they finally emerged, they were all smiles, casting thank-yous over their shoulders. One of them said good

luck to Triple Threat, and that was it. Their time had come.
Seth could only hope that Prynne's recovery was sufficient
to allow her to shine.

The agent was a tattooed woman given to lots of fringe
that hung about her clothes in a leather rainfall. Her name
was Freda Windsarm, which suggested Native American
birth, but she didn't look even vaguely Native American since
her hair was bleached to the point of no turning back and
her skin was so pale she looked like one of those Japanese
dancers who wear white masks. She was at the window of
her office, blowing cigarette smoke into the street below,
and when she said to them, "Give me a sec," they had a
chance to check out the space, which was characterized by
photographs galore: Freda with Kurt Cobain, Freda with
Macklemore and Ryan Lewis, Freda with Snoop Dogg, Freda
with Jay Z, Freda with Britney, Freda with Cher, Freda with
Queen Latifah, Freda with Michael Jackson, and on and
on. It was sort of strange, Seth thought, because in each
picture she looked exactly the same no matter how long ago
it had been taken.

They set up to play for her in an area designated for
this: a square of hardwood floor sitting beneath an enormous
poster from *Star Wars*, Han Solo and Chewbacca at the
controls of the *Millennium Falcon*. By the time they were
ready, so was Freda Windsarm. She sat down behind her
desk, gave them a nod, and said, "Let's see what you've got
then, Triple Threat."

Not much, as things turned out. What they had wasn't a
disaster, as Jackson and Dane had thought it would be. But
what they had was marginal. Prynne did her best, but her
performance was riddled with mistakes that the rest of them
tried to cover. And even when Freda Windsarm said with
a frown, "Let's have the fiddler sit the next one out," the

rest of them were so stressed that they weren't anywhere in the same hemisphere as their best. Thus all of them knew what the outcome would be even before Freda Windsarm said it: "We'll be in touch. Thanks for coming in," after which she shot a look at Steamer Constant that clearly said, What the hell were you *thinking*?

They plodded back to the SUV in silence: stony on the part of Jackson and Dane, sorrowful on the part of Prynne, crushed on the part of Seth. It wasn't till they got to the vehicle and piled inside that Jackson turned to Prynne and said, "You sabotaged us. Happy about that?" For a moment no one said anything. Then Jackson went with a choice epithet said under his breath, which caused Seth to spring to Prynne's defense with a "Hey, back off," which caused Dane to suggest Seth would say or do anything just as long as he got laid. This put Seth into a real state – Hey, what do you think? That his thing with Prynne was all about sex or something? he demanded – which caused Dane to remark, "You said it, we didn't, man," which caused Prynne to say "I *tried* to tell you," which caused Jackson to shout, "Shut up, Prynne," which made Seth want to punch his lights. He made a lunge for him, but Prynne put a stop to that.

"It's not Seth's fault! It's mine!" she cried, and having said that she dumped out her shoulder bag, found the bottle of weed oil, and drank the rest of it in front of all of them.

31

Becca began to understand that a quickening was happening, just as the book given to her by Diana Kinsale had explained. After the Mutt Strut, she pulled that book – *Seeing Beyond Sight* – from the bookshelf in Ralph Darrow's former bedroom that now was hers. She opened it, and she refreshed her memory with the words: "A verbal exploration and subsequent interpretation of the visions will lead the visionary to propel events forward to a safe, desired, or happy conclusion that might not otherwise occur should the visions not be explored completely and understood with a sharp degree of accuracy. This is what we call a quickening."

The quickening appeared to be going on everywhere. It was as if everyone's life was geared up so that Becca could see exactly what was happening. How to propel events forward so that the conclusion would be a good one, though . . . ? That was trickier. And how the quickening applied to her own life was trickier still.

When she'd arrived back at Grand's house after seeing Mrs. Banks and her grandchildren, the first thing she'd done was to make certain that she was interpreting things correctly. She waited till she and Grand were alone on the porch, where he'd indicated he wanted to sit and enjoy the sight of his garden. By his side on the bench beneath one of the windows, she said, "Banks is a person, isn't she? You didn't mean banks like in the places where people put their money. You meant banks as in So-and-so Banks. She was at the Mutt Strut today with her grandkids."

Ralph was slightly slumped on the bench but as she spoke, his spine became straighter. He smiled lopsidedly and said, "Go banks."

What at once accompanied these hesitant words was a vision: papers spread out, Ralph's hands on either side of them. Becca thought of a will. Grand was of an age when a will would be a crucial thing to have. But why this was important to him now when he was alive and kicking, she didn't know. Unless he wanted to change that will. Or unless he knew that he wasn't going to be alive and kicking very much longer, which was a thought she couldn't bear addressing. But say it *was* a will. Shouldn't there be a copy somewhere? In the house, maybe, locked in some kind of box that was fireproof? Except wouldn't it be smarter to have that box somewhere else, *beyond* the house? She thought of the possibilities for this, but there seemed to be only two: Ralph's workshop and his garden shed.

She said to him, "Did Mrs. Banks make a will for you, Grand? Is that what you've been trying to tell us?"

"Houch," he said.

She said, "Houch?"

Ralph slapped his good hand against the building behind them. "Houch," he said. "Banks. Houch."

"Oh God, of course!" she cried. "*House.* Mrs. Banks did something about a house. Can you tell me what?"

"Pay," was all he said. He sounded desperate to be understood.

Banks, a woman, a drive through the forest, a stairway up the side of a cedar-shingled building that clearly looked like a house. Those were the clues Becca had. She knew she needed to work upon them to bring events concerning Seth's grandfather to a conclusion that didn't destroy his family.

Mrs. Kinsale had told Becca that she couldn't do anything about her visions until the time when she was fully able to block whispers without aid of the AUD box. But what Becca told herself now was that desperate times called for desperate action, and these were desperate times, especially for Grand.

But they were also desperate times for Jenn, and Becca had known this the moment Jenn had brought up Mr. Sawyer's visit to Jenn's home. She'd also known what was coming before Jenn had made her request to couch surf at Mr. Darrow's. What she hadn't been able to tell her friend, though, was that she – Becca – could not bring more drama or even the potential for drama into Ralph Darrow's life. She couldn't risk it, not only because of his health and what stress could do to it but also because if Brenda Sloan found out that someone was couch surfing in her father's house, she would have yet another reason to plant incendiary devices along the path of Grand's recovery. Becca had intended to tell Jenn this, but her friend had walked off in anger before she could do so.

She'd realized soon enough that there was someone else who might be able to help out, however. But because she didn't want to get Jenn's hopes up until she knew for sure, she had to talk to Diana Kinsale first.

Jenn's situation, along with Becca's growing understanding of what Ralph Darrow was trying to tell her, was not the only sign that a quickening was fast approaching. The next day at school, Derric was waiting to talk to her at the end of her first class.

Wordlessly, he dropped his arm around her shoulder and they walked in the direction of her next class. She fastened her arm around his waist, and he kissed the side of her head and said, "I showed her the letters. She didn't want to look at them at first. But I wouldn't budge and I wouldn't get into it with her till she read them. It took, like, I don't know . . . it took a while."

"And?"

"She cried. I cried." Derric's face said he was reliving the moment and so did Becca, for she saw the vision of Rejoice sitting on the swinging bench on her family's front porch, and she held in her lap a stack of letters that Becca recognized only too well. Then the vision was gone because Derric went on. "I took the album with me when I went. You know which one?"

"The one your mom made that shows your adoption and coming to the island?"

"We went through it, and she saw how it was: how I met them, Mom and Dad; how Mom kept coming to Kampala as long as it took for the adoption to go through; how everyone was at the airport when we finally got there; how I grew up. And the rest was there, too, pictures Mom took at the orphanage. Rejoice was in them, just one kid along with the rest of us. And I was . . . Becca, I was never looking at her. Never. She cried about that, too, and so did I. I told her how sorry I was. I said I hated myself for what I did, leaving her like that. But I think she could see – Rejoice could see – that I meant everything because what she said was . . ." A muscle worked in his jaw. "She said she could see it'd been way harder for me than it had been for her because she didn't remember she had a brother while I knew all the time I had a sister."

"Whoa, that's nice," Becca said. "Bet that helps her let it go, Der. Do her parents know? Did you guys tell them?"

"I got to tell my own parents first. I've been waiting for the moment, but I'll do it."

She raised her eyebrows. This had always been the real issue for Derric: telling his parents. He caught her expression and said, "I'm ready. I want them to meet her. I just want things to be normal."

Normal was the key, Becca thought. Wanting things to be normal seemed to be the theme of everything going on around her.

This was what she understood when she saw Diana Kinsale that afternoon. She'd phoned Prynne at Ralph's house and she'd asked if a couple of extra hours there would be asking too much, since Prynne had been there since seven that morning. Prynne said, "Oh . . . I was hoping . . . Before Seth gets home . . ." But then she changed course with, "No problem. It's okay."

She went to Diana. She found her kneeling in her front garden, planting primroses along the flagstone path to the front door. As Becca watched, she nearly tipped over as she got to her feet. Becca hurried forward to help her up.

Diana sighed. "I *hate* this damn business of getting old." She was wearing her baseball cap and an old South Whidbey High School letterman's jacket. She had a scarf around her neck and heavy gloves on her hands, although the day didn't call for this much protection. "Is this a practice day? Have I forgotten?"

"Nope. I just wanted to talk to you. I can come back later if you're too busy."

Oscar had been lying on the lawn, head on paws, watching Diana. He'd risen as Becca helped Diana to her feet and now he came to her.

Someday soon came from Diana in perfect clarity as did *can't take something from a younger person.*

"What's there to take from a younger person?" Becca asked her.

Diana stopped walking on their route toward the mudroom door. "You weren't supposed to hear that."

"Was I supposed to block you? You didn't say."

"No, no," Diana told her. "It's fine." *Must be more careful.* "The power you have is growing. Let's do a little practice."

"Shouldn't we go into the house for it? Shouldn't we be in your room?"

"Perhaps. But to block successfully, you must be able to do it anywhere. Why don't you try it here and now and see what happens?"

So Becca began the mantra: *Empty of all there is, there is. Empty of all there is.* She glanced at Diana to see that she looked placid. They walked steadily toward the back of the house where the view was expansive and there was plenty to distract her and to disrupt her blocking. Becca kept with the mantra and then released it slowly to see what would happen.

Nothing. She held on to it. Again, nothing. She locked herself to the nothing. Blocking the whispers like this made her start to sweat. It made her heart pound. She began to feel like a runner near the end of a race.

Next to her Diana stumbled. The blocking was gone and *how much more* was what Becca heard. When she took Diana's elbow to keep her steady, what she saw was tubing going into an arm. This tubing ran from the arm to a large machine. A second or two, then the vision was gone. But it was enough to tell Becca what she'd known without wanting to know for at least a year.

She said at once before she could lose her courage, "Mrs. Kinsale, are you sick? Do you have cancer or something?"

Diana glanced at her. She smiled one of those fond relative-not-your-mom smiles. "Or something," she said.

"Are you . . ." Becca didn't even want to say it.

Diana did so. "Dying? Not yet. But I will eventually. Just like everyone."

"That's not what I meant."

"I know that. But it's all I'll say for now. Let's get the dogs, shall we? It's time they had a romp on the beach."

Diana went to the run and released the four other dogs. She picked up two well-chewed balls and handed them to Becca. She said, "All dogs come," and they did just that.

They made slow progress across the field next to Diana's house. A well-used path led through the lush springtime grasses, beaten down by Diana and the dogs over years so that nothing now grew upon it. The dogs knew where it led, though, and they began to gambol like lambs. They were a joyful sight, yipping and leaping on their way to the beach at Sandy Point. Here the tides met, where the waters of Saratoga Passage and the waters of Possession Sound carved to a depth of six hundred feet, allowing space and depth for orcas and gray whales to dive.

On their way, Becca told Diana about Mrs. Banks, about Derric and Rejoice, and about her thoughts on the quickening. She didn't bring up Jenn. She felt she couldn't yet, although she wasn't quite sure why. Diana was silent as she spoke. Then she released a thought, *Are the visions and the whisp* –

Becca blocked it at once. She felt a swirling of delight all over her body. She said, "I stopped you, Mrs. Kinsale! Before you finished the word *whisper*."

Diana said, "Excellent. You've been practicing."

"When I can."

"Do you think they relate, then?"

"The visions and the whispers? Mr. Darrow's do."

"What kind of understanding are they leading you toward?"

"Doing something. Mrs. Kinsale, I *got* to do something. I think Mr. Darrow wants me to. He's telling me the best he can. And then there's Jenn. She . . . well, she *asked* me . . ."

"What?" Diana said when Becca hesitated. They were across the field now and following the lane that would take them down to the beach. The dogs were far ahead of them, snuffling the sand, all except Oscar, who maintained his pace at Diana's side.

"If the quickening is about propelling events to a good conclusion . . . if that's what I'm s'posed to do . . ."

"When everything's *mastered,* that's what you're supposed to do," Diana said. "You've been given extraordinary power, Becca. I believe you're beginning to see that. But to be hasty in a situation when the ramification of any action you take could be serious . . . ? This is something over which you absolutely must maintain control."

"Control over what?"

"Impetuosity in the face of something you don't yet clearly understand."

They were silent for several minutes after that. Becca gnawed on this. She felt like a dog frustrated to get to the marrow of the bone. She and Diana descended the rest of the way to the beach, where Becca took the two balls and began to hurl them south as the dogs tore in that direction in anticipation. She tried to take in the beauty that surrounded them: far to the east the Cascade Mountains still topped with snow, closer to Whidbey the soaring cliffs at the south end of Camano Island, a bald eagle riding a current of air, the extraordinary calm of the water on this day, the cumulous clouds lazing in the sky.

"What if someone *asks* for action?" she finally said. "If I know a quickening is going to happen and someone asks me to do something, then what am I supposed to do? It's not like I can walk away."

Diana leaned against a cottage's three-foot-high stone wall, an inadequate bulwark against anything more than a casual high tide. She shivered although the breeze was mild on the beach and despite the heavy jacket she was wearing. Her complete lack of energy was apparent and it was deeply uncharacteristic of her. Once again Becca thought of *normal*. Normal was not who Diana had been for months.

Diana said, "That's a different issue, isn't it? If someone asks for action, what is the visionary supposed to do? *Has* someone asked for an action?"

"Like I said, Mr. Darrow."

"But not exactly. Is that right?"

"He can't ask directly. He can't say all the words. But I've seen his memories in visions and they seem to relate to what he *can* say."

"And his whispers?"

Becca knew this was the tricky part. She bought time by wresting the balls away from the dogs and hurling them again. The animals shot after them, splashing into the water and out again.

"His whispers are broken up," she admitted. "They're like his words. It's the whole language thing. But he seems so desperate."

"For you to do something?"

"For me to understand something."

"Then doesn't that tell you where to begin?"

"With understanding?" And when Diana nodded, Becca said, "Can I act once I understand?"

"You can act at any time," Diana said. "But understanding *why* you're acting and *how* you must act need to be in place if a quickening is to occur."

The visionary cannot be afraid, my dear. Diana had released another thought and Becca had allowed it because of the word *visionary*.

"Afraid of what?" she asked.

"Did you try to block that?"

"No."

"Why?"

"It seemed related to what I said."

"*Are* you afraid, then? I ask this because you're being hesitant with me about something, and that's going to make our work more difficult. Hesitation is like indirection, and indirection is a half-measure, Becca. I believe you've been gifted in the way you've been gifted because you're intended to take full measures."

"I came here because I wanted to ask you if Jenn could stay with you." Becca told her the story, including in it the details of her conversation with Jenn and concluding with, "She needs a place to stay because her mom's freaked out that Jenn works for lesbians, so she says Jenn has to be baptized into her church. Jenn says she needs a place to stay just to get away from her for a while and she asked me if she could come to Mr. Darrow's. But see . . ."

"Yes," Diana said.

"What?"

"Of course she can stay with me, but only if she understands that she and her mother must try to reach some accord on all this. I would want her to work on that while she was with me. Do you think she'd be willing?"

"I can ask her."

"Do that. But there's something else, another solution to Jenn's situation that you've not looked at in your haste to" – and here Diana smiled – "'propel events to a safe, desired, and happy conclusion.'"

"What? I don't think I overlooked—"

"Listen, dear. Because of how Jenn reacted when you spoke to her, and because of how *you* reacted to her reaction, you turned away from the true direction, which you already gave her – quite admirably, I must tell you – during your conversation. Can you see what it is?"

Becca thought about this. She saw the truth in Mrs.

Kinsale's point about her own reaction to Jenn's reaction. Jenn had reacted to Becca's hesitation about her request, and in very short order, Jenn had rejected *her*. It was the rejection that Becca was reacting to and she was choosing an action based on that.

She sighed. "This is very tough, Mrs. Kinsale."

"Believe me, no one can make this journey easy."

"You mean the quickening thing?"

"I mean life. No one can make anyone's life easier, at least not in the way that you'd like to do it. But you did give Jenn very good advice. Can you think what it is?"

There was only one topic that Becca could come up with that might have fit the idea of having given advice. She said, "I told her to talk to someone in the club, the Gay Straight Alliance."

"There you have it. And although Jenn is upset with you now, you've made that the only option she has. Painful as it is for both of you at the moment, you *propelled* her. Congratulations, my dear. You've taken a necessary step. A little ahead of schedule, it's true. But you've taken it all the same."

32

Jenn was in her English class, trying to appear fascinated with a presentation on the burning topic of various ways to create an introductory paragraph for an essay on Lady Macbeth, Macbeth, Macduff, Banquo, or the witches – your choice – when she was called to the office. She shoved her notebook and her text of the play into her backpack in the hope that she wouldn't have to return to finish the period, and out she went. The call slip was from Mr. Vansandt. Getting sent for by the principal never meant anything good.

She had to cool her heels for five minutes outside his office. She could hear him talking, and because no one was replying, she figured he was on the phone. When the door opened, it was Mr. Vansandt who did the opening. He beckoned Jenn inside his sanctum, told her to sit, and left the room. His office smelled of lilacs, the scent coming from one of those bottles with oil inside and incense-looking sticks popping out of it. This sat next to a picture on the principal's desk. It was turned away from Jenn, but when she sneaked a peek at it, she saw it was of the principal and some kid in a U-Dub football jersey, presumably his son.

"Here we are then," Mr. Vansandt said as he re-entered the room. One of the two school counselors teetered in front of him. This was Tatiana Primavera, the A–L counselor. She'd long been known for her crippling footwear in the land of sandals-and-socks or hiking boots. She favored necklines that featured five inches of cleavage and made it a challenge to direct your eyes somewhere else.

Because Jenn was an M-for-McDaniels, she and the counselor knew each other only by sight. Jenn didn't understand what she was doing there. She also didn't understand why – if a counselor was needed – her own counselor wasn't entering the room along with the principal.

Mr. Vansandt must have seen confusion on Jenn's face because he said, "You're not in trouble, Jenn. You know Ms. Primavera, don't you?"

Jenn knotted her eyebrows although she said, "Yeah. Sure." She waited to hear why she'd been sent for.

Mr. Vansandt said, "Why don't we sit over here?" and indicated a round table in the corner of the office. "This isn't an inquisition," he added with a smile. "It'll be more comfortable."

Jenn didn't see how, since the chairs were identical to the chair she was sitting in, facing his desk. But she went along and crossed over to the table. She dumped her backpack next to a chair, plopped down, and waited. The other two sat at two angles from her. They all formed a triangle whose sides crossed the surface of the table.

"You're just finishing tenth grade," Mr. Vansandt began. And when Jenn nodded, he said, "Been a good experience so far? South Whidbey High School and all the rest?"

Jenn nodded again. Maybe this was part of his job, she thought, checking into the experience of each kid on campus, talking to three or four every day to make sure everything was okay. Could be this was an answer to the bullying that sometimes went on in schools. Mr. Vansandt would want to stay on top of that, nipping it in the bud wherever there was the potential for conflicts to bloom among students.

He leaned forward and clasped his hands together. Ms. Primavera cocked her head of black curls and smiled in a way that looked like sympathy. Jenn felt a little churning in her stomach.

"Let me ask you this, Jennifer," Mr. Vansandt said. He was using a tone of voice that Jenn could only call delicate. "Has anything happened to you against your will while you've been at South Whidbey?"

Jenn wanted to say that every test she'd taken was taken mostly against her will, but she decided that wasn't what he meant. "Bullying, you mean?"

"Not exactly." Mr. Vansandt looked a little uncomfortable. Ms. Primavera looked placid, like a sleepy cat. She cleared her throat, but she didn't speak. There was nothing for it but Mr. Vansandt to go on. "You're a player on the soccer team. Isn't that right? Varsity soccer even as a freshman?"

"Yeah."

"I understand that you're training pretty heavily for the All Island Girls' Soccer team as well."

"It's the best way to get noticed by college coaches," Jenn said. "I mean, being on the team, not just training for it."

"And this is something important for you?"

"I need a scholarship if I'm gonna go to college."

"Have a college picked out? U-Dub? Western? One of the private schools?"

"I'll end up going wherever I c'n get a scholarship."

"Grades looking good?"

"Well . . . yeah . . . guess so."

"Three point one," Mr. Vansandt said. "You'll need to bring them up in the next two years."

"Sure. I want to."

This was so bizarre, Jenn thought. It felt more like making stabs at conversation, like something that would happen on a blind date . . . if she ever agreed to go on a blind date, which she never would.

Then Mr. Vansandt clarified things a bit. He said, "You've been training with Cynthia Richardson and Lexie Ovanov, I understand. How's that working out?"

"Good. Cynthia's a great player. Our positions are different, but she's been helping me with my moves."

"What about Lexie? She's not a soccer player, from what I've learned."

From what I've learned rang a few alarm bells in Jenn's head. Why was Mr. Vansandt checking into Lexie at all? And what did it matter who Jenn trained with? "Track and field," Jenn said. "She's been helping me build speed. She weight trains with us, too. She spots, mostly."

"Sounds like you're fond of her."

A few more alarm balls went off. "I like her, sure."

"Cynthia, too?"

Jenn looked from him to Ms. Primavera. The counselor's face was unchanged, and her head was still cocked. Jenn thought she'd end up giving herself a stiff neck, and she wanted to reach across the table and right the counselor's head before that happened.

She said, "Yeah. Cynthia's great."

"Good of her – and Lexie, of course – to help you out, then," Mr. Vansandt said.

Jenn said nothing. She nodded, though. Then she waited. Somewhere along the line, the principal was going to have to get to the point, if there was a point. Her armpits were getting a little sticky as she waited for it.

Mr. Vansandt steepled his fingers. He, too, cocked his head. There was a lot of head-cocking going on. Jenn wondered it this was an adult thing, an unconscious movement that indicated something . . . only she didn't know what that something was.

Mr. Vansandt finally made things clear when he said, "I've had a phone call from your mom, Jenn. She has some concerns about your relationship with Cynthia and Lexie. Particularly with Lexie."

Jenn felt her face turning into stone. She didn't reply.

"Frankly your mother feels that you're being coerced into a lesbian relationship," Mr. Vansandt went on. The skin just above his shirt collar flushed. The red climbed his neck but went no farther. "She believes that you might have been talked into a sexual relationship in exchange for a job at G & G's, over in Freeland. We know Lexie Ovanov works there, so it seems that if you *have* been coerced in some way, Lexie might have been the person who's done the coercing."

"No way!" Jenn cried.

"'No way' what?" Mr. Vansandt asked. "No way that you were coerced? No way that you're having a sexual relationship with Lexie? Which is it?"

"No way to everything!" Jenn declared. "I can't even *believe* my mom . . . I'm working there because I need the money. I got to have money to be on the All Girls' team. There's hardly any jobs for kids on the island and *this* job fell right into my lap. No way in hell was I not going to take it when they offered it to me."

"Lexie's your transportation to get there on time, isn't she?"

"So what? Look, my mom's all . . . all . . . She's all about the Bible and being baptized and going to church. Anything that looks to her like the path to hell freaks her out. When she came to the restaurant, she saw some lesbians and went ballistic. Then she invited her minister to pray over me or whatever and I can't *believe* she called you! Cynthia and Lexie aren't interested in me – like, sexually – and I'm not interested in them except as friends and athletes. I'm a normal human being—"

"Let's not start referring to some people as normal and

some as abnormal, please." It was, finally, Ms. Primavera speaking. She added, "If you'd like to come to the Gay Straight Alliance, you'll see for yourself that everyone in the club is just like you."

"I'm not gay!" Jenn shouted.

"I didn't say you were," Ms. Primavera replied, in a friendly fashion. "I meant just like you as in just a normal human being, Jenn, going through what every high school student goes through. The same kinds of experiences, the same kinds of problems."

Jenn seriously doubted that. She would have been willing to bet her position on next year's varsity soccer team that no one in the club had a mom like hers.

"That's the purpose of the club," Ms. Primavera said. "Mr. Vansandt wanted me to be here to invite you to attend a meeting. Cynthia's president, by the way. Lexie Ovanov is a member."

"Whatever," Jenn said, but she crossed her arms over her chest. Her gesture said this conversation was over. She and her mom had some talking to do . . . if Jenn ever went home again, which she didn't intend to after this scene.

Mr. Vansandt said, "Well, your story matches Lexie's, Jenn. It matches Cynthia's as well. I've spoken to them both."

Jenn reeled at this one, smacked in the face by a perfect wave of humiliation. That her two friends would be called into the principal because of whatever insane thing her own mom had claimed on the phone . . . ? It was almost more than she could bear.

At lunch, she marched right by the table of her regular lunch crowd over to Cynthia and Lexie. They were sharing a turkey wrap. A container of chopped fruit accompanied this. Both of them had a carton of nonfat milk.

Jenn didn't wait for them to say hi or to ask her to sit. She pulled a chair out and plopped herself down. She said to them, "I'm seriously sorry. My mom's insane. I don't know what else to say."

Cynthia said, "Ah. You got talked to by Mr. Vansandt."

"He didn't tell me he'd talked to you guys till the end," Jenn said. "He was all 'Has anyone messed with you?' and stuff like that. He told me my mom'd called him."

"G & G's?" Lexie speared up some pineapple.

"Those two ladies having dinner for their anniversary?" Jenn said. "To her it was like they'd invited Satan to have dessert with them."

Lexie laughed. So did Cynthia. Jenn couldn't believe they both weren't steaming.

"This has nothing to do with you guys anyway," Jenn said. "It's all my mom and her minister and saving my soul. They got a baptism lined up for me. I bet they'll show up here any day now, kidnap me, and drag me off. I *got* to get away from her."

"A cooling-off period," Lexie noted. "That's what you need. I had to take one of those. I still do, sometimes, when my mom starts talking about an updo, heels, makeup, and a date to the prom."

"I asked my best friend if I could use her couch," Jenn said. "Just for a couple of nights, but she said no way."

"That's a little harsh," Lexie noted.

"Not much like a friend, you ask me," Jenn agreed.

"Come to my house," Cynthia said. "A few days? No problem. My mom'll be fine with that, and we c'n just trade rooms with my brother while you're there."

"Oh gosh, you mean it?" It was like an answer to a prayer she hadn't yet made, Jenn thought.

"Like I said, no problem. You have to be okay with bunk beds, though. That's what's in Brian's room. And . . .

well . . . he's a little odd. Asperger's." She smiled. "You wouldn't believe the stuff he says sometimes."

"It can't be any more odd than what my mom says," Jenn declared, "especially when she's speaking in tongues."

33

At lunch, Derric was the one to say, "What's with Jenn?" when she walked by them without a word and joined Cynthia Richardson and Lexie Ovanov at their regular table across the room.

Squat was the one who responded darkly, "Don't even ask, man," before going back to his burrito.

Becca got to her feet with a quiet "Be right back." She crossed over to Jenn and asked if she could talk to her. Jenn looked up like someone who hasn't the first clue about the identity of the person standing before her. Her response was, "I don't think so," before she turned back to Cynthia and Lexie.

Cynthia, though, said, "Jenn," in that way that suggested someone was being unreasonable.

Jenn sighed and swung around to Becca. "What*ever*," she said. "What d'you want?"

"It's sort of private?" Becca inclined her head in the direction of the Old Commons stairway that led to classrooms above. "Could we . . . Maybe over there . . . ?"

An eye roll greeted this along with another "What*ever*." After that, though, she followed Becca, past their regular table where Derric and Hayley Cartwright said hi and Squat just threw an indifferent look their way before diving back to burrito-land.

At the stairway, Becca didn't waste time, since she could tell how little Jenn even wanted to be with her. She eased the earbud from her ear, though, and she told Jenn she'd found her a place to stay.

"I didn't want to say before," Becca said. "I wanted to check things out first."

The response was a string of swear words that came distinctly from Jenn's whispers and this was followed by *just like everyone else when it comes to this* which made Becca want to say how unfair that accusation was. When nothing came from Jenn as far as spoken words went, Becca stumbled on. "See, I couldn't take you to Mr. Darrow's house because his family is in this huge fight over where he's going to live from now on. Seth and his dad and his aunt and attorneys . . . ? There's all sorts of bad feelings, and with Mr. Darrow's blood pressure needing to stay normal—"

"Like I'm going to raise his blood pressure, Becca," Jenn cut in acidly.

Becca ignored this. "So I talked to Mrs. Kinsale because I knew she has a guest room in her house. I stayed there once, and it's real nice. She's real nice." Becca smiled at Jenn encouragingly. "You just got to like dogs because she has five. Anyway, she says you c'n stay there long as you want. Her house is on Clyde, right above Saratoga Passage and your room would—"

"I have a place to stay," Jenn snapped. "No thanks to you."

"I know you're mad at me," Becca said, nearly flinching from more whispered swear words. "But I didn't want to get your hopes up before I talked to Mrs. Kinsale. And Mr. Darrow . . . Jenn, I couldn't bring any more craziness into his life."

"Oh *thanks*, Becca. So now I'm crazy."

"I didn't mean that. I meant your mom and how ticked off she'd get if you weren't at home. See, if she turned up at Mr. Darrow's on top of Seth's aunt who keeps turning up and on top of everything else like the court and now Seth's dad is trying to get guardianship of Mr. Darrow away from Seth's aunt and—"

"So? No matter where I stay, my mom will probably turn up when she finds out where I am. Mrs. Kinsale's going to be happy about that? What is she, anyway, about two millions years old? Why would I want to stay with some decrepit old lady?"

Probably smells was totally unfair of Jenn, but Becca didn't engage her on that. She said, "Don't talk about her like that. She's old but she's totally nice and she says that as long as you at least try to reconcile with your mom—"

"*What?*" Jenn shrieked. "Oh right, Becca! That's a real help. And I *told* you. I have a place to stay, okay? Just *forget* about me."

Becca watched her walk off. She followed her. She saw her surge past their regular table, push through two freshman girls, and rejoin Cynthia and Lexie. For her own part, Becca went back to her friends. Derric read her face and said, "She kick your butt?"

Squat said, "*Anyone* who tries to talk to her gets their eyeballs singed."

Hayley said, "She's in a bad mood?"

"Who the hell cares?" Squat commented.

I do, Becca thought.

When Becca considered Jenn's reaction, she couldn't come up with a way to have done it better. So she had to set aside her concerns about her – at least for the moment – so that she could go at the problem of finding the Mrs. Banks she needed to talk to. She used the South Whidbey phone book as a place to start. If she could find the right Mrs. Banks, she was in business. She wanted to do her talking in person, though. Otherwise her only option would be to call and say to whoever answered: "Do you know Ralph Darrow by any chance and can you tell me why he keeps saying your name?"

When Becca opened the island phone book, she saw an immediate problem. Ninety-five percent of the names listed had only the phone number and the town lived in accompanying them. There was no address. This caused her spirits to plummet when she gave a glance to the very first page. Then she noted that directly under some of the names, a business name was printed in all caps and in red. She concluded that these businesses were related to the name above them: with one of the three Andersons listed connected to Anderson's Counseling Services in Langley and with one of the seven Arnolds listed associated with Arnold's Septic Services in Freeland.

With high hopes, then, she turned to the Bs. There it was: Banks, Betty, followed by Clinton and a phone number. Beneath this, BANKS, BETTY ATTY was printed in all caps and in red. There was still no address, but there was a phone number, and this number *had* to be of Betty Banks's office. Becca knew that she could call in the morning and ask for the office's address. But first she had to talk to Grand.

She went to his room, where Celia was helping him into bed for the night. She was chatting away in her Celia fashion, telling him a tale about her Balinese cat and the mischief he caused on a regular basis. "If I don't play with him every morning for at least an hour, he's just the dickens, Mr. Darrow," she was saying. She glanced over at Becca and said, "Look who's come to say good night to you. Hey, d'you want the Galapagos book to look at before you go to sleep?"

He shook his head and waved her off. It was Becca he wanted to see, he seemed to be saying. Celia got the message and left them. Becca quickly approached the old man's bed.

She said, "Is Betty Banks your attorney, Grand?" And when his beatific smile, although lopsided, told Becca that she was correct, she went on directly with, "Have you been trying to tell me that I need to talk to her?"

Ralph nodded vigorously. "Houch," he said.

Since it was the business number she needed to call, Becca knew she couldn't do it until the following day during office hours. So when the time arrived, she borrowed Derric's smartphone and called after her first class. She learned that the attorney's office was on Cedar Lane, off Humphrey Road. Becca's heart did a little dance at the name of the street: Cedar Lane. She knew this could be the unpaved road lined with cedars that she'd seen in the vision she'd picked up from Ralph.

She asked Derric where Humphrey Road was. When he told her it was just before you reached the ferry to go over town, she knew she had her work cut out for her. She wanted to ask him to drive her there, but since she didn't exactly know what her purpose was in going and since she didn't have the first idea of what might happen when she got there, she understood she had to find the office alone. This meant asking Prynne to stay late at Grand's, which she hated to do. Something had gone wrong in her relationship with Seth again, but what Prynne seemed to be worried about was where her next hit was going to come from. At least that was what her whispers were saying.

Derric saved her on this score. When she told him she had to go to Clinton, he offered to drive her. She merely switched his offer to an offer to stay with Ralph instead so that Prynne wouldn't have to. No problem, was how he responded.

Becca did it by bus and by bike, and she thought at first that she was in luck because the island bus had a stop right at Humphrey Road. But there her luck abruptly ended. The road rolled before her in a series of climbs and drops as it paralleled Possession Sound. She had a feeling that the ride was going to be a long one, and this proved to be exactly the case. For safety's sake, she removed the earbud and switched off the AUD box, as she usually did when riding her bike.

She was in excellent condition after nearly two years of biking on Whidbey Island where, as far as she knew, there existed only three or four level streets. The rest of the place was steep ascents, steep descents, curves, and deer jumping in front of you. When she finally reached Cedar Lane – which felt like ten miles of hard riding but was probably only three or four – she saw that she would have to walk the rest of the way. For the unpaved road made a climb that only someone from the Tour de France could have conquered.

Her spirits were high as she began the ascent. She knew this place because she'd seen it. Grand had been here, it remained in his memory, and it had transferred to her through his vision.

At the incline's third turn, she found the address she was looking for. It offered more of a climb on a car's-width gravel track, but at its top was a welcome sight. Here was the cedar house Becca had seen and there was the stairway that ascended on the side to the second floor of a building that appeared to be a garage.

At the top of the stairs, she knocked on the same screen door she'd seen in the vision. Someone called out, "No need to knock," and in she went. But the woman who sat behind the desk she encountered within the office was not the grandmother whose grandkids had shown her dog at the Mutt Strut.

As Becca was about to back out the door with apologies,

someone called out, "Shelley, can you make an appointment with Judge Welsh up in Oak Harbor?" and Becca realized that *this* woman – Shelley – was a secretary. So when she asked if she could help Becca in some way, Becca told her she was hoping to see Mrs. Banks for a minute. Before this request could be replied to, she added, "Ralph Darrow asked me to come."

Shelley hesitated. *One of his grandkids* drifted easily from her, and to this Becca gave her a winsome smile and said nothing else. Rising from her desk, the secretary asked her to wait and disappeared behind a door that was across the reception area. Less than a minute brought her back to Becca. "Go on in" gave her access to Betty Banks.

34

The very same dog from the Mutt Strut was there. Uncostumed, he was lying on a rug to one side of the desk. He looked up, seemed to find no issue with Becca, and settled his head on his paws.

Betty Banks folded her hands on her desk and nodded at a chair that stood in front of it. She said, "Shelley tells me you're here for Ralph Darrow?"

Becca said that she was. She also said that it was awkward but Ralph Darrow had been saying the name *Banks* for weeks and none of them – the family, the caregivers, and Becca herself – knew what he meant. "Then we saw you at the Mutt Strut," Becca told her. "Me and my boyfriend? We were there. We saw your grandkids and the dog. Then we saw you, and I realized *banks* might be a person instead of what we thought, which was, well, banks as in going to the bank." It sounded lame. Becca wished she could have come up with a way to decorate the facts so they'd be more appealing.

"Are you a member of the Darrow family?" Mrs. Banks asked after *more than irregular* and *pretty little thing* greeted Becca's opening gambit.

Becca shook her head. She explained that she lived with Ralph Darrow and was one of the people who helped take care of him.

At this, Mrs. Banks drew her eyebrows together. *Take care of him?* "Has something happened to Mr. Darrow?"

"He had a stroke," Becca told her. She went on to explain the rest. She didn't add anything about the dispute between Rich Darrow and his sister regarding their dad's living situation. But she did tell her about Jake and Celia and about the progress Grand had made in his recovery. She ended with, "So I know he wanted me to come to see you, only I don't know why. I was hoping you could tell me because it seems really important to him."

Betty Banks looked thoughtful. She took thirty seconds before she replied. Becca picked up a vision of Ralph Darrow sitting exactly where she herself was and looking so much like the Grand of old that she felt heartsore when she compared the sight of him then to how he was now. Still, she was hopeful about this, more hopeful when a whisper of *he would want* accompanied it. But that hopefulness didn't last.

"I can tell you that Mr. Darrow is a client of mine," Betty Banks said. "I can tell you that I did some work for him. But I'm afraid I can't talk about anything else. It's called attorney-client privilege, you see. I can only speak about it if Mr. Darrow gives you written permission."

When she got home, Becca found that Derric hadn't been needed after all. For Celia Black's car was in the upper parking area. So was Jake's. So she coasted down the new driveway and entered the house. Jake was doing dishes in the kitchen, and Celia was working with Grand on word exercises.

Becca couldn't bear to tell Grand that her mission to see Mrs. Banks had been a flop, so she was glad he was occupied. She went to him and kissed his cheek as Celia said, "Now this is going to be a toughie, Mr. Darrow. You listen up. Bet you can't get it. Bet you five bucks. Gorilla, chimpanzee, baboon, howler monkey, orangutan." And to Becca,

"We're onto word *topics* now. I say the words and he's gotta get the topic they fall under." And to Grand, "What d'you say, good looking?"

He said quite clearly, "Ape."

Celia hooted. "Smarty pants! Okay. I owe you five. But no way're you gonna get this next one. Here goes: Manx, Mexican hairless, Maine coon, Siberian white."

Becca thought *cats* but Ralph Darrow said, "Fee-luh."

"Nope." Celia shook her head and grinned. "I get my five back. It's *felines*."

Ralph slapped his hand on the table. "Fee-luh!" he said. "Fee-luh!"

"Ooops. That's what you meant? Okay. I'll give it to you. Get ready for the next: coal, iron—"

"Hey, Becca." Jake was just coming down the stairs. "I talk to you for a sec?"

Becca said sure as Celia and Grand went on with their topic exercise. Jake turned on the stairs and climbed back up. Becca followed him as he went into the room that used to be Ralph's but now was hers.

"What's up?" she asked him.

"I found this in the shop," he said. "I was looking for a washer to stop a leak in Mr. Darrow's shower, and I thought he might be keeping stuff like that in this."

This was a tobacco tin, decades old by the look of it. It was about the size of a baking soda box, and it was pitted by rust. Jake picked it up from the center of Becca's bed and handed it over to her. "Take a look," he said.

She opened it. Inside were three grayish lumps of what looked like stone streaked with a coppery color. With these she saw a square of tin foil, a Bic lighter, and another piece of tin foil rolled into a tube the approximate length of a cigarette. She didn't have the first clue what she was looking at, and that's what she told Jake.

His response was to tell her to unfold the square of tin foil, which she did. She saw that it was crisscrossed with lines, and for a dumb moment she wondered if this was a message she was supposed to decipher. She said, "Okay, but I still don't get it." To which Jake replied, "It's heroin."

Omigod was what she wanted to say and she also wanted to drop the tin onto the bed, as if it were contagious. But instead she felt a moment of confusion and said, "But isn't . . . I thought heroin was white. And powdery. Isn't it a powder?"

Jake said, "This is black tar heroin."

"Are you sure?"

"Oh yeah. The foil and the lighter? That's how you use it."

"But there's no spoon and needle and . . . I don't get how . . . ?"

"You put some in the larger piece of foil, you use the lighter to heat it from beneath. That makes smoke and you use the tube to inhale the smoke. Bingo, you're high."

Becca frowned. She admitted she didn't even know this stuff existed. Jake said it was the most common kind of heroin in the state. It was, he told her, practically everywhere.

When she heard this, Becca said, "You *can't* be thinking that Grand . . ."

"Not Mr. Darrow," Jake said. The gravity of his voice and his expression was enough to tell her the rest. Still, he said, "You and I know it's not Mr. Darrow. Seth's got to be told but I sure as hell don't want to be the person to tell him."

It was one more terrible thing to face. Becca was getting tired of terrible things. It was only later when she was getting ready for bed and reaching up to remove the earbud of the

AUD box that she realized she'd never replaced the earbud once she'd taken it off earlier in the day. It was still in her backpack along with the AUD box, where she'd placed it when she'd begun her ride to Betty Banks's office.

Yet she'd heard nothing of anyone's whispers once she'd arrived back home. She'd managed to block them without knowing she was blocking them. She'd made another step in gaining power over the strange talent that fate had given her.

35

Prynne had done what she could to make things right after the debacle at the music agent's office. She'd called Steamer Constant the next day, explaining that she had been ill but that none of them had wanted to cancel their appointment because they were so excited that a music agent wanted to hear them play. As a result of this call, Steamer Constant agreed to let them try again. But, she told Prynne, Freda Windsarm was now in Los Angeles working on a deal for a recording contract and from there she was going to festivals in South Carolina and Georgia, followed by a stay in New York. She would return in eight weeks. Triple Threat could come into the city and play for her then.

"So we have eight weeks to get ready," Prynne told Seth. "And . . . I didn't want to tell you this before, but I've been working on a new piece. I can't play it for you yet because it's not quite ready, but in maybe another week . . . ? I think you'll like it."

Seth forgave her. She'd made a mistake in taking too much of the marijuana oil, but she'd only done it to settle her nerves and who could blame her? There had been a lot on the line: potential representation by a real music agent, possibly a recording contract, a chance to cut a CD in an actual studio. They'd *all* been nervous that day, and Prynne had only tried to do something to make herself less so.

Things went back to normal, or at least as normal as they could get, considering the risk of Aunt Brenda's forcing her will on everyone. So far Grand's attorney had managed to throw up a few roadblocks to stall Aunt Brenda, but he wasn't going to be able to do that forever. It would come down to a battle in court unless another path was found or forged that would make it impossible for her to intrude on her father's life. So when Becca came to him and told him about what the word *banks* had actually meant and about what Betty Banks had told her about attorney-client privilege, his first conclusion was that Grand thought this Betty Banks would be a better lawyer to handle things in the conflict with Brenda. He checked this out with Grand, saying to him, "D'you want me to talk to this Betty Banks, Grand? D'you want me to get her to help us?"

Grand's nod was accompanied by, "Houch."

Seth took off work an hour early, and he stopped at Grand's, where Becca was waiting for him fresh from her school day. Celia hadn't yet arrived to take Jake's place, so Prynne told them all that she would wait at the house for Celia's arrival. Jake could go, Becca and Seth could go, Prynne would happily hold the fort. Seth was cool with this, but Jake intervened with a casual, "I've got no problem hanging till Celia gets here," and he and Becca exchanged a look that could have meant something, but Seth didn't know what. He was just happy that Prynne was free to go with them down to Clinton. Only, Prynne said she'd go home instead. She had her scooter with her, after all, and she could help Amy with the dinner.

Off they went. Jake remained on the porch until Prynne's Vespa coughed, started, and could be heard puttering up the hill on the new driveway. Meantime, Seth and Becca climbed to the upper parking lot, where Gus was snuffling in the bushes on the trail of a rabbit.

Becca explained that she'd called in advance to make an appointment with Betty Banks. She'd told her secretary that she would be bringing a member of the Darrow family with her. She said to Seth that they were on rocky ground because of the problems attached to attorney-client privilege, but since Grand had indicated that he wanted Seth to see the attorney, it couldn't hurt to talk to her and reveal what was going on with Aunt Brenda. They had nothing to lose and everything to gain.

Seth agreed with this. So off they went. Becca was pretty silent on the route there, and Seth could tell something was on her mind. He said to her, "Everything okay? Nothing going on with Derric, is there?"

She replied with a brief chuckle and, "Something's always going on with Derric."

"Uh-oh. Some new babe trying to get his attention?"

"Sort of. But it's nothing bad."

She settled more determinedly into her seat as they drove. Seth had the feeling she wasn't telling him what was really going on.

It was about twenty minutes from Grand's house to the attorney's office. When they arrived and jounced up the unpaved driveway, Gus made his usual time-for-play noises. Out of the car, the Lab began galumphing around the wooded property. Seth called out, "You stay close, dog," and Gus looked up as if he actually meant to obey.

Shelley admitted them to Mrs. Banks's office. That was a good sign, Seth figured, but the good sign faded when he saw the expression on the lawyer's face. Before either he or Becca could say a word, Mrs. Banks said, "I'm sorry you came all this way. The situation is, I'm afraid, what it was before. Unless Mr. Darrow can put it writing that—"

"We know," Becca interrupted. "But I was thinking . . . See, Rich Darrow hired a lawyer for Grand to change the guardianship situation. And Seth here thinks what Grand maybe wants is for Seth's dad to hire you instead."

"Are you Seth?" Mrs. Banks asked, not unreasonably. "You're Mr. Darrow's grandson?" And when Seth nodded, the lawyer went on to say surprisingly, "What a pleasure to meet you! Your grandfather obviously thinks the world of you. I hope he's explained everything about the property: how the taxes will be paid, what kind of fund he's going to set up for maintenance . . . ?"

All Seth could say to this was "Huh?" He had no clue what she was talking about.

Mrs. Banks looked concerned, and maybe a little confused herself. She said, "You signed the paperwork, didn't you? You must have, because when he brought it back, it was notarized. I offered your grandfather Shelley's services – she's a notary – but he said he wanted to go over everything with you first and when he returned the paperwork to me, it was done officially, so you had to have signed."

Seth felt like the idiot of the century. "Paperwork? I dunno. I don't even remember . . ."

Mrs. Banks got up. She went to a file cabinet, pulled open a drawer. She began to riffle through the files within it, and she finally brought out the one she was apparently seeking. This, she brought back to her desk. Removing the paperwork within, she flipped through its pages to the very last one and showed this to Seth, saying, "This is only a copy, but you can see . . ."

He was looking at his own signature, no doubt about it. There was Grand's signature as well. And there was a stamp with someone's name scrawled beneath and the State of Washington in some sort of seal, too. He'd definitely signed this thing, but he couldn't remember having done so, and he didn't have the first clue what he was looking at anyway.

"Is this your signature?" Mrs. Banks was asking him.

He nodded, said, "Sure is, but I don't remember . . ."

Then he spied the date. It was right in the middle of his agonizing break-up with Hayley Cartwright that he'd signed this paperwork. He hadn't known up from down in those days. It was no surprise to him that he hadn't remembered having gone some place to sign some papers with his granddad. He said, "Oh. This was when I broke up with my girlfriend. What is it? Grand's will?"

"It's a property conveyance." Mrs. Banks pointed to the date that Seth had already taken note of and added, "On this date your grandfather signed all his property over to you. You didn't read this before you signed it?"

Seth just stared, first at the paperwork, then at her, then at the paperwork. Next to him, he heard Becca murmur, "Omigod."

He said, "I got learning problems," to Mrs. Banks. "I mean, reading is . . . and legal language . . . and whatever . . . ? Uh, no. I didn't read it. And Grand didn't tell me what it was. Why, though? Why didn't he tell me?"

"Perhaps he didn't want you to know yet."

"I don't get what it means, to tell you the truth."

Mrs. Banks smiled. She looked, Seth thought, like someone who knew what it meant when a person has troubles learning. She said, "It means your grandfather's property is yours, to do with as you wish. He assumed that you and he were of one mind and that what you would wish to do is what he wished to do: to keep it as it is. The house, the gardens, and the forest."

"But what if someone wants to sell it? Like, another relative. In order to . . . I don't know . . . to get the money?"

Mrs. Banks shrugged. "Unless that person is you, that can't happen."

Seth turned to Becca. Her eyes were like teacup saucers in her face. She said, "Grand was so smart, Seth. He must've *known* what would happen if he got sick."

"Damn." Seth shook his head in wonder. Grand had always been a step ahead of everyone.

When he and Becca got back to Grand's, they found him playing Monopoly with Celia. Grand appeared to be cleaning Celia's clock. Seth grinned when he saw this, not only because his grandfather was winning but also because of the fine motor skills involved in playing at all. "Now that's looking grim," he told Celia.

"Oh, he just better wait" was her reply. "I got more tricks up my sleeve 'n he's got hairs on his head."

Grand, Seth saw, seemed delighted that he was beating the pants off his home health care aide. Seth said to him, "So we talked to Mrs. Banks, Grand."

Ralph looked at him with that old sparkle in his eyes. "Gud," he said.

Seth replied with, "Thanks, Grand. Like . . . I don't even know what to say except you got no worries, okay? About anything."

Ralph said, "Fahv-it may granchill."

"*Only* male grandchild," Seth reminded him. He bent, kissed his grandfather on the forehead, and felt the old man's grip on the back of his head. Then he left the two of them to their Monopoly battle.

From all of this, Becca had hung back. As Seth turned to leave, he saw her standing on the stairs. She had an expression on her face that wasn't about celebrating Seth's change in circumstances, and at first Seth thought she was figuring she'd have to leave now, since he could move into Grand's house with Prynne and there was only one bedroom which they could use to effect this.

She said, unsurprisingly, "C'n I talk to you?"

He said, "Sure. But hey, no worries, Beck. We'll work out where—"

"It's not that," she replied as if she'd read his thoughts about moving into the house with Prynne. "C'n you come upstairs?"

"Sure."

She led him to her bedroom where she closed the door. From the chest of drawers, she brought out an old tobacco tin. She handed it to him. She said, "Jake found this in Grand's shop."

Seth opened it. He knew at once what he was looking at: the number one drug problem on Whidbey Island, the replacement drug for those for whom Oxy had become either too costly or too hard to get. It was cheaper than everything except contraband weed grown in someone's back yard. It was also easy to come by if you knew who to ask. Seth heard again the voice of that guy Steve in Port Townsend: "I can't even *get* it anymore, Prynne. It's way too risky."

What he thought was *no no no* in an ever growing wail of silence in his head. What he said from the dryness of his mouth was "Geez, he found this in Grand's shop? I better check to see if someone's living out in the tree house."

"Seth." Becca sounded way too sympathetic. "You know it's not some doper who might be living in the tree house. Why would someone be living in the tree house but keeping his heroin in Grand's shop?"

"Well, it sure as hell isn't Grand's. Do you think Jake is trying to make us think . . ." He couldn't finish the question because he couldn't come up with anything Jake might have in mind.

Becca said, "Think what? Are you saying Jake's been doing heroin here and he wants us to think it's someone else? Come on, Seth. We both know who's using."

"I don't think Celia's a druggie."

He saw that Becca's gaze was sympathetic but it was also

driving holes into his head. He felt as if she was invading his mind with that look of hers, and what came over him was a tsunami of fury. It was followed by one of pure despair. Still, he said, "Beck, I don't think . . . And this stuff . . . It hasn't even been used!"

"Look at the foil, the folded-up square. Look at everything. Jake told me it's all for inhaling the smoke."

Seth sought words to fight off what was fast approaching. "So Jake knows all about how to take it, huh? What d'you think *that* means? Man, when I tell Dad . . . when I tell the place Jake works for . . . when they find out and he gets his ass kicked . . ." But he couldn't finish the rest. He knew not a word of it was true. He said hopelessly, "D'you think Aunt Brenda might've put it there to make things look bad for Prynne?"

Becca watched him for a very long time and the question hung between them, unanswered. Finally she said, "I'm so totally sorry."

He said, "I don't want to believe it, Beck."

She said, "I don't blame you."

36

From the upper bunk bed in Brian Richardson's bedroom, Jenn stared at the constellations on the ceiling. She figured Brian had put them there himself. She discovered at dinner that what Cynthia's younger brother liked best was to talk about the universe. He was very big into astrophysics. He went on about black holes and alternative universes and the expansion of the universe and the potential travel to other galaxies, and Jenn was about to ask him if he was into the whole *Star Wars* thing and which of the films did he like best? – she had to say something to the kid, after all – when his mom said, "Jenn's had enough for now, Brian," and Cynthia said, "Cease and desist, Bri," and Brian himself grinned and said to Jenn, "Oh. You got to tell me when I'm s'posed to stop. I've got Asperger's. I can't read social signals so if you sigh or roll your eyes or say something like 'Thanks, that's interesting,' I won't know what you mean. You won't offend me because I'm used to being told. Sometimes Mom says I'm having an Asperger's moment. It's what I do. Hey are you a lesbian like Cynthia? I think close to sixteen percent of the girls at the high school are lesbians, by the way."

To her surprise, Jenn laughed along with everyone else. Mrs. Richardson laughed the most until she could only weakly say, "Apsperger's moment! Asperger's moment!"

They were an amazing family, Jenn thought, nothing like hers. After dinner, Cynthia and her brother used the dining room table to do their homework, both of them excused from washing dishes because of the heavy class loads they carried. Cynthia helped Brian with his French. Brian helped Cynthia with her advanced math. Their parents talked quietly in the kitchen while their children worked. There was no music, no television, or anything else that might disturb them.

Particularly there was no brawl on the living room floor engaged in by Petey and Andy. There was no dad lining up his brews for tasting on the same table where Jenn had to work. There was no Mom reading the Bible aloud or setting off to a church meeting or returning from delivering a passenger somewhere in the island taxi. Best of all, there was no reason for Jenn to rustle up a dinner in advance of all this with whatever had been available and picked up yesterday by her mom at Good Cheer Food Bank.

It was so heavenly an environment that Jenn whispered into the darkness, "You still awake, Cynthia?"

"Hmmm. Barely. You doing okay?"

"I guess." She really wasn't sure. At Cynthia and Mrs. Richardson's insistence, she'd called her mom to say where she would be spending the night. To her mom's reply of a recitation of the fifth commandment, Jenn had tried to explain that she *did* honor and love her parents. To this Kate had quietly answered, "Come home, then, and demonstrate that." But Jenn knew what such a demonstration would entail, and she couldn't do it. So, *was* she doing okay? Maybe. But again, maybe not.

"Good." Cynthia turned on her mattress. Jenn felt the quivering of the bunk beds as she did so. As Cynthia had said they would, they'd traded rooms with Brian because she had only a single bed in hers.

"Thanks for letting me stay here," Jenn said. "Your family . . . Everyone's amazing. Especially your parents.

They seem, like, so accepting. I mean not only you but your brother's Asperger's."

"They've always been the-glass-is-half-full kind of parents," Cynthia told her. "They wouldn't like it if we decided to take up robbing banks – Brian and I – but as long as we each have a sport and our grades are good, we c'n more or less forge our own way."

"Wow. *Seriously* perfect."

"Nothing's perfect," Cynthia pointed out. "But my mom and dad come close."

"Wish I could live here forever," Jenn said, more to herself than to Cynthia.

"You can stay as long as you need to, you know," Cynthia told her. "They get it. They know most of the kids from the Alliance, so they also know how parents can be."

Jenn gritted her teeth at this reference to the club, but she didn't go there in conversation. Instead she said, "I *got* to get on that team, Cynthia." Outside the house, an owl's cry sounded: *whoo whodoo whoo.* Jenn listened for a moment before she added. "It's the only thing I got right now and the only way I'll ever get anywhere."

"Don't even worry about it," Cynthia told her.

"I didn't make it last year. I screwed around too long with other stuff."

"That was last year," Cynthia said. "This year's different, and you'll be picked the first round. Guaranteed." A movement below her suggested that Cynthia was getting out of bed. Her shadowy form rose, and she leaned against Jenn's upper bunk as she continued. "You know the drill anyway. For the tryouts."

"I got cut so fast last year that alls I remember is a bunch of coaches standing around with clipboards."

"There're five of them," Cynthia told her. "They're going to decide together who gets on the team. You only need a majority of them to think you're good enough and you're in. You can't really think you won't impress three coaches."

Cynthia reached out and caressed Jenn's head. Jenn felt the caress like a warmth through her body. "You're just going through a bad time," the older girl said. "This whole thing with your mom and getting called into Mr. Vansandt's office and everything he asked you . . . ? It's like it put you into a crisis when there's no real crisis at all." She touched Jenn's cheek with her fingertips. Her voice altered to a murmur as she said, "Just relax about things. School, soccer, training, tryouts, your mom, Mr. Vansandt . . . everything. Really, that's all you ever have to do. Relax and let things take care of themselves."

"I wish they would."

"They will. Nothing stays the same. Changes come, changes go, and changes make way for other changes. That's just life."

"That how it is for you?"

"That's how it is for everyone."

Cynthia was silent then, but she didn't move back to the lower bunk. She stayed by Jenn's bed and her fingers drifted along Jenn's jaw and then, so delicately, over her ear and down her neck. Jenn got the shivers, but she felt like a cat. She wanted the caresses to go on and on.

Then Cynthia said, "I want to kiss you."

And Jenn found that she wanted to be kissed.

37

Becca was in her earth science class, having serious trouble staying tuned in to the group's discussion of California's record-breaking drought. At this stage, she had worries aplenty. She worried about the black tar heroin she'd handed over to Seth. She worried about how he was coping with the news that the likeliest user of the drug was his own girlfriend. She also worried about Jenn and how whatever was going on with her was putting dents into her old friendships, especially into her friendship with Squat. She knew there wasn't much she could do about what Jenn was going through, but she hated to see Squat pay such a price for having made a few stupid remarks.

Becca was thinking about this instead of thinking about climate change when the classroom door opened and a message was delivered to the teacher, Mrs. Glass. Without missing a beat in directing the discussion, she read the message, carried it to Becca, handed it over, and complimented one of the female students on a salient point she'd made about the desalinization of ocean water.

Becca opened the note to see it was from Debbie Grieder. Debbie had called the school with a message that Becca King was to come to the Cliff Motel when her classes were finished for the day. *Important* was part of the message. It was underlined.

She rode her bike there after her last class. She found Debbie in the kitchen with her grandkids, who were working on their grade school homework while she made quesadillas for them. Becca's appearance was an unexpected pleasure for Chloe and Josh. Chloe jumped up and ran to her for a hug while Josh looked past her for Big Brother Derric before he decided she was an acceptable substitute.

"I got a new LEGO," he informed her, pushing his chair away from the table.

"Grammer found a bowling outfit for Barbie!" Chloe crowed. "Even the shoes, which're sort of funny looking 'cause of her feet but do you want to see? I c'n get her if you want to see."

"You skedaddle back to that table if you want a quesadilla," Debbie informed her. "I need to talk to Becca and this is big girl business. You two got that?"

They grumbled but succumbed to their grandmother's orders. Soon enough they were back in their seats, each of them with a quesadilla neatly cut into triangles on a plate before them. Then Debbie nodded in the direction of the kitchen door. This led out to the back of the property, which overlooked the marina. There a handful of boats gently bobbed on the water.

Debbie lit a cigarette that she took from the pocket of her sweatshirt. She seemed to place herself between Becca and the possibility of Becca's being seen from Camano Street, some twenty yards away. She looked around and then shook her head. All of this made Becca prepare for bad news. It wasn't long in coming.

"Had a visit from a young woman 'round eleven this morning," Debbie told her. "She was asking about a girl and her mom, wanting to know if they'd stayed with me a while back, like near two years ago. Here at the motel. She said the girl was called Hannah and the mom was called Laurel and this young woman herself . . . ? Said she was a reporter up from the San Diego."

Becca felt the blood draining from her face. The world spun for a moment, and she wondered if she was going to faint.

Debbie dug her hand into the back pocket of her jeans and brought out a business card, which she handed to Becca. Becca knew what was going to be on it before she looked. She looked anyway and there was Olivia Bolding's name and the name of the paper for which she worked.

"What did you tell her?" Becca assured herself that she'd changed substantially. Even if Olivia Bolding went around describing her to people and even if she'd put her hands on a picture of the former Hannah Armstrong, the girl who'd fit any description the reporter might give was long gone.

"'F course I told her I didn't have the first clue who she was talking about," Debbie said. "But that's not where I'm heading with this, darlin'. See, she had some computer artist guy in San Diego mess around with a school picture of this Hannah person, and he did one of those things you see when kids are missing for years."

"You mean an age progression?" Becca didn't see how helpful this would be, since she hadn't been missing long enough to have changed substantially in the eyes of someone who was attempting to make her look like what she was: less than two years older than when she lived in San Diego.

"Yeah." Debbie paused to pick a bit of tobacco off her tongue. "Only with these pictures, hon . . . ? It wasn't her age that the computer person altered. It was her looks."

It turned out that Olivia Bolding had been smart enough to ignore the age part entirely. Setting that issue aside, she'd instructed the artist to make Hannah Armstrong thinner than she'd been when she'd fled from San Diego. He'd produced that altered picture, and he'd come up with various hair styles and hair colors on her, Debbie said. Obviously, this Olivia Bolding was dead set on finding her.

"I don't get why she came to the motel," Becca said, more to herself than to Debbie.

"Makes sense when you think about it. The motel's the first place to stay that you come to on the island. She prob'ly thought this Laurel Armstrong and her daughter might've stayed here."

Becca was aware that Debbie wasn't saying anything directly about the coincidence that one Becca King had come to the island at relatively the same period of time as when Hannah Armstrong had gone missing. She also wasn't mentioning that Becca King's excuse for being on the island at all was that she was waiting for her mother. But Debbie wasn't an idiot.

"What did you say when you saw the pictures?" Becca asked.

"It's not what I said, darlin'. That's what I wanted to tell you. It's what Chloe said. See, Chloe was there. Not at first, but she came in just when the reporter whipped those pictures out. And you know Chloe. Curiosity killed the cat. She scooted over and had a look and she upped and said, 'Hey, there's Becca, Grammer!'"

Becca stared at Debbie. She couldn't come up with anything to say. She felt the need to run and she felt it acutely: to run as far and as fast as she could to get away from this place.

Debbie appeared to read this because she said, "Whoa, there, darlin'," and she put her arm around Becca's shoulders. Becca saw the vision immediately and knew she was looking at Olivia Bolding because there was no mistaking the young woman with her California blond-streaked hair. The reporter was handing over the pictures to Debbie and Debbie's gaze went down and what Becca saw through Debbie's eyes was the picture on top of the stack, which was a very good image of what she looked like now, only with far darker hair.

Debbie said, "When Chloe said that, I just laughed. I said 'Hon, our Becca's your cousin, and she doesn't come from San Diego. This girl in the picture . . . she's someone else.' Then I grabbed her and gave a big kiss on the forehead and said whatever else I could think of 'fore she could make anything more of it. I don't know what the reporter thought, but anyways she left."

That was it. But that *wasn't* it. For Becca knew that she owed Debbie an explanation, just as she'd owed her an explanation when Jeff Corrie had shown up on Whidbey Island not terribly long after Becca had left her cell phone in the parking lot of Saratoga Woods. She said, "I didn't do anything bad in San Diego. Neither did my mom. But we had to leave because—"

"You don't need to tell me a thing, darlin'." Debbie waved her words off like flies in the summer. "But you do need to watch your step now this woman's on the island 'cause I got the impression she wasn't planning to leave any time soon."

"Where'd she go from here?" Becca asked. "Did she say anything about that?"

"I figure she had to find herself a place to stay. From her looks, I c'n tell you she's not a Cliff Motel kind of girl. Maybe Saratoga Inn or the Inn at Langley? You give those places a wide berth, okay? Till I find out what she's done with herself. And keep your head down because I couldn't tell if she believed me about the cousin thing. *And* when she asked me what my 'niece' Becca's last name was, I had to tell her."

To this, Becca wanted to shout *Why why why*? But she knew why. Debbie could hardly have claimed that Becca was her niece and then refused to give the reporter her last name when asked. Why on earth would Debbie Grieder want to hide the last name of her own niece?

The present moment had an urgency to it that Becca felt right to her fingertips. She was the fox, and the hounds were closing in.

She had agreed to go to Derric's for dinner that night, and she could hardly back out of it, even though what she wanted to do was hide away and lay some emergency plans for the moment when Olivia Bolding confronted her. She had very little doubt that a confrontation would be soon, especially since the reporter had been clever enough to come up with the idea of photos.

When Derric showed up to take her over to his parents' house, she almost faked illness to get out of going. But his expression told her that tonight was indeed going to be when he took the first step of introducing his parents to Rejoice, even if Rejoice herself was not going to be there. He couldn't just spring her on his mom and dad, he'd told Becca. He had to go at this in his own way.

He went at it in his own way just before dinner. He'd brought out the picture album/scrapbook that his mom had made for him, the one that chronicled his advent into the Mathieson family. It began from the first time Rhonda and Dave had laid eyes on the little Ugandan boy who'd stolen their hearts, and it concluded with Rhonda's arrival at SeaTac Airport with Derric a few years later, when the family had been there in baggage claim with signs and balloons and a gigantic teddy bear and welcoming arms. Luckily, Becca had never seen the album before, so it wasn't an oddball moment when Derric began to show it to her.

Becca had asked him why he wanted to do things this way. She knew that he'd earlier pointed out to his parents an older girl in one of the album's pictures and he'd told them she was the Rejoice he'd written letters to. So, she asked him, wasn't it going to be strange when he pointed out a *different* Rejoice now? They're going to ask you about that, she'd warned him.

He said he'd tell them that when they first asked him about a girl called Rejoice to whom he'd been writing never-sent letters, he thought they'd conclude he was a pervert if he'd pointed out a little girl in the pictures and told them *she* was the Rejoice he'd been writing to. Becca couldn't actually see how this was a better plan than simply bringing Rejoice over from La Conner, but she figured that the best thing for her to do was just go along and see what happened.

They looked at the album in the kitchen, where Rhonda was preparing dinner. When he got to the first picture that had Rejoice in it, he said to Becca, "And this is Rejoice, right here. Pretty small, huh? She used to follow me all over the place. I figured she had a crush on me."

Rhonda picked up on this, as he intended. She said, "Didn't you tell us that Rejoice was one of the older girls, sweetie?"

Derric hung his head, then looked at his mom sideways. "It was 'cause of those letters I'd been writing to her, Mom. I figured you guys might've thought I was . . . I don't know . . . a pervert or something if you saw I was writing to a five-year-old. Anyway, here's something amazing. She lives – Rejoice lives – up in La Conner."

"You're kidding!"

"Becca and I met her," and before his mom could question them about how they'd met a girl from La Conner, Derric went on. "Becca found her when I told her about the letters. So we went up there and met her and her family. To surprise her, you know? You want to meet her sometime?"

"I'd love to," Rhonda said.

That took care of step one. Derric looked relieved as he put the album away, and Becca was relieved for him. Soon, she hoped, all of the truths would be out on the table and Derric could go on with his life instead of spinning his wheels in guilt.

They were laying the table for dinner when Derric's dad got home from Coupeville, where the sheriff's office was. He called out a hello and tramped up the stairs answering his wife's "Dinner's ready" with "Got to get into some more comfortable clothes."

They had everything ready and they were seated at the table when Dave Mathieson came into the dining room. He hesitated at the sight of Becca then covered his hesitation with, "I didn't know Derric's main squeeze would be here." He smiled, but there was something about that smile that made Becca feel uneasy. He didn't give voice to anything, though, because Rhonda immediately told him Derric's story about his fellow orphan from Uganda. "The girl he was writing those letters to," Rhonda concluded. "Isn't that incredible that she's practically just up the road? And Becca found her, Dave. I think that's twice again incredible."

Dave directed his gaze at Becca and said, "Our Becca is a very resourceful girl."

Becca hoped to escape with her identity intact. But that was not to be. After dinner, cleaning the kitchen, and engaging in three rounds of Mexican Train dominoes, she was gathering her school stuff for the ride back to Grand's place. Dave Mathieson stopped her. "Derric, can I borrow this young lady for a minute?"

Derric looked surprised. It wasn't like Dave to want alone time with Becca. Obviously, he didn't know how to take this. So Becca said cheerfully, "Sure can," and followed Dave into his home office just down the corridor.

He closed the door behind her. He walked to his desk and stood behind it. He looked at her the way Becca thought a judge might look, then he opened a briefcase that was on the desk. From this, he removed a manila folder, and he handed it over to Becca. He nodded at her in a way that told her she was meant to open it, so she did. She found herself looking down at a picture of herself, of how she looked now but with a different haircut of a different color. It was identical to the picture she'd seen in Debbie's vision.

"A reporter from San Diego came to the office," Dave said. He went on, but Becca didn't hear the rest. Instead, she looked at the picture. She realized that no one who knew Becca King and who saw the picture would hesitate to identify her.

Suddenly Dave's words worked their way through Becca's rising sense of panic. ". . . owe it to Derric to tell him yourself."

She raised her head. Dave was watching her gravely in that way adults have when they want to say how disappointed they are in you. She said, "What? I didn't hear . . ."

"I'm not telling Rhonda yet, and I'm not telling Derric at all," he said to her. "You're doing that."

"Why . . . why did she come to see you?" Becca asked. "I don't get it. How would she know . . . ?"

"She learned about the cell phone in Saratoga Woods. She wanted to know if the owner had been tracked down."

"Oh." Becca's voice sounded small to her ears. She felt small, too. She also had never felt so alone.

"She wanted to know who found it, too, because she wants to talk to him."

"C'n I ask . . . I mean . . . What did you tell her?"

"The truth. Which is what you'll do when it comes to talking to Derric."

"But I mean, like, what did you tell her when you saw the picture?"

He was silent. In that silence they were eyeball to eyeball.

Becca longed for a whisper or a vision that could help her understand what Dave Mathieson was thinking and what he was planning and what, above all, would happen next to fracture her carefully constructed world on Whidbey Island. But there was nothing. There was only the void.

"I told her I'd pass the picture around," he finally said. "But I'm hoping you don't make me have to do that."

38

S eth spent a little time trying to tell himself that the black tar heroin didn't belong to Prynne, that she just did weed. Besides, he decided, if this black tar heroin that was now in his possession *did* belong to Prynne, wouldn't she be desperate for it? Wouldn't she be going into withdrawal? Wasn't that how things worked?

He didn't want to consider what he knew about Whidbey Island: black tar heroin was the cheapest substance to buy if you needed to score some, and you could find it by simply asking around. With this tin box of dope gone missing, if Prynne *was* the person using, it would be easy for her to get more.

He decided to go to Port Townsend to get to the full truth about Prynne. He did what he never before had done and called in sick to work. As far as the household knew, however, he set off for his job site with Gus like always, but this time, he didn't drive to Wahl Road but rather up to Admiralty Bay.

Once the ferry docked in Port Townsend, Seth made his way to the house where Prynne had gone to on the day he'd followed her. His driving felt automatic, as if the VW knew the way and all he had to do was to go along for the ride. When he reached the right street and spied the big hedge and the arbor, he got a large rawhide bone from the glove compartment and gave it to Gus to keep him occupied.

The same van was in the driveway. Seth went around it

to the door in the side of the garage. On this fine day it
was standing open, and from within came an ancient song
by the Doors. He saw that a large worktable ran the width
of the double garage and at this table the same guy he'd
seen before was working. He was bent over a square of
unfired tile, meticulously carving a design into it. To his
left were tiles waiting for design. To his right were finished
tiles waiting for a glaze. The garage was hot from a kiln
that stood in one corner. In front of it were boxes packed
with finished tiles. They bore funky dogs on them, as well
as orcas, octopi, dolphins, sea stars, mermaids, foxes, and
funky cats. This, Seth figured, was one of the ways that
Steve – that was the name, he remembered – supported his
family.

Steve looked up. He frowned. It seemed to Seth that the
other young man figured he'd seen him somewhere but
couldn't remember exactly. He also seemed to figure Seth
was some kind of customer, since he slid off his stool and
said, "Happening, man?" in a way that wasn't unfriendly.

It was exactly the friendly nature of that greeting that
prompted Seth's fury. He wanted to take the guy down and
pound his head on the concrete floor. But what he was there
for was the truth. So he took the tobacco tin from the pack
he was carrying and he tossed it to Steve, saying, "Look
inside."

Steve didn't cooperate. He said, "What the hell? Who
are you?"

"Open it, dude."

"Man, I don't know what you want, but . . ." He seemed
to put the pieces together then. A light bulb went on, and
he said, "Oh hell. Did *Prynne* send you? I told her—"

"Open it!" Seth raised his voice.

"Chill," Steve said. "I got kids in the house and a
pissed-off wife who wouldn't mind punching my lights

today. Okay?" He opened the tin. Seeing the black tar heroin within it, he said, "I told her no more. About six times I told her no more. So if you're here to buy more for her or for yourself or whatever, that game's not on."

"When did you sell this to her?"

"I didn't, man. I used to sell it, yeah, but it got too hot. Besides, my wife'd drop-kick me into the next time zone if she knew I was dealing anything but weed. So I stopped, okay? And this stuff here? This amount? It wouldn't've lasted Prynne a week, so if I'd've sold it to her, it would be long gone by now."

"You expect me to believe any of that?"

"I don't care what you believe. I'm telling you the truth. Believe what you want."

Seth's vision seemed covered by a veil of red then. He shouted, "You *did* this to her. She *only* did weed before you but—"

"Crap's sake! Shut up! What the hell's wrong with you?" Steve brushed by Seth and closed the door. He went on with, "*She* found *me*, man. I didn't go looking for her. I don't need to go looking for anyone. And don't ask me how she found me because I don't know, okay? Dopers? They can smell it in the dark."

"You got her hooked!"

"You got to be kidding. She came to Port Townsend *because* she was hooked. You don't believe me, go talk to her parents. They're in Port Gamble and they kicked her to the curb years ago when she wouldn't give the stuff up. She told me she tried to a few times, but she couldn't hack it and that was that."

"And you sold to her anyway?" Seth asked, incredulous. He couldn't even begin to process the information that Prynne had been gone from Port Gamble for years and not just for the few months she'd claimed. "You knew she was trying to get straight and you sold to her anyway? Is that what you're saying?"

Steve cast him a look that said he was nuts. "I'm a businessman, dude. It's all economics to me."

Seth drove straight to Port Gamble. It was a forty-minute drive south on the Quimper Peninsula and a turn that took him through one of the area's Indian reservations. Beyond this, Port Gamble stood, a tiny town at the top of Teekalet Bluff.

Seth had never been there, so he didn't know that Port Gamble was more a history lesson than a habitation. Its main street boasted a short string of widely separated houses that bore historical markers. These identified their dates of construction as well as their early owners. This same little street featured a museum, a former firehouse, a mercantile, and a building that appeared to function as the tiny town's municipal offices. There were only a couple more streets in the place, and every one of them was deserted. Some of the houses looked like holiday rentals. Nearly all of them had been restored. As had been the white, steepled church, which advertised on a notice board outside that it was a superb place for weddings.

It seemed that while Port Gamble had once been a thriving little mill town, it now was a living museum offering a glimpse into what life might have looked like in a previous century. It existed to serve the interests of tourists and wedding planners. Prynne's parents, as it turned out, were there in Port Gamble to meet the needs of both groups.

It was easy enough for Seth to find them. He and Gus sauntered over to the museum with its enormous anchor and well-kept bronze bell in front. As Gus searched for dog smells along the building's foundation, Seth ducked inside and asked a man sweeping the floor if he knew of the Haring family. "Rooster Tea," was the man's reply.

This turned out to be the short version of what he might have said, which was that Prynne's parents ran the Rooster Café and Tea Room. It was three doors away and across the street. Seth hoped at least one of the Harings would be there.

He was in luck. He'd made it to Port Gamble before everything closed up in the late afternoon, and although it seemed as if tea time itself was over, he saw that lights were still on in the back of the place. Figuring there had to be a back door, he went in search of it, with Gus loping ahead between the café and the building next door, which appeared to be someone's home. As he reached the corner, Gus gave a sharp bark. Seth recognized it as his want-to-play bark and picked up his pace to see a curly-haired man smashing a garbage bag into a plastic can that was mostly full.

Seth said, "Are you Mr. Haring?" and the man looked over. He'd been watching Gus galumphing around the lawn behind the café, his ears flapping and his tongue lolling cartoonishly out of his mouth. Seth called, "Gus! Get back here! Now!" As usual the Lab completely disregarded the command.

The man said, "Ben Haring," as he tightened the lid on the garbage can. "Who are you?"

"Seth Darrow," Seth said. "That's Gus, my dog. Well, obviously. C'n I talk to you for a minute?"

"We're not hiring. We'll need someone later on in the month if you want to come back. Now, the weather's still too iffy for a lot of visitors."

Seth told him that he wasn't there about a job, that he was a finish carpenter on Whidbey Island. When Ben Haring assumed this meant he was looking for carpentry work and began to speak about that, Seth corrected him once again. "It's Prynne," he said and he added dumbly, "your daughter."

Ben Haring's face altered. A steeliness came to it. Seth couldn't tell if the man was preparing himself for the worst or arming himself from some kind of onslaught. He said, "What's happened? Who are you?"

Seth gave him only the facts that seemed important enough to share: He was a musician, Prynne was the fiddler in his gypsy jazz group, they lived together on Whidbey Island, and she was helping care for his grandfather after a stroke.

Ben Haring said, "So what can I do for you? You can't be here to tell me Prynne's finally found a cure that took. Not that it wouldn't be good news but I expect she'd come to tell us herself. That's more her pattern."

Seth didn't like the use of the word *pattern*. He also didn't much like Mr. Haring. He started to feel that he was taking part in the biggest betrayal of his life, but he had to know what the true situation was, and Prynne's parents were probably the only people who could tell him.

Ben Haring opened the back door of the café and said, "You better come in," and he led the way. Seth whistled for Gus and called out, "Milk Bones!" which did the trick. He pulled one from his pocket and leashed Gus to the railing of the old house's back steps. When he followed the way Ben Haring had gone, he found himself in a large professional kitchen.

Seth didn't know how to begin a conversation that could lead him to ask about Prynne and heroin. It turned out that he didn't need to. Prynne's mom, who was as pale in the face as the flour she was measuring into a mixing bowl, said to him, "Has she overdosed?" the moment Prynne's dad explained who Seth was. With an agonized glance at her husband, Mrs. Haring went on. "Or has she stolen something?"

That pretty much confirmed things. Seth felt hollow inside, as if someone had taken the self out of him so that all that remained was a shell.

"She's into heroin," he said. He felt he needed to lean against the wall and hoped he didn't slide down it to the floor. "She says she's not, but we found some. And I followed her once when she went to a house in Port Townsend where there was this guy . . . ? He said I should talk to you."

"Here." Mrs. Haring sounded quite compassionate. She brought a stool out from beneath the kitchen's island work counter and said, "Sit here, dear." She went to a large restaurant-size fridge. She took out some orange juice and poured him a glass.

"He said she moved to Port Townsend in the first place because of heroin, because you guys threw her out. I want to help her. I want to make her okay because if I don't . . . I love her," he said simply. "I figure if you can tell me what to do . . . or if you know how to help . . . or anything?"

Ben Haring leaned against the counter in front of the large stainless steel sink. He said, "You can't help her, Seth. You can't, I can't, her mom can't, her brother can't. She can help herself, but she has to want that, more than she wants to use."

Quietly, then, the Harings told Prynne's story, and Seth recognized it from so many similar stories that had played out on Whidbey over the years. Prynne, they said, was their troubled child. She began stealing alcohol from them when she was eleven, so they both stopped drinking. She then switched to weed – this was when she was twelve – and then she got into prescription opiates. At that point, they sent her into a recovery program. There, she learned about black tar heroin, and when she got out, she went after that. They put her through two more recovery programs, but nothing helped her. The need for drugs had become a hunger so ravenous she had to keep feeding it. When she turned eighteen years old, they asked her to leave.

"I think the eye started it," Mrs. Haring said. "Losing it so young, being in the hospital all that time, with all the drugs involved . . . I think that's where it all began."

"It's why we put up with everything for so long," Ben Haring said. "The rest of us – Prynne's brother, her mom, myself – we all felt guilty that she'd suffered so much. That one thing – our guilt – it's what kept us going. It kept us trying to find a way to help her."

"We finally decided that until she was invested in her own recovery," his wife added, "we wouldn't send her into any more programs and we wouldn't see her. It must sound cruel to you because you love her. We love her, too, but something . . . It just seemed to us that sometimes the life you save has to be your own."

39

Jenn tried to put the kiss out of her mind. She also tried to put out of her mind the fact that, when asked, she'd said yes to the whole *idea* of being kissed by a girl. Much more than that, though, she tried to put out of her mind that in that instant when Cynthia had asked if she could kiss her, Jenn had been longing for exactly that.

She hadn't thought twice about saying yes, and it had turned out to be a real kiss. It wasn't just a peck on the cheek between friends or even a peck on the mouth that happens when a kiss intended for the cheek accidentally gets misplaced.

That one kiss had segued into another. That kiss had evolved into a third. Jenn had found herself all pulsing heart and throbbing veins. Then Cynthia had murmured, "Have a good sleep," and returned to the lower bunk. Her breathing, becoming regular and deep within minutes, told Jenn that she'd gone quickly to sleep.

Not so for Jenn. She'd wanted to ask Cynthia what it meant that she – Cynthia – had felt like kissing her – Jenn. But to ask that question would indicate that the kiss itself and those that followed meant something to her, and she didn't want to go there in her brain let alone in a conversation. She thought, at the end of a night spent mostly observing Brian Richardson's ceiling constellations, that it might be best to forget the whole thing.

The next day comprised their final training session before

tryouts for the All Island team. Despite the fact that they'd trained for weeks on end, they didn't take a break to rest on the day before tryouts. They worked as hard as ever. Cynthia knew the various stations that would be set up to test the girls' skills and their overall athleticism, and she pushed Jenn hard. Lexie did the same. At the end of it all, Jenn was dripping sweat and the other two girls were in the same condition.

In the locker room afterward, Cynthia stripped in that unselfconscious way she had, shedding workout clothes as she went: tank top first, sports bra second, shorts third, undies fourth. By the time she reached her locker, she had only her athletic shoes and socks on, and she kicked these off before she opened the locker and grabbed her soap, towel, shampoo, and conditioner. She said to Jenn, "You looked super good out there today," and Lexie said, "You'll kick butt tomorrow, Jenn."

Lexie strode off to the showers ahead of them, but Cynthia remained at her locker. Jenn found that she wasn't sure where to look because the thing about Cynthia was that she was sort of like someone you make up in your head. She was also like someone you wanted to look like. She had breasts that were . . . what? Well, they were luscious. That was the word. Her hips were slender and her legs were long and her stomach was a board. Between her legs the hair was darker than her head hair and . . . Jenn turned away. She grabbed her soap and towel. What she knew was that it was completely wrong for her to be noticing Cynthia Richardson's body.

Cynthia said to her, "Jenn . . . You okay? I mean . . ." and it was the very first time that Jenn could remember Cynthia sounding anything but 110 percent self-assured.

Jenn said, "Sure. Yeah. Why?" But she had some trouble meeting the other girl's gaze.

"Oh. Good," was Cynthia's response. Then, "You seem a little different today."

Now, Jenn thought, was the moment to ask those questions that had kept her awake. But she just couldn't do it. So she said, "Nope. I'm cool."

Cynthia said, after a moment, "Good. I'm glad," and then Lexie yelled, "I'm almost done in here. You guys coming or what?" from the showers where water was blasting against the tiles.

Lexie was fast on this day. When Jenn and Cynthia got to the showers, she was finished. Although she and Jenn had a regular work night at G & G's, both Gertie and Giselle knew that the following day was tryouts for Jenn, and they'd insisted she take the night off in order to be thoroughly rested.

Lexie, however, still had to work, so she was toweling herself off by the time Cynthia ducked her head into the stream of water she'd been using. Lexie threw her towel over her shoulder and said, "I'm outa here, you guys. Good luck tomorrow."

"You coming?" Cynthia asked her.

"Got a Skype date with Sara-Jane," she said.

"More Europe plans?"

"Endless Europe plans." Then she was gone, saying, "Later, 'kay?" The other two girls were left in the showers.

Jenn flipped another shower on and stepped beneath the water. She dunked her head into it while next to her, Cynthia removed the scrunchie that held her hair back from her face, allowing it to fall to her shoulder blades. She squeezed shampoo into her palm. She said, "You've got the funds for the All Island team now, right?"

"Thanks to Gertie and Giselle," Jenn said. "Yeah, I'm good. If I make the team, I can—"

"When, not if," Cynthia told her. "You've got to go into the tryouts with confidence. And there's not a single reason for you to be anything less than totally sure you're going to make the team."

"Easier for you to say than me," Jenn told her. "I got plenty of ways to screw things up."

"Don't think about those ways, then," Cynthia said. "Here, want some shampoo?"

She handed over the bottle and began to suds up her hair. She worked up a large amount of lather, which oozed down her breasts and across her stomach and between her legs. Jenn said, "Thanks," and turned away. Not that she had anything to hide from Cynthia or anyone else, since she was flat as a board with boobs the size of mushroom caps. The rest of her had no shape at all, a source of unending embarrassment to her.

Jenn squeezed a dab of shampoo into her close-cropped hair. She began to do the sudsing thing. She said, "At least this year I've done everything I can to put myself into a position to make the team. So if I don't make, it's not like I didn't give it everything."

"What happened last year?"

Jenn didn't want to say. The distracting proximity of Annie Taylor was too embarrassing to go into. Annie Taylor and her presence in Jenn's life and in the life of Langley was the main reason Jenn had completely blown the tryouts last year, and she didn't want to come close to that happening again. She settled on saying, "I was an idiot is basically what happened."

"I don't believe that."

Jenn glanced in Cynthia's direction. She was covered with shampoo suds, which she was apparently also using as her soap. She dunked her head under the water again, saying, "God, it feels so good when the sweat's washed off."

Jenn rinsed her hair of shampoo. "Well, it's true," she said in reference to her idiocy.

Cynthia reached for another plastic bottle and squeezed a quarter-size daub of something into her palm. She gestured for Jenn to extend her own hand, saying, "Conditioner. You want? Never mind. Wait. I'll do it for you."

She worked it into her own hair and then crossed to Jenn's to do the same for Jenn. The other girl's fingers were strong, and the pressure of them against Jenn's skull was soothing. She figured this was what a massage was like, and she thought how she could just stand there forever with the warm water beating against her and her head loving the stroke of someone else's fingers upon it.

"Feels good, huh?" Cynthia said. "Next time, I'll make you do me."

Since tryouts were tomorrow, Jenn didn't see how there would be a next time. She wondered if Cynthia wanted there to be one. She wondered if she did, too.

The next day dawned glorious. The tryouts for the team were taking place up in Coupeville, on the field at the high school. Girls could easily converge upon this spot: driving south from the northernmost town of Oak Harbor, driving north from the southernmost town of Clinton.

To Jenn's surprise, all of the Richardsons intended to go along and to cheer their efforts to make the team, so shortly after seven-thirty she and Cynthia climbed into Cynthia's Honda while the rest of the family piled into their SUV. They headed for the highway where the annual invasion of Scotch broom made bursts of bright yellow flowers along the road's shoulders and within the island's empty fields.

There were going to be two full days of activities. At the end of the first day there would be an A team comprising girls who had definitely been chosen by the coaches and a B team comprising girls whom the coaches would like to see on the second day.

"The key is to try to get chosen the first day," Cynthia told Jenn. "So make sure you don't hold anything back."

"You, too," Jenn said.

"Oh. I'm not trying out," Cynthia told her.

Jenn stared at her, completely nonplussed. "What? But then why did you . . . ?"

"I need to stay in shape for UV," Cynthia said. "Plus, there was you."

Jenn wasn't sure what she meant by this. "Me?"

"I wanted to help you out. So did Lexie. It was a challenge for us. Well, mostly it was a challenge for me, and Lexie went along, since she was working out anyway."

"Don't you want to be on the team?" Jenn wasn't sure how she felt about being on the All Island Girls' Soccer team if Cynthia wasn't going to be there with her.

She had her path already, Cynthia explained. During the coming summer, she would stay in shape, but no way did she want to risk getting hurt when University of Virginia was waiting for her to join their team.

"But how come your family . . . ?"

All of the Richardsons were going to the tryouts in a show of support for Jenn, Cynthia told her. Cynthia glanced at her, then back at the road and the family's SUV before them. "You make the A team, and we're celebrating, you and me. That's why we're going in separate cars. The rest of the fam . . . ? They'll have had enough soccer at that point, believe me."

In Coupeville, the family set up a picnic area about thirty yards away from the tryout activities. This featured a card table and camping chairs with cup holders in them, one for every member of the family and another for Jenn.

There were more people at the All Island tryout than Jenn had expected. Fifty girls had shown up, and it seemed that each of them had brought along supporters, whether family, friends, boyfriends, or personal coaches. There was even a team of little girls who'd come to watch and perhaps get some pointers. They had their uniforms on, and they were jumping around energetically.

Jenn looked among the throng. She told Cynthia that she was checking everything out, but the truth was that she was thinking about what it all meant or if it had to mean anything at all that both Cynthia Richardson and Lexie Ovanov had shown such kindness to her.

Five women with clipboards and whistles came onto the field from the parking lot. One of them blew her whistle and yelled, "Let's get this going," and gestured for the potential players to gather around. She turned out to be the head coach, a former UW player who worked privately with girls on the Olympic team. Without any formalities, she assigned the girls and the other coaches to individual stations around the field where their skills would be tested.

Jenn shot looks at her competition as she walked with them to the first station. Some of the girls she recognized because she'd played against them before. Some were strangers to her.

From the number of girls and the number of stations, Jenn could tell that this first round of tryouts would last the entire day. During this time, the coaches would be looking at everything: shooting, ball control, speed, flexibility while running, aggression with the ball, guarding . . . the entire package.

As Jenn made her way through the first three stations, she recognized how much she owed Cynthia and Lexie. She was in the best shape she'd ever been in. Her speed had increased, her ball control had improved, and her coordination was excellent. As she went through the paces being demanded of her, Jenn found herself getting back to the joy of playing soccer.

There was a break for lunch. Jenn rejoined the Richardsons, where Cynthia's mom was unpacking an impressive picnic basket onto the card table while Brian Richardson voiced his concerns over the length of time the potato salad had gone without a serious control of the temperature which, he intoned, should be no more than thirty-eight degrees, although a brief period at a higher temperature would not actually hurt anyone, since the eggs had only just now been added and most people knew that eggs kept in their shells could—

"*Bri*an," the rest of his family said at the same time.

"Whoops. Asperger's moment," was his reply, and he lowered his gaze to the astronomy book he'd brought with him.

Jenn laughed with the others. Then she heard a cry of "Jenn! Jenn!" and she swung round to see Petey hurtling across the lawn from the parking lot. Andy was not far behind him. At some distance to the boys, Jenn saw her dad sauntering in their wake.

Away from what Jenn thought of as his natural habitat, Bruce McDaniels was even more of an oddity than he was at Possession Point, with his long gray hair ringing a very bald pate and his outfit comprising a striped T-shirt, white patent leather loafers of a vintage Jenn could only guess at, striped black-and-white knee socks, and khaki shorts over which his beer belly burgeoned like a life preserver. He'd shaved in honor of the occasion, and no matter his get-up and overall appearance, Jenn was happy to see him.

"Greetings one and all," he said magnificently and with a bow. "Bruce McDaniels, paterfamilias. We've come to offer our support to Jennifer. I hoped to do it from a distance, but I fear Jenn's rambunctious siblings escaped my control."

From this little speech, Jenn knew how out of place he

felt. She went to him and hugged him hard. "Thanks for coming, Dad," she said into his ear.

"We miss you at home, Jennie-Jenn," was his quiet reply. "Your mom intended to come today, but she got a call for a ride over town, and you know how it is."

What he meant was that Kate had to go because of the money. She couldn't turn down an expensive fare whenever it happened, even if it had been the middle of the night.

Jenn wanted to believe that her father was telling the truth about Kate, but she couldn't quite get there. The fifth commandment still hung between them.

Mrs. Richardson was giving each of the boys a leg of fried chicken and smiling at their whoops of joy. She asked Bruce to join them, but he held up his hands in a gesture of refusal. "Ate on the way," he told her. "So did the boys. The last thing they ought to be doing is eating more."

Jenn knew eating had consisted of PBJs, but she still felt embarrassed that Petey and Andy fell upon the food like members of the Donner party. Bruce called the boys to him. At least they came, happily gnawing and casting longing looks at the rest of the spread. Mrs. Richardson said, "Are you sure?" and Mr. Richardson said, "There's plenty to go around."

But Bruce was firm, and he was equally firm about where they would go to watch the second half of the tryouts, which was at a distance from anything edible, such as the Richardsons' bag of oatmeal raisin cookies, at which Petey and Andy were liable to throw themselves. He made another bow, and they walked off, with Petey shouting "Good luck, Jenn!" and Andy talking loudly about potato salad.

When the whistle blew for the second half of the tryouts to begin, the activity to which Jenn's group was sent dealt with control of the ball. If she was going to play the position she wanted – center midfielder – Jenn knew she had to be a star here. She was grateful when Cynthia walked her over to the activity, reminding her of what to pay attention to when she was performing. At the end, when it was time for Jenn's group to move to the next station, the coach at that station, who was writing something on the paperwork her clipboard held, looked up and said, "Good job, McDaniels," and Jenn heard Cynthia, close by, whoop. Then she punched the air.

That filled Jenn up unexpectedly, more than the coach's words. She grinned to herself and made easy work of the rest of the tryouts. Nothing could touch her. She was invincible. Still, she was thrilled when her name was the second one called to be a part of A team and therefore not required to attend the next day's tryout. The Richardsons surrounded her. The McDaniels contingent broke through. Jenn felt herself swept up in her father's arms, her little brothers hugging her around her waist.

"Jennie-Jenn-Jenn," her dad said in triumph. "What a day for you, my girl!"

"It's because of Cynthia," Jenn told her father. "I couldn't've done it without her help."

"Indeed, indeed," Bruce agreed. He embraced Cynthia as well.

Jenn wondered if he would have done so had he known about the confusion of feelings she had for the older girl.

40

Becca knew Derric's dad wasn't going to change his mind about her revealing her true identity to his son. The only thing that *might* keep him from insisting she do it n-o-w was if he understood the dangers facing Hannah Armstrong because of what she could hear when she wasn't using her AUD box and what she could see when visions came upon her. Yet Becca couldn't tell him any of that.

She was still trying to develop some strategy – *any* strategy – a day later when a car passed her on Newman Road and made the turn into Ralph Darrow's driveway some 150 yards ahead of her. It was a car that Becca didn't recognize, so she felt cautious. Her caution morphed into having a bad feeling, mostly due to her previous conversations with Debbie Grieder, Dave Mathieson, and Mrs. Kinsale. Because of this, she slowed down, and when she got to the property and saw the car parked next to Jake's, she glided down the new driveway and decided not to enter the house till she knew what was going on.

Leaving her bike at the side of Grand's house, she crept around the back of it where the window to the bedroom above and the bedroom below looked into the forest. She reached the house's north corner. From here, the space was open. Lawn gave way to a few of Grand's rhodies and some of his specimen trees. But not far from the house, a massive cedar drooped its lacy branches nearly to the ground.

Becca darted to this tree. Under the cover of its curtain-like boughs, she was able to get a very good look at the living room window. She was unsurprised at the sight in the living room of a young woman with sunny California blonde-streaked hair. Dave Mathieson would have told the San Diego reporter that Ralph Darrow was the man who found the ringing cell phone in the parking lot of Saratoga Woods. It would be Olivia Bolding's logical next step, and here she was.

She was at the chess table where Grand was sitting. She was showing him what Becca figured were the altered photographs of Hannah Armstrong. Grand was fingering them but he didn't appear to be acknowledging the resemblance between Hannah Armstrong and Becca King.

Prynne passed the table on her way to the kitchen. She, too, didn't seem to be saying anything about what she saw printed. But the fact that the reporter showed them to Prynne at all was enough to tell Becca that at some point someone was going to see the pictures, recognize who was in them, and betray her. It wouldn't be done maliciously. More likely was the possibility of someone saying, "Hey. That looks like Becca King."

Olivia Bolding didn't remain long in Grand's house. Becca saw her head away from the chess table, and in a moment, she could hear voices on the front porch. Olivia and Jake were speaking, and although Becca couldn't make out the words, they seemed to constitute a casual goodbye. She thanked her stars that Jake Burns was there and not Celia Black. She could only imagine Celia giving the pictures a glance and saying in her Celia way, "Oh hey, isn't she the spitting image of our Becca!"

Becca waited until she heard a car start in the parking area at the top of the hill. Even then she waited another two minutes to make certain it was safe to leave her hiding place. She quickly crossed the lawn to the house and made fast work of getting inside.

Everything seemed normal. Prynne was the one to tell her that some reporter had been there talking to Grand about a cell phone he'd found in the woods something like eighteen months ago. She showed them all some pictures of this Hannah chick who looked like she'd had an amazing television makeover, Prynne added. But all that came of it was Grand saying *ring woods*, and the reporter chick had decided this meant he'd heard a phone ringing in Saratoga Woods. She said she was heading there next, although Prynne couldn't figure out why.

As she spoke, nothing came from her in whispers. In fact, nothing had come from Prynne in whispers since Becca had given Seth the black tar heroin. Becca couldn't work out what this meant, but she understood that Prynne *couldn't* become her problem. She didn't want her to be an addict, but what was going to happen with her and with Seth had moved out of her hands the moment Becca had given Seth the tobacco tin.

She crossed the living room to Grand. He watched her with those twinkly eyes of his. She caught his whisper – *Green Gabe* – and for a moment, she didn't follow his meaning. But then she saw his memory in the quickest of flashes. His hands were holding her childhood copy of *Anne of Green Gables*, the only item from her life in San Diego that she'd brought with her. Those hands opened the book and through Grand's eyes within the vision, she saw the inscription to "my sweet Hannah" that her grandmother had written.

She knelt by his chair and put her head in his lap. She murmured, "I just couldn't tell you," and she felt his hand descend with infinite gentleness onto her hair.

41

S eth figured that since his family was paying Prynne for the hours that she was at Grand's, she'd been able to buy dope all along, and she had to have it hidden all over the place. But she also had to know that someone had found that one tin in Grand's workshop and removed it. So she was probably waiting to be unmasked. And Becca and Jake were waiting for him to do the unmasking, which Seth knew he had to accomplish before someone else – like Aunt Brenda – came across another stash somewhere. Brenda hadn't been around much since being awarded guardianship of Grand, but Seth knew that was only Round One. She'd be back when *whatever* her plans were stood in place.

Seth was too bummed after talking to Prynne's parents to engage in any search of Grand's property. He figured there wasn't any dope at his own parents' house, but if there was, Prynne was probably going to keep it close.

It was a phone call from Steamer Constant that set Seth on the path to a confrontation with Prynne. The talent scout called to tell him that the music agent Freda Windsarm was back in town. She'd talked her into giving Triple Threat another listen. Seth told the talent scout that it would have to be just the guys this time as Prynne wasn't doing so well. In reply to this Steamer Constant revealed that it was Prynne who'd taken them over the top. *Terrific musician* and *excellent technician* were the words she used and she added, *even when Prynne obviously wasn't at her best.* "So give us a yell when she's feeling better" was how Steamer Constant ended the call. Seth said he would.

He'd learned from Prynne's parents that they'd run through their savings sending her into recovery programs. They were well into her brother's college fund trying to help her when they came to understand this wasn't the route that was going to save anyone. From this Seth took the knowledge that Prynne would die if she didn't recover. He also took the knowledge that she would die if she didn't *want* to recover.

When he got to Grand's house that afternoon, he shoved the tin of black tar heroin into a canvas satchel. He found Prynne in the garden with Jake and Grand, sitting in lawn chairs enjoying the sun.

Gus was with him, and he loped to the porch where the bone box was. Instead, Seth rooted for a ball and handed it over. Gus dashed onto the lawn and dropped the ball at Grand's feet. Ralph bent slowly. With his good hand, he picked it up. He gave it a toss that he couldn't have given two months ago. Jake and Prynne said "Way to go!" and "Wow!"

Seth shouldered the satchel and went to them. He kissed Grand on the top of the head and said to Prynne, "Want to go for a walk?"

She jumped to her feet. "Where to?"

Seth decided on the tree house. She'd never seen it.

He could feel Grand watching him in that way he had as he and Prynne set off into the woods. No one knew him better than his grandfather. Grand had picked up that something was wrong.

Seth didn't talk much as they walked the path, other than to say he needed to get out here and do some work on it. The way of path-keeping in the forests on Whidbey was to fight reclamation by nature. Within three years, any path made by man would be overgrown if someone didn't make the attempt to get the plant life under control. Seth told Prynne this in fits and starts. Had to bring the chain-saw out to remove a downed tree, had to yank out some yellow archangel before it took over, had to pull out that English ivy.

Prynne said nothing other than *hmmm* and *oh*. It was in this manner that they arrived at the clearing where Seth had built his tree house under the watchful guidance of his grandfather.

Seeing the building nestled between two hemlocks, Prynne said, "Seth, this is *amazing*," and for the first time in days, she seemed enthusiastic about something. "C'n I go up and see inside?"

"That's why we're here." He went first up the stairs in order to open the trap door onto the deck. He was happy to see that the wood was holding up strong and true.

Inside, the place smelled musty from disuse, and there was a fair amount of dust because the stove that heated the single room in winter had been left ajar and a film of ash from the last fire within it had been blown out. Seth opened one of the windows. He noticed that jays were chattering *shaark shaark shaark* in the trees. A crow called out a warning to the rest of his gang and flew off as if in indignation at the human invasion into the woods.

"How come you've never showed me this before?" Prynne went to the cot. She sat and tested its strength. "Do you ever sleep here? It would be fun. I always wondered where the trail went. I walked a ways along it, but—"

"Why?" Seth asked.

"Why what?"

"Why did you walk a ways along it? Were you looking for something?"

Her face became wary immediately. "What would I be looking for?"

Seth opened his satchel and brought out the old tin. "A place to hide something like this," he said.

She said nothing at first. She managed to look supremely confused. Finally, she said, "What's that?"

"A tobacco tin," he told her. "A real old tobacco tin."

"An antique? Is it valuable?"

He wanted to laugh. He could feel laughter's nastiness bubbling up. "What's inside is worth money. Not a whole lot but probably more than the tin. Want to see it?"

"I don't know . . ." and there she faltered.

"You don't know what? What's inside? Where we found it? What don't you know, Prynne?"

He opened the tin. He dumped the contents next to her onto the sleeping cot. When she started to say something, he jumped in. "Don't even bother. I've been to Port Townsend. I've talked to Steve. He sent me to your mom and dad, so I went to Port Gamble and talked to them. If you want to tell me this isn't yours, go ahead, but we both know it'll be a lie because we both know lying is what you do best."

Her good eye filled. "It isn't mine. I don't even know what that stuff is. I don't know where it came from. I don't know where you found it. I don't know what it's used for. I don't *know*."

"Oh yeah right." Seth grabbed up the square of aluminum and a small chunk of the heroin. He snatched up the Bic lighter from beside her leg. He said, "You don't know, huh? Want me to show you? You think it's mine?"

"I didn't say that. It could be anyone's. It could be Jake's. Or Celia's. Or Becca's. Or . . . or. . . ."

"How 'bout Grand's? Grand's smoking heroin in his free time these days?"

Her lips trembled spasmodically. She clenched her fists in her lap and lowered her head so her hair spread around her like something meant to protect her from what would come next. She said brokenly, "You're the best thing in my life, Seth. You're the *only* thing in my life. You and my music and if I lose you . . . I can't lose you, Seth."

"You lied to me about everything," Seth said. "Right from the first. You claimed all you did was weed. You said that whole thing with my mom's Oxy was just giving it a try when the truth was you hadn't found a heroin source on Whidbey yet. You *had* to use the Oxy and you would've kept using it if Mom hadn't needed to renew the prescription."

"All I have is you and my fiddle," Prynne said, and this time she looked up. She'd started to cry and she didn't cry prettily. She went all red in the face, her neck got splotchy, and she had to wipe her nose on her arm. "You have to know that you – Seth, *you* – are the most important thing in—"

"*Dope* is the most important thing to dopers," Seth said. "Everyone knows that. Like Steve, like your parents, like *everyone*. Where the hell did you get this stuff? How'd you figure out . . . ?" It came to Seth even as he was speaking. "Langley," he said. "I bet it was the music store. You said you needed strings and rosin and you kept me from going in with you. That was when, wasn't it? Someone in the music store knew where to find this stuff. Someone told you and you made contact and that was that."

"Please," Prynne cried. "Please don't leave me. I'll stop. I swear it. I *can* stop, Seth. I've done it and I can do it again. I can. I will."

"Your mom and dad said you've been in recovery three times. *Three* times and they spent their savings and some college money trying to get you straight. Do you know that, Prynne? *All* their savings before they gave you the boot."

"They . . . they should have told me. They *never* told me. They should have told me. I didn't know. I swear. If I knew, I would've—"

"What? Been cured because they'd used up all their money trying to get you cured?"

She rose creakily. She extended her hands in a gesture that looked like someone pleading for a handout on the street. "Please help me," she said. "Do you think I want to be this way? Do you believe that I haven't tried and tried and told myself . . . but they sent me to the wrong kinds of places. I went and I did *everything* they told me to do and it didn't take. But something will. I know something will. I swear I'll make something work for me. You have to believe that. Just don't . . . Oh God please don't give up on me. I know we can make it together. And what's changed? Nothing, Just this. I have a problem. I'm trying to solve it. Help me solve it."

Seth began to gather what he'd dumped from the tin. Prynne touched his arm so tentatively that it felt like the touch of a frightened kitten. "If you give up on me, too, I won't have anyone. And you and me . . . we'll lose our chance at happiness, Seth. And we were happy. *I* know we c'n be happy again."

Seth closed the tin on its foul contents, but what he saw in his mind's eye was Prynne playing her fiddle that first day he'd encountered her. He saw the liveliness of her, the joy in her music, the way she carried her audience effortlessly with her. He saw her in her gypsy shirt and her old blue jeans, tapping a foot shod in a cowboy boot. He saw her when she was asleep in the morning and when she sat up in bed at night reading a book. He saw her helping his mom cook dinner, throwing the ball for Gus, showing Grand his flash cards, and more than anything else, he saw her believing in *him*.

What he knew was that he couldn't let her go. What he knew was that he didn't know how to keep her.

42

O n the day designated to introduce Rejoice to his parents, Derric took Becca with him to pick her up in La Conner. Rejoice didn't get into the car at once, though. Instead, she stood before Becca and looked her directly in the eyes. "I got something I have to say to you," she announced.

Becca had been wearing the earbud, so she hadn't a clue what Rejoice wanted to tell her. Before she could reply, though, Rejoice rushed on with, "I acted bad with you a bunch of times and I'm really sorry. I was, like, gynormously dumb. Der was trying to be cool with me and to make sure he didn't do anything to give me the wrong idea. I was totally the one to try to make something happen between us. And I got to say now . . . I'm *so* happy to have a real brother. I mean a real brother from the same parents. It makes me feel like I have a place in the world, if that makes sense."

"It totally makes sense," Becca told her.

"C'n we be friends, then?" Rejoice said.

"Like, forever," Becca replied.

The two girls hugged and Derric cried, "Group hug!" and threw his arms around both of them.

Becca felt what the word *bittersweet* had to mean: the joy of Rejoice's homecoming into a family comprising her only sibling and the sadness of having no sibling of her own and of having no knowledge of where her family – in the person of her mother – was.

They piled into the car for the drive to Derric's house near Goss Lake. When they arrived, Becca saw the building through Rejoice's eyes, pleasantly gray-shingled in a clearing made to contain it, with the land surrounding it left in its natural state of ferns, salal, wild huckleberries, and grasses. Rejoice, she saw, was taking it all in.

Once inside the house, Derric called out "We're here" and his parents responded with "In the kitchen" and "In the office." He and the girls chose the kitchen, and trooped in that direction to find Rhonda icing a cake meant for their dessert that evening. She looked up as Derric said, "Here's Rejoice, Mom."

Becca could never have predicted what happened next. Rhonda said nothing for a moment. Her lips parted, then closed, then curved in a smile. She said, "My holy God. You've found your sister," and then she cried out, "Dave! Come here!"

She crossed quickly to Rejoice and took both her hands, saying, "You are lovely, sweetie. *Welcome*."

Derric, Becca saw, was completely dumbfounded. So was she. They looked at each other wordlessly as Dave Mathieson hurried down the hall from his office, coming in answer to the insistence he'd heard in Rhonda's voice. He stopped short at the sight of Rejoice. Then he said, "Good Lord. They were right."

Dave went to Rejoice, saying, "Well, you're the image of him. We should have known. *Had* we known, things would've been different."

Next to Becca, Derric stirred. He said, "You guys want to tell me what's going on?"

"Let's go to the living room," was Rhonda's reply.

There she explained, and her explanation was simple. The director of the orphanage had suspected that Derric had a sister among the children who were picked up off the

Kampala streets on the day he'd been taken to the orphanage. But there were twenty-five children brought in to Children's Hope of Kampala on that hot afternoon, and among them at least twenty were sobbing their little hearts out, terrified because their world was undergoing an upheaval again. All of them had lost their parents – mostly to AIDS – and getting along on the street had become a way of life. Now they were thrust into yet another world, this one peopled by strangers who were examining them, administering strange syrups and pills to them, inoculating them, bathing them, finding clothes for them, assigning them to beds, assessing them for everything from language skills to the ability to follow simple directions. Derric, five years old at the time, had been put at once into Sick House. He'd come into the orphanage with pneumonia and a fever raging at 105 degrees.

"You talked about a sister," Rhonda said, "but you were so ill that it seemed you might be imagining her or she might have died along with your parents. Had we known . . . Oh sweetie, I hope you know we *never* would have separated the two of you. We would have adopted Rejoice as well. But then later on, you never mentioned a sister and none of the girls ever said they had a brother."

"She was too little," Derric told his mom. His face looked totally haunted. "Like I said before, Becca was the one to find her in La Conner. See, when I fell in the woods? When I was in the hospital all that time? Becca was there that day when I fell and she went back to the woods to try to figure out why I'd been there. I had a hiding place where she found the letters and . . . Becca always wanted me to tell you but I was scared because . . ." Tears began to course down his cheeks as he spoke, and he seemed to be unaware of them.

"Oh, sweetheart, why?" Rhonda asked him.

"Because I left her in Kampala when I could've maybe

brought her here," he said. "Because I never said when I *could've* said. Because I made it all about me coming to America and I liked you and wanted you to be my mom. . . ." He turned away from them all, raising his arm to cover his face.

Rejoice scooted along the couch where they were sitting. She put her arms around him. She said, "Big bro, it's *so* okay. I came to America anyway. You *tried* to tell them right when we got there to the orphanage. And me? I forgot I even *had* a brother, so I was always okay. We were both always okay."

"All's well that ends well," Dave Mathieson said.

"I think we owe a lot to Becca," Rhonda added.

Becca had a small hope that Dave Mathieson might be of a different mind in the aftermath of the reunion and reconciliation among all of them. But that hope didn't live long. Dave took her aside for a moment as Rejoice and Derric walked out to the car to make the drive back to La Conner.

Dave said to Becca, "I need to thank you."

She was surprised. "What for?"

"For finding Rejoice for him. Rhonda and I should have put in more effort, especially when those letters turned up."

"I had the advantage," Becca said. "You knew he was writing to someone called Rejoice, but I knew Rejoice was his sister. And you *did* ask him about her. I think you did everything you were s'posed to do."

He ran his hand back through his salt-and-pepper hair. Up ahead, Derric and Rejoice laughed and bumped shoulders together and Rejoice cried out, "Oh totally no *way!*"

Dave said, "One way or the other, you did a good thing. We're grateful for that." And then when Becca would have left in good spirits, he said, "Have you told him yet? Olivia Bolding and her search for Hannah Armstrong?"

"I promise I will."

"I hope you keep that promise," Dave replied. "Things need to be made right everywhere, and in this case, you're the best person to do it."

43

When Jenn was next at school, she knew that she had two things that she absolutely had to accomplish. As soon as she saw Becca, she set about accomplishing the first of them. She didn't want to become some dumbo who crashed through her life burning personal bridges right, left, and center, and she understood that she'd come pretty close to doing this with more than one person in her immediate group of friends.

In their shared English class, she passed a note to Becca – *Talk to you whenever???* – and waited to see what would happen. Becca looked over at her and nodded. She mouthed the word *lunch* and Jenn nodded back.

They met outside. They went to the back of the school where they could watch the potheads slithering up to the woods of South Whidbey Community Park. It was the kind of day that suggested an early summer instead of twenty days of nice weather beginning sometime after the Fourth of July. In Washington, though, you never knew, so they held their faces up to the sun while it was available to them.

"My life's getting . . . well, it's sort of complicated," Jenn said.

"Yeah?" Becca lowered her head. She took her earbud thing out of her ear and started searching around in her backpack till she brought out a pipe cleaner that she used on it. Jenn waited. Becca looked up. "I c'n hear you good without this," she said. "Especially when it's just you and me."

"Oh! I didn't know that. Did you tell me before?"

"Prob'ly not. I forget to sometimes. Anyway, what's happening?"

Jenn wasn't quite sure how to put it. How do you tell someone who's your BFF that you keep thinking about a girl, in a way you never thought you'd be thinking about a girl? She was drawn to Cynthia Richardson. She wanted to explore what this meant. But she was afraid of that exploration. So she also wanted to protect herself.

Becca said slowly, "Hey, c'n I say something, Jenn?"

"Sure."

"This might sound like la-la land, but Mrs. Kinsale's always telling me that life is just life. People are who they are. No one's s'posed to try to change anyone into being a way they *aren't*, if you get what I mean."

Jenn nodded. She started at the only place she could think of to start. "I made the team," she said. "The All Island team? I got picked second."

Becca dropped the earbud to her side in her haste to throw her arms around Jenn. "Awesome!" she cried. "I always *knew* you could do it!"

"I wouldn't have, though," Jenn said. "Not without Cynthia and Lexie. They worked out with me and pushed me and Lexie . . . ? She even helped me get the job at G & G's. And then when it came time for tryouts, Cynthia took me there and didn't even try out herself."

"How come?"

"She said she never meant to try out. She just wanted to help me because she thought I could make the team. She said she needs to stay in shape anyway 'cause of her scholarship to University of Virginia, so training me helped her to do that. But I'm not sure that was . . . well . . . all of it."

Becca blinked. For several seconds her eyes got all strange, like she'd stopped being able to see Jenn at all. But then she blinked another time and she was back to normal. She said, "I bet anything she did it for you."

"She thinks I'm good enough to get a scholarship if enough people see me on the All Island team, and—"

"Sure, but it's more than that. I bet she did it for you 'cause she's into you."

"You think?"

"Yeah. You're into her, too, huh?"

Jenn touched her fingers to her lips. "I keep telling myself I don't want to be. Only, yeah, I might be. I want to, you know, be with her sometimes and other times I'm . . . I guess I'm scared."

"But scared's not bad, is it?" Becca pointed out. "I mean, scared's just . . . scared, right?"

"I get that. Only my mom's so freaked just 'cause I'm working for Gertie and Giselle. She's gonna think they turned me into a lesbian or something if she knows I'm into Cynthia. And then . . . ? She'll never let me go back home. But I can't stay with the Richardsons forever. So I don't know where . . ." Once she'd said that, Jenn realized how it sounded: like a manipulation. She hastened to add, "I got to apologize to you, Becca. I totally get why I couldn't stay with Mr. Darrow. I got it right when you said it, but I was too mad and I expected that if you were my friend—"

"I *am* your friend."

"—that you'd say sure to anything I needed. But sometimes friends have to say no and I get that it doesn't mean anything other than saying no." Now for the difficult part, Jenn thought, because if there was another no involved, she didn't know where else she would turn if she had to find a place to live permanently.

Before she could ask, Becca said, "You know, that room at Mrs. Kinsale's house is still open. Alls you have to do is say it's okay for her to at least try to get you and your mom back together. And really, Jenn, d'you think that's a bad thing?"

"Nah. I can see it's pretty smart to try. It might be totally hopeless but it's not bad. I'm okay with it all. Mrs. Kinsale, my mom, whatever."

"She'll prob'ly want you to help take care of her dogs, though."

"I c'n get behind dogs."

"There're five of them. Well four, really, because Oscar hardly counts as a dog. You want me to ask her when you can move in?"

"I'd like that." And as Becca stood and Jenn stood as well, she said to her, "C'n I ask, Becca . . . ?"

Becca turned. "What?"

"C'n I get you to be my BFF again?"

Becca laughed and gave her a lighthearted punch on the shoulder. "Duh. Like I ever stopped?"

That took care of the first accomplishment that Jenn had promised herself she would make. The second came on the day that the Gay Straight Alliance met. Jenn understood that it was a huge and scary step for her, but she figured it was one she had to take. After she survived her conversation with Becca, Jenn was ready.

At lunch, she took her brown bag to room 210. There, she slid to the back of the classroom and decided she would just lurk and listen. But it turned out that this was impossible. There were only twelve kids present that day, and their sponsor, Tatiana Primavera, had a counseling motto that seemed to be "Tell everyone your truth as soon as possible." Thankfully, the first truth she required of Jenn was only her name, which she mumbled at Ms. Primavera's beaming, "And *who's* our visitor today?" Then the counselor repeated it for all to hear: "Jenn McDaniels. Welcome, Jenn."

Cynthia mouthed the word hello at Jenn and glanced at Lexie, who raised her eyebrows and gave Jenn a thumbs up. The rest of the kids didn't seem to notice or even care. They were busy with committee reports on the subject of the Rainbow Prom. The head of ticket sales was saying something about the LGBATQ community on campus. She wanted to know whether enough outreach was being done to the Qs.

Jenn frowned at all the letters. She got L and G: lesbian and gay, but the rest pretty much mystified her. So she merely took everything in and asked herself what she'd been asking herself every day for months. Where did she fit in?

Then the chair of the advertising committee stood to give his report. She'd seen him before: a senior boy who'd started a website featuring bow ties that he designed and made. The *South Whidbey Record* had done a story on him when he'd outfitted the entire Seattle Men's Chorus with bow ties for an upcoming concert. He was wearing one of his creations now: sort of a Tommy-Bahama-married-to-Jerry-Garcia. He blended this with a tight-fitting vest and white dress shirt. His jeans were black. His shoes were yellow PF Flyers. He looked, she decided, pretty amazing. His name was Jeff but he insisted on Rupert. "Fits me better than Jeff," he said.

Now he was announcing that they had to increase their publicity if they wanted to bring in kids from Coupeville, where ticket sales were lagging. A dozen more posters were needed within two days, and they had to be good. "Volunteers?" he asked. "You don't have to draw the images, just do the lettering and the colors. Believe me, a kinder-gartner could manage this."

Jenn looked around. It came to her that there were all types of kids in the room. It also came to her that she couldn't distinguish which of the alphabet soup of letters that designated sexuality applied tò which kid. They were just part of South Whidbey High School. There was no big deal with who they were or what they were, unless someone – like her – made it one.

She raised her hand. Rupert's face lit up. "Have I managed to convince someone that lettering posters isn't a death sentence?"

"Think you have," Jenn told him. "I'll do it."

"Available today?"

"Today and whenever," Jenn replied.

44

After their last conversation, Becca fully intended to keep her promise to Dave Mathieson. But she wanted to find the best opportunity to do so. She told herself she wasn't avoiding anything in not telling Derric immediately about Hannah Armstrong. There were, after all, many other things going on.

First of all, there was getting Jenn settled at Diana Kinsale's house. After that, there was helping Seth figure out what to do about Prynne. Beyond that problem, there was the practice she had to continue: blocking whispers, trying to interpret the visions, trying to integrate the whispers and the visions, trying to understand what truly constituted a quickening. These were *pressing* issues. These were *serious* issues. They needed her attention first and foremost.

Only, she knew that all of this was just an enormous jumble of avoiding what she had to do. In the middle of this jumble was the ugliness of her continuing to lie to Derric. Not only to lie to him, at this point, but also to lie to herself about the relative importance of all these things she just *had* to see to before she could see to the boy she loved.

She went over in her head the trail of discovery that Olivia Bolding had been forging. So far she'd been to the Cliff Motel. She'd been to see the sheriff and after that she'd showed up to question Ralph Darrow, who had sent her on a useless mission to Saratoga Woods. There was really only one more place for Olivia Bolding to go in her search for Hannah Armstrong: the high school.

Here, Becca had been most careful. She'd skipped photo day at school both of the Septembers that she'd been there. She'd never joined a club that would put her picture in the yearbook. She'd been caught by a photojournalist last year when a fire broke out at the county fairgrounds, but she didn't see any reason why Olivia Bolding would start looking through old issues of the *South Whidbey Record* on the chance that Hannah Armstrong had been photographed at some time without her knowledge. So since the journalist knew her age – sixteen years old – she would have to come to the high school next. Becca could only hope that whoever looked at the pictures she was showing would either not recognize Becca King in the updated pictures of Hannah Armstrong or they would keep their mouths shut. Olivia Bolding was, after all, a reporter. Becca King was, after all, a minor. That had to count for something.

She was able to cling to this belief for three days. On day number four, her world came crashing down.

She and Derric were walking to his car. He was explaining that the Vicklands and the Mathiesons had met and were planning a large double-family get-together at Deception Pass State Park. He was in the midst of telling her that he really wanted her to go as well, when a woman's voice spoke behind them.

"You must be Hannah Armstrong at last."

Derric and Becca swung around. The reporter stood there. She wore a long, crushed linen blouse and Capri-length leggings. Inside her sandals, her toenails were painted red with a flower design rendered on each of the big ones. She held an iPhone in one hand and a stack of photos in the other.

Derric said, "What?"

She said, "You're Derric, aren't you? Sheriff Mathieson's son? I did think he wasn't quite telling me everything." She shoved the iPhone in her shoulder bag and she fingered through the pictures, selecting one and handing it to Derric. She said, "Not bad, is it? Teenage girls generally want to lose weight. That's how I saw it, and it seems I was right." She turned to Becca. "Ms. Ward gave you up," she told her, naming the school's registrar. "One look at the picture and she said, 'I knew Debbie Grieder was lying that day,' and she told me the name you were using was Becca King and if I wanted to find you, I just needed to look for the sheriff's son. Ms. Ward said Debbie Grieder had Rebecca King's transcripts and a copy of her birth certificate and the rest was supposed to come in the mail but it never did. What I can't work out is what her part in this is. I mean Debbie Grieder's part. She's certainly not your mom in disguise. But is she nearby, Hannah? Is your mom here on the island? In Everett? In Bellingham? Maybe in Seattle?"

Derric said to Becca, "What the *hell* is going on?"

Becca had been using the AUD box, but she now removed the earbud because her entire life as she'd known it depended upon her ability to read every nuance of the next few minutes. If this wasn't her personal quickening, she was going to have to make it her quickening.

Later, Becca wouldn't be able to recall the exact order in which things happened and in which things were said in those critical moments. Most of it was a blur. She knew she began with "I don't know what you're talking about," which she said to Olivia Bolding. She knew that Olivia responded by saying to Derric, "Her real name is Hannah Armstrong. She hasn't told you, has she? She hasn't mentioned San

Diego and what happened there: her stepfather Jeff Corrie. His partner Connor West. A whole pile of missing money."

Derric looked sick to his stomach. Becca said to him, "What she's saying isn't true. Derric—"

Olivia cut in, saying, "Lies have a way of catching up with you," which Becca knew was the absolute case, because Derric's lies had caught up with him. Only, his lies had had a happy ending, whereas hers weren't going anywhere close to that.

Whispers were everywhere. They were coming too quickly for Becca to be able to process them and to attach them to the thinker: *No way no way but always knew I could last night there was always a moment to get her away from here she knows the truth there's a story how much I wanted we were always going to be this is it* . . . In the past, there had been moments in which Becca could work with what was flooding her head, and when she couldn't do that but instead needed to think clearly, she had the AUD box to help with that. But she couldn't risk the AUD box now because she couldn't risk losing the opportunity that *might* arise from within someone's thoughts to lead her to the proper next move. She felt as if she'd lost every power she'd ever had to hear whispers in a way that would help her, to see visions, to recognize who was thinking what, and to determine if only vaguely what they intended to do.

Derric said faintly, "Why?" and that was it. Before Becca could reply, he had simply walked away.

She faced Olivia Bolding squarely. She knew that there was no way the reporter could actually prove anything. No one on the island aside from Diana Kinsale was aware that Becca King could hear whispers as well as see the memories of other people in the form of visions. So all she had to do was keep bluffing.

She said, "I don't know what you're talking about."

Timeline was the only whisper in response and then, "Your stepdad does, though."

"What stepdad?"

Olivia smiled. "You must mean which one of the five you've had. I've done my homework, Hannah. That's what I do. It's what I'm good at. Just like you're good at what you do."

Becca said nothing. She also picked up nothing. She wondered if this meant that Olivia's thoughts matched her words or if the reporter had worked out how to keep them from escaping as Diana had done.

Olivia went on to say, "Your neighbor in San Diego didn't know the exact date that you and your mom left, but Jeff Corrie did. Allowing for a meandering drive from there to here to confuse the trail, it sounded reasonable to me that it would take a couple of weeks for you and your mom to get here. It was only a matter of logic. And I've always been very logical."

Becca said nothing. She glanced in the direction Derric had taken. She was in time to see him drive off, practically spinning the wheels of the Forester in his haste to get away from her.

She knew she'd dealt their relationship a death blow, and she figured he was going directly to his father in order to confirm what Olivia Bolding had said to him. She also knew that all she'd ever had to do was to tell Derric the truth about who she was. Not about the whispers and the visions, but at least about her name and about her flight from San Diego.

Instead of seeing Olivia's memories, Becca suddenly saw her own. Foremost among them was that first night on the ferry, coming over from the mainland to Whidbey Island. She'd turned from the view of the massive trees rising up into an evening sky, and she'd seen an unmistakably African boy in the passenger seat of a sheriff's car. They'd locked eyes briefly, and her life had never been the same.

Olivia's words intruded into that memory. "What I've heard from Connor West is that you've got a very interesting talent. What I've heard from him is that you can read minds." *Can you read mine do you know what Connor West told me Hannah would you like to know.*

Becca blinked but otherwise kept her face impassive. If she showed no sign, Olivia knew nothing.

Would you like to know I think you'd like to know he's not your friend not like I can be if you let me.

Becca remained firm. It was like being tempted by the devil.

Olivia said, "What I know is that you read minds for his company for three years, going in and out of the conference room at your stepdad's investment company, an innocent girl with an afterschool job and a summer job bringing coffee and tea and whatever to people of a certain age who wanted their money to go further in their retirement so they came to Corrie West Investments to see how this might be possible. I know your part was to listen carefully. Your part was to report what you picked up from their thoughts. Your stepdad and his partner would then design a package that quelled the old folks' every unspoken fear about ending up in life without any money and living under a bridge."

Becca saw that in silence lay power. There was simply nothing Olivia Bolding could do as long as she kept her face a perfect blank.

"It was a great idea. It might have gone on forever. But something happened to bring it all to an end. So you and your mom went one way, Connor West went another, and Jeff Corrie remained in San Diego, where he ended up holding the bag. Which he didn't much like. Understandably.

Who would?" Olivia paused. She glanced at her smart-phone, as if expecting a message. Becca figured she was doing it for effect. She then went on. "What I haven't been able to work out is why all of this happened. Not bilking money, of course. People are greedy. I get that. But I don't get the running-off bit unless someone – like you – knew the whole scheme was about to collapse and unless someone – like your mom – knew how to put her hands on Jeff Corrie's half of the money and run off with it."

"No way!" Becca cried. "We—" And then she stopped herself. She whirled around, set to run.

Olivia grabbed her. The vision was there: that final used-car lot where Becca and her mom had traded for the last car, the one that had brought them to Whidbey Island, the 1992 Ford Explorer. *How* had she found that place? Becca asked herself. In that moment, she missed her mom so badly that she cried out with the pain of it and in that cry, she knew she'd given the game away.

Olivia linked her arm tightly with Becca's. There was no way that she could escape. Even when she pulled, Olivia held her fast.

The visions began to come one up after the other, like a motion picture being run too fast: talking to their next-door neighbor in San Diego; talking to Connor West; looking at a photo album in which Becca could see the pictures of her as a child and a hand removing those pictures and passing them over and then the sight of Jeff Corrie as the person doing it; talking to someone in an office with piles of papers and awards on shelves.

"I'm just after a story," Olivia said. "I'm not trying to wreck your life."

"You just wrecked it," Becca said.

"I haven't. And only part of the story is here, right now. I'm not writing it till I have the rest. There's no point. My editor wouldn't take it, and I don't write anything my editor won't take."

"So?"

"So I need to find the other half of this story. I need to find your mom."

Becca laughed bitterly. "Good luck with that. I've been trying to find her since the night I got here. I got no clue where she is."

"I can find her," Olivia insisted. "When I do, will you talk to me?"

"How can you do something that no one else can?"

"I found you, didn't I?" Olivia said. "I can find her. Will you help me do it?"

"What's in it for you if I do?" Becca asked her.

"An exclusive. That's all I want."

"That and a Pulitzer Prize," Becca pointed out.

Olivia shrugged, a delicate movement that Becca could imagine won hearts and souls and the trust of people she interviewed. "If that happens, I'll take it. What do you say? Do you want my help in finding your mother?"

"I don't see I have any choice," Becca told her.

45

The thing was, Seth loved her. The thing was, you don't abandon someone you love just because life gets tough. If you find out they have a problem, you step up to the plate to help them solve it.

He believed Prynne. He believed *in* Prynne. He believed her when she said she'd tried, that she didn't want to be an addict, and he believed she had the power inside her to win the coming battle. He understood that she had to keep doing heroin until he could find the best recovery place for her. If she didn't do that, she might catapult herself into a withdrawal that none of them would be able to handle. She protested at first when he told her that he was looking for a recovery place for her, one that would work this time. She said, "I should be doing that at least" to which he replied, "Your hard work is coming. Let me do this part."

She told him she loved him and she would always love him: for caring so much when others had discarded her. "You're the best," she said. "There's no one like you."

What Seth did first was talk to Jake. He made Prynne talk to Jake with him. The plan was that she would smoke just enough junk to keep herself from going into withdrawal. In the meantime, Seth would search for the best place for her to get over it.

Jake didn't like this plan. He didn't like the idea of anyone doing heroin anywhere near Grand. But after listening to both of them swear that this *would* work and that Prynne *was* serious, he reluctantly said he would keep the peace and not let anyone know what was going on.

Seth couldn't bring himself to tell his parents. His mom had been right in voicing her early concerns about Prynne. But she had been wrong in thinking that sticking with Prynne was going to mean permanent trouble for him.

So Seth worked on finding a place for her to go into recovery. He looked at programs in Seattle, Portland, Eugene, Spokane, Pullman, Ellensburg, and Bellingham. He rejected them. Some were too vague with their promises and others were too far away. He wanted Prynne near enough for him to visit her because he wanted to be able to encourage her. The program that looked the most promising turned out to be in Burlington, well within striking distance of Whidbey Island.

The cost was staggering, though. He discovered that depending upon the person's need, the price tag would be between $10K and $40K. Need was determined in an intake interview, physical exam, and conversations with a psychologist and an addiction specialist. An individual program would then be designed, and the addict would first go through withdrawal under the care of a physician. After that, the real work of recovering would begin.

"But it works?" Seth said.

That would always depend on the addict, he was told. The individual would have to spend the rest of her life fighting the hunger for heroin. This was impossible to do alone.

"I'll be there for her."

Which was nice, he was told. But the addict needed the support of other addicts who were also in recovery. Giving up heroin did not stop a person from being an addict. That person was just someone currently not using the substance to which he was addicted. That was why the addict needed the support of other similar people trying not to use again.

Seth felt discouraged at this news. His picture had been that Prynne would go somewhere, get the heroin out of her system, and return to him as the Prynne he'd first met, the love of his life, his partner and his friend. That this would not be the case was something he needed to talk about, and he wanted Becca to be his listener.

But he was on his own. Something had happened with Becca. He knew it wasn't good, and he knew it was about Derric, who was totally missing in action. But when Seth asked her about it, Becca only shook her head and got teary-eyed. Seth didn't want to force the issue. So he let it go because of his own concerns, the biggest one of which was how to come up with the money to pay for the program in Burlington.

Oddly enough, it was his aunt Brenda and her husband who gave him the answer, on an evening when Seth and Grand were having a go at playing chess again. Seth had just taken the second of Grand's castles, when a triple knock at the front door – taptapTAP – told him trouble was on its way.

Brenda had been keeping her distance, but the rest of the family hadn't taken heart from this. They knew that Brenda wasn't the kind of person who was going to give up easily, since mostly she never gave up at all.

When she and Seth's uncle Mike entered, Aunt Brenda was all smiles. She was wearing her Medina best: from the sunglasses perched on the top of her head to the designer stilettos on her feet. Seth gawped at these and wondered how the heck Brenda had got down the hill in them. Uncle Mike was duded up as well: *GQ* central, right down to the three-day-old beard thing that he had going.

Brenda came over to the chess table. She knelt at Grand's side, took his good hand in her own, and said to him, "I've been a mule about everything, Dad. I hope you'll forgive me."

Grand's bushy eyebrows moved toward each other. He didn't say anything. Neither did Seth. Celia was puttering around in the kitchen and she called out something about coffee and cake, which everyone except Uncle Mike turned down.

Brenda said, "I completely understand that you want to stay here in the house, Dad, and Mike and I have finally come up with a way that you can do it. It's a compromise, but I believe it's one that all of us can live with."

There was something about her approach that Seth didn't like. She was being too *oily*, he thought. It was the only word that he could come up with to describe how smooth her presentation was. He said, "I c'n call Dad so you c'n tell him whatever you got to say."

Brenda looked at him brightly. "Of course you can," she said. "But we don't have a lot of time right now. Mike?"

Seth's uncle pulled a chair over to join them. Together they unfolded their plan: Grand would *definitely* stay in his house. In fact, he would stay in his house till *he* gave the word that he wished to live elsewhere. Since the current setup had people coming and going all the time – Jake, Celia, Becca, Seth, Prynne – and since there was no real expert there to work with Grand, an honest-to-goodness nursing and physical therapy staff was going to be employed for him. There would be a twenty-four-hour nurse on the premises along with an aide. A physical therapist and a speech therapist would come and go on a regular basis. Nutritious meals would be provided. The only thing that would *really* change was that family and friends would not be responsible for his care and could thus be able to get on with their lives.

Seth was seething at the end of this. Grand merely looked

confused. Seth said, "So how's this all supposed to be paid for? Did you and Uncle Mike decide to fund it?"

"We do have three children in college, sweetie," Aunt Brenda said coolly.

"What*ever*. So how's this plan of yours going to be paid for?" Seth felt hot under the collar with the way she'd spoken to him.

"Mike will explain," she said.

This was, obviously, where they'd been heading. Uncle Mike spoke directly to Grand. Ralph, he said, was sitting on over 170 acres of forest, and Mike had a buyer who wanted to purchase 165 of those acres for a destination resort. He'd be putting a hotel and spa at the highest point on the property, so Ralph wouldn't have to see it. No one would see it, in fact, until they actually arrived. This resort would have a 360-degree view that would encompass the forest below it, the waters around Whidbey Island, the Olympic Peninsula, Camano Island, and the Cascades with the crown jewel of Mount Baker shimmering in the distance. It would have a yoga studio, a thirty-thousand-square-foot spa, two swimming pools – one outdoor and one indoor – trails for hiking, lawns for lounging, quiet rooms for reading and napping. . . .

"The whole nine yards," Uncle Mike finished. He added that a resort of this kind would bring an enormous amount of money to Whidbey Island. People would come by boat and be picked up at the Langley marina; they would come by car from the mainland; they would come by bus from Canada. The resort would be a destination, and creating this destination would be good for them all. Grand's 170 acres merely needed to be platted appropriately so that he would retain the five remaining acres and live comfortably upon them.

"So," Brenda said in happy conclusion, "you won't ever

have to leave home again, Dad. I get how important that is to you."

"Uh. . . . 'Scuse me?" Seth said. "Thing is, Aunt Brenda, you don't get everything."

She put a manicured hand to her chest and said, "Exactly what don't I get?"

"Grand gave the property to me."

Such utter silence greeted this that you could hear the wind stirring the branches in the nearby cedar. Brenda finally gathered herself enough to say, "What do you mean, he 'gave' it to you? One doesn't just 'give' property to someone. There're procedures to be followed. You've probably mistaken a conversation you had or a remark he made."

"Nah," Seth said. "You c'n check it all out. See, Grand kept saying 'banks' to us and we kept thinking he was telling us to go around to the banks for some reason. You knew that, right?" He didn't wait for a reply because he was sort of enjoying watching his aunt trying not to fall over, since she'd never risen from her position in front of her father and her stilettos were tough to keep her balance on, considering the shock she was in the process of having. "Well, the thing is, he didn't mean banks like in where you keep your money. He meant Betty Banks."

"Who the hell is Betty Banks?" Mike was still seated but he'd leaned forward and he thrust his face in line with Seth's.

"She's the land attorney who did the paperwork. This was about two years ago. I signed it but I didn't know what it was. You know me: too dumbnuts to read all that legal stuff. I thought maybe it was his will or something."

"Let me get this straight," Brenda said evenly. "You signed a document and you had no idea what it was."

"Like I said, I'm dumb," Seth told her. "Anyways, Grand took me to someone, and I signed and he signed and there was this person who stamped it and made it all official and recorded it in a book and the whole deal. So the thing is . . . ? It's not up to Grand when it comes to selling property. It's up to me."

Brenda took this in with ever widening eyes. She turned to her father, who was watching her as he'd been watching her since she'd entered the house. She said, "But . . . *why*? I'm your daughter. Rich is your son. *What* were you thinking? You had to have been . . ." She whirled on Seth and nearly fell over for good. "You tricked him!" she cried.

"I didn't trick anyone," Seth said. "I wouldn't even know how. I'm way too dumb. Like I said, check it out. And just to add . . . well . . . no one's building anything around here."

They left with promises of lawsuits and court appearances and blah blah blah. But Seth knew that Grand was smart enough to have hired an attorney who knew how to do things right. So the land was safe. Only . . . there was still Prynne, her recovery, and the cost of it.

He had to tell Grand about her, and he did. He told the whole story, leaving nothing out. Addiction, heroin, Port Gamble and her parents, Port Townsend and Steve, his mom's Oxy, the failed trip to Seattle to play for the music agent, Jake's discovery of the heroin, his confrontation of Prynne, her need for treatment, his search for a place she could go. And finally the cost.

Ralph didn't flinch from any of it. Seth knew that his grandfather wanted to talk to him in the old way, in the warm and supportive and loving and wise way that he'd always employed in the past. But he hadn't progressed far enough with language to do that, and chances were that he never would. Seth nearly lost his courage then. To continue, to get to the crux of the matter, felt like a blow he'd be dealing Ralph, felt like a betrayal of him by the very person his granddad had decided to trust. But a human life *had* to be worth more than land. And he knew he couldn't live with himself if he allowed his own actions to discount that fact. So Seth told him he would have to sell some of the property in order to get the money to send Prynne to a recovery program. He *knew* his grandfather understood what he meant, but he wondered how Ralph would find the words or even the way to give a reply.

There was silence for a bit. Seth waited and watched. Please, he thought. Please understand. Ralph finally raised his good hand. He reached onto the table where the chess set was. He toppled his own king. Seth watched him do it and then raised his eyes to meet the blue eyes of his grandfather that had shone with love upon him for his entire life.

Ralph smiled and spoke, for the first time, quite distinctly. "Favorite male grandchild," was what he said.

46

When Cynthia invited Jenn to go to the Rainbow Prom with her, Jenn hesitated. It was one thing to attend meetings of the Gay Straight Alliance and to help Rupert with the posters. Going to the prom itself – not to mention going with Cynthia – meant moving forward in a way she wasn't sure about.

It was Mrs. Kinsale who persuaded her. She said, in that Mrs. Kinsale way of hers that Jenn was becoming used to, "You've taken a step, Jenn: the meeting at school. This is just another that you might want to take. It might help to remember that to get anywhere, you always have to take the steps." When Jenn had asked her where she was supposed to be going, Mrs. Kinsale smiled and replied, "Where we're all going: into greater understanding and into the future."

Jenn hadn't expected to like this old lady. She'd decided she would keep her distance. She figured she would merely do her bit in exchange for a place to stay. Her bit was the dogs: cleaning their run – they pooped like hell on wheels, she discovered – exercising them either in the back yard or in the field next-door or down on the beach, feeding them, and making sure they had water. She also did some gardening under Mrs. Kinsale's careful direction. She also kept the pots watered and the flower beds weeded and the lawns mowed. Mrs. Kinsale did the cooking, though. Jenn's skill there was limited to making something from nothing, and faced with a refrigerator and cupboards and a pantry that were well stocked, she was out of her depth.

Her dad had come twice to see her, once with Petey and Andy, who tumbled on the lawn with the dogs, rolling in ecstasy with furry playmates who were only too happy to wrestle with them. The other time, he and Jenn and Mrs. Kinsale had sat in her sunroom, and Bruce and Mrs. Kinsale – to Jenn's astonishment – had tested a brew and Jenn had sampled her dad's newest venture, which was homemade soft drinks.

During that visit, Jenn's dad had told Mrs. Kinsale that he was a live-and-let-live kind of person. He said that, frankly, he didn't care one way or the other what Jenn decided about her sexual preference, but the real difficulty lay with Kate. "She has beliefs like we all do," was how he put it, "and I respect that. I can keep trying to bring her around, but right now she doesn't want to see Jennie, and that's how it is."

Mrs. Kinsale said that she understood, and what could Jenn do but say the same? Mrs. Kinsale also said, after Bruce McDaniels had left, that time and patience sometimes surprised one with the changes they could bring about. Jenn had her doubts about that, but since she was a guest, she went with the program and said she hoped that would apply to her mom.

When it came time for the Rainbow Prom, Jenn went with the program again. She accepted the invitation with Cynthia and was relieved when she learned that Lexie and Brian were going with them. There remained, then, only a costume to create, and in this, Jenn discovered that Mrs. Kinsale had a whimsical side to her. Once she heard from Jenn that the theme was steam punk but that the kids really didn't *have* to go in costumes, Mrs. Kinsale pointed out that costumes were at least 50 percent of the fun and they would design something together.

They began with an ancient – and truly epic – flight jacket that had belonged to Mrs. Kinsale's father. To that they added an old pair of her black jeans that she turned into something that she called jodhpurs. A trip to Senior Thrift up in Freeland unearthed a pair of knee-high brown boots that they polished to a dazzling shine, and the finishing piece was a baseball cap that Mrs. Kinsale turned into an old-fashioned flight helmet. To this, she added a pair of swim goggles, and Jenn was set. When she put it all on, she felt bizarre, but Mrs. Kinsale said, "Just you wait. You'll be the best outfitted young lady there."

When Cynthia arrived in her Seahawks-decorated Honda, Brian and Lexie trooped up to Mrs. Kinsale's front door with her. It turned out that this was to be a group activity from start to finish: "One for all and all for one," was how Lexie put it. She was outfitted as a steam punk ballerina, in a black leather bustier, lace tights, a tutu dyed black like the nasty *Swan Lake* bird, and Doc Martens boots. Cynthia and her brother had chosen matching tuxedos. They wore top hats, tails, white silk scarves, and white gloves. They'd somehow come up with matching monocles, too. Jenn didn't know what their get-ups had to do with steam punk, but it didn't matter when you looked that good, she figured.

As they came in the door where Mrs. Kinsale was waiting with her camera to document the event, Brian greeted Jenn in his typical way. "You were welcome in my bedroom as long as you didn't mess with the constellations, you know. Did they offend you? Was it me? You know I always just talk and you've got to tell me when I say the wrong thing because I don't know whereas Cynthia is someone who can tell when she's said the wrong thing so of course I rely on her."

"It wasn't you," Jenn said. "But you know . . . house guests and fish?"

Brian said, "House guests and fish . . . Is this a form of syllogism?"

"They both stink after three days," Lexie told him.

"But if a person bathes and wears deodorant, there wouldn't be a stink," Brian pointed out. "Don't you wear deodorant?" he asked Jenn. "Antiperspirants have caused concern in some corners, but deodorants don't—"

"Asperger's," Cynthia told him. "Jenn meant that guests shouldn't hang around too long."

"But aren't you two in love? It seems to me that if two people, no matter their sexual inclination, have feelings that—"

"Asperger's, Aspergers!" Cynthia declared. To Jenn's surprise, the older girl was blushing.

Mrs. Kinsale was the one to intervene. "Pictures, everyone," she said and shepherded them into her living room to memorialize the Rainbow Prom with photos before she sent them off into the evening.

Deer Grange was the site of the prom, a smallish building that sat above Lone Lake. It was right off the road with a small parking lot in front, and Jenn saw when they pulled into it that the prom was going to be successful. Not only were there cars parked in virtually every space, but kids were also being dropped off by their parents. Some were in costume, some were in prom clothes, some were just in jeans and T-shirts.

They trooped toward the building. Through the windows Jenn could see the decorations that had been devised. There were steam punk flying machines, steam punk trains, steam punk clocks, and steam punk motorcars. She could hear the music and the voice of the DJ that the Alliance had hired. It was like any other dance that might occur on Whidbey Island. At the same time it was unlike any dance she'd ever seen.

Cynthia said to everyone, "So. It's happening. You guys ready?" although she looked only at Jenn.

"Born ready," was Lexie's reply.

"Dressed and dapper," was how Brian put it.

Jenn swallowed and wondered what it would mean to walk through that door in Cynthia's company. She was her date, after all, no matter that they'd come with the others. But she remembered what Mrs. Kinsale had said about taking steps. You didn't get anywhere if you weren't willing to move yourself forward in some way.

She held out her hand. Cynthia took it. "Let's do this," Jenn said.

Inside, much to her surprise, the first person Jenn saw was Becca. She wasn't in costume. She also wasn't with Derric. She waved hi, though, and Jenn went over to her, saying to Cynthia, "Be right back."

"OMG," Becca said as Jenn joined her. "You look *amazing*. Did Mrs. Kinsale help you make that? How's it going so far?"

"She's cool. For an old lady." Jenn looked around. "So where's the man?"

"Derric?"

"Uh . . . is there another?"

Becca offered a sad smile. "I think we're over."

Jenn lowered her flight goggles, as if for a closer examination of her friend. "No *way*, Becca. He's like . . . I mean he's always been totally *into* you."

"He's not into me anymore, and I don't blame him," Becca said. "Anyway," she added with forced good cheer, "you look terrific. I wanted to see everything. It's totally great. Where'd you guys get all the stuff for the costume?"

"Becca . . ." Jenn began in a don't-avoid-me voice.

But Becca shook her head and gave a wave of her hand

that said she wouldn't talk about Derric. Not now. Not here. She said, "I have a date, though. Around here somewhere. Oh yeah. Here he comes."

Jenn swung around. To her surprise, Squat Cooper was approaching, two cups of punch in his hands. In spite of herself, Jenn grinned when she saw him. What he was wearing made any other reaction impossible. He had on a wet suit, underwater goggles, a snorkel, and hiking boots.

"Holy crap," she said when he joined them. He handed Becca one of the paper cups and offered the other to Jenn. She took it. "*What* are you supposed to be? And what the aitch are you doing here anyway?"

"Posters said anyone could come," Squat told her. "Me and Becca decided we were part of anyone. We didn't communicate about the costume part though. She's showing remarkable forbearance in being seen with me."

"Geez, Squat. Aren't you hot in that get-up?"

He grinned. Then he leered at her in that old Squat way. "Do you think so? *I* did. Thanks."

They laughed together. Becca joined them in the laughter although she looked sad around her eyes. Jenn said, "I already said this to Becca, but I know I got to say it to you, too. I'm sorry, Squat. I've been treating you bad."

He shrugged. "Believe me, that's nothing new. Anyway, I mouthed off a bunch. I'm sorry, too."

"Friends, then? Like me and Becca?"

He looked from her to Becca and back again. "Works for me," he said. And then he added to Becca, "You care if I . . . ?" and nodded at Jenn.

Becca, in that way of hers, seemed to know exactly what he meant. "Go for it," she said. "I want to look closer at the steam punk train."

She went off to do so, leaving Squat and Jenn alone. Squat glanced in the direction of the DJ, where Cynthia and Lexie had begun to dance. He said to Jenn, "You want to dance? I mean, I guess I'm the wrong sex, but we could always pretend."

"Pretend what exactly?" Jenn asked him curiously.

He seemed to think about this before he replied. "Whatever you want," he said.

Do you wish this wasn't the end?

Join us at www.hodder.co.uk, or follow us on
Twitter @hodderbooks to be a part of our community
of people who love the very best in books and reading.

Whether you want to discover more about a book
or an author, watch trailers and interviews, have the
chance to win early limited editions, or simply browse
our expert readers' selection of the very best books,
we think you'll find what you're looking for.

And if you don't,
that's the place to tell us what's missing.

We love what we do, and we'd love you to be part of it.

www.hodder.co.uk

@hodderbooks

HodderBooks

HodderBooks